Why America Lost the War on Poverty—And How to Win It

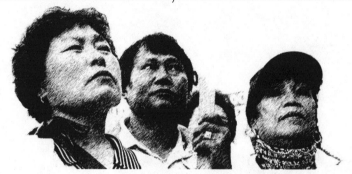

Why America Lost the War on

FRANK STRICKER

Poverty—And How to Win It

THE UNIVERSITY OF NORTH CAROLINA PRESS • Chapel Hill

The publication of this book was supported
by a generous grant from the Division of
Academic Affairs, California State University,
Dominguez Hills.

An earlier version of chapter 7 appeared as "Why
American Poverty Rates Stopped Falling in the
70s, and Why a Better Story Was Not Told
about It," *Journal of Poverty* 4, no. 4 (2000): 1–
21; an earlier version of chapter 10 appeared as
"Staying Poor in the Clinton Boom: Welfare
Reform and the Nearby Labor Force," *Journal
of Poverty* 7, nos. 1–2 (2003): 23–49, and in Keith
M. Kilty and Elizabeth A. Segal, eds., *Rediscover-
ing the Other America: The Continuing Crisis of
Poverty and Inequality in the United States* (New
York: Haworth Press, 2003).

The paper in this book meets the guidelines for
permanence and durability of the Committee on
Production Guidelines for Book Longevity of the
Council on Library Resources.

Library of Congress Cataloging-in-Publication
Data

Stricker, Frank.
Why America lost the war on poverty—and how
to win it / Frank Stricker.
p. cm.
Includes bibliographical references and index.
ISBN 978-0-8078-3111-3 (cloth: alk. paper)
ISBN 978-0-8078-5804-2 (pbk.: alk. paper)
1. Poverty—United States—History—20th
century. 2. Poor—United States—History—20th
century. I. Title.
HC110.P6S78   2007
362.5'560973—dc22   2007012426

cloth   11 10 09 08 07   5 4 3 2 1
paper   11 10 09 08 07   5 4 3 2 1

To my wife,

DEBORAH SCHOPP,

and to all good people

who fight for a real

government war

on poverty

CONTENTS

ILLUSTRATIONS, FIGURES, AND TABLES

ILLUSTRATIONS

FIGURES

TABLES

PREFACE

I was not poor when I grew up in the 50s, but I know that my family felt cramped. We had five people in a small house with two bedrooms. My father, a house painter, worked hard and usually steadily, but he probably did not charge his customers enough. The family never had a vacation together. I remember my mother using a wooden egg to darn a patch where we had holes in our socks.

I have rarely been unemployed. For most of my high school and college years I worked in the university library or as my father's assistant. I recall that at one point in the early 1960s my dad was paying me $5 an hour; that was the equivalent of more than $30 today. My father was too generous as an employer, as he was too generous to his customers. But the high pay for an apprentice house painter seems appropriate to that better time for American workers.

Although I suffered only one year of real unemployment in my life, I had more than a decade of worries about keeping the academic position I accepted at California State, Dominguez Hills, in the fall of 1972. California's finances were on a three-decade seesaw, and faculty and staff often worried that they would be laid off. Most weren't, but the dark cloud of unemployment stayed with me for a long time. And it stayed over the California State Universities, although its shape has changed; now Cal State makes extensive use of under-employed and underpaid part-time professors.

Poverty and living standards have been an interest for many years. In the 70s and 80s I participated in meat boycotts, worked with unions, studied the latest inflation and unemployment crises, and learned about Marxism. I have never taken an economics course, and perhaps it shows. But I learned a lot about economics and history from friends in the New American Movement and in the Westcoast Association of Marxist Historians.

By the time I decided to write this book, I had been teaching and writing about poverty, incomes, and unemployment for two decades. Although I am undeniably comfortable today, I have not forgotten where I came from or that life is an economic struggle for most people, even in this, the richest nation in the history of the world. I hope this book finds many different audiences, but above all, I want it to be of political use to working-class students like those I teach.

So many people helped along the way. First are my students at California State University, Dominguez Hills. They read chapters and offered suggestions, especially on how to make the book more reader-friendly. Years after taking my courses, they remembered I was writing a book and asked how it was coming. It was nice that they wanted to know when they could buy a copy.

Next are colleagues at California State University, Dominguez Hills. Lois Feuer, Don Lewis, Linda Pomerantz, John Auld, Myrna Donahoe, and David Churchman are among those who read chapters and offered valuable suggestions. Also at Dominguez Hills, colleagues on awards committees were sometimes generous. Several administrators offered financial and moral support. Deans Richard Palmer and Selase Williams encouraged me, as did department and program chairs. Don Castro came up with a grant that gave me a boost; Allen Mori and Laura Robles helped support this book. Sabbaticals and partial-pay leaves were extremely important. Marilyn Brady, Jean Butler, and Ineki Fike, all wonderful staff people, helped out in direct and indirect ways. The librarians at my university provided efficient support, perhaps most of all those in the Interlibrary Loan Department, led by Faye Phinsee-Clack. Finally, I was blessed with exceptional research assistants. These students were smart and eager; they never said no when I asked them to find something. I hope I have not forgotten anyone: Jane Lexow, Liz Tamoush, Linda Jackson, Glenn Britton, Dan Kenney, Kathryn Katsenis, and Daniel Gardner.

Charles Grench, American history editor at the University of North Carolina Press, his assistant Katy V. O'Brien, associate managing editor Paula Wald, and copy editor Grace Carino helped me get through a long journey to final publication. The outside reviewers for the University of North Carolina Press, Melvyn Dubofsky and Edward Berkowitz, were generous critics and made me read more widely. Historian and old friend Doug Monroy read chapters early on. Pat Palmieri was supportive all the way, and she encouraged me to link up with Charles Grench. Two economists helped out. Tom Larson gave valuable criticism, especially of chapters 4 and 5, and Jim Devine tried to answer my queries. Gordon Fisher helped me understand poverty lines and adequate budgets. Joan Williams applied a fine-tooth comb to several sections. Sociologist Ellen Reese commented especially on chapter 8. The staff of the *Journal of Poverty*, led by Keith Kilty, gave me pointed criticisms on several occasions. So did participants at the annual conventions of the Southwest Labor Studies Association, notably the late Tim Sampson. Librarians at the

John F. Kennedy Library sent copies of documents relating to the War on Poverty. Many people, including Martha Bishop in Ohio and Larry DeWitt at the Social Security Administration in Washington, helped me acquire illustrations. Above all, members of the Los Angeles Social History Study Group read every chapter at least once and patiently offered trenchant criticisms. I learned much from the critical process of the group. It has endured for a quarter of a century, and its recent membership included Hal Barron, Carla Bittel, the late Clark Davis, Bill Deverell, Phil Ethington, Nancy Fitch, John Laslett, Nelson Lichtenstein, Margot McBane, Jan Reiff, Seth Rockman, Troy Rondinone, Steve Ross, Diana Selig, Bob Slayton, Jessica Wang, Tom Zakim, and Leila Zenderland.

Antipoverty workers who spoke to my classes shaped the way I thought about the book. Nancy Berlin, Bob Erlenbusch, Alton Donatto, Valerie Grab, and Paul Freese all inspired me with their tenacity, deep knowledge of people, and moral strength. Finally, my family helped me complete this work. Although they might not understand some of it and they would disagree with many of its conclusions, my parents, now deceased, would be proud of this book. My brothers and their partners, Bert and Margot and Jim and Debby, will also disagree with much, but they have been supportive of my career. My mother-in-law, Virginia Bragg, helped out in ways that she may not even know. My son, Vonn Schopp, helped with technical support and much else. My daughter, Alexis Schopp, did research and often helped me become a little less computer-illiterate. Finally, my wife, Deborah Schopp, read many chapters and offered loving support every step of the way. She is a patient, steadying force in my life.

INTRODUCTION

Historical Overview

Two hundred years ago, poverty was a pressing issue in the United States. Influenced by Enlightenment rationalism, Protestant evangelicalism, and American self-confidence, reformers believed that they could cure poverty. In those years, as in other times, the causes of poverty were debated, but most people chose one of two big explanations. The first blamed the poor; laziness or foolishness caused them to be impoverished. The second emphasized political and economic structures that failed to provide enough jobs and that dealt too much income to the rich and too little to the majority.[1]

Today we are vastly richer than we were in the early 1800s, and our governments operate dozens of programs that help the poor. But if much has changed, much remains the same. In every year of the past fifty, at least 11% and often much more of the U.S. population has been poor. (This is according to official U.S. poverty lines, which meant that in 2004 a family of four with more than $19,157 a year was not poor.)[2] The 37 million officially poor in 2004 did not include millions of Americans in a state of near poverty, above the miserably low government poverty lines but below a decent standard of living.

This book is about the past half century of our national debate about poverty. In the 1950s we were not much concerned about the poor. Anticommunism stifled critical economic thinking, and our leaders had faith in the economic growth machine. But when growth faltered in the late 50s, a serious discussion began about the causes of poverty and unemployment. Conservatives had their views, too, but much debate occurred among liberals and liberal scholars. How much poverty and unemployment was caused by the fact that the economy was not growing fast enough? How much was due to specific factors such as racism, regional decline, automation, and people's lack of schooling and skills?

In the late 50s and early 60s, liberals and leftists prepared the way for the War on Poverty, but they sometimes misled the public by emphasizing the defective mentality of the poor. In *The Affluent Society* (1958) liberal economist John Kenneth Galbraith claimed that the poor were just a handful of people outside the economic mainstream. Socialist writer Michael Harrington seemed at times to agree. Elsewhere Harrington pushed for economic growth and urged government to create jobs, but in his most famous book, *The Other America* (1962), he prepared the ground for a War on Poverty that focused on poor people's defects.

The 1960s were the last period of triumphant liberalism in our history. President Lyndon Johnson and his economists adopted a three-part recipe for prosperity: tax cuts to spur economic growth, the War on Poverty to rehabilitate and train the damaged poor for the jobs that growth would generate, and programs like Medicare, Medicaid, and food stamps to fix the problems that remained. We shall see whether this liberal project succeeded or whether, as conservatives maintained, it caused laziness and poverty.

At points in the 60s and 70s, some liberal intellectuals and politicians inched toward a more radical position: growth would never eliminate unemployment and job-related poverty. Government would have to create jobs directly. A small group led by Harrington and Daniel Patrick Moynihan had urged this approach in planning the War on Poverty, but to no avail. Moynihan reportedly suggested that the U.S. Postal Service bring back two mail deliveries a day, for that would create 50,000 good jobs. The urban riots of mostly poor people in the late 60s also put job creation on the agenda. Secretary of Labor Willard Wirtz's survey of real inner-city unemployment showed appalling levels of misery. These seedlings might have refocused poverty policy toward direct job creation.

Although President Richard Nixon eliminated components of the War on Poverty, tentative steps were taken toward a new antipoverty policy in the early 1970s. Nixon's plan for a guaranteed income failed in Congress, but presidents and Congresses approved large hikes in Social Security benefits, an Earned Income Tax Credit for working poor families, and a program of government jobs for the poor and the unemployed.

Despite these victories for government antipoverty ventures, the political balance was shifting against liberalism in the 70s. Backlash to radical movements of the 60s played a role, but so also did soaring inflation and rising unemployment. Conservative scholars such as Martin Anderson argued that government social programs discouraged hard work and entrepreneurship. As the decade came to a close, there was still strong backing for Social Security, but popular support for programs serving the poor wavered. Meanwhile, business mobilized against government regulations and social programs, the conservative movement was growing in sophistication, and liberals seemed confused.

By the mid-80s, with Ronald Reagan in the White House and author Charles Murray doing the talk show circuit, conservatives began to shape public debate on poverty, welfare, and unemployment. In effect, they encouraged white workers to turn against the average poor person of color. But why didn't labor and liberals make political hay out of global changes, deindustrialization, and recessions, which clearly did not stem from people's laziness or overly generous welfare programs? Perhaps liberals and leftists had not, in the 60s and early 70s, significantly modified popular beliefs about individual blame for being poor—or even their own beliefs. Had the liberals won the legislative battles but lost the intellectual war? Or perhaps liberalism's penchant for government action was, as conservatives maintained, fundamentally flawed.

In the 80s and 90s, almost no one talked about direct government job creation to solve unemployment and poverty. That seedling of the 60s and 70s had wilted. Liberals as well as conservatives did little to stop the influx of cheap foreign imports. In the Clinton boom of the 90s almost no one spoiled the party by asking whether positive reports on welfare reform, poverty, and unemployment ignored a lot of reality. There was more talk about the harmful effects of welfare than about the harmful effects of unemployment.

In the first years of the new millennium, the great American job machine again faltered. Between the start of recession in March 2001 and the spring of 2005, the private sector showed essentially no net job increase. Not only did the total increase in jobs trail the average of other postwar recoveries, but all the net gain was in government jobs—a curious outcome for an administration that claimed to be conservative.[3] Meanwhile, poverty began inching up again, but even in the presidential campaign of 2004, there was not much debate about poverty or jobs. And little was said about the fact that the United States had the highest poverty rate of all the rich democracies.

Assumptions and Intentions

This book is intended primarily for concerned citizens and upper-level college students. It describes the political, economic, and intellectual history of poverty and unemployment over five decades. But it is more than a descriptive history. It explains why things turned out the way they did. And it suggests that other roads might have been taken.

Staying out of poverty is only in part a matter of individual effort; it is also and more so about institutions and structures that allow individual aspirations to bloom or die. Most of this book assumes that, all other things being equal, the level of individual effort has not changed much in fifty years. But structures and institutions have, and so most of what follows is about big causes.

I believe that several approaches are necessary to solve poverty, but I often focus on jobs because I believe that many antipoverty approaches are futile without good jobs and because I believe it is necessary to confront the conservative command to the poor—"*Get a Job!*"—with reality. I show in several chapters that unemployment was higher than we were told and that we often had a labor glut. I believe that whenever full employment seems within reach, the authorities curb economic growth in order to combat wage and price inflation. That is, the growth remedy for unemployment and poverty is never allowed to work long enough to complete the task that its defenders claim for it. So there is always a job shortage, and as long as there is a job shortage, there will be poverty among people who want to work.

I have learned a great deal from many scholars and activists, but my model of unemployment and job-related poverty comes mostly from reading Marxists and liberal writers and from studying the course of history since the mid-nineteenth century. The historical record demonstrates that a substantial amount of unemployment is normal for capitalism; capitalists don't want a thirties-style depression, but they do want a fair amount of unemployment in order to control workers and suppress wages. If this is true, then the years of relatively low unemployment—for example, in the early 50s and the late 90s—are the exception; except during big wars, unemployment never stays low for very long. And in recent decades, when faced with stiff competition from abroad, American businesses have traveled the globe in order to enlarge the available labor force. In effect, capitalists take advantage of the worldwide labor surplus, that is, of high unemployment around the globe.

As long as the cozy relationship between government and capital continues, job-related poverty is not likely to be solved. With a few tweaks here and there, Social Security can eliminate poverty for people who have finished working; it has just about done so already. But for those who need and want to work for pay, poverty rates are about where they were in the 1970s.

It seems to me that our leaders must be forced to promote enough economic growth to bring a long period of full employment, or take alternative steps to create jobs and raise wages. While each approach would require a broad political movement to compel action, the latter, direct approach may be easier. As to the first, I am convinced that when faced with a choice—and without counteracting pressures—our economic rulers at the Federal Reserve and in the White House will always choose less inflation over less unemployment and they will always favor capital over average Americans with subsidies and tax cuts. Barring government policies to promote a long economic boom that creates millions of permanent high-wage jobs, our leaders should admit that our government-coddled private markets cannot erase poverty. Then, if the fit of honesty continues, they can do either of two things. One is to confess to the public that they think it is best that we live permanently with 20% of the population poor and nearly poor. The other is to work with movements that support redistribution of income away from the very rich and toward the poor, direct government job creation, and government efforts to protect unionization and require higher pay.

Much more than job creation must be done to wipe out poverty. We can improve the schools and do better at retooling people's skills. But while more training and better schools are essential, they won't help the poor if the jobs aren't there.

Of course, much poverty is not job-related. As another part of any anti-poverty program, we must redesign rather than cut social programs. For example, some people cannot escape poverty by finding traditional jobs. Caretakers —parents caring for their children, children caring for aging parents, all who nurse sick friends and neighbors—deserve income.

And we need a national health program; on health care we spend more per capita, more in total, and more on administration than any other nation on earth, but we don't have the healthiest people, and millions are without secure access to medical care. Rising health insurance costs inhibit employers from hiring more workers, and they may make domestic businesses less competitive with foreign businesses in which health insurance costs are controlled and more universally shared. Did liberals err in the 60s by not trying for national health insurance to cover all?

To state the issue more broadly, we need less economic inequality and a frank recognition that a tiny class of rich people lives off the insecurities of a large class we might call the economic majority. The reader can judge whether liberals were politically shrewd or sadly mistaken in deemphasizing class and not making economic equality a bigger issue in the 60s. It seemed then that economic growth would create enough income to help the poor without having to take from the rich. But over the 80s and 90s, it became clear in the economic statistics that the richest took so much new income that there wasn't much left for the rest. Wages for most workers stagnated while executive pay soared. That meant more poverty.

At times liberals acted as though solving poverty was not a political issue and not, in some broad sense, a class issue. But it is both. It was not just impersonal forces that allotted more income to the rich and less to the middle and the bottom. Since the early 70s the rich and the wannabes have organized with great energy and ruthlessness to win many political battles. They are still winning them in the early 2000s. That has meant more inequality and more poverty. To solve poverty, some people are going to have to be made to give up some of their riches. More good jobs and more income for the poor cannot be created out of thin air.

Conservatives acted as though classes were nonexistent or not important, and liberals tried to run around the issue, arguing that everyone would gain from growth and good social programs. But if growth fails to create enough jobs or cure much poverty, what then? This situation became more likely in the 80s and 90s, when there were many years of high unemployment and corporate policy became leaner and meaner. In the 50s and 60s, it was possible to believe that corporate success would lift everyone; people at the top took less than they do now, and those at the bottom did better. But with intense foreign competition and rampant capital flight, life became more tenuous even for those who considered themselves middle class. Although many stayed middle income, many suffered volatile income swings. They were like the Jacobson family, which earned $60,000 in one year but, because of health crises and bad job markets, was forced the next year to beg for charity in order to meet house payments. Or the Ryans, who earned at least $100,000 a year in the late 80s but later were rocked by corporate collapses and medical catastrophes and had to declare bankruptcy twice. Or like millions of working poor and not poor Americans, whose incomes gyrate much more wildly than they did thirty years ago.[4]

Whether American politics and culture will change enough to confront increasing economic insecurity is up for grabs. In 2005 there was a disconnection between economic reality and public debate. In part this was the effect of living in a very rich country where there is a lot of income, a lot of material goods, and a lot of debt. But it also involved the mental frameworks that shape the way we think about class and power. Will our tradition of individualism and our desire to belong to the middle class inhibit the development of a "Coalition of the Economic Majority" against the top tenth that grows richer day by day? Will people find enough economic compensation from two-earner families and low-priced imports, enough warmth in religion, and enough escape in entertainment that they can ignore not only other people's poverty and joblessness but the hugely unequal distribution of incomes and their own shaky situation? In 2025 will we still be wondering why nothing is being done about the health insurance crisis and our 40 million poor people?

part one

The Golden Age

of Laissez-Faire?:

The 50s

chapter one

THE 1950s
Limited Government, Limited Affluence

For many Americans the decade of the 1950s has an agreeable image. As people stumbled through the turmoil of later years, they remembered the era of Dwight Eisenhower and Lucille Ball as a time of prosperity and moral calm. Two books published in 1986 reflected this warm popular assessment: William O'Neill's *American High: The Years of Confidence, 1945–1960* and J. Ronald Oakley's *God's Country: America in the 50s.*

Of course, there were negative reviews; they included claims that anticommunism and consumerism quashed critical thinking and that economic advances were limited. Lawrence Wittner wrote of a "blackout of critical opinion," and Douglas Miller and Marion Nowak assailed the decade's celebration of "people's capitalism," the myth of a fair and democratic economy. These authors pointed out that millions of Americans remained poor and that economic power was still exercised by a tiny group of corporate leaders.[1]

My chapter is in the second school. It challenges our cheery image of the 50s by examining poverty and how Americans defined poverty. It judges whether the economy of the 50s cured poverty, and whether it did so without significant government assistance. Were the 50s proof that individual willpower and laissez-faire policies were sufficient antipoverty programs, as conservatives later claimed? We will see that growth was strong and that it cured much poverty, especially in the early 50s, but also that government's role was vital in both promoting economic growth and lifting the destitute. Success against poverty evaporated in the late 50s when the president refused to spend.[2]

Linked to the issue of what government should do, a discussion began whose outcome would profoundly influence antipoverty policy. The discussion involved a big question. Were the high unemployment and persistent poverty of the late 50s due to discrete problems of specific groups (such as racism) or to large defects in the economy? Were people poor because of skill deficits and dysfunctional lower-class cultures or because they were simply the most distressed section of a large working class that suffered from deeply based income inequalities and a long-term labor glut? In short, was poverty caused by defective individuals and subcultures or by capitalism?

The 50s as Economic Utopia

The economy of the 50s seemed robust. Real (that is, after eliminating the effects of price changes) gross domestic product (all the goods and services produced in the United States) was 41% larger in 1960 than in 1950. Because the average tax bite did not rise much and because income inequality did not worsen, after-tax real income for the average family grew by an amazing 41%.[3]

The 50s were especially good for male workers, in part because the baby bust of the 20s and 30s meant less competition for good jobs. The male work force grew by less than 1% a year. At the same time, and contradicting widely held views that women belonged at home, the female labor force grew by almost 25%. While wives had more babies, more wives worked for pay, too. More than a third of all adult women were in the labor force.[4]

Men monopolized the growing number of elite white-collar and unionized blue-collar positions, and their pay advanced faster than women's. Average weekly earnings of employees in the male-dominated construction industry rose 62% to $113 in 1960; weekly earnings in a sector with many women, retail trade, rose 45% to $58.[5]

Historically, economic growth has been a popular method of solving poverty because it jibes with the American work ethic and because it often uses tax cuts and subsidies to businesses and the rich to spur investment and job creation. The benefits are supposed to trickle down. And a booming economy normally lifts people who are poor because they have not been working and earning, and it raises wages because demand for labor is up and employers must pay more to attract and keep workers. Also, increased output expands the income pie; if enough new income goes to the poor in the form of jobs and higher wages, the poverty rate will fall.

And fall it did in the 1950s. The proportion of the U.S. population that was poor declined from 30.2% in 1950 to 22.2% in 1960. (See figure A.2 in appendix 1.)[6] It is hard to argue with the notion that the 50s, an age of limited government, had a good record against poverty. But is the case finished?

What Made Poverty Fall in the 1950s?

Higher earnings from the main breadwinner were a major factor lifting families above the poverty line.[7] Increased earnings reflected growth in national output, productivity increases that made workers more efficient, and upward career moves. Some of the biggest advances in earnings came for blacks who migrated from the southern countryside to northern cities. It did not take much to rise above a sharecropper's annual earnings of $300. The poverty rate for African American *southern* families was 74.6% in 1949; for African American *northern* families in 1959 it was 31.7%. This did not mean that all was well for black migrants, but average incomes were higher.[8]

Migration, occupational advances, and earnings growth depended, in part, on general economic growth. Why was economic growth healthy in the 50s? Pent-up consumer demand from the 30s and early 40s still fueled the private sector, but government also helped. Spending on the Korean War (1950–53) created an economic boom; spending on highways employed thousands, and highways facilitated commerce and suburban construction. The G.I. Bill subsidized education and homes for millions of families. Eisenhower went along with increases in Social Security, the minimum wage, and unemployment compensation. He talked of limited government, and Treasury Secretary George Humphrey lauded the free market, but government jobs at all levels were growing twice as fast as all nonagricultural jobs. Growth was working, but government spending fueled it.[9]

Growth, migration, and training did not directly help groups that were likely to be out of the labor force. Two such groups were older Americans and female heads of household who wished to stay home with their children. Both groups grew in the 50s, and they made up almost half the American poor (figure 1.1). Each had some claim on public support, the aged because they had once worked, and female heads because they were raising children. Were government payments curing poverty in these two groups?[10]

The American welfare state seemed backward. As historian James Patterson put it, Europeans "tried to maximize coverage and minimize the stigma of accepting public aid . . . [Americans] sought to cut expenses and exclude from the rolls all people considered able to care for themselves."[11] Nevertheless, governments provided income to female-headed families, the blind and disabled, the unemployed, and the elderly. Spending on Social Security and disability insurance (the Old Age, Survivors, and Disability Insurance program [OASDI]) increased ten times in the 50s. The number of families on welfare (Aid to Dependent Children [ADC], which later became Aid to Families with Dependent Children [AFDC]) inched up from 644,000 to 787,000, and one

Figure 1.1. Poor Families by Type of Head of Household, 1959

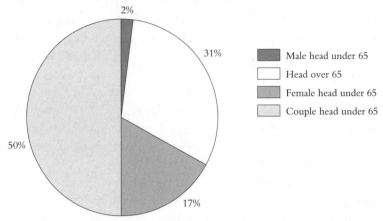

Source: Based on data in Herman P. Miller, *Rich Man, Poor Man* (New York: Thomas Y. Crowell Co., 1964), 65–66.

economist claimed that transfer payments lifted 30% of the poor out of poverty in 1961. But monthly payments to welfare families still averaged only $108 a month in 1960, roughly $1,300 a year. That was extreme poverty. Especially in states like Mississippi, where annual payments were only several hundred dollars, welfare did not cure poverty.[12]

With Social Security things were different. The recipient population multiplied, and benefits were liberalized four times in the 1950s. Average benefits increased from 59% to 83% of the poverty line for older couples. A retired female worker on her own was paid only $626 a year in 1957; she was probably still poor. Couples with Social Security and other income, however, were less likely to be poor by the end of the 50s.[13]

Total beneficiaries of ADC and OASDI jumped from 2 million to 18 million over 1945–60.[14] Although more people were being helped, the welfare state may have been hardening the division between a "deserving" poor (the elderly) and a "less deserving" poor (welfare families). The former were already getting a better deal. Whether the split would congeal would be determined by interplay of ideas, organizations, and politics. Could liberals offer a vision that combined generous support not only for unemployed and retired blue-collar whites but also for poor African Americans? Would the welfare poor be degraded and isolated?[15]

Seeds of a Debate

Although the economy was generally strong, a third to a fifth of the population was poor, and another fifth was on the edge of poverty. That was enough for a debate about economic policy. The welfare system was doing little to lift families out of poverty. That the poorest 40% of families received only 15% of all national income challenged the popular idea that everyone was middle class. Although they did not increase as in later decades, wealth inequalities were wide; the richest 1% of all adults held 33% of all assets by 1962.[16]

For most of the decade questions like these were smothered by Cold War anticommunism, good feelings about prosperity, and conservatism in the professions. Anticommunism made it dangerous to be critical of America, and prosperity seemed to make it unnecessary. Not only did many Americans think that socialism and Marxism meant low living standards and totalitarianism; many believed also that affluence was eliminating class divisions.[17] While it was not surprising that politicians and business apologists were uncritical of capitalism, the retreat of critical thought and broad sympathy among some social scientists and social workers was troubling. Even in the Great Depression, most social scientists were not particularly radical on economic questions about class and capitalism, but in the late 40s and 50s, having to fight the Cold War by affirming American virtues blinded otherwise intelligent scholars. In 1955, prominent sociologists David Riesman and Nathan Glazer found no underprivileged except in "enclaves" in the southern Alleghenies and the rural Deep South. Poverty, in other words, was not much of a problem. Sociologist Robert Nisbet declared in 1959 that the United States was largely an egalitarian society: "The conception of class is largely obsolete." For many writers America had but one class, a huge middle stratum running from the lowliest worker to the richest coupon clipper. Such a formulation drowned the worries of the working class in a sea of affluence and shoved the poor out of the mainstream.[18]

Not long ago intellectual historian Richard Pells praised Riesman, William Whyte, and other 1950s social critics who gave our language catchy phrases like "the lonely crowd," "the power elite," and "the organization man." These writers *were* creative thinkers, but their creativity flowed in narrow channels, as did their collective obsession with the identity problems of the middle class. Few investigated the economic insecurities of the working class or the poor. This myopia of the intellectuals narrowed social policy in the 50s.[19]

While some in the helping professions worked with federal officials and union lobbyists to expand the social welfare state, many in the field of social work were more interested in the psychiatric rehabilitation of the needy.[20] But there were two noteworthy governmental initiatives against poverty. In 1956 Democratic governor Averell Harriman of New York appointed a committee on low-income problems. Its job-training experiments for the unemployed and underemployed and other pilot projects apparently improved the lives of 4,500 poor people. It is difficult to judge the effectiveness of those programs, but the Harriman effort anticipated programs of the 1960s by using training programs to restore "chronic welfare cases to economic self-sufficiency," by targeting "one of the main causes of substandard incomes," racial discrimination, and by establishing community development projects to focus local resources on the poverty problem. Most of all, the experiment showed that it was possible to crack the crust of complacency.[21]

The other initiative emerged from a congressional subcommittee on low-income families headed by Senator John Sparkman of Alabama. In 1949, the subcommittee pioneered the effort to develop explanations for poverty that were both humane and constricting. Economic deprivation, in this view, afflicted groups that, for reasons ranging from race and age to regional economic decline, were left behind as the economy expanded. Ending poverty was a problem not, as in the thirties, of the mainstream millions who were poor because of a faulty economy but of people who had social handicaps or faced discrimination that kept them out of a prosperous economy.

This handicapping approach was based on realities; there was, for example, an association between poverty and female-headed families, and race, sex, and age discrimination limited opportunity. But if the handicapping emphasis became the main approach to poverty, larger economic causes affecting millions of working-class Americans would be ignored. Furthermore, while it touched on such deep problems as racial discrimination, the handicapping model risked marginalizing poverty. In class terms, this categorical approach pushed aside the idea of a big working class of unemployed and employed but vulnerable people and created a one-class-plus model: most Americans were employed, successful, and middle class; outside this huge class were the poor, people who lacked drive or faced special impediments that kept them from pulling themselves up by their bootstraps.

The Sparkman committee seemed to reflect this one-class-plus approach, which risked marginalizing the poor and ignoring the working class.[22] An alternative came from a group of social workers and charity leaders who offered Sparkman's committee a study of one hundred low-income families in the early 50s. Their idea of the poor "included fathers who are heads of small enterprises such as a machine shop, a pickle works, laundries. Others are salaried employees or skilled or semiskilled wage earners—for example a goldsmith, a mold maker, tool and sheet-metal workers, bakers, truckmen, postmen . . . GIs on the way up; mothers keeping broken homes intact; together with a score of farm families and operators, sharecroppers and migratory workers. . . . Over a fourth of the urban breadwinners were skilled workers . . . one third of our urban family breadwinners had worked a full year . . . without earning as much as $2000."[23] This was a helpful way to picture the low-income population—as a broad spectrum of occupations and conditions, including many regularly employed people. It suggested a large, durable political constituency for egalitarian politics. Whether a broad or narrow view would frame policy remained to be seen.

Recession and Unemployment Raise Questions:
The Late 1950s

Throughout much of the decade conservatives tarred government social programs as communism, but in the late 1950s, anticommunism weakened. The Cold War with the Soviet Union continued, but in new forms; the Russians beat the Americans when they launched the Sputnik satellite in October 1957, and that fueled a national debate about American schools.[24]

Other events put equality and poverty in the news. These included the Montgomery Bus Boycott of 1955–56 and, a year later, the confrontation over school integration in Little Rock, Arkansas. There was mounting concern about urban decay, rising welfare rolls, and juvenile delinquency.[25] And what gave wider publicity to many of these issues was the recession in 1957. The slump was severe; truck and car sales fell by half. Unemployment rose above 6%, and for black Americans it exceeded 12% (figure 1.2). Twice as many Americans (4 million) were looking for jobs in the late 50s as in the early 50s. Full recovery would not take hold until 1962.[26]

Economic crisis roused audiences for reform. Recession accelerated plant closures, prefiguring the catastrophes of the 1970s and 1980s. High unemployment rates helped Democrats win congressional victories in 1958. The kinds of unemployment and poverty that predated the recession now seemed worthy of attention with the whole country in trouble. Liberals pushed not only to end the recession but also to ease long-term economic problems.

The idea that some kinds of poverty and unemployment were resistant to economic growth and required direct aid had appeared in the first reports of the Sparkman committee. In 1952, Pennsylvania had a program to train the long-term unemployed. The idea that "depressed areas" had been left high and dry by economic change and deserved government aid was first introduced into Congress in 1954; a year later Illinois senator Paul Douglas proposed a depressed areas act (retraining programs, subsidies for public works and new businesses). Eisenhower vetoed the bills in 1958 and 1960, but the idea that poverty and unemployment would remain even in good times was becoming common in reform circles.[27]

Meanwhile, labor unions were pressing for action on unemployment. Dem-

Figure 1.2. National and Black Unemployment Rates, 1948–1965

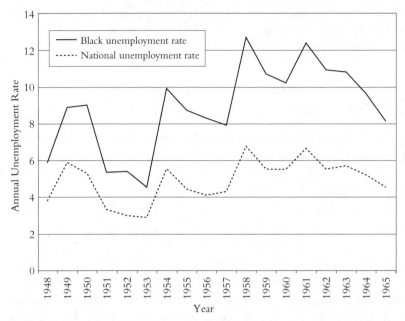

Source: U.S. Department of Commerce, Bureau of the Census, *Historical Statistics of the United States: Colonial Times to the Present*, pt. 1 (Washington: Government Printing Office, 1975), 135.

ocratic Senate majority leader Lyndon Johnson found a way to deflect the pressure; he appointed a committee under Minnesota senator Eugene McCarthy to study the problem. The Senate's Special Committee on Unemployment Problems toured the nation in 1959 and 1960 to listen to politicians, business leaders, union officials, academics, and the unemployed. The committee collected nine volumes of testimony.[28]

The Senate hearings were part of a rising debate about the causes of unemployment and poverty. Some economists, following the theories of British economist John Maynard Keynes, argued that enough aggregate economic growth would fix many of these problems. On the other side were those who talked of "structural unemployment," by which they meant that people were held back by discrimination, regional economic decline, lack of training, or other specific causes that persisted even in a booming economy. Those whose favored antidote to poverty and unemployment was pumping up general or *aggregate* economic growth I call "aggies." Those who wanted to focus on specific causes of poverty and unemployment such as lack of training or regional decline I call "stues" because they liked to talk about the problem of *structural unemployment* and poverty, which would last even in a booming

HILLBILLIES INVADE CHICAGO

One group that became a focus of antipoverty interest in the 60s was facing hard times and meeting the class equivalent of racism as it moved north. While migrations to the North were often an advance for southern blacks, many of whom came from desperately poor sharecropper families, some southern whites had a different experience. Many who had been farmers had been poor, but those who had worked as miners had probably once been better off. As mining jobs in Appalachia were cut in half in the 1950s, thousands moved north, carrying poverty with them. One favored destination was Chicago, which prided itself on being a place where one could find a job. But jobs were being moved to other areas; Appalachian whites, like southern blacks, faced unemployment, poverty, high crime and disease rates, and the hostility of Chicagoans. One police captain claimed that "they are vicious and knife-happy." The *Chicago Tribune* weighed in with an attack on this group: "The Southern hillbilly migrants who have descended like a plague of locusts in the last few years, have the lowest standard of living and moral code (if any), the biggest capacity for liquor, and the most savage tactics when drunk, which is most of the time." These were moral and cultural rather than economic views of poverty.

Sources: Albert N. Votaw, "The Hillbillies Invade Chicago," *Harper's*, February 1958, 64–67; Donald A. Crane and Benjamin Chinitz, "Poverty in Appalachia," and Robert J. Lampman, "Population Change and Poverty Reduction, 1947–1975," both in Leo Fishman, ed., *Poverty amid Affluence* (New Haven, Conn.: Yale University Press, 1966), 124–49, 18–42.

economy. In general, the aggies had better academic credentials and better theory than the stues, but the stues told stories with human interest. People knew that the Packard factory in Detroit closed its doors forever in 1956, that meatpacking plants were shutting down, that mining jobs and railroad employment were sinking, and that the older unemployed had a hard time of it.[29] Aggies argued that these problems would be solved if total economic demand improved enough, but the drama of human suffering inclined politicians toward the view that specific kinds of unemployment needed special programs right away. There wasn't much narrative power to the aggie argument; there was in John Alderson's story of looking for work: "When you tell them you're 61 years of age, regardless if you are able bodied, they seem to look at you and say, they don't tell you but they just give you the smile that you ought to have better sense than to ask."[30] In contrast, the aggies' talk of "billions in deficits" and the multiplier effect of federal spending seemed abstract. Also, aggie solutions were not directed at politicians' backyards—at the jobless of Detroit, Michigan; Altoona, Pennsylvania; and Illinois's Little Egypt. Under the aggies' rigorous scholarship, trouble spots might appear temporary or, in the words of conservative senator Barry Goldwater, as problems "perfectly normal to the economic cycle of American enterprise." But people in southern Illinois saw nothing normal about a decline in coal mining jobs from 9,596 workers to 2,908.[31] Even if economists who emphasized aggregate growth turned out to be right about the long run, people had to eat in the short run.

Galbraith, Keyserling, and Lampman: Liberals Debate Poverty

In the later 50s there was no consensus about whether poverty was a serious problem and whether its causes were primarily economic or personal. One liberal economist took the view that there weren't many poor people. In his best-selling book *The Affluent Society* (1958), John Kenneth Galbraith argued that the United States had solved the problem of producing enough for everyone; in fact, advertisers had to create false needs to stimulate buying.

Galbraith made a noble effort to move economic policy from its obsession with producing more goods—part of what he called the conventional wisdom —to concern for the quality of public goods. He drew a striking contrast between luxury in the private sector and poverty in the public sector. The family that took "its mauve and cerise, air-conditioned, power-steered, and power-braked automobile out for a tour passes through cities that are badly paved, made hideous by litter, blighted buildings, billboards, and posts for wires that should long since have been put underground."[32]

Galbraith was one of a small number of liberal writers who had anything to say about poverty. But his general themes cramped his view of poverty. He held that if the economy produces plenty and if most people have enough, it might follow that poverty is not due to economic causes but rather to personal defects or cultural lag. And if affluence prevails, poverty must afflict a very small group. Perhaps to help his case, Galbraith set his poverty lines at a very low $1,000 a year; that was about half the lines other scholars were proposing.[33]

Galbraith divided poverty into two categories: case poverty, in which poor people were mentally or socially defective, lacking skills and schooling, or victimized by alcoholism or "excessive procreation"; and insular poverty, which afflicted communities left behind by economic change and people who refused to migrate to better opportunities. Galbraith concluded that neither group's problems were likely to be solved by a "general and tolerably well-distributed advance in income," for a "specific individual inadequacy precludes employment and participation in the general advance."[34]

This focus on the defects of poor people was a common one. It came very close to degrading all poor people as inferior beings and led to ineffective antipoverty programs in the 1960s. It built a fence between the poor and the economic majority, for the view that the poor were defective blended nicely with the view that normal people were doing fine. In fact, millions were doing better than in the 1930s, but the affluence view exaggerated the prosperity of the nonpoor and supported what was becoming a new conventional wisdom: the working class had become middle class. The separation of the poor and the working nonpoor was not only bad social science; it was shaky support for political action. If the economic needs of the majority were ignored while attention was paid to the very poor, the economic majority would feel aggrieved. As its members struggled with medical bills and layoffs and college expenses, they might come to resent paying taxes to help the very poor.

There were facts enough for a perspective that linked poor and nonpoor as part of an economic majority that stretched out along a continuum from extreme to moderate economic insecurity. Senator Paul Douglas of Illinois and socialist writer Michael Harrington showed that the poverty population was much larger than Galbraith claimed. Others understood that most blue-collar workers and many white-collar workers were neither affluent nor middle class. The average auto worker, labor writer Harvey Swados remarked in 1957, took home less than $2 an hour, or about $4,000 year. That sum, just under median family incomes, was by no means lavish or middle class. (The sum of $4,000 in 1957 equaled $27,000 in the purchasing power of 2005 dollars.) Instead of talking about the middle-classification of the worker, we should be talking, Swados said, about "how a family man can get by in the Fifties on that kind of income."[35]

Galbraith seemed uninformed about what life was like for millions who were neither poor nor affluent. There were a lot of things for people to buy—monster cars with sharp fins, big refrigerators, TVs, TV dinners, and TV tables—and plenty of advertising; it was easy to conclude that almost everyone's basic needs were covered. But Galbraith made no effort to estimate whether most of people's budgets went for necessities or luxuries.

The Affluent Society had begun with a Carnegie grant to explain why the poor, especially farmers and Appalachian people, were poor; by the time Galbraith had finished, the poor had almost disappeared from his book—as they had in much of what the decade of the 50s said about itself.[36] Galbraith misled the reader: the poverty population was large, millions moved in and out each year, and economic growth could still make permanent cuts in poverty rates. Yet despite the flaws, Galbraith had done something useful; he had provoked debate about national purpose and about the existence and causes of poverty. This was no mean feat in the 50s, when it was easier to be utopian about capitalist success than critical of its failures.

In the debate about poverty, close to Galbraith's position were conservatives like former New Dealer Raymond Moley, who denied the existence of involuntary poverty, and liberals like historian and Democratic Party activist Arthur Schlesinger Jr., who agreed with Galbraith that poverty was pretty much a thing of the past.[37]

On the other side were radicals and liberals like Harrington and Swados and economists like Leon Keyserling. Keyserling had helped write the 1935 Wagner labor relations act, had been chair of Truman's Council of Economic Advisors (1949–53), and now ran a liberal think tank, the Conference on Economic Progress. Keyserling urged more government spending as a full-employment growth policy; he kept the focus on economic causes and off personal defects. He suggested that there were 17 million more poor people than Galbraith claimed. He was certain that economic growth was essential to cure poverty. He judged that the United States had a "dismally low rate of economic growth," and he meant not the late 1950s recession but the prosperous mid-50s. He enlarged the economically insecure population beyond the very poor. (Table 1.1 is my version of Keyserling's broader definition of the poor and the deprived.) Keyserling's definition supported a broad constituency for political action. Keyserling did not ignore social "handicaps" like racial prejudice and skill deficiencies that affected the poor, but he contended that these were not the ultimate causes of poverty and unemployment but rather screens by which the class system apportioned scarce jobs and income.[38]

Another economist who took poverty seriously and who would later play an important role in the War on Poverty was Robert Lampman. In 1959 the University of Wisconsin economist wrote for Congress *The Low Income Population and Economic Growth*. From census data Lampman concluded that the rate of poverty had fallen from 26% to 19% between 1947 and 1957. Young family heads (25–34 years old) did very well; their poverty rate declined from 24% to 12%. They succeeded because of economic growth, migration, productivity and wage advances, job mobility, and educational advance.[39]

Like most students of poverty, Lampman highlighted structural or handicapping characteristics that were associated with higher poverty rates for some groups. People 65 and over, female-headed families, nonwhites, and those with

Table 1.1. Poor and Nearly Poor Families in 1960

Very poor	17.5% of American families had less than $2,500 yearly income
Nearly poor	24.5% of American families had between $2,500 and $4,999 yearly income
Total deprived	42% of American families had less than $5,000 yearly income

Sources: Poverty lines from U.S. Department of Commerce, Bureau of the Census, Current Population Reports, P60-181, *Poverty in the United States, 1991* (Washington: Government Printing Office, 1992), A-6; income breakdown from U.S. Department of Commerce, Bureau of the Census, Current Population Reports, P60-127, *Money Income and Poverty Status of Families and Persons in the United States: 1980* (Washington: Government Printing Office, 1981), 13. See also Helene H. Lamale and Margaret S. Stotz, "The Interim City Worker's Family Budget," *Monthly Labor Review* 83 (August 1969): 785–808; Donald Light, "Income Distribution: The First Stage in the Consideration of Poverty," *Review of Radical Political Economics* 3 (Summer 1971): 44–50; Oscar Ornati, *Poverty amid Affluence* (New York: Twentieth Century Fund, 1966), 20–22, 191; Leon Keyserling, *Poverty and Deprivation in the United States: The Plight of Two-Fifths of a Nation* (Washington: Conference on Economic Progress, 1962); and U.S. Department of Commerce, Bureau of the Census, *Historical Statistics of the United States: Colonial Times to 1970*, pt. 1 (Washington: Government Printing Office, 1975), 169, 173.

Note: In the 60s the federal government adopted poverty lines that were just over $3,000 for a family of four. The figure was based on a skimpy food budget. Like Keyserling, I wanted a more realistic estimate of people in need. I used government income distribution figures to estimate how many families fell below $5,000. That large number probably included 8 million employees who earned $3,000 a year or less (about $1.50 an hour). Many were heads of households. They worked in clothing factories, in laundries, in hotels and motels, in variety and general merchandise stores, in drug stores, and on farms. Millions of other workers earned more but were hardly affluent. The average weekly wage in manufacturing came to $4,500 for fifty weeks.

This table suggests that not only were 17.5% of all families poor and often unable to pay their rent or food bills, but another 24.5% were lacking essentials of the American standard of living. Below $5,000 year, a family often had no TV, no car, no savings, and little furniture. It could take but one vacation a year, a fifty-mile rail trip. At $5,000–$6,000, the family neared what the Labor Department considered a "modest but adequate budget" for an urban family. Little was allotted to savings except health insurance and life insurance, but the family had income for better furniture, a TV, a used car, and a one-week camping trip. In short, families below $5,000 a year, especially in big cities, felt pinched. Above $5,000, they had more comfort but little for a rainy day.

little schooling were more likely to be poor than others. But Lampman was confident that trends were good for nonwhites; it was clear that their educational attainment was rising.[40] That left two groups, about half the poor, that might be immune to the benefits of economic growth—the aged and female-headed families (figure 1.1). Lampman claimed that the poverty rate for female-headed families, although still high, had fallen by a fourth. He was not pessimistic about this group.

The second group that seemed immune to the curative power of economic growth was the aged. Of all aged family heads, half were poor, and of all aged individuals on their own, 90% were poor. Lampman found little improvement over 1947–57, despite rising numbers of Social Security recipients. He claimed that benefits were still low, that Social Security encouraged people to leave the labor force—so job earnings fell—and that it allowed seniors to live alone, a situation in which they looked poorer than as members of their children's households. Lampman sometimes underestimated the antipoverty effects of Social Security, but he was right that government payments often eased rather than cured poverty.

Lampman was convinced that Galbraith's notion of a new poor, impervious to the benefits of economic growth, might be true for the aged and, to some extent, female-headed families. For the rest, Galbraith was wrong: poverty rates were falling; economic growth worked. Insular poverty declined as millions migrated, and Galbraith's case poverty was falling as educational levels rose. On the whole, Lampman was an optimist; poverty would continue to fall if the economy stayed healthy, if people got more schooling, and as productivity advanced.[41] While his categories sometimes implied too much division between the poor and the nonpoor, Lampman usually avoided negative stereotypes. In the future, would poverty thinking drift toward Galbraith's narrow categories of a handful of social abnormals, Lampman's middle-range view that normal economic growth could cure a lot of poverty, or Keyserling's large group of deprived Americans—almost half the population—that required more government spending and brisk economic growth?

Why Did Poverty Rates Stop Falling in the Late 1950s?

Poverty rates almost stopped falling in the late 50s. In 1956 22.9% of the population was poor; in 1960 the rate stood at 21.9%, a drop of only 1 percentage point. In contrast, over 1950–56, the rate had fallen more than a point a year to 22.9%. Why had success against poverty slowed? Were government payments too low? Or were they so high as to lure poor people into idleness? Perhaps unions caused unemployment. The following evaluates four detailed explanations for the weak antipoverty record of the late 1950s.

1. Government payments to older Americans were not lavish, but they were improving, and they were curing more poverty. Richer benefits would have cured more, but payments were growing, not shrinking. Welfare payments rarely cured poverty, but they were not moving in such a way as to cause more poverty.

2. Migration and more schooling normally meant less poverty. Had their impact lessened in the late 50s? State-to-state migration dropped a bit but not by much. Exits from the generally poorer farm population were only slightly slower than in the early 50s.[42] As to education, median years of completed

Table 1.2. Percentage of Female-Headed Families by Race

Year	White	Black	Nonwhite
1940	10.1	17.9	20.6
1950	8.5	17.6[a]	23.7
1960	8.1	21.7	21.9
1970	9.1	28.3	27.6
1980	11.6	40.2	32

Sources: White and black data adapted from William Julius Wilson and Kathryn M. Neckerman, "Poverty and Family Structure: The Widening Gap between Evidence and Public Issues," in Sheldon H. Danziger and Daniel H. Weinberg, eds., *Fighting Poverty: What Works and What Doesn't* (Cambridge, Mass.: Harvard University Press, 1986), 235; nonwhite data from Christine Ross, Sheldon Danziger, and Eugene Smolensky, *The Level and Trend of Poverty, 1939–1979*, Discussion Paper #790-85 (Madison, Wis.: Institute for Research on Poverty, 1985), 26, table 12.
[a]Black and "other."

school continued to rise, from 9 to 11.1 for men and 9.7 to 11.6 for women (1950–62). Migration and education were moving against poverty.[43]

3. It is unlikely that increasing numbers of people made themselves poor to get on welfare. It is true that the number of families on welfare increased by 22%, from 644,000 to 787,000 (1950–60), but the totals were small, and there is no evidence that these people had not been poor before welfare. Whether the overall share of female-headed families was rising is not even certain (table 1.2). The share of white female-headed families barely changed in the 50s; calculations for two categories of nonwhites show an increase and a decrease. At the very least, the proportion of female-headed families in the 50s was increasing slowly.

4. Some economists claimed that unions raised the cost of labor so much as to force employers to lay off workers. More unemployment meant more poverty.[44] But if so, why did exits from poverty slow in 1956–61 when union membership declined from 25.2% to 22.3% of the labor force? After-inflation compensation in manufacturing grew 12.5%, but since worker output per hour grew almost as much (12.1%), labor costs were not rising. On the other hand, in 1950–55, real compensation increased by 20.5%, faster than worker output per hour (14.1%). If rising labor costs caused poverty, why didn't poverty rates rise in the early 1950s and fall in the late 50s? The reason is simple: rising labor costs did not cause more poverty.[45]

The size of the poverty population had much to do with four big factors. First, the stues, who emphasized such causes as regional decline and training deficits, argued that the economy was undergoing rapid structural change that was leaving millions behind. The stues were not able to show that such change was faster than in the past, but it was there, in the depressed mining communities of Appalachia and in the shuttered factories of older cities. Add the impact of racism and sexism on employment opportunities, and structural causes account for a fair amount of poverty and unemployment. Second, and on the other hand, aggies claimed that full-employment growth required strong government action. While the aggies acknowledged that regions and industries were in decline, they believed that strong overall growth would solve many apparently structural causes of poverty. Third, Marxists offered a pessimistic version of the aggie story; not only was economic growth too slow in the late 1950s, but it would never erase unemployment and poverty. Fourth, in any economy there are people who cannot work, and even in the best economy there is unemployment, and that causes poverty. Since natural events (such as disease and aging), economic inequalities, and deep-seated unemployment are ever present, institutions must compensate. To the degree that compensating programs and organizations like unions don't function well, more people will be poor.

All four of these explanations were true. Structural unemployment and poverty would always be important, as long as some businesses declined and some grew, as long as there were regional shifts in economic activity, and as long as there was discrimination. The last could be eased by civil rights legislation, the first two factors by improved unemployment insurance and labor market policies.

Meanwhile, aggregate growth normally cut poverty rates, and recession raised them. The 60s showed how economic growth lifted the poor and the early 80s how depression raised unemployment and poverty rates. However, economic growth may not be enough. As we shall see, in the later 80s (illustrating our fourth factor), with the balance of power tilted against the working class as unions declined and good jobs were exported, economic growth did not always eliminate much poverty.

As to the third explanation, this history will show that growth is never long and strong enough to eliminate unemployment and job-related poverty. Growth in the 80s and 90s would be slower to cure poverty, and it stopped while poverty rates were still more than 11%. In the 50s and 60s there was still room for the growth medicine to cure a fair amount of poverty, but in later decades, the Marxists were right that growth alone would not eliminate what was left of poverty because there would never be enough of it. One of two events usually interrupted the boom. Overproduction led to lower investment and recession; or growth brought inflation and higher wages, and the Federal Reserve Board responded by creating a recession that raised unemployment and poverty.

African Americans and Deindustrialization: Structural Unemployment and Poverty

Structural causes undoubtedly made people poor. This was apparent in two areas. One was the way women were treated in labor markets and family matters. Another, the focus of this section, involved the impact of racism and economic change on African Americans.

The structural argument that unemployment and job-related poverty were best explained by specific causes rather than overall economic growth seemed to make sense in some cases, but it was not well developed in research and theory. Its advocates often argued that aggregate growth was adequate and that there were plenty of jobs; structural unemployment resulted not because there were too few job openings but because the jobless were in the wrong place, lacked appropriate skills, or suffered discrimination. In 1959, John Ross of the Evansville, Indiana, Employment Security Division testified that there were vacancies for 6,100 unemployed in his community, but, he claimed, the jobless lacked skill or schooling for such vacancies as mechanical engineer, legal secretary, hospital orderly trainee, and snackbar counter girl. This alleged mismatch between jobless people and job vacancies provides a perfect example of what was meant by structural unemployment in the 1950s.[46] It also reveals a partial weakness in the stue argument, for it is hard to believe that people lacked skill and training to become orderlies and counter workers.

Despite claims that jobs went unfilled, experts were unable to develop a convincing measure of job vacancies, and they never proved that skill requirements were rising faster than educational levels. Also, the stues rarely acknowledged the example of World War II, which showed that during periods of rapid growth employers provided or job seekers found the training they needed. Enough growth—the aggie recipe—solved a lot of skill problems.

Despite these weaknesses in the stue argument, people observed striking examples of structural unemployment and structural poverty. Mining employment was sinking in Appalachia, in southern Illinois, and on the Minnesota iron range. Four thousand Packard workers lost their jobs in 1956, a generally prosperous year. Two years later, only 44% of them had jobs; the unskilled, blacks, and the aged had a hard time finding new employment, and many slipped into poverty.[47] These were powerful examples of structural joblessness.

The American job structure was tilting away from solid blue-collar jobs. In the 1950s, professional and related categories grew by 65%, and clerical and related occupations grew by 28%. Blue-collar job growth stopped.[48] In manufacturing, total output and white-collar positions climbed, but the number of blue-collar positions was the same in 1960 as it had been in 1950.[49] Productivity advanced faster than prices fell or markets grew, so more workers were not needed. The result was automation unemployment. Some economists thought worries about automation were silly, but blue-collar workers understood the threat.[50]

In the late 40s and the 50s, whites moved to the suburbs and to the South and the West, but two-thirds of black migrants moved from the South to the Midwest and Northeast, often to cities that were leaking industrial jobs. Some locales where minorities and the United Auto Workers Union had made job gains were vacated by the car companies. The big three automakers built twenty-five plants in the metropolitan area of Detroit, but in search of pliant labor and cheap land, they built every single one in the suburbs. Detroit's manufacturing production force fell by half, from 281,500 to 145,000 (1947–63). This loss of jobs meant more poverty. Of the ten largest cities, only Los Angeles gained manufacturing production jobs (55,000); the other nine lost 680,000 positions. In East St. Louis, Fargo, Chicago, and Oklahoma City, 30,000 meatpacking jobs disappeared in 1956–59. Chicago lost a third of its blue-collar factory jobs (1945–63), and the number of blacks in Chicago manufacturing fell by 2,000 (1950–60). The South gained 944,000 manufacturing jobs; 12,000 went to black women and none to black men. Government jobs provided increasing opportunity for African Americans, particularly for educated women, but industrial work was leaving northern cities and was almost closed to blacks in the South.[51] When jobs were suburbanized, it was hard for blacks to follow. Federal housing agencies did not support shelter for blacks in the suburbs. (Federal taxes subsidized the highways and housing that made suburbanization possible, so Americans were paying for discrimination and poverty.) Job flight and racism slowed progress against black poverty and aggravated inner-city troubles.[52]

The mix of racism, economic transformation, and, in the late 50s, weak economic growth was poison for minorities. The ratio of black to white male unemployment averaged 1.69 during the Korean War, but it was 2.0 in the late 50s (1958–61). Growth in the median real earnings of white males slowed in the late 50s (2.7% over 1956–59), but it actually turned negative for black men (−6%).[53] Black family income fell from 55.2% of white family income to 53.2%.[54] The late 1950s was not such a golden age for the working class, and especially not for blacks.

The stues were right that economic transformation was hitting factory workers. Potentially this was a political unifier, for whites as well as blacks suffered job loss. But racism allotted more pain to blacks than to whites, and there was less incentive for whites to confront the conditions of economic insecurity that threatened everyone. If they needed to feel they were better off

DETROIT'S WELFARE EMPIRE

Once spending on Korea tapered off and as automakers accelerated urban deindustrialization, the welfare rolls crept up. The result was heaven-sent for critics who helped whites scapegoat African Americans and ignore what was happening to the economy.

The cases that author Ray Moseley picked for his welfare exposé in Detroit were atypical—yet they soon became typical in white folk tales. There was Maude, herself illegitimate, who produced nine children with seven men and lived with her family in four rooms with one bed. There was 300-pound Bernice, with eleven children, some of whom already had their own illegitimate babies. And so on. The homes of many welfare clients were "nothing more than breeding grounds for crime, immorality, and severe emotional illnesses, all being subsidized with public money."

Writers like Moseley did not play fair. Some poor blacks on welfare had bad values (as did people in corporate offices); many, however, were blocked by harsh labor markets and residential apartheid. The idea that white taxes supported black immorality and laziness was good politics. In 1960 Louisiana's governor tried to eject from welfare women who had children out of wedlock; 95% of the victims were black. The action was halted by federal officials. A year later, the city manager of New-burgh, New York, went after African Americans. Newburgh was losing jobs, losing whites, and gaining black residents. City Manager Joseph Mitchell, hoping to scare people, ordered all recipients to pick up their checks at the police station. He proposed that no one without a firm job offer be allowed to settle in Newburgh. Mitchell became national news. Arizona senator Barry Goldwater praised him for fighting the chiselers. President John Kennedy recognized that welfare could cause political trouble, and his administration worked on reforms to keep families together and rehabilitate workers.

Sources: Ray Moseley, "Detroit's Welfare Empire," *Atlantic Monthly*, April 1960, 43–46; "Temporary Assistance to Needy Families," at <www.acf.dhhs.gov/news/stats/3697.htm>; Edward D. Berkowitz, *America's Welfare State: From Roosevelt to Reagan* (Baltimore: Johns Hopkins University Press, 1991), 100–107.

and just plain better, white workers had politicians and journalists who were demonizing black people. What could have solved some of these problems was a combination of aggregate, structural, and institutional approaches. The aggies wanted to end the recession and promote growth; that always cured some poverty. But to advance equality and economic security it was also necessary to have strong civil rights laws, better unemployment insurance, transition assistance for workers pushed out of good jobs, and unionization in expanding areas of service and clerical work. That package might have been pie in the sky in the late 50s, but many pieces would be on the table in the 60s.

Ike and Conservatives Choose More Poverty: Poverty Is a Political Choice

In the debate between stues and aggies about whether structural or aggregate growth problems explained low incomes, a pragmatic view made sense. As President John Kennedy later said of unemployment, "Some of it is structural and some of it is not."[55] Aggregate growth was important, but whether the economy was growing or not, it was necessary to attack structural problems, especially discrimination and deindustrialization. Eisenhower vetoed bills to aid depressed areas, and he did little to advance civil rights.[56]

There was still plenty of antipoverty work that growth could accomplish. A fourth of the population was poor in 1958, and millions were nearly poor. A moderately conservative political leader like Eisenhower could have worked for strong economic growth to create jobs, cure poverty, and help minorities.[57]

I stated earlier in this chapter that the 50s' record on economic growth was positive, but if the decade is broken down into smaller segments, the picture is mixed. Over 1956–60, growth was just so-so, with the exception of one sparkling year (7.2% in 1959). Korean War spending accounted for some of the decade's strongest growth. After that, there were three recessions, all under Eisenhower: 1953–54, 1957–58, and 1960. This might come as a surprise to people brought up on the view that the decade was an economic golden age, but we now understand why Keyserling labeled the 50s a period of "abysmally low growth." It may also come as a surprise that total real increases in output during Eisenhower's presidency (20%) were less than under the Clinton (28.6%) and the Kennedy and Johnson administrations (43%).[58]

Why were growth rates weak in the late 50s? It was not because of pressure on profits. Although pay for salaried workers shot up, wages for many workers fell behind productivity, so labor costs were not eating into profits.[59] Corporations had ample funds for new investment, but investors grew "cautious." That was not because of a security-conscious management—as in *The Organization*

Man or *The Man in the Grey Flannel Suit*—but because companies had already added productive capacity beyond potential demand. Sales of big consumer items jumped by 6.6% a year over 1947–55 but only 0.9% a year over 1955–59. More money was going to rent and services. Without hefty income increases, consumers could not rapidly increase their purchases of cars, televisions, and refrigerators.[60]

Also, there was a paradox at the heart of investments that generated rising productivity. Increases in efficiency from investment in technology might mean more output but not more workers. Without a greater share of income going to average- and low-income consumers or shorter work weeks, more investment meant overproduction. Marxist economists Paul Baran and Paul Sweezy argued that "capitalism's basic law of motion"—its inherent tendency to overproduction and stagnation—had reasserted itself in the late 1950s.[61] As in the late 1920s, the economy was in a crisis from which it could not escape without government spending. The laissez-faire ideal of conservatives was stumbling.

One countermeasure to recession and unemployment was to tax the rich more and redistribute the income to low- and middle-income Americans, that is, to people who spent most of their incomes. That would have spurred economic growth. But the Robin Hood strategy did not have broad support in the late 50s. Still, government could have found other ways to increase civilian spending; one option was borrowed funds, that is, deficit spending. Big deficits had erased unemployment and cured a lot of poverty in World War II and the Korean War. Some in the labor movement and business circles as well as Democrats like Keyserling were ready for deficit spending.[62]

Even some Republicans wanted more federal spending to stimulate the economy. Vice President Richard Nixon, former Council of Economic Advisors' chair Arthur Burns, and even the generally conservative Raymond Saulnier, head of the Council of Economic Advisors, favored more spending. But they were in a minority. They faced Republicans who wanted to eliminate even the deficits that accompanied recession as tax revenues fell. Some conservatives believed that deficit spending was immoral and even pro-communist; they would not support increased government spending that would have created more jobs.[63]

Cuts in the military budget during the Korean wind down and Republican antispending policy caused a shrinkage of federal stimulus. Defense expenditures jumped from $13.3 billion in 1949 to $48.7 billion in 1953 but sank to $41.2 billion in 1954. Over the next five years they advanced only to $46 billion. Total federal purchases of goods and services more than doubled between 1949 and 1954 (+136%) but grew only 13% between 1954 and 1959. It was an achievement that Eisenhower resisted demands for higher military spending, demands fueled by the Sputnik scare and Democratic grandstanding about the missile gap. His success shows what he might have done against hysteria over deficits and inflation. In Galbraith's *The Affluent Society* or in publications by conservative writers concerned about America's cultural heritage, the president would have found popular spending opportunities in park building, highway beautification, school and museum construction, and much more. But Eisenhower's worldview linked anticommunism and tight budgets: fighting communism demanded economic strength; inflation threatened strength; federal deficits and low interest rates caused inflation. Eisenhower's budget policy and Federal Reserve chair William McChesney Martin Jr.'s use of high interest rates to keep inflation low raised unemployment and poverty. Even when 1,120,000 were added to the ranks of the unemployed in January 1958, Eisenhower responded with what *Time* magazine called "puny antirecession" measures.[64]

People who urged more federal spending and easier credit to boost the economy were sometimes accused of being Reds; anticommunism still restricted debate. Liberals attacked Eisenhower's slow-growth policies, but they were a minority. Senator Paul Douglas's program for a temporary $6 billion tax cut was trounced in the Senate, 65 to 23, on June 18, 1958. Eisenhower vetoed Democratic bills to provide federal aid to depressed regions.[65]

Ike's decision to fight inflation rather than unemployment and poverty was not a neutral or technical one. It was a political judgment that hurt people at the bottom most. It was to be a common judgment for American leaders in 80s and 90s. Eisenhower and those of like mind judged the negative threat of inflation and rising wages more important than the positive prospect of aiding the poor and unemployed. The rate of exits from poverty could have been accelerated by policies that were not too far from even the narrow economics of many Republicans and Democrats. But Eisenhower resisted antirecession programs. And Martin, in the midst of recession, chose to fight wage increases and inflation by making credit more expensive, even though it was not clear that high interest rates cured inflation (prices would soon climb despite tight money in this recession) or that deficits caused inflation. There were alternative mainstream explanations for inflation—for example, that big businesses, acting together like monopolies, "administered prices" to keep them high even as consumer demand fell. But debating the issues was not an option around Eisenhower. People who opposed the president, like Nixon, were ignored.[66]

In the late 50s and early 60s, the big poverty and unemployment question among scholars was which helped more: aggregate growth or programs targeted at structural unemployment and discrimination. But those two options did not exhaust the list of explanations. Few asked whether unemployment and poverty were built into the economy and its class system and would require, therefore, as a cure a larger welfare state and direct job creation. In the next two chapters we examine how politicians, scholars, and activists in the 60s understood the causes of poverty and the character of the poverty population. Attacks on the poor and welfare cheats seemed to be getting more vitriolic ("Hillbillies" and "Detroit's Welfare Empire"), but the poverty problem was not yet racialized, the narrow focus on people with social handicaps had not hardened, and the poor had not been fully marginalized as a group outside the class structure. Across-the-board remedies for poverty, unemployment, and other economic problems that afflicted a large working class were still possible. And for a while healthy economic growth could still lift a fraction of the poor out of poverty.

part two

Wars on Poverty:

The 60s

chapter two

PLANNING THE WAR ON POVERTY
Fixing the Poor or Fixing the Economy?

Early in 1964, President Lyndon Johnson declared unconditional war on poverty. Before learning about the programs that followed, the
reader might reflect on the best ways to solve poverty. One way to start thinking about antipoverty strategies is to learn about what made people poor.
There will be theories and facts in the rest of this book to help the reader
answer these questions, but here's something concrete. In February 1964,
Newsweek magazine profiled nine poor households. (In judging these cases, it
helps to know that experts were thinking that the annual poverty line for a
family of four would be $3,000 to $4,000 and for an individual about $1,500.)[1]

1. A Maine couple, Alice and Howard Neipert, were in their seventies. They
lived on $1,700 a year in Social Security payments and worried about crushing
medical expenses.

2. In Spanish Harlem, Pauline Veliz raised six children on welfare benefits of
$3,000. Three of her children had chronic illnesses. Pauline's parents had emi-
grated from Puerto Rico.

3. In San Francisco, 68-year-old Esther Strom lived on less than $1,500. She
had emigrated from Finland in 1928 and worked as a cook before retiring.

4. Twenty-one-year-old Thomas Ray Spray of Des Moines, Iowa, had a
learning problem that kept him out of the military and hindered him from
earning a high school diploma. He lived with his mother, who earned $1,500 a
year as a baker. When Thomas looked for work at the state unemployment
office, "all they ever say is they ain't got nothing. Leave your application, and
we'll be calling you, they say, but nobody ever calls."

5. In Detroit, Joseph Crowley had been laid off from a good warehouse job.

Now he searched for work and cared for his five children. The family lived on his wife's wages as a housekeeper—about $3,000 a year.

6. Slim Lemert was a "Main Street wino in Los Angeles." He had pretty much given up on life and seemed proud of it.

7. Handyman John Kester was a respected figure in his Oklahoma community, but his regular pay, which did not surpass $3,000 a year, had to support a family of nine.

8. In rural Georgia, African Americans Tobe and Claudie Mae Lowe and their eight children lived in two rooms. Tobe had worked for twenty-one years in the sawmills, but the local industry was in decline. Often the Lowes had no cash at all, and never enough for the operation Mrs. Lowe needed.

9. Finally, in Granny's Branch, Kentucky, there was 42-year-old Jim Smith, unemployed miner, and his ten children. Thousands of Appalachian miners lived like he did, without work and dependent on government aid.[2]

In this sample of the poor, five households needed jobs or better jobs: Tom Spray (#4), the Crowleys (#5), Mr. Kester (#7), Mr. Lowe (#8), and Mr. Smith (#9). The older Americans and the welfare family needed more generous government income programs and health insurance. Half of these households might have been better off economically if they had been smaller, but lack of jobs and income was the key. Only one of them, Slim Lemert (#6), seemed so psychologically damaged that a job or government subsidy would not have improved his life.

From this informal survey, one might guess that the War on Poverty would have included three things: family planning, new jobs with good pay, and more income in the form of cash and free medical care for people who could not work. In fact, the federal government did some of these things in the 60s. It increased spending and cut taxes to stimulate job creation, and that was a vital, if sometimes unacknowledged, part of its war on poverty; it also lifted people's incomes by raising the minimum wage and Social Security benefits and creating Medicare and Medicaid. But the programs that were publicized as the War on Poverty and that are the main subject of this chapter excluded direct job creation and income supports. They were about fixing the attitudes and skills of poor people and community institutions.

If we think of the War on Poverty not only as a program of assistance to the poor but as a story to educate the public, we can judge whether it taught Americans about the sources of poverty and inequality. In this and in other chapters (5, 7, 10), we will analyze job data to test whether the focus on poor people's lack of skills and proper attitudes was the right one. At this stage we can say that the focus on poor people's bad attitudes, what some were calling "the culture of poverty," did not appear to fit the *Newsweek* households.

Poverty discussion and the War on Poverty itself reflected what one author called the "liberal consensus" of the 1950s and 1960s. The consensus was that economic structures were sound or could be made so easily, that the paths to success were not blocked by class barriers (and race barriers were being torn down), but that poor people lacked skills or drive. Some radicals challenged this view in the mid-1960s, and a small band of dissenting economists (discussed in chapter 4) developed a more critical view of the economy in the late 1960s. But that was in the future.

In some ways the War on Poverty was a magic show. Most of the talk about fighting poverty focused on training programs; meanwhile, behind the curtain, mass movements, liberal politicians, and government bureaucrats were improving programs that worked simply by giving people cash or services. Welfare payments rose, Social Security benefits increased, and Medicare and Medicaid were created. These changes mimicked the direct methods used in Western Europe to combat poverty and address social needs. But they fell short of what was needed, and they were less discussed as antipoverty methods than the War on Poverty and other misleading stories. One misleading story was that work cured poverty (sometimes it did not); another was that "handouts" were a label appropriate for welfare benefits for the poor, but not for tax breaks to the middle class and big oil companies. Johnson and his people tried to keep the antipoverty story as old-fashioned as grandma's apple pie, but that disguised hard facts: cash handouts cured poverty; the affluent received handouts; and there were not enough good jobs to cure poverty.

Kennedy Methods: Aggregate Growth and Structural Programs

It was President John Kennedy who planted the seeds of the War on Poverty. When he took office in January 1961, Kennedy indicated that he would concentrate on foreign affairs, not domestic problems. But he had won the election partly on a promise to fight recession and bring down unemployment. If that effort was successful, poverty rates would fall too. Also, during the presidential campaign he had been shocked by conditions in West Virginia, and he pledged that within sixty days of taking office he would ask Congress for aid to people of that state. But he promised no comprehensive attack on poverty. In his inaugural address, he used the word "poverty" three times, but he meant the poor in "huts and villages" around the globe, not at home. On civil rights, which involved antipoverty considerations, Kennedy was cautious, even though the black vote had been vital to his narrow victory over Richard Nixon. Kennedy's domestic program, The New Frontier, promised to outlaw segregation in federally supported housing but not much else for civil rights. It included other liberal programs that might help the poor: a higher minimum wage, federal aid for low-income housing and education, and hospital insurance for retirees.[3]

Congress and the president quickly implemented three initiatives that, we can see now, prefigured the War on Poverty. The first consisted of efforts to reform welfare. Concerns about rising costs and welfare dependency, as well as sensational attacks on welfare clients in New York and Louisiana, led to federal action. In 1961, the Aid to Families with Dependent Children–Unemployed Parent program (AFDC-UP) made it possible for two-parent families to receive welfare. Unfortunately, the program was optional for the states, few fathers fit qualifications that included a recent history of employment, and the program was never large. Meanwhile, in 1962 the administration won congressional approval for public welfare amendments that increased federal funding for training social workers and expanding services to recipients. The amendments aimed to get people off welfare by fostering conventional families and jobs; the method would be intensive case work that involved counseling for self-esteem and life skills and that might include job training and job placement. There was no proof that welfare recipients' lack of training rather than a job shortage was the main problem, and researchers would find little evidence that the new approach worked, but that discovery came later. The people who would shortly plan the War on Poverty forged ahead with same assumption: that the poor needed services and personal rehabilitation rather than a federal jobs program and more money.[4]

The second initiative was another program that linked concerns about structural unemployment and poverty. Liberal politicians and union leaders hoped to aid declining economic regions; Illinois senator Paul Douglas, who wanted something for unemployed coal miners, led the way. Congress passed the Area Redevelopment Act, and Kennedy signed it on May 1, 1961. Depressed mining, textile, railroad, and fishing communities could apply for grants and loans to improve public facilities and attract new businesses. It was a small program and one whose effect would be controversial, but regardless of its effect, it showed that Kennedy was more reform-minded than Eisenhower, who twice vetoed depressed areas bills.[5]

The third initiative that prefigured the War on Poverty was the Manpower Development and Training Act (MDTA) of March 25, 1962. Behind this one was the belief that rapid technological change—often called "automation"—was pushing well-paid workers out of jobs and into poverty. It was a popular analysis with union, liberal, and socialist writers. How well the Manpower Development and Training program worked out will be analyzed in chapter 3, for it soon became a program for the poor and disadvantaged. Its enactment showed that the possibilities for liberal reform were better than they had been for a decade.[6]

Despite approval of these targeted programs, White House economic advisers were led by centrist Keynesians—aggies who had more faith in macroeconomic stimulation (strategy #1 in the "Seven Government Antipoverty Strategies" sidebar) than structural (#6) or targeted approaches and who proposed to boost economic growth in ways that satisfied business leaders. Walter Heller, chief of the President's Council of Economic Advisors, urged that the federal budget run a deficit to pump more money into the economy than government collected in taxes. That would boom the economy, create jobs, and cut poverty. But in choosing the method of tax cuts rather than expanded federal spending on social programs aimed at the poor and working class, Heller was taking the conservative Keynesian route.[7]

At first President Kennedy was wary of deficits, but he knew that in 1960 Eisenhower's refusal to raise federal spending had hurt Nixon, who lost big in cities with high unemployment, so Kennedy sped up surplus food distribution and income tax refunds, won support in Congress for new spending—$20 billion for defense—and signed the Revenue Act of 1962, a billion-dollar investment tax credit for business. The economy picked up. When it seemed in danger of slipping again, Heller urged more tax cuts. On June 7, 1962, after the stock market took a dive, Kennedy offered a bill to cut personal and corporate income taxes and to produce a recession-fighting deficit. Not surprisingly, business leaders jumped on the bandwagon. Unionists and liberals like economist Leon Keyserling questioned the cuts, not because they feared deficits but because the bulk of the tax savings went to the rich and corporations and because they wanted increased spending on public goods rather than lower taxes. Despite opposition, in February 1964 President Johnson signed the Revenue Act of 1964. Although the public did not always understand this, the administration's taxing and spending policy for economic growth was its biggest antipoverty weapon.[8]

Improving overall economic growth could help the unemployed and the poor who needed jobs or better jobs. Growth had the advantage of seeming to be apolitical; it appeared not to set class against class, as did the Robin Hood strategy of taxing the rich or the middle class to aid the poor. Yet the growth strategy was deeply political in whom it helped most and first, especially in Heller's version, which cut taxes most for the affluent in the hope that they would invest and buy. Eventually the benefits of growth were supposed to trickle down in more jobs for the poor. But there were alternatives to the trickle, even among Keynesians. Galbraith and Keyserling urged spending on

SEVEN GOVERNMENT ANTIPOVERTY STRATEGIES
WHEN THE PRIVATE SECTOR FAILS

1. Use federal control of the budget and interest rates to boom aggregate economic growth, which in turn creates jobs and lifts wages (varieties of Keynesianism).

2. Give people money and services to lift their incomes above poverty lines.

3. Create government jobs that pay above-poverty wages.

4. Encourage unionization and raise the minimum wage to make work pay more.

5. Cut every tax including Social Security taxes on low-income Americans, raise taxes on the wealthy, and use the income to enrich public goods like schools, bus service, health care, and improved welfare and Social Security benefits for those with a poor wage history.

6. Eliminate everything that interferes with the smooth operation of labor markets, whether people's lack of effort or lack of training, job discrimination, or the geographical misfit between workers and labor demand. These impediments were sometimes called "structural" problems.

7. Empower people in local and national organizations to organize their own programs and to confront governments and businesses that poorly served them.

The antipoverty effort of liberal Democrats and Republicans in the 1960s included #1, #2, a bit of #4, and almost none of #3 and #5. Most of the War on Poverty involved #6 and #7.

public goods such as schools, parks, and museums and tax cuts for people with low rather than high incomes. They lost out to people who did not care much about helping the poor or who claimed that it was hard enough selling tax cuts and deficits without giving direct benefits to the poor.[9]

Whether the tax cuts cured poverty would not be clear for a while, but their bias toward the rich was obvious. Heller felt that the administration had to do something for poor people, and Kennedy wanted something new for his 1964 reelection bid. In December 1962, he told Heller: "Now Look! I want to go beyond the things that have already been accomplished. Give me facts and figures on the things we still have to do. For example, what about the poverty problem in the United States?" Later Kennedy ordered Heller to evaluate claims by Keyserling and Michael Harrington that poverty was more widespread than people thought. From then on, Heller, the high priest of aggregate economic growth, became the missionary for programs targeted at special populations that growth bypassed.[10]

Many Streams Led to a War on Poverty

There were experts, experiments, and books galore to shape the War on Poverty. Concern about welfare dependency was growing. The absence of robust economic growth over 1958–62 pushed unemployment issues to the fore. Foundations and community activists were analyzing urban decay and urban renewal. Juvenile delinquency provoked discussion, as did the problems of depressed areas. Liberals and unionists worried about automation unemployment. The Manpower Development and Training Act, which had been enacted to provide for job retraining, was running out of experienced older workers and becoming a kind of war on poverty for the "hard-core" unemployed.

There were also two big factors that created a context for the War on Poverty. Few commentators doubt that affluence nurtured America's confidence that it could solve poverty and that it should do so. Surprisingly, the role of the civil rights movement is more controversial. Social scientists Frances Fox Piven and Richard Cloward argued that the War on Poverty was part of a presidential electoral strategy to calm protest and win black votes, but some antipoverty planners denied that civil rights activism catalyzed the War on Poverty.

Piven and Cloward may have had the exact mechanisms wrong, but the civil rights movement was clearly one catalyst for the War on Poverty. In 1963 when Kennedy began to think seriously about civil rights, he learned that low incomes were a crucial part of the equation. Lyndon Johnson sometimes conceived of the War on Poverty as a device to get money and services to blacks without arousing white resentment. Furthermore, daily headlines about economic discrimination and demonstrations made the antipoverty effort seem urgent. A key demand of the 1963 March on Washington was for jobs.[11]

Another stream flowing into the river of programs against poverty was the 1950s effort to deal with urban problems. A few urban planners worried that slum clearance was wiping out low-income housing and generating popular resistance. Meanwhile, in northern cities, whites and jobs were leaking out to the suburbs. Newly arriving African Americans and Puerto Ricans found a shrinking tax base and bleak job prospects. Urbanists were enamored with the idea that comprehensive programs that coordinated a variety of services and approaches were the solution.[12] Often their remedies were politically timid, but their rhetoric sounded advanced and scientific.

Despite these shortcomings, scholars and service professionals were beginning to take a more humane view of delinquency. In the late 50s, the Henry Street Settlement in New York City sought funding for a comprehensive attack on gang delinquency. Echoing the harsh psychiatric view that was common at the time, the Henry Street staff considered delinquency a mental disease. They portrayed girl delinquents as "provocateurs and handmaidens of violence" who were "too severely disturbed" for traditional casework methods and would have "to be taken out of the community and given intensive psychotherapy and care in institutions."[13]

But there was change in the air. Officials at the National Institute of Mental Health, a federal agency, doubted that psychiatry could cure delinquency; under the influence of sociologist Leonard Cottrell, they invited proposals for community participation and rehabilitation. Meanwhile, Richard Cloward and Lloyd Ohlin of the New York School of Social Work at Columbia University were arguing in *Delinquency and Opportunity* (1960) against psychiatric models and for the view that delinquent subcultures arose because youths were blocked from fulfilling the American dream. Delinquents were not deviant; on the contrary, they had strong aspirations to succeed—hence their extreme reaction in drugs, crime, and violence when conventional routes to success were blocked.[14]

Cloward and Ohlin's simple insight was a major advance on models that portrayed delinquents as mental defectives; it made their book seem new. But in retrospect, *Delinquency and Opportunity* seems tame; there was little about job creation, as one might expect in a book about opportunity. Much of *Delinquency and Opportunity* was not about a system of class inequalities that channeled the poor into poverty but about broken systems of authority and discipline that allowed frustrated young people to run wild. Cloward and Ohlin usefully changed the focus from individual delinquents to group structures that affected young people, but as they talked about reorganizing slum communities and erecting new structures of social control, misleading medical metaphors crept back into their work. At times Cloward and Ohlin concentrated more on social control than on improving incomes. At times they encouraged the idea that poverty was problem of culture, not cash.[15]

Still, Cloward and Ohlin's step away from psychiatric explanations landed them the job of revising the Henry Street Settlement's proposal to the National Institute of Mental Health. Their 600-page plan proposed a multifaceted approach called Mobilization for Youth.[16] Prefiguring the War on Poverty's community action agencies, the authors urged better delivery of social services through Neighborhood Service Centers. Bowing to psychological theories, they admitted that poor people sometimes had bad attitudes, "self-defeating modes of adaptation" that cut them off from real opportunities; they suggested that delinquency was rooted in the breakdown of authority in immigrant communities. Finally, they proposed a youth jobs center to publicize employment opportunities; a coffee house for young people; skill training for adults; a program to help poor people overcome their "lack of such 'middle-class' graces as good speech, promptness, neatness, and politeness"; and community programs to empower lower-class residents.[17] These proposals were a preview of the War on Poverty.

The Mobilization for Youth strategy was more about helping the underprivileged obtain good jobs than about creating such jobs. At times, Cloward and Ohlin recognized that new jobs might have to be created, and they knew that the youth labor supply would grow by 40% in the coming decade, but most of their emphasis was on young people's lack of job preparation. The authors talked about a shortage of skilled workers in New York City but said nothing about the seepage of good jobs from the city. The Mobilization for Youth proposal was an advance on psychiatric models, but it did not go much beyond cultural and psychological approaches. After the anticommunist 50s, Cloward and Ohlin's humane approach looked like a challenge to the foundations of the social order, but it was so only in part.[18]

Mobilization for Youth personnel were important in the birth of the War on Poverty. Early in 1962, Ohlin was running the White House Office of Juvenile Delinquency, which had $30 million for comprehensive antidelinquency programs that targeted institutions rather than individuals. Cloward and Ohlin's Mobilization for Youth proposal received the first antidelinquency action grant on May 31, 1962. With funds from New York City, the National Institute of Mental Health, and the Ford Foundation, Mobilization for Youth had $15 million for three years.[19]

Experience would soon radicalize the organization. Increasingly it involved neighborhood residents in militant confrontations with public agencies. In June 1963, it put solving poverty rather than reshaping delinquents at the top of its list of priorities.[20] This was a paradigm shift, from curing deviant individuals and weak neighborhoods to confronting government institutions that did not help people escape economic poverty.

The Other America: A Foreign Land

Were the poor simply people who lacked income? Or were they prisoners of a culture that interfered with their ability to find and keep a good

Michael Harrington in the mid-1960s (Courtesy of National Archives)

job? In 1962–64, policy makers could study at least eight recent books and articles for an answer.[21] It is curious that of all these the work that captured the most attention, *The Other America* (1962), was written by Michael Harrington, a Marxist and member of the Socialist Party. Marxists claimed to have a deep understanding of how capitalism normally generates unemployment and poverty. Would Harrington create a new model, something different from the liberal view that poverty was rooted in people's cultural and social handicaps and exacerbated by sluggish economic growth?

Harrington was no newcomer to poverty or politics. In the 50s he participated in Dorothy Day's Catholic Worker movement, whose members lived in poverty and served the down-and-out on skid row. Later, he hoped for a political realignment that would turn the Democratic Party into a version of European social democratic or socialist parties that supported generous social programs.[22]

Much of *The Other America* was not very Marxist and not very economic. Often Harrington simply followed common practice by describing the links between poverty and such social handicaps as inadequate education, old age, work in a low-wage industry, broken families, and racial background. The emphasis was both accurate and misleading, for the correlations were real but what caused what was not always clear. (Did broken homes cause poverty or vice versa?) Also, the handicapping perspective implied that the nonpoor had no social handicaps and that people without social handicaps must be comfortable. This raised a wall between "the two nations," the poor minority and the majority that was not so poor but also suffered from unemployment and medical emergencies. The bigger the conceptual gap between the poor and the economic majority—the more that poor people's problems were made to seem very different—the weaker the political alliance between the two.

Even more harmful than the handicapping approach, sections of *The Other America* emphasized to an extreme degree that the poor lived in a different mental world, a culture of poverty. Poor people, Harrington asserted, "should be defined psychologically . . . [as] internal exiles who, almost inevitably, develop attitudes of defeat and pessimism and who are therefore excluded from taking advantage of new opportunities." The poor were progress-immune; they could not help themselves, and economic growth would not cure poverty if poor people did not get a helping hand. We needed commonsense reforms like national health insurance and a higher minimum wage; but we also needed something to help the poor overcome their "pessimism and fatalism." In other words, antipoverty work was as much about psychological rehabilitation as about fixing economic institutions.[23]

Harrington borrowed the culture-of-poverty theory from anthropologist Oscar Lewis. Lewis based the theory on a handful of cases, and he gave the culture of poverty so many attributes that at times it seemed synonymous with poverty itself. (What was cultural about "a chronic shortage of cash"?) Lewis argued that poor people's fatalism and their hunger for immediate gratification blocked their way out of poverty. And he made the alarming assertion that it was "much more difficult to eliminate the culture of poverty than to eliminate poverty per se."[24]

Elsewhere, Harrington stressed the need for jobs and incomes, but in 1962, Lewis's model dominated *The Other America*, and the jobs issue stayed in the background. The poor lacked money, but worse, they were "internal aliens," "twisted spirits" with "a culture that is radically different from the one that dominates society." They are "a different kind of people. They think and feel differently." They are "pessimistic and defeated . . . victimized by mental suffering to a degree unknown in suburbia." Immune to the lures of a booming economy, they are "depressed human beings . . . who cannot move and . . . who lack the will to do so." They are trapped in a "vicious circle of the culture of poverty." It was wrong for the middle class to "condemn the poor for their faults," for they lived beneath moral choice . . . society must help them before they can help themselves."[25]

Of course, some of the poor *were* psychologically damaged, but so were some of the rich. And was bad attitude the best explanation for the situation of 40 million poor? There were plenty of facts for an economic view, and Harrington knew them. For one thing, many of the poor were working. For another, many escaped poverty without the aid of therapy. Except for the mentally ill and individuals brought down by drugs and alcohol, most of the poor needed jobs, higher wages, or better government income supports, not a change of attitude. Harrington knew they needed substantive economic and social programs too, but at times the psychiatric view overwhelmed everything else in the book.[26]

Why did a man who was knowledgeable about the economic causes of poverty opt for an approach that now seems regressive? I think there were two main reasons. First, the culture of poverty must have been part of a strategy to make a broad appeal. It blamed no one, and it explained why the poor could not meet the demand that they lift themselves up by their own bootstraps. The image of pathetic people trapped in an oppressive culture tugged at the heartstrings. Harrington was the Charles Dickens, not the Karl Marx, of this moment in antipoverty history. Socialism was not on the agenda; the Socialist Party was tiny. It made sense to work on the feelings of the broad middle class and governing elites. And the appeal had an impact on the people planning the War on Poverty.

A second force behind Harrington's dehumanization of the poor was that the denigration of poor people's mentality—even if for positive ends—seemed to be the dominant model in the field. Even on the left it seemed acceptable to remove thought and agency from the poor. Movements of the 60s, especially those for civil rights and welfare rights, would recast social science models and redefine acceptable views of oppressed peoples. It would soon appear untrue and unfair to claim that the poor were outside the realm of moral choice and were, in effect, mentally ill. But in the 50s and early 60s, people who did not accept the dominant view had a difficult time getting a hearing.[27]

The culture-of-poverty idea ignored economic fundamentals and commonalities between the poor and not so poor. Millions moved in and out of poverty every year, not because of motivational rehabilitation but because of changes in their social and economic situation and the state of the economy. Meanwhile, millions worked hard but stayed poor, and millions of working-class Americans were not "middle class" if that meant a secure job and ample savings. It was common even for well-paid blue-collar workers to face seasonal or permanent layoffs. As historian Gabriel Kolko put it: "The basic economic fact of life for a majority of the population is insecurity."[28] The line between the poor and nonpoor was not sharp. Much that hurt the poor also affected the nonpoor.

Kolko's *Wealth and Power in America* showed that a different, more economic view was possible.[29] The book lacked the personal connection Harrington forged with the reader, but it was a better view of economic facts and long-term political possibilities, for it did not isolate the poor from the rest of the working class. But Kolko's views did not get much of a hearing. Harrington's *The Other America* got more attention, and it opened people's eyes to the existence of poverty in the midst of affluence. But it misled the reader about poverty's causes.

Constructing an Antipoverty Program

The Other America earned respectful reviews and sold several thousand copies after it appeared in March 1962. Following Dwight Macdonald's recommendation in the *New Yorker*, a second printing sold 7,000 copies. In the fall of 1963, it became the first Penguin paperback published in America. By then it was being read by antipoverty planners, and it helped move them from general programs for "Widening the Sphere of Prosperity" to a "unified program" aimed at the poor. Jack Conway, a union leader in the Kennedy administration, believed that after *The Other America*, "things kind of came together and had a different meaning." The book was "a real blockbuster."[30]

Serious planning began in 1963 when Lampman reported that there had been a dramatic slowdown in exits from poverty over 1956–61 (see figure A.2 in appendix 1). In June, Heller asked Lampman to develop "a practical Kennedy anti-poverty program."[31] Other events fueled antipoverty planning. In a closed meeting, James Baldwin, Lorraine Hansberry, and other black leaders assailed Attorney General Robert Kennedy for the administration's poor civil rights record. That spring and summer aggressive civil rights demonstrations moved north. Finally, Kennedy submitted a civil rights bill to Congress. He hoped to calm the demonstrators. In June he ordered a review of hiring on federal construction projects; Labor Secretary Willard Wirtz responded with grim data on black unemployment and the stagnation of black incomes at half the white level. The administration worked hard to tame the great march on Washington of August 1963, but demonstrators carried signs for both civil rights *and jobs.*[32]

It was not just civil rights and not just *The Other America* that pushed things toward a war on poverty. Harry Caudill's book about Appalachia, *Night Comes to the Cumberlands*, appeared in 1963, and in October, Homer Bigart reported on poverty and welfare in Kentucky in the *New York Times*. Kennedy found emergency funds for unemployed miners and their families, and the *Times* called for new programs.[33]

Sometime in October or November 1963 Kennedy approved a full-blown program against poverty. He was assassinated on November 22. One day later, Heller got President Johnson's agreement to "move full speed ahead."[34] Antipoverty planners floundered until David Hackett presented a thirty-nine-page plan on December 1. Hackett assumed that they did not know how to solve poverty; they could discover how to do it by listening to the poor. Hackett proposed that a limited number of task forces conduct field studies in urban and rural areas, among Native Americans, Alaskans, Mexican Americans, and others. The task forces would then choose communities for development corporations. The program could start without legislative authorization: a cabinet-level committee would find the money in existing programs.

Hackett's proposal was attractive. It gave the Keynesians who opposed big new job and income programs something to support. Community-based demonstrations seemed innovative, were inexpensive, and did not appear to threaten major political and economic interests. They might include comprehensive, coordinated approaches, which were trendy in antipoverty circles.[35] On December 20, Heller suggested a modest program of five urban and five rural projects and a cabinet-level coordinator. During Christmas week Heller and Budget Director Kermit Gordon flew to the president's Texas ranch, where they convinced him that community action would work.[36]

Once sold on the idea, Johnson ran with it. He was not interested in testing social theory in ten cities. For reasons of politics and glory, he wanted something big. In his first budget message to Congress (January 21, 1964), Johnson announced that *any* community that wanted a program could have one. The hope of scholars and funders that antipoverty efforts would be part of a controlled social science experiment was doomed.[37]

On February 1, 1964, Johnson appointed the director of the Peace Corps, R. Sargent Shriver, to finalize the War on Poverty. Shriver summoned the experts. Someone mentioned Harrington, and Shriver asked, "Who's that? Get him in."[38] Harrington and his friend Paul Jacobs spent two weeks with the President's Task Force on the War against Poverty. Despite the therapeutic emphasis that dominated *The Other America*, Harrington knew that good jobs were essential. He, Jacobs, and Daniel Patrick Moynihan in the Department of Labor urged Shriver to push for massive public works projects. Secretary of Labor Wirtz raised the idea with Johnson in a cabinet meeting. The president ignored him, taking phone calls all the while.[39] The antipoverty effort would not focus on direct government job creation.

Johnson had practical reasons for rejecting a big jobs program. Direct government job creation might require a tax increase. Johnson had just won a tax cut from Congress that his economists claimed would create lots of jobs. Unemployment was falling. If people could not find jobs, it would not be because of lack of jobs but because of structural and personal impediments. Civil rights bills and the War on Poverty would fix those.[40]

Nor would the War on Poverty include direct efforts to equalize incomes. People who had other ideas suppressed them. Economist Lampman decided that a politically acceptable program must avoid terms like "inequality" and "redistribution of income and wealth."[41] The same went for cash handouts. Experts estimated that $11 billion a year in income grants could lift everyone above the poverty line. But that was eleven times what would be spent on War on Poverty programs, and the grants might have generated opposition, especially if they looked like welfare. The War on Poverty was sold as a hand up, not a handout. Johnson ordered his assistant Bill Moyers: "You tell Shriver, no doles." At Johnson's instructions, Council of Economic Advisors' staff economist Lester Thurow removed from the 1964 *Economic Report of the President* all references to cash handouts to the poor.[42]

LYNDON JOHNSON (1908–1973) AND THE GREAT SOCIETY

As a young man, Lyndon Johnson directed Franklin Roosevelt's National Youth Administration (NYA) in Texas. The NYA provided work to depression-era students. Johnson won a seat in Congress in 1937 and, just barely, a Senate seat in 1948. He idolized Roosevelt, but he mixed support for liberal measures with service to conservative business interests. He worked hard to master the machinery of the Senate and rose to become Democratic majority leader (1955–60).

John Kennedy chose Johnson as his running mate in 1960. Johnson hated the job, but in the fall of 1963 he became president. In the days after the assassination he skillfully employed people's feelings for the dead president to push more liberal reforms than the country had seen since the 30s. In 1964 Johnson trounced conservative Barry Goldwater.

Johnson was the greatest American liberal president of the post–World War II era. He created a vast empire of laws and agencies called the Great Society. They ranged from the War on Poverty to the war on billboards. They targeted everything from highway safety to improving the arts and humanities, from expanding the welfare state with new programs like Medicare and Medicaid to improving old programs like Social Security. Johnson spoke eloquently about the quality of life, reflecting a theme that Galbraith had popularized in *The Affluent Society*. Above all, he was the first American president thoroughly committed to civil rights for black Americans.

Johnson represented the core notion of modern American liberalism that the federal government could make life better for people. But he was also a prisoner of liberalism's Cold War dogmas. He could not think outside the anticommunist box. Johnson sensed that victory in Vietnam was unlikely, but he claimed that if he pulled out of Vietnam, conservatives would use anticommunism to destroy the Great Society. But the war stifled antipoverty programs anyway, and it killed 50,000 Americans and a million Vietnamese. And it forced Johnson out of politics.

Society and politics cracked in the late 60s. Even without Vietnam that might have happened, but things would have been less chaotic. New programs needed time and money to develop. The people needed to be told about the meaning of vast new social reforms and how they were part of a broad transformation of the American state and American values. That did not happen, in part because Johnson had hoped to extend social programs without upsetting anyone and in part because he was obsessed with Vietnam.

So the War on Poverty would not mainly be a jobs or an income program; it would be an experiment in training, education, and motivational rehabilitation for a relatively small group of individuals outside the regular economy. If there were enough jobs but people were stuck in poverty, there must be something wrong with the people. The president's economists used culture-of-poverty rhetoric to describe a "vicious circle. Poverty breeds poverty"; "lack of motivation, hope, and incentive is a more subtle but no less powerful barrier than lack of financial means." Shriver told Congress that the new training program—the Job Corps—would "change indifference to interest, ignorance to awareness, resignation to ambition."[43] This was the culture of poverty in the service of liberal antipoverty programs that would not challenge the privileges of the very rich or corporate America.

Antipoverty legislation marched through Congress. The war would cost only $500 million, and it had widespread public support. Johnson selected an antiunion southerner, Georgia's Phil Landrum, to lead the fight in the House. Racists feared integration in the Job Corps, but Landrum responded that no one had to enroll. Shriver agreed to give southern governors a partial veto over antipoverty programs. President Johnson advertised the program as lily-white by touring the Midwest and Appalachia, where he sat on the front porch of Tom Fletcher, whose family of ten lived on $400 a year.[44]

Meanwhile, conservative Republican senators John Tower and Barry Goldwater claimed that there were millions of job vacancies and no need for a War on Poverty; they charged that the Job Corps, by taking young people away from their families, was using Nazi and Soviet methods. Republicans taunted Sargent Shriver as a "Poverty Czar" with all-encompassing powers. Shriver responded, playing on his first name, that he was only a sergeant and did not want to be czar; look at what happened to the Russian czars. Johnson's strategy and the liberal tide—energized by Kennedy's assassination—rolled over the opposition. The president signed the Economic Opportunity Act on August 20, 1964. The law created a new agency, the Office of Economic Opportunity (OEO). Shriver would be its director, and he would have a cabinet-level position directly under the president.[45]

A Preview of the War on Poverty:
A Program for Young People

The broader War on Poverty turned up in dozens of new programs outside the OEO itself, including Medicare and Medicaid, Model Cities, the Elementary and Secondary Education Act, and Job Opportunities in the Business Sector (JOBS). Existing programs like food stamps, welfare, and Social

**"IF YOU HAD ANY INITIATIVE, YOU'D GO OUT
AND INHERIT A DEPARTMENT STORE."**

"If you had any initiative, you'd go out and inherit a department store." In this cartoon, Herblock satirizes Arizona senator Barry Goldwater. (From *Straight Herblock* [Simon and Schuster, 1964]; reproduced by permission of Herb Block Foundation)

Security were improved. Some of these are evaluated in later chapters. Here is a preliminary assessment of characteristic programs of what people thought of as the War on Poverty.

Important parts of the War on Poverty focused on the young, especially young men. Title 1 of the Economic Opportunity Act created the Job Corps to remove young people (16 to 21) from the harmful effects of their communities and to teach them school subjects and good job habits and to train them in welding, auto repair, and other blue-collar trades. The initial proposal for the Job Corps applied only to young men. Only after women in Congress protested was the corps opened to women, although their training was for "women's jobs" outside and in the home.[46]

Planners, like most people, assumed that more education meant less poverty. The Neighborhood Youth Corps offered part-time and summer work in landscaping, painting parking meters, and cleanup jobs to low-income youths who stayed in school. Upward Bound offered summer programs to high school juniors and seniors to enrich their cultural package and help them succeed in college. For low-income college students there were grants, loans, and jobs, including the Work-Study Program, in which the federal government paid 90% of the wages for up to fifteen hours a week for full-time college students in good standing; almost 400,000 students were soon involved in this program.[47]

A sometimes controversial element of the antipoverty war, and one that was not focused on young people, involved community action agencies. For many planners, this component was the most innovative part of the War on Poverty and the one that best embodied the idea of comprehensive attack on poverty. It included the commonsense idea that services to the poor should be available in one place. Many agencies would also operate programs dreamed up by the Community Action Program office in the OEO in Washington, such as Head Start and Neighborhood Legal Services. Sometimes they employed organizers from the OEO's Volunteers in Service to America (VISTA) to launch literacy programs, organize tenant unions, or fight strip mining. Action agencies were options for communities anywhere, urban or rural. There were soon sixty-three agencies serving 129 Native American reservations.

In addition to their service orientation, community action agencies had a more elevated role as organizations run by poor people. In planning sessions social scientist Richard Boone had harped on the idea until he wore down his colleagues; the final law specified that community action programs had to be "developed, conducted, and administered with the maximum feasible participation of residents of the areas and members of groups served."[48] The idea was in tune with militant demands for political participation made by the civil rights and the student movements, and the poor would have demanded participation even if it had not been included in the legislation. But antipoverty planners had other reasons to support participation. Some thought the poor would deliver services more fairly than welfare agencies, or they hoped that the poor could confront agencies that were not doing their jobs. Others feared that if antipoverty organizations were not run by the poor, segregationist politicians would subvert them. Perhaps most important was the idea that participation could be a therapy of empowerment to break the culture of helplessness and pessimism, the culture of poverty.[49]

Yet words about control by the poor did not always mean what they said. Some planners intended only that the poor be kept informed or hired for part-time agency jobs. Maximum feasible participation did not mean that poor people should run things. James Adler, a young lawyer on Shriver's task force, recalled: "I had never really conceived that it (participation) would mean control by the poor of the community action represented on the community action organization itself. . . . I expected that the poor would be represented on the community action organization but that such representation would be something in the order of 15 to 25% of the board. . . . *Moreover, I don't think it ever occurred to me, or to many others, that the representatives of the poor must necessarily be poor themselves.*"[50] As it turned out, the poor would not control many local antipoverty agencies, but in some locales they would spend a lot of time fighting for control.

An equally fundamental issue about poor people's control was, control of what? What power would local agencies have to challenge dominant economic interests? Although occasionally an agency would cause enough of a ruckus to upset local politicians, poor people rarely had the power to reform business institutions that created and destroyed jobs and services in poor communities. The concept of poor people's mobilization might have made a difference in power relationships had it been allowed to develop, but few of the planners wanted federally supported community organizations to pressure General Motors to rebuild plants in the city of Detroit or to compel cities and states to make big real estate interests pay their fair share of local property taxes. Anyway, were the root causes of poverty local, as the community action model assumed? Elizabeth Wickenden, who had decades of experience in welfare circles, wrote to an official at the White House: "The problems of poverty are only in limited instances localized in character. They are for the most part widely distributed, related to economic and social factors that operate nationwide, and would require more than local action for solution."[51] Her view was ignored.

Administration leaders and even one socialist believed that it was politically unwise to rile important economic interests. A program for all workers, poor and nonpoor, unemployed and employed, demanding good jobs for all, a comfortable minimum wage, and a shorter workweek would, said socialist Harrington, "set off all kinds of class antagonisms, real and imagined, on the part of business."[52] In this light the OEO narrative was a shrewd effort to avoid class conflict and win broad support. But if low wages and joblessness were rooted not in racism or lack of training but in a class system that functioned to allot more pain to the poor and working class than the affluent, what then?

War on Poverty programs offered little assistance for adults who were poor because of low wages or joblessness. There was a program of loans to farmers for improving farm productivity, building homes, and rural manufacturing, and Congress added funds for sanitation, housing, and adult education for the poorest and most exploited of all employees, farmworkers. Beyond that, little direct aid was provided for the working poor.[53]

Of course, many poor adults were assisted by other programs: Social Security, welfare, a higher minimum wage, and prosperity. The president's economists noted that 70% of all poor families included one earner and for them, "high employment and vigorous economic growth are still of major importance."[54] But if the emphasis on improving skills and attitudes was misdirected and if the economy into which the poor were being sent generated unemployment and working poverty regardless of the values and skills of the poor, then the War on Poverty might be something of a swindle.

Was the War on Poverty Designed Just for Men?

About a third of the poor were in female-headed families, but little was done directly for them. War on Poverty planners assumed a patriarchal model that focused on young men. Such a focus had the potential to reverse the trend toward more poor female-headed families. We have seen that initial plans for Job Corps training did not even include young women. (For other categories of poor people that were underemphasized, see appendix 2.)

However, the War on Poverty included many programs and thousands of workers, clients, and volunteers. It would be astonishing if women had not been included in many activities. In terms of direct approaches to getting people off welfare, there was the Work Experience Program, which connected women and men on welfare to the job market. Thousands did pass through the program, and some found low-wage jobs, but it is doubtful that they were more successful than they would have been without the program. More important, thousands of women found employment in community action agencies, in Head Start, and in other programs, some of them through New Careers, an effort initiated in 1966 to employ community people who lacked formal credentials but had skills, experience, and knowledge of their commu-

WHO WAS MOLLIE ORSHANSKY AND
HOW DID SHE MAKE HISTORY?

Few Americans know about Mollie Orshansky, but she wrote an important page in American history. Orshansky grew up in a large poor immigrant family in Brooklyn in the 1920s. On scholarships she completed a B.A. at Hunter College in math and statistics. After graduate work in economics and statistics, she began a long career of government employment that brought her to the Department of Agriculture in 1945. In 1958, just as Galbraith and Lampman were raising public awareness about poverty, she came to the Division of Research and Statistics in the Social Security Administration. Soon she was pouring out a steady stream of important articles about how much income people needed to stay out of poverty.

Of all family budget expenditures, those for food were the area in which experts believed they had a scientific view of human need; for decades they had been studying what people of different ages and income levels needed to afford a diet that would give them essential calories, minerals, and vitamins. The Department of Agriculture had created four model food budgets, the two stingiest being the low-income and the emergency economy budget. Knowing also from Department of Agriculture studies that the average family spent a third of its budget on food, Orshansky decided that a quick way to estimate a poverty line (or "threshold") would be to multiply model food budgets by three. She did this for different family types and sizes, for farm and nonfarm families (but not for regional variations), and for each of the two lowest food budgets. She ended up with 248 thresholds. For the nonfarm family of four the poverty line in 1963 was $3,165 using the emergency food budget and $3,995, about a fourth higher, using the low-income budget.

Orshansky's work came at the right time. In 1965 Sargent Shriver's Office of Economic Opportunity adopted the lower of Orshansky's measures to guide its own work. In 1967–68, Social Security Administration officials argued for higher lines, but the Bureau of the Budget directed all federal agencies to use the lower thresholds. Higher lines would have raised the number of Americans counted as poor and eligible for government benefits. Except for price changes and minor adjustments, the poverty lines have not been increased in thirty-five years. For a family of four the line was $19,971 in 2005.

Mollie Orshansky was proof that someone doing solid scholarship without much fanfare could have a big impact. We must remember, however, that her influence was shaped by larger forces. She was surprised when her research was used to make the poverty line so low. She came to believe that the official poverty line omitted millions of needy Americans. While conservatives in the 1980s argued that income data overestimated the numbers of poor people because they did not include noncash items like food stamps, progressives argued that the line itself was terribly low, especially for someone living in a high-rent area. The reader can judge whether, for example, $25,000 was adequate for a family of four in 2005. The government asserted that such a family was well above the poverty line.

Sources: Deborah A. Stone, "Making the Poor Count," *American Prospect*, Spring 1994, 84–88; Gordon M. Fisher, "The Development and History of the Poverty Thresholds," *Social Security Bulletin* 55 (Winter 1992), at <www.ssa.gov/history/fisheronpoverty.html>.

nity. These jobs did not pay well, but many women had been doing the same work for free.

So the War on Poverty was not for men only, but just as it could not solve the basic problem of too few good jobs and the deep problems of inequality in income and power, so it could not solve—in fact did not address—what made many women poor, the devaluation of women's work in and outside the home. To have fixed this last problem might have required, first, that women's unpaid labor in the home and community be compensated through a universal system like Social Security rather than through a welfare system that degraded poor people; and second, that labor markets be reformed to guarantee to women and minorities access to good jobs *and* to low-cost or publicly funded child care and social services. Although the legal foundations for attacking job inequalities were being established in the mid-1960s and a new feminism would push a revaluation of women's work, little would reverse the fact that an increasingly large fraction of the poor were in female-headed families.[55]

Newsweek Meets the War on Poverty

Of the nine *Newsweek* portraits that opened this chapter, only three matched the War on Poverty diagnosis. Young Tom Spray needed a steady job in the baking industry, but he might have been helped by more schooling or Job Corps training. Slim Lemert, the self-admitted "wino," had bad attitudes—an extreme case of the culture of poverty. He might have used local war-on-poverty agencies to find appropriate services. Miner Jim Smith probably needed a job as much as he needed training, but his children might have benefited from training and service programs.

Of the other six *Newsweek* cases, two were aged and needed higher Social Security payments and a subsidized health program. These improvements were on the way, but not as part of the War on Poverty. Five of the nine were very large families. The woman on welfare with six children required higher welfare benefits and a health program.[56] The other four families needed jobs or better jobs. In three of them the man had been thrown out of work, and in one he worked regularly but at poverty-level wages. In these four families, experienced workers needed jobs that paid a decent wage, not training. In the nation, millions of poor people were ready to work; many of the heads of poor families had a connection to the labor force.[57]

If you had used the nine *Newsweek* cases to design the War on Poverty, you might have concluded that the best war on poverty was one that offered

- Birth control: Five of these families were large; to the extent that they did nothing to plan their families, they may have been ensnared in a fatalism like the culture of poverty; if the government wanted to attack this culture of poverty, it needed to provide birth control information, and that was not, at first, a prominent part of the War on Poverty;
- Higher welfare and social security payments and a national health program;
- Government creation of permanent jobs at decent pay for poor people.[58]

The War on Poverty was built on the idea that poor people needed skills and a motivational upgrade; it sometimes assumed that they needed help in overcoming their aversion to work. But many poor adults worked, and many others wanted to find good jobs. Neither the War on Poverty nor other programs like Medicaid did much for the working poor. It was hoped that economic growth would provide jobs and better wages. But if it did not? The notion that the working poor might be a permanent part of the population was not discussed, and it did not fit well with official antipoverty ideas. Nor did the idea that there might not be enough good jobs even in prosperous times.

If, for the sake of argument, we grant planners' assumptions that the able-bodied, nonelderly poor were poor because they lacked job skills and correct attitudes, their remedies made some sense, but if the poor were trapped in a culture of poverty, handed down from generation to generation, War on Poverty solutions were too timid. It took years of psychoanalysis and thousands of dollars to alleviate middle-class neurosis. If the culture of poverty were as tenacious, then the War on Poverty was underfunded, even in terms of its own strategy.

Social engineering of the kind envisioned by creators of the War on Poverty was difficult, and circumstances made the road even bumpier. Johnson hoped that antipoverty funding would grow year by year, but that did not happen. A collection of infant programs just learning to walk had to crawl back to Congress every year to beg for money. Shriver was a sitting duck for congressional critics. It was difficult to plan when funding was on such a "sudden-death basis."[59] But the OEO's defects were not only a matter of underfunding. Johnson and Shriver did not prepare people for a program that would stumble. Johnson was secretive, and he overpromised in order to win support. Later he told a biographer that he wished "the public had seen the task of ending poverty the same way as they saw the task of getting to the moon, where they accepted mistakes as a part of the scientific process. I wish they had let us experiment with different programs, admitting that some were working better than others."[60] But Johnson did nothing to instruct people this way.

In another respect, liberal antipoverty warriors missed a chance to convey a broad view of economic security by focusing on people with social handicaps. There was nothing wrong with paying attention to the social correlates of the worst kinds of poverty, such as being unemployed in Appalachia. Certainly African Americans, people with low education, farmers, and female-headed families had above-average poverty rates. But scholars and nonscholars alike often confused cause and effect. Sometimes it was difficult even for specialists to avoid focusing on defective people rather than defective social, political, and economic systems. Antipoverty expert Lampman wrote, after a standard list of handicaps associated with poverty, that poor and nonpoor "populations are not so different as one might think. . . . The poor population is only a slightly distorted cross-section of the general population. The poor are like other Americans, except that they are poor."[61] But Lampman then emphasized the power of such social handicaps as a nonwhite or farm background to cause poverty. It was natural and useful that students of poverty catalog the handicapping correlates of poverty, and there is no doubt that race and gender bias made millions of Americans poor. But too much focus on the social correlates of poverty turned attention away from class structures that contributed to economic inequality, unemployment and poverty. More attention to deep economic causes, along with an expansive view of economic need, made for a unifying story. While racial, ethnic, age, gender, and many institutional factors (craft unionism, educational credentialism) allotted much more poverty to some groups than to others, many nonpoor people were affected by recession, structural economic change, weak social programs, and the persistence of economic inequality and unemployment even in prosperous times.[62]

Better than the view that the poor needed rehabilitation, and that the employed did not need much government help, was the idea of a continuum of the economically vulnerable, from the desperately poor to the auto worker facing a plant shutdown. Economist Barry Bluestone argued that the poverty line "should not be taken seriously. It is nonsense to assume that once a family's income exceeds the poverty line by a few dollars, it is out of the woods."[63] Another added, the poverty line "is the most arbitrary kind of figure possible. And it seems to divide the interests of those labeled poor—and thus eligible for a vast array of meager programs—from their neighbors who are also quite poor, but slightly above the arbitrary line."[64]

Antipoverty liberals missed a chance to focus on programs that could assist all Americans as they responded to economic change; they did too little to educate people about the realities of welfare and modern government; and they missed the chance to show that people in every class received "unearned" income—whether free schools or mortgage interest deductions, more Social Security benefits than they contributed, subsidies to tobacco farmers, business-friendly bracero programs, tax breaks to oil companies, or military protection of corporate profits at home and abroad. Americans could have been moved toward a value system that frankly recognized people's continuing need for help and government's role in a complex system of interdependencies. The War on Poverty was a positive step; it sparked the idealism of thousands of Americans in VISTA, Head Start, and community action programs. But people needed an up-to-date, big-picture story about the entirety of government benefits, the pervasiveness of economic risk, and how dependent people were on one another and on government.[65]

But that is getting ahead of the story. It does not follow that because antipoverty planners often segregated the poor from the rest of the population, the War on Poverty would not work. No one knew how programs would turn out. History tricks pessimists, just as it makes fools of dreamers. In the 60s, the nation was in the midst of huge social and political changes. The civil rights, student, and feminist movements were opening reform possibilities that had not been seen for three decades. No one knew what energies would be released by the crusade to end poverty.

chapter three

EVALUATING THE WAR ON POVERTY
The Conservatism of Liberalism

In its heyday, the War on Poverty spent billions of dollars and much political capital to wipe out poverty. From 1964 to 1969, poverty rates fell from 20% of the population to 12%. That sharp decline seemed to prove that the War on Poverty was a winner.

But the success of the War on Poverty remained controversial. Ronald Reagan asserted a decade later that government had declared war on poverty and poverty had won. Real victories against poverty, conservatives claimed, stemmed from individual willpower and economic growth, not government programs. From Michael Harrington on the left came the view that because of Vietnam, War on Poverty programs were underfunded and never given a chance. Others, like political scientist John Schwarz, concluded that cash programs such as Social Security and welfare, not economic growth and training programs, produced most of the 1960s' success against poverty.[1]

Later in this chapter, we will evaluate other poverty cures, but first I want to assess the programs that were usually associated with the War on Poverty, those that were, for the most part, run by Sargent Shriver's Office of Economic Opportunity (OEO). In particular I will analyze job-training efforts, Head Start, Neighborhood Legal Services, and community action programs. These had three goals: to offer poor people training and motivational rehabilitation so that they could obtain jobs in the booming economy; to improve services to the poor; and to empower poor people to help themselves and to pressure local governments for better treatment.

Liberals often assumed that the able-bodied poor were poor because they lacked skills or motivation for work, but many heads of poor families who were not elderly worked all or part of the year. The press featured stories about poor people lining up around the block for jobs when a new grocery store opened near them. Was there a shortage of willing and able workers or a shortage of good jobs? Probing this question did not seem so urgent after economic growth took off in the early 60s. But the success of training programs depended not only on effective design but also on the accuracy of assumptions that jobs would be plentiful. If there were too few jobs or too few good jobs, then the War on Poverty might be a diversion from real issues of unemployment and inequality. It could frustrate poor people, and it could bring reproach to all liberal programs.

And there was a second issue. Was it a good idea to focus public attention on the problems of the poorest, while assuming that things were good for most workers? Why not a broad attack on economic insecurity, embracing not just the very poor but the nearly poor, the working poor, and the whole working class?[2]

The 1960s shaped up as one of those rare periods in history when millions of Americans were open to major reforms. The civil rights movement got people thinking about economic opportunity. The public was supportive of the War on Poverty. On college campuses, idealism defeated careerism; thousands of students were engaged in civil rights activities and community organizing. The decade was the most opportune time since the 1930s for creating new institutions and fixing old ones. Some of what planners and politicians did with their opportunities is sketched in this chapter.

Training Programs: The Manpower Development and Training Act and the Job Corps

An essential part of the War on Poverty was job training. The poor had less education and training than the nonpoor, and it seemed common sense that if poor people had the right skills they would get good jobs and rise out of poverty. Yet Stanford professor of education Harry Levin, after reviewing the literature on the War on Poverty, found a "basic failure of existing approaches toward education and training in alleviating poverty."[3] What happened? To find an answer, we examine the Manpower Development and Training Act and the Job Corps.

The Manpower Development and Training Act (MDTA) was signed into law by President Kennedy in the spring of 1962, two years before the War on Poverty. It grew out of concern in the late 1950s that technological unemployment was worsening. Yet, as Labor Secretary Arthur Goldberg claimed, there were chronic labor shortages in "transistorized circuitry, inertial guidance, ferret reconnaissance, human factors science," and other areas that sounded very advanced. The MDTA spent $1.5 billion in six years; but as economic growth picked up, many displaced workers found new jobs, and increasingly the MDTA served not the newly jobless but poor young people. Many of these lacked the educational background for advanced training, so the MDTA offered remedial subjects before it trained enrollees in auto mechanics, food services, machine operation, office work, and health services.[4]

In six years, 600,000 Americans completed an MDTA course. What was the outcome? Some studies showed that graduates improved annual earnings by $1,000 or more; others found a gain of only $269. Because few evaluations included control groups, it was impossible to tell how the same kind of people were doing without the MDTA, but one effort using Social Security data found that MDTA graduates did worse than the control group! The safest overall conclusion came from two sympathetic students of the MDTA: "After 10 years, there is still no *definitive* evidence one way or another about MDTA outcomes."[5]

Some MDTA training programs were poorly run, and students had weak educational backgrounds or drug problems. But the MDTA was fundamentally flawed. It was based on the theory of structural unemployment: people were jobless and poor because they lacked the skills to take existing jobs. Yet MDTA women were being trained for low-level jobs in clerical and health fields and men in auto repair, welding, and the like; in some of these occupations, there were usually plenty of job seekers, so the main impact of successful training was to give MDTA graduates an advantage over others. Since MDTA did not create jobs, it increased the number of people applying for some positions. In the job market as a game of musical chairs, a successful MDTA added more people but no more chairs.[6]

Unless there were significant job shortages for which the poor could be trained, antipoverty training programs might not lower total poverty rates. This did not mean that training programs were useless or that the nation did not need an efficient system of job information and training open to everyone.[7] But if there was a shortage of decent jobs, training could not solve much poverty. It seemed, at times, that the unemployed poor were being trained to become the working poor. "Why train us for $1 an hour in health services?" one woman asked.[8]

A second prominent training program of the 60s, the Job Corps, had similar flaws. Shriver made the Job Corps Title 1 of the War on Poverty because he thought it would "yield instant results and cover him in quick glory. He never made a greater mistake."[9] The Job Corps was designed for youngsters trapped in poor communities. Some commentators noticed that youth unemployment was climbing as the baby boomers joined the labor market. In January 1964, the President's Task Force on Manpower Conservation claimed that the military

Typing class at Woman's Job Corps Center. (Courtesy of National Archives)

would reject one of three young men for physical and mental deficiencies. Perhaps a Job Corps could remedy those deficiencies.[10]

The Job Corps removed young people (16 to 21 years old) from the negative influences of their communities and brought them to residential campuses for basic education, vocational training, and health services. Enrollees had their living expenses covered and received a small stipend. There had been much debate in Congress about what the camps would do, and in the end there were three kinds: those for young women, who would be trained mainly for white-collar positions; "rural" camps run by the Interior and Agricultural departments to offer remedial education and conservation work to boys whose skills fell below the fifth-grade level; and "urban" camps (usually in rural areas), run by corporations like IBM and General Electric, for better educated young men, who would be trained in auto repair, construction trades, and the like.[11]

The Job Corps began with high hopes; 300,000 young people applied for 10,000 slots. People had not been defeated by a culture of poverty and despair, even if things looked pretty hopeless back home. An Appalachian mother told her son, Ray Martin, "Don't come back, son. There's nothing for you here." Camp conditions were spartan, and kids became homesick. One youth from Baltimore left and then returned. "I hate this lousy place, but it's better than the lousy place I come from."[12] Burglaries and fights were common in the early days. Trainees brought problems with them; 7% of the first 10,000 had been involved in "serious crimes."[13] Many were school dropouts. But these were exactly the kind of people that the corps was supposed to help.

On the physical side, the program worked. Trainees gained weight, and a third were fitted with glasses. One 16-year-old had fourteen teeth extracted soon after he arrived. Many enrollees had never been to a dentist.[14] But the corps did not exist mainly to offer free health services. It was an educational and training institution. Teachers and counselors had a difficult task: take young people, many of them lonely and resentful, and convince them—often in the absence of realistic prospects for a good job—to behave and to study hard.[15] Shriver, congressional critics, and the press wanted training programs to show quick results; they would not tolerate an extended process of educational experimentation to find the best methods. Much was demanded, and the methods were not always inspiring. Some of the teachers were authoritarian and hostile to students.[16]

Results reflected these problems. Two-thirds of Job Corps enrollees never finished the course. Graduates earned wages that were the same as no-shows who had been accepted into but had not entered the program. Some studies showed better outcomes, but generally the results were not good. To add fuel to the flames, critics claimed in the *Congressional Record* in 1967 that the costs of educating a student in the corps were as much as sending someone to Harvard.[17]

In fact, the Job Corps tried something more difficult than educating a Harvard student. And it was handicapped by the missing link to good jobs. This was the downfall of antipoverty training programs. It may have been a good idea to modernize young people from low-income families—to improve their schooling, polish them up for the job market, and address their health needs. But many trainees already had middle-class job aspirations; if job offers did not follow, they would grow more cynical. The Marine Cooks and Stewards Union ran a successful Job Corps program in the early 70s; it offered real jobs at the end of the program. But training alone could not create jobs, and there was no shortage of applicants for working-class occupations in services, construction, and manufacturing. We examine national data in chapter 5, but the anecdotal evidence is striking. One employer tested the labor market in Scranton, Pennsylvania, with an ad for workers; 14,000 returned the coupon in the ad, and 10,000 filled out job applications, all without knowing the name of the company; 400 were hired. At GM's Lordstown plant in 1966, 57,000 applied for 5,700 slots.[18]

The economy of the 1960s mixed progress and poverty. Official unemployment rates fell, but even in the 60s there was a huge underground of unem-

School dropouts having lunch at a Maryland Job Corps Center. (Courtesy of National Archives)

ployed and part-time workers. Most heads of poor families had a connection to the world of work. In 1963 only 36% did not work at all, and some of these were aged or disabled (table 3.1). Concerning the rest, 28% worked full-time all year; 22% worked full-time part of the year, and 14% worked part-time. As income expert Herman Miller put it, "Although today's poor are frequently presented as psychologically or spiritually handicapped, the fact is that about 50% of them are headed by a full-time worker whose wages are simply too low to support a family."[19]

Along the same lines, there were seven or eight times as many black women in the labor force (3,218,000) as there were heading welfare families (400,000 to 450,000), but the media began to pay more attention to those on welfare than those at work. Many of these women workers were poorly paid. Even those who worked regularly averaged only $2,949 for a full-time, year-round job. That was below poverty lines for a family of four.[20]

As we will see in chapter 5, a Labor Department survey in the fall of 1966 showed that huge numbers of the urban poor were unemployed, were part-time workers wanting full-time work, had stopped searching for work because they could not find it, or were full-time workers earning poverty wages. The national unemployment rate was 3.8%, but these subemployment rates ranged from 24.2% in Roxbury (a Boston neighborhood) to 47.4% in the slums of San Antonio.[21]

If there was a surplus of workers, antipoverty training programs were doomed. A successful training program might have perverse effects. If it raised worker efficiency, that meant more trained workers fighting for the same jobs. Society gained lower prices, and people who found a job got a lift, but that did not solve the aggregate job problem.[22] Antipoverty planners had assumed that there would be enough jobs for all and that the jobless poor just needed help getting them. As it turned out, there were more jobs but not enough, and things worsened as baby boomers flooded job markets in the late 60s.

Many poor people needed good jobs or a realistic prospect of them. The minority that could not handle job offers because of mental or physical disabilities would not be helped by six months of training; they needed special services. By the late 60s, pushed by the worst riots in U.S. history, some political leaders gave more thought to the need for government to create jobs directly or to subsidize job creation in the private sector, but old assumptions were deeply rooted.[23] In the 1960s antipoverty warriors—and many Americans for that matter—were apostles of the human capital theory that emphasized the importance of education and training. The training myth behind the Manpower Development and Training program and the Job Corps kept Americans from thinking about the limits of a capitalist boom as an antipoverty weapon,

Table 3.1. Work Experience of Poor Family Heads in 1963

Work Experience	Percentage
Worked full-time year-round	28
Worked full-time part-year	22
Worked part-time	14
Worked	64
Did not work at all	36

Source: Data from Mollie Orshansky, "Counting the Poor: Another Look at the Poverty Profile," *Social Security Bulletin*, January 1965, table 2.

for they focused on defects in the worker rather than those in labor markets. But if economic booms could not erase unemployment, they would not wipe out poverty. The War on Poverty kept Americans from understanding that. So also did the sense of generalized prosperity and the fact that the media began to color poor people and clients of the War on Poverty black. These factors confined antipoverty thinking to narrow channels.[24]

Operation Head Start

The branch of the Office of Economic Opportunity that won the most political support was Head Start. Shriver had an interest in early child-hood education, and it looked like all Community Action Program funds would not be spent that first year of the War on Poverty, so there was money and motive for a prepackaged program to get community action agencies going.[25] Half of the nation's poor were children; early intervention might break the cycle of poverty that "perpetuates itself" year after year. Head Start would be a preschool enrichment program to offset cultural deprivation, the negative influence of low-income families and communities.[26]

Head Start turned out to be more than a system of schooling. It diagnosed and sometimes treated medical and dental problems. It offered one nutritious meal a day. And as part of the OEO's Community Action Program, it mandated poor people's participation, and it employed parents as aides and paraprofessionals. Some staff members of the OEO's Community Action Program hoped that Head Start would become part of a "movement among the poor of our country to take control of the course of their lives including the education of their children."[27]

Head Start evoked tremendous support. Its introduction as an eight-week summer program was rapid. Scholars wanted a carefully designed pilot program for 2,500 tots, but Shriver thought the moment of opportunity would be brief. Head Start opened in the summer of 1965 for half a million 4- and 5-year-olds.[28] Speedy implementation was possible because of people's willingness to donate time. In the spring of 1965, hundreds of volunteers and government interns worked night and day under difficult conditions (one group used a bath tub as a filing cabinet) to broadcast the availability of funds and help applicants draft their proposals. Idealism and optimism cut red tape and minimized fraud. For the first summer program 44,000 teachers, many of them schoolteachers on vacation, got six days of orientation and went to work. That summer 200,000 people signed up to serve as unpaid aides. Soon Head Start became a full-year program, and in 1968 it was serving 218,000 children.[29]

Head Start was based on local control. Most units were supervised by community action antipoverty agencies, although school systems often ran the programs. Local control allowed a range of approaches. Success rates were sure to vary. Experts did not even agree on how to measure success. Furthermore, success with preschoolers would have little immediate effect on poverty rates (although adult employees of the program might gain enough income to rise above poverty lines). Psychologist Leon Eisenberg claimed that Head Start children gained ten IQ points in ten months. Others doubted that IQ could have improved so rapidly.[30] Soon researchers were developing a standard critique: early gains did not last long. Worse, in a general study of education, James Coleman came to the shocking conclusion that the quality of schools made little difference in student performance. Family background was much more important.[31]

The public remained supportive of a program that helped children succeed in school, but the battle of evaluators continued. In the 70s, psychologist Urie Bronfenbrenner found that Head Start gains faded after two or three years. Other scholars claimed that reading achievement and social adjustment were long lasting. Head Start kids seemed to be more eager, more involved, and more curious. Young adults who had gone through a Head Start–like experience at the Perry School, a preschool program for low-income African American children in Ypsilanti, Michigan, in the 60s, were more likely than a control group to graduate from high school, get a job, and avoid trouble with the law.[32]

Head Start was underfunded and its staff poorly paid. The Perry School was funded at twice the level of Head Start. With better paid and better trained teachers, less turnover, and more emphasis on academics, Head Start students might have shown better results. To counter the fade-out of cognitive advances, officials started a program called Follow Through, but it was not well funded.[33]

Whatever the academic outcomes or the impact on poverty rates, Head Start endured, and it eased the effects of poverty. Thousands of children saw their first doctor and dentist; thousands of families received free social services. Head Start employed parents, and so it was, indirectly, a job creation program. Many parents moved on from work as Head Start aides or board members to improve their own schooling. In 1965–80, 12,000 parents got college credit for their work in the program, and 1,000 earned A.A. or B.A. degrees. Thirty thousand paraprofessionals worked in the regular full-year program, and although they earned low wages at part-time hours, some became less poor.[34]

No matter how successful Head Start was, it could not revolutionize the class structure or create good permanent jobs for Head Start graduates. But as a Community Action Program emphasizing people's participation, Head Start had the potential to be an arm of a poor people's movement that could use government to reform the unequal distribution of good jobs and income. In some communities, especially in the South, Head Start began that way. In the Child Development Group of Mississippi (CDGM), civil rights activism, community involvement, Head Start, and the War on Poverty came together in a remarkable movement. With federal money and donations from some of the nation's poorest people, the CDGM opened eighty-three Head Start centers in forty communities in 1965. It was an extraordinary achievement.

The CDGM was, in part, a civil rights effort to empower poor black Mississippians. It educated preschoolers and mobilized low-income blacks as aides, teachers, and supporters. It became a test of whether federal officials would stick up for poor people against white racists like Mississippi senators John Stennis and James Eastland. The CDGM seemed to fulfill one goal of antipoverty planners: providing a direct link between the poor and the federal government. Had Mississippi's poor depended on local and state authorities, there would have been no CDGM and no Head Start in the state. But President Johnson needed Stennis's support for the war in Vietnam. So when Stennis and other conservatives attacked the CDGM for bad accounting practices and for mixing Head Start and civil rights activity, Johnson and Shriver listened. What really bothered Stennis and the segregationist establishment of Mississippi was the fact that the CDGM gave power to blacks, that its staff was integrated, and that the staff demanded that white officials treat black people with respect. The CDGM *was*, as Stennis charged, part of the civil rights movement, but any effort to improve the lives of black people in Mississippi had to involve civil rights awareness; surely one goal of Head Start was empowering poor blacks to stand up to racism and inequality. That was always dangerous. In Mississippi people were killed trying to register to vote. In 1964, the bodies of three civil rights workers, Michael Schwerner, James Chaney, and Andrew Goodman, had been found after a long search. State officials had never shown concern about violence against black people. They had vowed never to accept antipoverty

HEAD START SUCCESS IN MISSISSIPPI

Tracy Whittaker, a CDGM Head Start teacher, wrote on August 18, 1965: "From a mass of withdrawn, repressed pre-schoolers who had never ridden a seesaw, worked a puzzle, drawn a picture, we have, with few exceptions, a happy, cohesive group of kids full of vitality (and now, at last, food) who spend their day creating, pretending, playing, singing, looking, listening, and wondering. We don't pretend to be a super educational machine at Holly Grove—the children did not learn to read and write in our eight weeks. However . . . we tried to show these children that they were important. . . . Almost all have a measure of human dignity that they didn't have before."

Source: Polly Greenberg, *The Devil Has Slippery Shoes: A Biased Biography of the Child Development Group of Mississippi* (Washington: Youth Policy Institute, 1990), 244.

money. The governor announced that Mississippi needed "to teach some of our Negroes that they are wasting their time staying in Mississippi."[35]

Johnson and Shriver caved in to reactionary forces. The CDGM was forced to cut civil rights activity, its director was fired, and Shriver secretly manufactured a replacement group of moderate whites and blacks. One of the moderates, Hodding Carter III, recalled that Shriver told him, "I need somebody to get my ass out of this sling . . . and we're going to have to dump this one [CDGM]." In October 1966, a full-page protest appeared in the *New York Times*, "Say It Isn't So, Sargent Shriver," signed by a long list of religious and labor leaders led by Walter Reuther of the United Auto Workers Union. The protest brought a temporary compromise, but the moderate group, Mississippi Action for Progress, Inc., was favored. Within the CDGM, problems and conflicts intensified, and it withered.[36]

While it flourished, the CDGM was an instrument for childhood education as well as new careers and prideful activism for thousands of very poor adults. In its first year, there were three times as many black children in Head Start as in the first grade of all of Mississippi's schools; the CDGM was bringing education to many who would not otherwise have had it. And much more. As onetime Head Start official and advocate Polly Greenberg recalled, the CDGM aimed to "build the iron egos needed by children growing up to be future leaders of social change in a semifeudal state." For this aim to be accomplished, poor black kids needed to see black parents in responsible positions. Parental competence and authority fulfilled one goal of the War on Poverty: to empower poor people so that they could transform themselves and their environments. In fact, the CDGM embodied what "Shriver and his poverty warriors have been battling for all along."[37]

It was not the poor who failed but the federal government. The destruction of the CDGM and its replacement by a more compliant organization proved that, while the poor would help themselves, the federal government would not defend them, even against openly reactionary forces. The culture of American politics, with its subordination to racist politicians, was a much bigger problem than the culture of poverty.[38]

Neither Head Start nor the CDGM could solve much poverty, even in Mississippi, where there was so much to solve, but the CDGM helped, offering income to parents and staff. And the work it did educating and inspiring children and fighting racism would make a difference when opportunities expanded. But massive forces having nothing to do with Head Start were ejecting Mississippi blacks from agriculture and creating more poverty. In the 60s, infant mortality was rising for blacks in Mississippi. Some federal programs caused more poverty. The Food and Fiber Act of 1965 gave the state's richest farmers subsidies of $39 million in 1966 to reduce acreage, and the 1967 extension of the minimum wage law to farm labor made herbicides cheaper than workers. The demand for farmworkers sank. White leaders told blacks to leave the state. The state gave little aid to the poor, and many blacks could not come up with the cash that was necessary in those days to buy food stamps.[39]

Although the CDGM could not solve these problems, it was doing the kinds of things the War on Poverty was supposed to do. It emphasized education and empowerment, but federal officials did not stand behind it. And Mississippi was not exceptional; in 1965–67, the principle of poor people's control in community action was under attack at the national level.

What Happened to Community Action?

Radical Democrats had managed to include in War on Poverty legislation not only community action but also a requirement for "maximum feasible participation of the poor." How much real control poor people would have emerged in 1965–67, often through bitter conflict. If people were poor because they were excluded from major institutions and mistreated by officials, poverty might be solved if the poor had "a real voice in their institutions,"[40] but exactly how community action would solve poverty had not been clearly thought out. Poverty agencies had no control over investment capital—over resources to rebuild communities and supply good jobs—and they lacked the "leverage to attract private investment back into inner-city communities."[41] So community action, the instrument that made the War on Poverty seem innovative, might be a sideshow to fundamental economic issues. Yet *because* it was a sideshow, it fit Lyndon Johnson's idea of a war on poverty that, far from being unconditional, was not supposed to upset the middle class or corporate leaders.

Planners and theorists had many reasons for wanting community action in the War on Poverty, not the least of which were that it looked new, was cheap, and was a good alternative for planners who did not want comprehensive job programs. Of rationales having something to do with helping the poor, there were three. First, community organizations could improve social services, for it was argued that schools, welfare agencies, and other institutions mistreated the poor. The service emphasis also played to the idea that if many services were brought together in a coordinated fashion, poverty could be solved. Second was the political action model: community organizations could organize the poor to reform institutions that affected them. The third rationale involved the therapy of participation. Poor people's involvement in running community agencies, on boards of directors, as paraprofessionals, and as agitators, would create a sense of empowerment and offer positive models for young people. That would counteract the culture of poverty; it would lead to the reconstruction of community discipline and thus to less crime and delinquency.[42]

While it is difficult to generalize about the 1,000 community action agencies in existence by 1968, some things are clear. Because of a few cases, community action agencies became controversial, but in fact most were under the control of local governments. An example was Chicago's agency, which was an arm of Mayor Richard Daley's political machine.[43] Most of the handful of community action agencies that independently mobilized the poor for demonstrations and other sorts of political activity were soon tamed. The Child Development Group of Mississippi was an example. Another was the pioneer of community action, New York City's Mobilization for Youth. Prior to the War on Poverty, Mobilization for Youth had been involved in demonstrations and rent strikes, but it was attacked as being communist-dominated by Mayor Robert Wagner. It was subdued, even before it became a part of the War on Poverty.[44] The same process affected the Syracuse agency, which worked with activist scholars at the university and paid for training sessions with renowned agitator Saul Alinsky.[45] While the *idea* of subsidizing the poor to engage in political action made sense in a democracy, since those with money already had influence, it was unrealistic to expect the federal government to finance attacks on mayors and other interests that were vital to the Democratic Party. As Harrington admitted, eventually the poor will "send a committee to their local Congressman," and then they will "picket the Mayor. Can you expect, given the political structure of this country, government funds being used to overthrow governments?"[46]

Some organizations were successful. Poor people in Newark limited a plan to destroy low-income housing and build a medical school. Community action agencies and antipoverty workers in New York's East Harlem, in Bedford Stuyvesant, and in other cities expanded welfare rights. But most of these organizations were like Pittsburgh's; there an investigator found "little evidence" of success in democratizing social welfare. That was no surprise, since the mayor and city bureaucrats controlled the community action organization, the Mayor's Committee on Human Resources.[47]

Scandals occurred in San Francisco and Harlem, where community action became a way to extort money and jobs from the government. In each case militants used harsh language and physical threats, without much payoff for the poor. Also not helping the public image of the War on Poverty, the Harlem agency subsidized LeRoi Jones's Black Arts Theater, which produced political dramas on the streets of Harlem. In a play called *Jello*, Jack Benny's valet, Rochester, rose up to kill his white oppressors.[48] This may have been good political art, but it did not sit well with white voters who increasingly perceived the War on Poverty as a "black" program linked to violence and riots.

Community action agencies did succeed as training grounds for a new class of urban black politicians, but the election of black mayors like Ken Gibson in Newark did not have much effect on urban poverty. Community action agencies also employed thousands of poor people in low-wage jobs and many middle-class Americans as bureaucrats and professionals. These jobs improved people's lives, although most were impermanent and, as in Head Start, part-time work at a minimum wage. Of themselves, they did not lift many people above the poverty line. Still, 68,500 nonprofessionals were employed on a year-round basis in various community action programs such as Head Start; another 75,000 came on in the summer. For some of the poor, jobs as paraprofessionals were steps to something better. It turned out that poor people, who were supposed to be beaten down by the culture of poverty, had very practical aims. Many wanted jobs more than they wanted political participation. Community action agencies were not designed mainly as job creators, but they generated thousands of jobs, and not all of them went to middle-class bureaucrats. These jobs, most of them low wage and often part-time, may have been the most substantial thing the War on Poverty offered to low-income communities.[49]

Community action agencies did a good job ordering up new services, especially programs drawn up by the OEO in Washington. Head Start (discussed above) and Neighborhood Legal Services (see below) were two such programs;

EMPLOYMENT IN THE WAR ON POVERTY
HELPED MARY LOU WILLIAMS

In 1965 Mary Louise Williams decided to get off welfare. When she heard about new antipoverty programs in Seattle, she applied and was hired as an organizer. In that job, she had earnings, and she honed her skills with the help of a stern supervisor. She even got started on a college degree. She worked for seventeen years in private and public social agencies until she was laid off from Seattle's Parks Department in the depression of 1982. She was eighteen months shy of retirement. For her government employment had been the ticket out of poverty and off welfare, and it appears that she had not needed special antipoverty programs to lift her motivation. She needed a job in 1965, and she needed one in 1982. She learned many of her skills while working, the way many people do.

Source: Kevin Roderick, "Case History of a 20-Year War on Poverty," *Los Angeles Times*, July 31, 1985, 1, 8–9.

they improved services to the poor. In addition, by the early 70s there were seventy Comprehensive Community Health Centers, which treated a million patients. Birth control services began to reach women through more than 300 community action agencies. Finally, the community agencies opened hundreds of neighborhood service centers to provide one-stop shopping for an array of programs like Head Start, Legal Services, health services, job training, and tutoring.[50]

Improving services *was* a worthy goal, but better services were no substitute for good jobs and more income. The other goals of community action were to agitate and to empower. But most agencies did not have the poor in controlling positions; many did not organize the poor to confront government or business over fundamentals like jobs; and many engaged in community organizing that did little to change institutions.[51]

Shriver and congressional leaders wavered in their support for poor people's control of policy making in the community action agencies. In many places, poor people had very little governing power at all, but the very possibility frightened local politicians. In 1966 Minnesota Republican Albert Quie got Congress to legislate that community action agencies had to have at least one-third representation of poor people (although the representatives did not have to be poor), but just a year later, led by Oregon Democrat Edith Green, Congress gave local governments the option of taking over independent agencies. In fact, so few agencies were independent that few governments had to take them over.[52] Meanwhile, Congress and the White House, with a nudge from labor leader Walter Reuther, created the Model Cities program. Model Cities would be an instrument of rebuilding the slums, but it assured local governmental rather than community control.[53] Both the Green amendment and Model Cities made poor people's control less likely, but it had always been tenuous.

The idea of community organizations trying to "change the system" was not a bad one, and there have been hundreds of effective community organizations since 1960. Most were independent of government. In 1960 Saul Alinsky helped to found the Woodlawn Organization (TWO) to win school improvements, jobs, and restrictions on the University of Chicago's right to encroach on surrounding neighborhoods. Farmworkers successfully unionized in the 1960s and 1970s, and their efforts to do so were as much a community movement as a unionization drive. Similarly, the Memphis Sanitation Workers strike in 1968 was as much a civil rights and community action as a labor strike. In 2000, a Los Angeles union of janitors organized community support to win a strike for substantial wage increases.[54]

But even good community organizations were limited in their power to respond to massive economic and political forces. The Woodlawn Organization could not stop the deterioration of Woodlawn. Crime rates increased, jobs declined, and people with good jobs elsewhere moved out. Perhaps only a massive reconstruction program could have turned things around, and that did not happen.[55]

Most community action organizations did not function as radical planners had hoped. Their power was limited, and so were their resources. Here was a war on poverty with empty guns; but even with a little more funding and more power, community action could not have solved a lot of poverty. Much poverty was not local, and it had only partly to do with local social services. The total quantity of poverty had to do with classes, class power, and the distribution of jobs and incomes; all that involved national politics and, often, big corporations. It is true that Head Start and community action agencies provided jobs for some of the poor, but that was incidental to their mission, and only a tiny fraction of the poor found work in the antipoverty agencies. To the extent that community action had little impact on real jobs, it was tilting at windmills.[56]

Community Action—Legal Services for the Poor

Often attached to local community action agencies was Neighborhood Legal Services. This agency fulfilled two of the OEO's goals: improving the delivery of services to the poor and promoting institutional change. Private legal aid societies were not meeting poor people's needs. By the end of 1967 Neighborhood Legal Services had 2,000 lawyers in 800 neighborhood law offices. It was limited to civil law, and almost 40% of its cases involved family issues, chiefly divorce and separation. A lot of what agency lawyers did was humdrum, time-consuming labor, but clients jammed their offices, and the need for the program seemed clear. How could it be said that Americans were equal before the law if some had lawyers and some did not?

But Neighborhood Legal Services, like the War on Poverty, not only offered services; it promoted reform. And this it began to do when its lawyers successfully challenged state residency requirements for welfare recipients (*Shapiro v. Thompson* in 1969) and regulations that denied welfare to recipients who had a man living in the house (*King v. Smith* in 1968). They established tenants' right to withhold rents when landlords refused essential repairs and services; as California Rural Legal Assistance, they proved that Governor Reagan had illegally cut medical benefits to the poor and aged; and for farmworkers they forced the Department of Labor to examine unrestricted admission of Mexican workers to harvest tomatoes. These were victories; some were worth millions of dollars to the poor. They probably did not bring the poverty rate down much, but they made the poor less poor and less miserable.[57]

There were limits to what the legal approach could accomplish without political transformation. Although philosophers and economists defended the idea of a guaranteed minimum income, no welfare rights lawyer won court approval for the principle that every American had a right to a living wage or adequate welfare. In fact, as the political climate cooled in the 70s, state governments allowed the after-inflation value of welfare payments to decline. In San Francisco, Legal Services delayed evictions or forced landlords to make repairs, but the housing situation overall "became a great deal worse."[58]

Neighborhood Legal Services accomplished as much as any other branch of the War on Poverty, but it revealed the limits of the War on Poverty approach. As Edward Sparer, the founding father of welfare rights litigation, put it, the Legal Services program assumed that the poor "were a very discrete section of our society, that the rest of the society was reasonably comfortable, that the problems of the poor could be remedied without greatly disturbing or burdening other elements." In fact, "most of the working class and lower middle class experience great financial overburdening"; they lack the services that the OEO was providing to the poor, and they were taxed to pay for those services. Legal work, Sparer argued, should bridge the gap between the very poor and the working and lower middle classes. It should focus not on welfare for the poor but on "income security" for all. Sparer's diagnosis of the limits of Legal Services was an apt critique of the whole War on Poverty.[59]

What Cured Poverty in 1965–1970: The War on Poverty, Growth, or Cash Transfers?

Between 1960 and 1969 the percentage of Americans in poverty fell from 22.2% to 12.1%. That decline was greater than the one in the 1950s (7.8 points). The poverty population fell from 39,851,000 to 24,147,000, a decline of more than 15 million. Had the 1960 rate of 22.2% remained in 1969, there would have been 44,293,000 poor people in America, that is, 20 million more than there were.[60]

How can we explain antipoverty success in the 1960s? As always, millions of people worked hard, went to school, and did a dozen other things to advance themselves. But the success of millions of private decisions depended very much on the state of the economy and government programs. We know that people did not change their attitudes toward work in the depression of the 30s, but millions lost their jobs and became desperately poor. Poverty stopped falling in the late 50s not because people's values changed but because the economy and government policy failed them. How did big factors operate in the 60s to cut poverty?

Expert opinion is divided. Conservatives who are hostile to government argue that strong economic growth in the private sector was the key. Political scientist John Schwarz claims that government income transfer programs cured the most poverty. Scholar Sar Levitan concluded that even the best friends of the War on Poverty would not claim it did much to cut poverty rates.[61] Most evaluations of the training programs showed that graduates did not earn much more than peers who had no War on Poverty training.[62]

How about the other two big poverty cures, economic growth and cash transfers? Experts have concluded that each contributed about equally to the fall in poverty rates over 1965–70. As a result of economic growth and the consequent increase in jobs and wages, poverty fell about 2.5 points. Government payment programs cut the poverty rate another 2.2 points. These numbers seem small, but the decline of U.S. poverty rates from 17.3% to 12.6% over 1965–70 was one of the best records ever—right up there with the previous decline of 4.9 points (1960–65).[63] Had the 70s been as good as the 60s, poverty rates would have been 1% instead of 11% in 1980.

The impact of growth and of cash benefits was uneven. Welfare payments were usually too meager to lift female-headed families out of poverty. Social Security payments were more effective for whites than blacks because whites were more likely to be covered and had better income histories. Over 1959–69, poverty rates for older blacks (65 and over) fell from 62.5% to 50.2%; for whites they fell from 33.1% to 23.3%.[64]

For African Americans, the impact of economic growth and civil rights was dramatic. Over the 60s black family poverty fell from 55% to 31%. Jobs, the gift of growth, paid off. White families in which both husband and wife worked saw their poverty rate fall from 17% to 8%; black families of the same kind cut theirs from 47% to 17%.[65]

But even during one of the longest expansions in our history, the benefits of income and job growth were not reaching everyone. Many black adults did not work or were underemployed. Inner-city unemployment rates for African Americans were falling but still 10% in the late 60s.[66] Baby boomers, white and black, were creating a glut of young workers. Civil rights laws existed, but past and present racism assured that poor blacks received an extra share of unemployment and unstable employment. Persistent unemployment and poverty, along with changes in social values, help to explain why, in an economic expansion, the proportion of black families that were female-headed increased.[67]

Some have argued that easier welfare caused families to break up, creating rather than curing poverty. Certainly the welfare rights movement of the late 60s raised poor people's sense of entitlement and put more of them on welfare. But social scientists cannot prove either that going on welfare caused family breakups or that family breakups caused poverty; most African American families that made a transition to being female-headed were poor before they changed.[68] One source of poverty was high unemployment or low-paying, unstable jobs. That, along with new ideas about marriage and about entitlements, contributed to rising welfare use and more female-headed families. The complex results of economic growth showed in the statistics: the poverty rate for blacks fell from 55% to 32% (1959–69), but rates for whites fell to 9.5%.

Even though blacks suffered higher poverty rates, we must keep in mind that many whites who were not poor were economically insecure and anxious and that a majority of the poor were white. Of the 24,147,000 Americans who fell below the poverty lines in 1969, 16,659,000, or almost 70%, were whites.[69] In that light, poverty looks like a mainstream problem. Unfortunately the War on Poverty assumed that those who really needed help were outside the mainstream and rather different than average working-class Americans.

The Limits of Johnsonian Liberalism

Lyndon Johnson oversold and underfinanced the War on Poverty. Worse, the war was conceptually flawed. Johnson and antipoverty planners censored alternative approaches. Notable in their thinking about poverty was "the absence of any mention of the economic system within which it operates." The antipoverty war targeted the poorest of the poor and segregated them from the larger population that also faced economic risk every day.[70]

Historian Irwin Unger claims that anything other than what the Johnson administration did was impossibly utopian. But there was nothing as utopian as programs that led nowhere; the poor learned that "once training is over, there is no job." Survey data showed that Americans would have supported other approaches; the War on Poverty could have emphasized government job creation or better income policies. Johnson and his economic advisers were at fault.[71] Political caution and a constricted ideology narrowed the antipoverty crusade. Johnson did not want social programs to threaten middle-class pocketbooks and business power. He and his economists were confident that tax cuts were creating jobs that would cure much poverty.

The Vietnam War had contradictory effects. It came to absorb Johnson's attention and grabbed funding that might have gone to fight poverty, but Vietnam spending cut unemployment, and that helped to lower poverty rates. Economists and politicians were not always frank about the fact that war spending was vital to job creation and poverty fighting.

The spectacular urban riots of 1964—68 showed that the War on Poverty and economic growth were leaving many behind, but the fact that most rioters were black helped to marginalize debate about the persistence of poverty and unemployment in the midst of prosperity. So did the training focus and the visibility of African Americans in antipoverty programs. The race angle and a condition of general prosperity meant that unemployment and poverty could be framed largely as problems of minorities who faced discrimination and lacked good schooling and training. And certainly these were vital issues. But too much focus on race meant no thinking about economic structures of poverty and inequality, that is, about class.

Johnson's Keynesian economists encouraged orthodoxy. They expected a growing economy to cut a lot of poverty. To some extent they were right. Economic growth was responsible for half the decline in poverty rates during the 60s.[72] Nevertheless, experts in and outside government sensed early on that growth and training programs would fall short. They called for direct government job creation or guaranteed minimum incomes or both.[73] The president continued to reject these strategies as unnecessary or unwise. One of the most liberal presidents of the century was not so liberal after all. On guaranteed incomes, he would only appoint a commission. On employment, the furthest he went was the 1968 program Job Opportunities in the Business Sector (JOBS). In this program government did not create positions; rather, it located the long-term unemployed and subsidized businesses to employ them. Limiting the program's focus to the "hard-core" jobless may have been well intentioned, but it narrowed the unemployment problem to a minority with special problems. In any case, business leaders quickly tired of the effort, especially as the economy slowed. Ultimately, JOBS was a flop.[74]

Two pillars of federal antipoverty policy—general economic stimulus and job training—constricted ideas about poverty, unemployment, and welfare. There were plenty of facts in the economy, union policies, and government programs to support a more inclusive ethic of mutual assistance. The unifying vision was missing, but the bricks existed for a new welfare state ethic and a broad attack on the economic risks that afflicted most people, not just the very poor. These bricks included the following.

1. As we will see in more detail in chapter 5, real unemployment was higher than widely publicized rates indicated. Millions of able-bodied Americans without work were not counted as unemployed. High unemployment was normal in good times. Thousands showed up to apply for a few good jobs.

2. Racial and ethnic minorities had higher poverty rates than whites, but whites were a majority of the poor. Also, millions of Americans, black and white, were nearly poor but not included in poverty rates. Poverty was mainstream.

3. The nature of work, merit, and welfare needed rethinking. Affluent Americans received huge tax breaks that sometimes dwarfed direct benefits that went to low-income classes. More was "spent" by government on tax breaks for mortgage interest than was spent on all housing programs for the poor. Tax breaks for private health insurance and retirement insurance were also huge. In general, the tax-break side of government subsidies was rarely debated, but had it been, Americans might have recast their idea of who got what for "free" and from where.[75]

In broader terms, the meaning of welfare and the link between merit and level of income needed rethinking.[76] In their hostility to welfare, people believed that there should be a close connection between income and work, but the connection was broken a thousands times a day. Millions collected more in Social Security benefits than they had contributed when employed. Medicaid and Medicare were not rewards for work but expressions of the principle that people had a right to medical care. Major industrial unions, led by the United Auto Workers, were winning Supplemental Unemployment Benefits, that is, company subsidies that, when added to unemployment insurance, guaranteed senior workers a full year of almost regular income for not working. Big farmers got paid for not producing. Most women who toiled in their own homes at housework and child rearing were not paid, although they might have been if they had done the same work in another's home.

Americans distinguished between the deserving and undeserving poor, and they resisted generous policies on welfare and food stamps. But in opinion polls they often said yes to more money for the poor and for government as the employer of last resort. Popular views on the welfare state were complex, ambivalent, and changeable.[77] But few organizations were broadcasting a new philosophy. Little was said about class interests or the fact that the poorest 40% of the families got only 17% of all income or that deindustrialization in Detroit put more people on welfare. The 60s youth culture and books like *The Greening of America* raised vital questions about the link between work and income and, really, about the point of living; but their reach was limited.[78]

The war, race, and decades of narrow thinking assured that a new politics based on progressive unions, advanced liberals, and pragmatic sections of the radical movements of the 60s would not coalesce around an ethic that combined the best of both worlds, the provision of reasonable income floors and decent jobs. Liberals and the Left muffed their greatest opportunity since the 1930s to make American values and institutions truly people-friendly. Much was done, but the War on Poverty itself failed to solve much poverty; it focused on the very poor and did not deal with the income and employment problems of average working-class families. So these families felt that their problems were being ignored, especially when it appeared that the poor were black and the working class was white. The antipoverty crusade did not conquer poverty, and it provided weapons to the enemies of liberalism. Beginning in the 70s and more so in the 80s, conservatives were winning media debates about antipoverty policy. It was ironic that they had success attacking the War on Poverty as a big-spending leftist program when it was neither very big nor very left.[79]

chapter four

MOYNIHAN, THE DISSENTERS, AND THE RACIALIZATION OF POVERTY
A Liberal Turning Point That Did Not Turn

In the decades after World War II, people in other capitalist nations like Sweden, Germany, France, and the Netherlands spent less time and energy than Americans talking about poverty. That was not because they did not care about it. Rather, it was because they were busy developing government programs to serve people with a variety of needs—the poor and the not so poor, the unemployed, those without health insurance, parents requiring child-care assistance, and so on. These nations devised extensive social programs that helped the truly poor in the process of helping everyone; such programs were less likely to isolate the poor than the American War on Poverty and the American welfare system. Today, even after more than two decades of discussion about funding problems and the effects of welfare programs on work and economic growth, the rich democracies of Western Europe have retained most of their welfare state apparatus. The contrast is most visible in the area of health insurance: the French and Italians, for example, have all but universal coverage and spend half or a third as much as Americans spend; Americans, meanwhile, spend more than any other nation on health care, in total and per capita, but are not the healthiest people in the world.[1]

In Western Europe, socialist and social democratic parties that represented workers and maintained close relationships to union movements had often been vital to building the welfare state. The United States had chances to move in a social democratic direction in the 1930s and the 1960s. Much was done in the 30s to build Democratic Party liberalism and to create a powerful union movement, but the effort to construct a comprehensive welfare state and a new social ethic was slowed in the 40s and 50s by the limits of liberalism and unionism, by racism, and by the repressive effects of anticommunism.[2]

In the 1960s new political possibilities opened as the civil rights movement shook people's minds about equality and democracy. Millions were in motion against racism and poverty, sexism and war. Although the different movements were sometimes at odds with one another, their combined weight supported new initiatives in social policy.[3]

Toward a New Liberalism?

Over the course of the 60s, many liberal politicians and policy experts became more liberal. Civil rights laws would guarantee that blacks had equal access and voting rights, but training and education programs would provide a helping hand through the gates of equal opportunity. President Johnson, in a commencement speech at Howard University in 1965 partly inspired by Daniel Moynihan's work on the black family, spoke of the need to equip people to take advantage of new opportunities.[4]

Johnson also expanded the welfare state with such programs as Medicaid and Medicare, but he refused to make direct government jobs creation and income subsidies part of his War on Poverty. Yet, despite Johnson's opposition, proposals for job and income programs multiplied in the 1960s. Moynihan supported them. Planners in the Office of Economic Opportunity, suspecting that War on Poverty methods were not solving much poverty, considered guaranteed jobs and incomes.[5]

This occurred while the political foundations for a new liberalism were cracking. By the mid-1960s, some young radicals, white and black, had given up on elections. Older socialists, on the other hand, had faith that the Democratic Party could be the instrument of a radicalized liberalism.[6] Among these hopefuls, Bayard Rustin, who had helped to organize the 1963 March on Washington for civil rights and jobs, and Michael Harrington agreed that old-style liberalism could not solve the race problem. Economic growth created jobs, but it also promoted automation, which eliminated jobs. Without a "qualitative transformation of fundamental institutions," without "radical programs for full employment . . . [and] new definitions of work and leisure," real equality for black Americans could not be won. But a successful political movement for radical change depended on many things, including whether unions and the white working class could overcome racism and whether the approaches of old and new radicals could blend. Older radicals like Rustin and Harrington were inclined to view the world from the top down and to act as though radicalizing a political party meant negotiating among leaders rather than mobilizing people for demonstrations, community organizations, and elections. The young New Left emphasized democracy from the bottom up, claimed that Democrats were part of the establishment that oppressed people at home and abroad, and had doubts about the liberalism of white workers. Young radicals were moralistic and sometimes inflexible; the older generation seemed eager to compromise with those in power. When Johnson escalated the war, some older radicals and most union leaders, including Walter Reuther of the Auto Workers Union, went along while New Left organizations became militantly antiwar.[7]

Two Efforts to Go beyond Civil Rights and the War on Poverty: An Introduction

The war would have fateful consequences for a new politics. But so also would ideas. The political history of the 1960s has been told in many books. Here we narrow the focus to explore two approaches to poverty that moved beyond the civil rights and War on Poverty models. The fate of each tells much about the development of ideas for a new politics. One model, outlined in Moynihan's *The Negro Family*, is well known.[8] The other, not so well known, involved efforts by scholars and government experts whom I call Dissenters to go beyond the skill-and-training model of the War on Poverty and to link racism to a new appraisal of unemployment and labor markets.

Daniel Patrick Moynihan and the Divisive Impact of The Negro Family

Daniel Moynihan was raised in Indiana and New York. His father fell victim to drink and gambling and deserted the family. Despite the kind of broken family that seemed damaging to young men in Moynihan's *The Negro Family*, Pat grew up to be a striver who seized his opportunities. He worked for Presidents Kennedy, Johnson, Nixon, and Ford. He was Democratic senator from New York for four terms (1977–2001).

Moynihan was a public intellectual who applied scholarship to social problems. He read widely but did not probe much. After the 60s, he had little to say about unemployment as a cause of poverty. Politically he was a loose cannon. A liberal Democrat in the 60s, he worked for two Republican presidents and became known as a neoconservative in the 70s. On foreign policy, Moynihan's positions were sometimes to the left and sometimes not. He opposed the war in Vietnam, but not loudly, and he did not associate with the boisterous antiwar movement. In the 70s, he was a vigorous defender of America and Israel against critics at home and abroad. Yet in the 80s he became a vocal critic of Ronald Reagan's invasion of the tiny island of Grenada, and he proposed a freeze on nuclear weapons production.[9]

On poverty issues, it is not easy to judge Moynihan's impact. During preparations for the War on Poverty, he joined the losing side, which wanted jobs and money; later he published a sour postmortem on community action, *Maximum Feasible Misunderstanding* (1969). He urged President Nixon to support a guaranteed income plan, but that was defeated in Congress. For the rest of the 70s Moynihan did not have much impact on social policy. But in the 80s, he led the Senate against Reagan's early efforts to cut Social Security, and in 1988 he helped to push through the Family Support Act, which required work and training for welfare recipients.

Moynihan spoke with feeling against the 1996 welfare reform, but he did little to organize the opposition, and his most famous book had fostered the image of the welfare-dependent black mother that was used to justify ending welfare.[10] Moynihan also did little to make the Clintons' health care reform a success. Thus, on two urgent issues of the 90s, the social policy expert was pretty much on the sidelines. In the spring of 2001, he surprised some people by agreeing to serve President Bush on a commission stacked with those who wanted to privatize Social Security, the government's most effective anti-poverty program. This seemed odd for someone who had advocated income programs as the best way to solve poverty.[11]

Moynihan was a gifted synthesizer of research. He had the media skills to lead the way toward a new socialist liberalism or social democracy, and he seemed to want that for a while. But he was a quirky individual. His bias for the male-dominated family put him out of step with emerging feminism, and he never forgave liberals and radicals who attacked *The Negro Family* as racist. In the mid-60s he began to associate with conservatives like Irving Kristol. Had there been a large social democratic movement pushing for such programs as a family allowance system, Moynihan's erratic temperament might have been checked. At times he seemed like a European social democrat. In 1968, among conservatives and Republicans in the *Republican Papers*, he castigated liberals— not for being too liberal but for not being liberal enough to press for the costly programs necessary to solve poverty.[12]

In March 1965, as assistant secretary of labor for policy planning and research, Moynihan completed *The Negro Family: The Case for National Action*. The report emphasized the corrosive effects of joblessness on urban black families. Moynihan hoped to put the Johnson administration out in front of the next phase of the civil rights movement, that is, going beyond laws ensuring access to positive efforts to improve people's daily lives.

The Negro Family used the work of prominent scholars like the black sociologist E. Franklin Frazier and the white historian Stanley Elkins to argue that because of slavery, racial discrimination, and unemployment, black family structure was abnormal. Moynihan focused on the rising number of female-headed families among urban blacks. He spiced his discussion with alarmist rhetoric. The black ghetto family was "crumbling"; it was "increasingly disorganized"; it had "all but disintegrated" and was "approaching complete breakdown."[13] Nonwhite illegitimacy ratios were eight times those of whites and rising. A larger share of nonwhite than white families was headed by females (23.2% against 8.6% in 1962). The result was "a startling increase in welfare dependency."[14]

Years of unemployment had so deranged the black family that it was now "a tangle of pathology" that perpetuated "the cycle of poverty and deprivation." At the center of the disease was the "matriarchy." Without positive role models, young men did not learn responsible behavior. Broken homes led to low school achievement, drug use, and crime.[15]

While Moynihan agreed that unemployment was the initial cause of poverty and social disorganization, over time broken families had themselves become a cause of poverty. One proof was the disconnection between rising welfare rolls and falling unemployment. If there were more jobs, he reasoned, there should be fewer people on welfare. Moynihan claimed that over 1962–64, nonwhite male unemployment fell but the rolls rose; this implied that the black family was disintegrating even as opportunities improved.[16]

Moynihan may have intended that his report never reach the public, but it leaked out in the summer of 1965, and there was a firestorm of controversy.[17] Although some white and black leaders defended Moynihan and praised his emphasis on unemployment, others flailed him. The new director of the Congress of Racial Equality (CORE), Floyd McKissick, charged that Moynihan was saying "that it's the individual's fault when it's the damn system that really needs changing." Psychologist William Ryan accused Moynihan of "a new form of subtle racism." He was seducing his audience into believing that the cause of racial inequality was "not racism and discrimination but the weaknesses and defects of the Negro himself."[18]

The Negro Family arrived at the wrong time. On the night of August 11, two days after *Newsweek* printed the first public summary of *The Negro Family*, the worst American riot in twenty-two years erupted in Watts, a Los Angeles neighborhood; over five days, thirty-four people were killed. By coincidence of timing, Moynihan's book looked like the administration's explanation for Watts. Civil rights radicals had been growing disillusioned with Johnsonian liberalism; some civil rights leaders felt guilty about ignoring poor northern blacks. Both were ready to attack someone, and Moynihan was a good target.[19]

Some of what the critics said of *The Negro Family* was true, but Moynihan was actually more liberal than he appeared in the book. In the ensuing debate about the report, there was a lot of shadowboxing. In fact, Moynihan did not advocate conservative laissez-faire solutions for the black poor, and he did not advocate psychiatry. He wanted job and income programs—but his readers could not know that from *The Negro Family*.

At times, Moynihan's ideas were not so different from those of African American psychologist Kenneth Clark in *Dark Ghetto: Dilemmas of Social Power* (1965) or Martin Luther King Jr., who asserted that oppression made the African American family "fragile, deprived, and often psychopathic."[20] But Moynihan was a white government official, and blacks were tired of being told by whites what was wrong with them. Were poor white families in better shape?

Moynihan never looked in the mirror when he handed out blame for the failure of *The Negro Family* to get a federal commitment to solving black poverty. He castigated black leaders who were "unable to comprehend their opportunity," white and black militants "caught up in a frenzy of arrogance and nihilism," and timid white liberals.[21] But some of the flak was due to defects in Moynihan's work. It was loosely argued and it did not probe or thoroughly link two main explanations: that unemployment was the cause of black poverty and crime and that black family structure was the cause of poverty and crime. Worse, Moynihan did not spell out his program of government solutions; had he done so, liberals would have been less likely to claim that he was blaming the victim. In short, while the times were tense and criticism was likely of any government report on poor blacks, the writer was partly to blame for the denunciations that rained down upon him.

Moynihan's main argument was not well defended, but it was not implausible. It was possible that poverty and unemployment had so damaged black family structure that it was itself a cause of further problems. That was akin to the culture-of-poverty theory and a pillar of the War on Poverty: the poor lacked not only jobs and incomes but positive attitudes and social habits. This was a defensible position, but Moynihan did not argue it well.

Also damaging, Moynihan ignored the positives: the superhuman struggles of poor women to serve their families against hostile bureaucracies, crime-ridden streets, and too little money. Moynihan was blind to the plight of millions of working women who were harmed by racism and sexism in low-wage labor markets. This plot line was not part of his story, possibly because Moynihan thought women's work was part of the problem. Women were "overemployed"; that robbed children of their mother's attention and under-mined the father's position. Moynihan would have been criticized less had he given low-income women more credit, but he didn't like the idea of working mothers. In a memo to the president, he even suggested that women's jobs be redesigned so that men could do them.[22]

Oddly, Moynihan wrote almost nothing about the War on Poverty helping or hurting people or about welfare payments relieving poverty. *The Negro Family* seems less a liberal antipoverty document than a conservative effort to maintain one idea of "a stable Negro family structure."[23]

Moynihan wanted to provoke. Complicated arguments would not have caught the attention of busy government officials. But one result of Moynihan's simplistic formulations was to incite hostility about things that may not have been true. A scholar might have guessed, for example, that the number of female-headed families on welfare was rising because more poor black and white families were taking advantage of their right to welfare, not because families were collapsing.[24]

A bigger question, one with huge implications for social thought, was whether "the black family," which Moynihan used almost as an independent cause, should be such an important category for the study of black poverty. If black families were in trouble, a family focus seemed right. But there were other pathways for social policy. Those would have come more easily if Americans had a tradition of thinking about economic class and class power. The start made in the 1930s and early 1940s in that direction was wiped out in the late 40s and the 50s by anticommunism, by prosperity and propaganda (everyone was middle class), and by the ease with which Americans substituted racial and ethnic categories for class categories.[25] From a tactical point of view Moynihan knew that programs advertised for blacks only would not be as well supported as those that were "color blind."[26] But in *The Negro Family* he was often narrowly racial. In an article published just one year later, sociologist Lee Rainwater suggested that class was as important as race (table 4.1). Blacks were about as loyal to traditional family structure as whites, but poverty and unemployment interfered with the fulfillment of the ideal. The numbers seemed to show the impact of economic class. There was much here that Moynihan would have agreed with, including the link between low incomes and "broken" families, but Rainwater's conception made the poverty issue partly a class issue. Race factors channeled more blacks into the low-income group, but once there, blacks and whites felt similar pressures against traditional families. A better book than Moynihan's would have been *Low-Income Families in America*.[27]

In *The Negro Family* race operated at times as an independent cause not only because class was missing but because Moynihan omitted his recommendations. A reader might have inferred that the sick black family required a combination of psychiatric treatment and punitive measures like welfare cuts to

Table 4.1. Percentage of Female-Headed Families in Selected Urban Racial/
Income Groups, 1960

Annual Income	Percentage Female-Headed
Blacks under $3,000	47
Blacks $3,000 and over	8
Whites under $3,000	38
Whites $3,000 and over	4

Source: Data from Lee Rainwater, "Crucible of Identity: The Negro Lower-Class Family," in Talcott Parsons and Kenneth B. Clark, eds., *The Negro American* (Boston: Beacon Press, 1966), 169, table 1.

Note: Even Rainwater's table may exaggerate racial differences; within each paired income group, average incomes were probably lower for blacks than for whites.

force black fathers to stay with their families. But that was not Moynihan's position. In planning the administration's direct attack on poverty, Moynihan had lined up with the losing side, which wanted job creation rather than training or community action. Around this time he told a colleague that the U.S. Post Office should reinstitute two mail deliveries a day, leading to 50,000 good jobs. Later, Moynihan was an enthusiastic supporter of Richard Nixon's guaranteed income plan for poor families.[28] Job and income programs appealed to liberals, civil rights leaders, and unionists, and they would have helped Moynihan avoid accusations that he was a conservative urging blacks to solve their own problems. Moynihan claimed that he left out his solutions in order to focus on the central goal of committing the government to fixing the black family, but perhaps another reason that he did not urge wider income programs and direct job creation was that his boss, Lyndon Johnson, had ruled out both options in planning the War on Poverty.

As to the personal and political impact of the squabble over *The Negro Family*, Moynihan never forgot the attacks from the Left, and he became more comfortable around conservatives and Republicans in the late 60s and 70s. His report inflamed civil rights leaders and liberals. Tensions were rising among black and white radicals anyway, but Moynihan missed a chance to direct social thought toward a new liberalism of programs that assisted the poor more effectively than the War on Poverty and that, putting class alongside race and gender, made for a more inclusive politics.[29] Of course, other, larger maladies caused the miscarriage of a new liberalism, but *The Negro Family* was one cause, and a symptom of the larger failure of American social thought.

Scholars later claimed that the harsh reaction to Moynihan's work pushed "the black family off the agenda of policy research," especially for liberals. But there were studies of black social and cultural patterns in the late 60s and the 70s.[30] Perhaps there should have been more, but some of the critics of Moynihan's critics required not open-ended research but a focus on black crime, illegitimacy, and welfare dependence. What was largely missing in the 70s was not more studies of how disorganized poor black families were but popular stories of poor and working-class blacks and whites tossed about by harsh labor markets and stingy social welfare programs.

In the 60s and 70s there would not be many liberal or socialist blockbusters on how economic forces victimized not just the poor but the whole working class.[31] There were a few, as we shall see, but there should have been books with titles like these: *Too Much Work, Too Little Reward: Why White and Black Americans Are Insecure about Health Care and Unemployment.* Or: *Work Hard and Worry: The Near Poverty of Fifty Million Whites and Blacks with Jobs.* Big books came in the early 80s, but they were conservative assaults on the poor and the welfare state. They carried titles like *The Underclass* and *Losing Ground*.

One positive result of the flap around Moynihan's book was to impel social scientists to reexamine cultural and moral explanations of poverty. It had not been unusual for liberals to use the model of a disabled lower-class culture to argue for economic aid. That was exactly what Harrington did in *The Other America*. But the backlash to *The Negro Family* inspired some researchers to question the culture-of-poverty theory. Sociologist Herbert Gans urged scholars to study "the economy that relegates many people to underemployment and unemployment and . . . leaves teenagers and old people without viable economic and social functions."[32] A small group of social scientists, mainly economists, began to do that in the later 60s and early 70s.

Labor Markets or People's Attitudes?: The Dissenters' New Model

One mainstream explanation of why able-bodied people were poor in the 1960s was that they lacked skills and will. The skills argument reflected human capital economics, which emphasized people's skill set as a form of intellectual wealth that could generate income. The willpower idea was as old as the Puritans and as new as the culture-of-poverty theory that found something wrong with the attitudes or family structures of poor people. The two models were welded together to form the main intellectual foundation of the War on Poverty.

Human capital and culture-of-poverty assumptions meshed with popular attitudes. When the culture of poverty had a racial twist, as in Moynihan's *The Negro Family*, it seemed to confirm whites in the belief that poverty was a result of bad black behavior. The human capital argument meshed with the faith that public education was a road to success. Both theories put much of the responsibility for poverty on the poor, although government would supply education and training. Both approaches emphasized fixing the poor rather than fixing economic structures.

Soon after the War on Poverty began, observers began to question human capital and culture-of-poverty assumptions. The discovery of massive unemployment in urban centers suggested that poverty was rooted not in weak skills or poor motivation but in lack of jobs.[33] One network of scholars and government policy makers whom I call the Dissenters worried that neither economic growth nor Johnson's poverty war would wipe out poverty. They understood that the lines between the poor and the nonpoor were fluid. And they suspected that unemployment, low-wage jobs, and even the culture of poverty were rooted in deep economic structures, not in people's attitudes. William Spring, staff director of the Senate Subcommittee on Employment, Manpower, and Poverty, summed up the emerging view. If you have one hundred applicants for ninety jobs, "ten people are going to be unemployed. They will probably be the ten with the poorest ratings on whatever scale is being used, education, skill, age, work experience . . . or race. But the basic problem would not be lack of training, but the lack of jobs." Therefore, the War on Poverty "was bound to fail."[34]

Thinking this way, Washington staffers like Spring and economists, anthropologists, and sociologists like Bennett Harrison, Elliot Liebow, Barry Bluestone, Michael Piore, and Ivar Berg began to develop a new model of deprivation rooted in labor markets but linked to racial discrimination. They challenged the idea that lack of skills caused poverty, and they found that there was not one labor market but two: a primary market where pay was good and jobs stable and a secondary market where pay was meager and jobs were unstable.[35]

The Dissenters' challenge to the skills argument was crucial. While it seemed self-evident that more skills and more schooling brought financial rewards—doctors earned more than janitors—human capital economists used circular argumentation to make their case. If people got higher pay, they assumed that those people had higher skills and that higher skills caused them to receive higher pay. Human capital scholars often ignored nonskill, nonmerit elements such as race, gender, class, luck, professional monopolies, and family wealth that gave some an advantage over others, regardless of skill or effort.[36] They ignored stories of low-skilled workers who did well and skilled workers who did badly. The white worker who moved from a southern textile factory to a unionized auto assembly plant in the North received a big pay increase without any increase in skills. The black southern sharecropper who went into the auto plant got an even bigger pay increase although his work as a farmer had probably demanded more skill.[37]

There was no evidence of a general skill shortage in the United States. Columbia University sociologist Ivar Berg, author of *Education and Jobs: The Great Training Robbery* (1971), found that sometime between 1956 and 1967 "the educational achievements of the workforce surpass[ed] the economy's requirements." He found also that corporate managers had no evidence that higher education led to higher productivity. They simply assumed it. In fact, while people with higher education got higher pay, they were not necessarily performing better than those with less schooling. Indeed, some overeducated workers became frustrated and inefficient workers.[38]

Perhaps lousy labor markets were more important than people's skill level. Dissenter research had begun with an effort to understand why urban blacks had been left behind in the 60s. As the urban ghettos exploded in riots, the question grew more urgent. Piore and Peter Doeringer decided that there was not one labor market in which everyone found the perfect job for his or her skills but two. In the primary labor market workers were generally well paid, often belonged to unions, and had stable jobs; in the secondary, or inferior, market, people often worked in nonunionized manufacturing, stores and fast-food joints, nursing homes, and a hundred other occupations that offered low pay, low status, frequent layoffs, and no career ladders. For a variety of reasons having little to do with people's abilities, millions were stuck in the secondary market. Racism, sexism, credentialism, and much else kept many of the poor locked in the low-wage sector, even though their skills were adequate for better jobs.[39]

In the late 60s and early 70s, Dissenters' ideas were in flux. Some Dissenters still believed that the poor were infected with the culture of poverty and that their lack of discipline helped to consign them to the low-wage sector. This view supported the War on Poverty strategy. Other Dissenters were beginning to locate the source of low-wage workers' attitudes in low-wage labor markets. It was not that workers with lousy habits and low skills caused lousy labor markets but that social conditions and institutions, including bad schools, poverty, and unstable, low-skill labor markets, generated and encouraged poor work habits. If some workers had little commitment to menial jobs, they were only treating the job "with the same contempt held for it by the employer and society at large." They had no compunction about quitting their job, but employers had none about laying them off. For each side, there was always more where that came from: more lousy jobs and more people needing work. Economic structures generated complementary cultures.[40]

Dissenters also deconstructed the idea that the poor were a different kind of human being by erasing the line between "workers" and "the poor" and between the very poor and the nearly poor. They argued that poverty lines were too low to include all who were poor; the lines artificially divided groups with common interests. Economist Bluestone noted that it was ridiculous to think that once a family's income had risen a few dollars over the poverty line "the family was economically secure."[41] William Spring warned that the poverty line was a purely arbitrary figure that artificially divided "those labeled poor—and thus eligible for a vast array of meager programs—from their neighbors who are also quite poor, but slightly above the arbitrary line."[42] Other critics noted that a third of poor family heads worked full-time year-round. This did not square with assumptions that people were poor because they did not work. On the whole, policy innovations neglected the working poor because their situation contradicted the "belief that work is the panacea for all societal ills."[43]

The Dissenters were slow to develop a view that linked poverty and inequality to class structures and in particular business's use of unemployment to discipline workers, but they were on the right track.[44] Both they and Moynihan began with the link between black poverty and unemployment, but Moynihan racialized poverty images. That was bad for black Americans because it undermined reforms that helped all working Americans. The Dissenters' analysis of the racial impact of labor markets promised to move the focus from bad black behavior to harmful economic structures; that led to a focus on the impact of labor markets on all employees. Nevertheless, since the impetus for Dissenter investigations was the puzzle of why urban blacks stayed poor despite government programs and economic growth, Dissenters were not yet paying much attention to whites.

It was a handful of writers outside Dissenter circles who punctured the 1950s–60s myth that white workers were affluent. Journalist Pete Hamill argued that white workers were not affluent and were not well served by government. Ignored by liberals and intellectuals, they turned their resentments against African Americans. In *The Myth of the Middle Class*, social scientist Richard Parker showed that in 1970 half of all American families lived below the Bureau of Labor Statistics intermediate standard of $10,700. That standard afforded a used car, a family movie every two or three weeks, but no savings for education or times of unemployment. Labor writers Patricia Cayo Sexton and Brendan Sexton pointed out that most white families (60%) needed two earners just to get past $5,000, not a very high standard. It seemed to the Sextons that not much was being done for white workers; meanwhile, Republicans had begun to appeal to their conservative racial views.[45] Could liberals focus more on the economic roots of poverty *and* the class exploitation of all workers? Could old organizations be remade and new ones created to advertise a new economics?

Race *and* Class

In the late 60s, it was apparent that Johnsonian liberalism, embodied in the War on Poverty, was not enough. But it was not clear that skeptics like the Dissenters could fashion a story about poverty and economic insecurity that was not only more radical in getting to the roots of the problem but also widely appealing. It was not clear as the 60s turned to the 70s that Dissent would become a Reformation capable of transforming institutions.

As journalist Thomas Edsall and others have argued, the identification of liberal Democrats with civil rights split liberalism and sent millions of white workers to vote for racist Democrats like George Wallace or for conservative Republicans. The Dissenters took the first steps toward a new model of poverty, but their emphasis on the way racism was rooted in a dual labor market was not enough to address these political problems. Dissenters focused on race and racism and said little about class and about whites who got bad jobs and low incomes year after year.[46] As long as they could not come up with something like a class view of things that showed that while blacks got the worst of it, they were part of a larger group of poor and insecure members of many ethnic backgrounds, the Left would not have a comprehensive theory or a political strategy to unite black and white, poor and not so poor. A new unifying liberalism had to pay more attention not only to racism and sexism but also to class exploitation. Fixing liberalism meant giving prominence to racism, sexism, *and* classism. For each of these and especially the last, the work of economists would be vital, and economists could find big-picture ideas about class in the Marxist tradition.[47]

Part of a new economics would be ideas, and part would be organization. Building an intellectual infrastructure for a radical but popular economics was under way. For example, in 1974, the Union for Radical Political Economics decided that its journal, the *Review of Radical Political Economics*, would develop Marxism. About the same time, radical economists founded *Dollars & Sense*; they hoped it could become the *Business Week* of the Left. In 1973, Congress created a program to give public service jobs to the unemployed (under the Comprehensive Employment and Training Act [CETA]), and that was a victory for the Dissenters.[48] Soon the United States was in the midst of its worst economic slump since the 1930s, an event that, in the words of a *Business Week* author, "breathed new vigor into radical economics." As the economy worsened and as business leaders turned boldly class-conscious in defense of their interests against workers, the Left's opportunity to lead the economic majority against big capitalists became clear. One could have predicted a bright future for radical economics.[49]

Some of the Dissenting scholarship that followed was impressive; Sam Bowles and Herb Gintis's *Schooling in Capitalist America* (1976), a roundhouse challenge to the national faith in schooling and merit, was widely discussed. But in general radical models of poverty and inequality were slow to develop. Dissenters had shown that low-wage markets encouraged bad behavior, bad pay, and poverty, but few of them wrote about general unemployment as a major cause of poverty. Useful models for this departure were available in the socialist tradition. Marxist Harry Braverman, in *Labor and Monopoly Capital* (1974), substituted a class explanation for the skills argument about why people succeeded or failed. Against those who raved about the value of education and the coming knowledge society, he maintained that low-wage sectors were growing faster than high-wage sectors. Above all he drew on two Marxist ideas: that unemployment helped capitalists dominate workers and that, by causing joblessness and low wages, the business system caused poverty. In the normal run of things, capitalism continually revolutionized production to dis-employ people; more workers than jobs kept wages down and poverty up. Unemployment and poverty were intrinsic to capitalism.[50]

Many younger radical economists did not put the problem of general unemployment in the foreground. Perhaps they were still basking in the sunshine of the 60s when it appeared that general unemployment had been cured and only special problems like automation and minority joblessness remained. If so, they were making these points even as maturing baby boomers and tougher global competition were enlarging the labor force and the ranks of the unemployed.[51]

As it turned out, Marxism never became important in public debates. *Washington Post* reporter Nicholas von Hoffman remarked that American capitalism was not well understood because "no Marxist regularly appears before Congressional committees."[52] In the 50s and 60s, mainstream scholars believed that class ideas and Marxism were irrelevant to a prosperous America. Today's readers may believe that Marxism was irreparably damaged by its association with Stalin and other communist dictators. But there is another way to look at these things.

Realism from Marxist Economics?

Marxist theory was not identical to Stalinism. Marxism was (and is) an exceedingly realistic way to understand power and economics, to understand in a general way who gets what and why. Other social theories knew about class, but none was so hard-nosed in its understanding of the long-term interests of classes. Marxism taught truths that conservatives and mainstream liberals didn't want to hear. The first was that the United States had classes, that is, socioeconomic groups with mostly persisting membership and each with its own broadly similar interests. Upward social mobility, especially from rags to riches, was more myth than fact. The country had a fairly stable group of big business leaders who ran much of the economy and whose goal was, as a General Motors vice president put it, "to get the most production for the least amount of compensation," while workers and their representatives tried "to get the most compensation for the least labor."[53] As the 70s moved on and business interests lobbied more openly for policies that undermined employee incomes and job security, the United States seemed a more openly class-dominated society.

A popular class analysis would have stressed that a handful of wealthy individuals had a prominent influence on the economy and made self-interested decisions about expansion and contraction, investment and disinvestment. A larger group of managers, intellectuals, lawyers, and politicians helped them run things. The largest class, a majority that consisted mostly of employees but also included many low- and middle-income self-employed people and many unpaid workers, generally received modest to low incomes. Their resources were limited in part because of the large sums that the ruling few and their assistants extracted from everyone's labor and in part because the tax system did little to equalize after-tax incomes.[54]

A Marxist approach would have emphasized that most people in the economic majority were subject to economic insecurities, of which unemployment was the worst. Those at the very top made decisions that meant more unemployment for those at the bottom. Those at the very bottom of the employee class generally experienced the most job and income insecurity; as a result, they were poor. In the media and popular culture the poor were often degraded and often racialized—which made it easier for people just above them to shift blame from rich economic decision makers to victims. Thinking the poor were a different kind of human being with different values encouraged better-off members of the working class to resent the family on welfare more than the CEO taking a million-dollar bonus for closing a factory.

One did not have to be a Marxist to understand all these things, but it helped. Conservatives assumed that most poverty would be solved if government just stepped aside, but that wasn't happening in the late 50s, and it had not happened in the Great Depression, which began in the late 20s. Some left-wing liberals had an understanding that was, in practical terms, not so different from that of Marxists, but many mainstream liberals were closet conservatives, convinced that capitalism could solve poverty with the aid of a modest level of government income support and training programs.

The fate of the War on Poverty and the spotty record of economic growth in reaching some of the poor suggested in the late 60s and early 70s that something more than liberalism was needed to understand and erase poverty. It did not have to be called socialism or Marxism, but it needed the idea that big business leaders and their government allies were acting in ways that benefited their common interests and that included the persistence of unemployment and poverty. The class that was running the economy, no matter how much its members gave to charity, thrived on a labor surplus at home and abroad. That created lower wages for many employees and no jobs for others. Such an understanding in the 70s and 80s might have kept citizens from allowing policies that attacked welfare, gave more income to the rich, and created more unemployment.

Many people understood bits and pieces of the class view, but the big picture that ties it all together and orients people on major public issues has never won over more than a minority of Americans. The United States never had a large socialist, communist, or social democratic movement to make class and class rule a central issue in public discourse. The void in American culture about class was both cause and result of socialist weakness. Also, Red scares in 1919–20 and in the post–World War II era as well as a murderous Stalinism damaged American socialism.[55]

But in the late 60s and early 70s things began to change. In the years before their assassinations in 1968, Martin Luther King and Robert Kennedy had been edging toward a new understanding of class and race. King talked more about class and economics and initiated the interracial poor people's movement. Kennedy was able, at times, to pull together an electoral coalition of black and white workers. These were just seedlings, and we cannot know what might have grown from them, but they might have blossomed into something new if they had been allowed to develop.[56]

Meanwhile, there was movement among radicalized youths. Most young radicals in the early and mid-60s had not been sympathetic to socialism; they claimed to be a *new* Left, an advance on the communist movement that had uncritically supported dictatorship in the Soviet Union. But as the war raged on, and as it appeared that success against poverty and racism was limited, many activists moved farther to the left. A handful of young radicals became revolutionary fanatics, but many searched patiently for ways to adapt class ideas to American contexts. Some activists moved from campuses to factories. But there was no big socialist movement linked to unions, civil rights organizations, and maturing new leftists—and there was insufficient infrastructure—to nourish and publicize the view that capitalism thrived on unemployment and could not wipe out poverty.

Of course, one did not need a radical model to support specific reforms. During the urban riots of the 60s, Sam Yorty, the conservative mayor of Los Angeles, testified that "facts are going to force us to provide employment for every person who is willing to work, and if they can't be provided with employment in the private sector, I think they ought to be employed in the public sector."[57] Others pushed guaranteed incomes, an idea that would become policy in the Nixon White House for a while. But while radical programs won an audience in odd places from time to time, what was not happening was the spread of a new story of unemployment, inequality, and class privilege.

Both a new politics and a new story were required. The new politics had to have multiracial appeal, and it had to reach out to the very poor, the broad working class, and liberals of all classes, especially with programs that served a majority, such as health insurance for all, progressive taxation, affordable child care, a labor market program that included high-level training and decent jobs, and, finally, replacing the welfare system with a guaranteed income floor. Why a new political movement for more economic security and less poverty never came together cannot fully be told here, but race, anticommunism, and Vietnam divided Democratic constituencies and retarded the education of liberals. Observers like Edsall have noted the potency of race, war, and taxes, but they may have underestimated the force of the liberal commitment to capitalism, the inertia of the union movement, and the political and intellectual underdevelopment of U.S. radicalism. American unions had 20 million members, but they were not doing much to broadcast a new vision or even, under labor leaders like George Meany, to unionize workers. On their side, many young radicals of the 60s had begun their careers thinking that the working class was part of a comfortable and oppressive establishment. That was changing as the 60s turned to the 70s and radicals discovered Marx, but a new movement uniting worker and student, black and white, was not coalescing as a political force.[58]

As the economy worsened in the 70s, it would become clear that liberals could not offer humane alternatives to rising imports, faster deindustrialization, and high levels of poverty. Meanwhile, radical views that emphasized economic structures spread only slowly. Could radicals conquer the airwaves with the view that poor people were mainly that fraction of the working class that bore the worst of the business system's low-wage, high-unemployment effects? Or would conservatives and liberals win with the opposite view: the poor were those who lacked modern skills and proper morals?

Two factors shaped the outcome. First, the history of the 60s and the longer history of American traditions and structures tilted things away from class models and toward the racialization of poverty. The energy with which blacks seized a place in War on Poverty programs publicized the link between poverty and blackness. Soon the call for Black Power and fiery urban riots scared many whites away from liberalism. The media played an important role, too, in racializing poverty. They gave the black urban poor more publicity than black numbers in poverty and welfare populations justified.[59] This found a ready audience, for there is no doubt that white racism remained strong, especially with regard to residential segregation. The white backlash of the 60s and 70s was not new, but working-class white racism in the North became more visible and politically more salient.

Second, the intellectual thinness of ideas and politics warped the War on Poverty and limited the cultural resources needed to advance to a broader understanding of class exploitation. The War on Poverty assumed that poor people were those left behind not because of a bad economy but because of racism or weak skills and values. Antipoverty planners focused on fixing the poor rather than economic structures; they marginalized the poor, and that was just a step away from racializing images of the poor.[60]

Racism was not an immovable barrier to the creation of an advanced left-wing politics. Racial integration had popular support in some areas, and a majority of whites in 1968 favored federal programs to tear down the ghetto and provide jobs for the jobless.[61] But the weakness of thinking about class and social welfare made it harder for people to move from focusing on the Lacking Black Worker to focusing on the Lacking Economy.

A class perspective would not have ended racism. But it would have given the Left a fighting chance to repel models that emphasized the blackness of poverty and the links between blackness, crime, and social disorganization. It would have helped demarginalize poverty and made the problem of low incomes an aspect of the larger issue of class inequality. The Dissenters were on the right track, but they had a long way to go, intellectually and politically. Moynihan's *The Negro Family* was a perfect example of how, without a firm class perspective, race overwhelmed everything. His view of the female-headed black family hooked on welfare would, over time, capture more media attention than the Dissenters' complex view of unfriendly labor markets.[62]

chapter five

STATISTICS AND THEORY OF UNEMPLOYMENT AND POVERTY
Lessons from the 60s and the Postwar Era

We cannot, finally, judge the War on Poverty or any anti-poverty effort unless we understand the problem we are up against. Unless we understand the unemployment problem, we will be doomed to talk about poverty without eliminating it. This brief chapter steps outside the historical narrative to elaborate on the underlying theory of the book: that unemployment is much higher than we are usually led to believe, that unemployment is a major cause of poverty, and that capitalism cannot by itself cure poverty because it cannot for long do without a significant amount of unemployment. While most social scientists and many politicians know that there is a link between unemployment and poverty, not many would agree with the Marxist idea that a small class of rich capitalists prosper from a system with a fair amount of unemployment—and thus poverty. Few would agree that substantial unemployment is the norm for capitalism and that truly low unemployment is rare in peacetime.

Unemployment is, of course, not the only cause of poverty. There are a variety of poverties. For example, there are people who do not work because they are too young, too old, too ill, or seriously disabled and who are poor because government income supports are skimpy. There are those whose work caring for children and relatives is not rewarded with money.

And low incomes have other causes besides unemployment. Political and economic forces affect how much national income goes to the top and how much goes to the rest of the people. For example, when wealthy households, big corporations, and economic conservatives wield extreme influence in politics, society, and the media, an extra large amount of income flows upward through tax breaks, feeble minimum wage laws, and weak unions. Such an extreme imbalance of class power is part of the explanation for the persistence of poverty and the acceleration of inequality since the early 70s.[1]

The other main determinant of income shares and of the bargaining power of employees is the subject of this chapter, the state of labor markets. Not everyone who wants work can find a job, or a full-time job, or a job that pays decent wages. Institutional and political factors, such as the strength of unions, play an important role here, as does the control of government economic policy by people who favor the rich over the poor and thus will cause high unemployment to bring lower inflation. The array of specific causes varies, but unemployment persists in periods of prosperity, and that maintains poverty. Full employment is the oddity, and many periods of strong demand for labor occurred during wartime, when authorities had no choice but to spend: World War II, the early 50s (Korea), and the mid- to late 1960s (Vietnam).

In this chapter we use information from the 60s and early 70s as the raw material for a general theory of unemployment and poverty. I argue that even in the boom times of the 1960s, significant unemployment persisted. Because official rates did not fully measure unemployment, because areas of high unemployment could be marginalized as the special problem of troubled locales (inner cities, Appalachia) and social groups (minorities, the unskilled), and because liberal leaders had faith that tax cuts were bringing full employment, few policy makers or scholars understood the dimensions of the unemployment factor or why neither economic growth nor training programs could eliminate poverty.

Unemployment and Poverty

Poverty and unemployment are linked, but they are not the same thing. Not all the poor are unemployed; half the poor work all or part of the year. However, while only a fifth of people who experience unemployment over the year are poor, half of all poor families have had some unemployment over the year.[2]

Unemployment factors hurt the poor directly in two ways and indirectly in a third way. First, unemployment leaves some people who want a job without work or steady work, and that means no or low earnings. Second, unemployment suppresses wages for employed low-skilled workers because there are plenty of jobless people available to the employer who does not want to raise pay to retain employees. Excess supply keeps the price of labor down. Third, the denial that there is much unemployment is the core argument of people who oppose government assistance to the poor. If there is little unemployment, at most the poor need the kind of help offered by the War on Poverty and the public schools. If people won't work, they should blame themselves. This antiunemployment story disorients the poor and short-circuits political support for programs to create jobs and raise low incomes.

For much of the fifty years covered in this book, especially since the early 70s, the United States has had a labor glut. More workers than jobs kept some people out of work and kept others from demanding higher wages for fear of losing their jobs to the unemployed. It is true that there is a counteracting force, and historically it has been one of the main remedies for poverty. That force is economic growth. As the economy grew strongly in the 1960s, more jobs and more income were created. Real hourly wages for the average worker rose 9% (1964–69).[3] As a result poverty rates fell. If the economy had expanded forever, economic growth could have cured what remained of job-related poverty in the late 60s. But growth does not last forever. Sooner or later, because, for example, government makes it hard to borrow or because consumers reach their limits and new business investment slows, booms turn into recessions or depressions. As unemployment rises, so does poverty. The boom ends before the last chunk of poverty is wiped out. That is one reason why the growth recipe, which helped to cut poverty from 30% to 11% in the 50s and 60s, could not cut it from 11% to 2% thereafter. The forces of recession have always intervened before growth reached the bottom.

Also, beginning in the 70s, new factors in the global economy and harsh business practices limited the antipoverty effects of growth. But regardless of specific changes, growth has not been long or deep enough to wipe out poverty. Indeed, the moment it starts to lift wages substantially is often taken as a sign of inflation, and the Federal Reserve raises interest rates to slow economic growth and raise unemployment and poverty rates.[4] That is, political and institutional forces cause and maintain poverty.

Did Social Handicaps Cause Poverty, Reflect It, or Merely Excuse It?

In the 60s and 70s the aged, female-headed families, nonwhite families, families headed by low-wage workers (domestics, laborers, farmworkers, service workers), people in the South, rural Americans, large families, and individuals on their own were more likely to be poor than others. A white family headed by a male professional had a one in fifty chance of being poor, while a black family headed by a woman had a one in two chance of being poor.[5]

Yet many poor families did not fit the handicapping stereotype. Of poor families in 1963, three out of four had a male head, and seven out of ten had a white head. The poor did have higher unemployment rates than the nonpoor, but half of the heads of poor families held a job. That suggested a desire to work, even at low wages.[6] Racial and ethnic minorities and women had higher than average rates of poverty, and that was for a variety of reasons including outright discrimination and the fact that child-care responsibilities rested on mothers rather than fathers. These things had to be fixed, but so did the economy that supplied too few good jobs.

It was difficult to distinguish causes and effects, and many scholars and policy makers never made the effort. Did the poor have less schooling because they did not value education or because the class system offered them inferior education and discouraged their aspirations? Did poor people's social characteristics (such as inferior education) explain "why too many are unemployed," or were they only an excuse for "why particular people are selected for unemployment when there are not enough jobs to go around"? I argue throughout this book that it is the latter, that the ultimate causes of poverty for many able-bodied adults are rooted in a persistent labor glut, not in people's shortcomings, most of which can be remedied over time.[7]

In the 60s, the War on Poverty often focused on the defects in people rather than defects in the economy or the welfare state. But if job shortages were the problem, training programs were misdirected. For much of the decade the economy grew, and millions rose above poverty lines, but the growth remedy was reaching its limits.[8]

Can Economic Growth Eliminate Unemployment and Poverty?

In the 60s the economy grew at 4.4% per year, the best record of any decade between 1950 and 2000. National unemployment rates dipped below 4% (1966–69); even most liberal economists thought that was about as low as unemployment could go without sparking inflation. It was assumed that the 4% was largely a matter of "frictional unemployment," that is, the normal process of people moving from job to job. And so it appeared that full employment had arrived, and if the jobs were there, it seemed reasonable to conclude that the unemployed poor were jobless because of employer discrimination or because of people's own defects. The War on Poverty was, at least initially, a tool to fix the skill and motivational defects of poor people. Economic growth would do the rest, by creating more good jobs.

When the economy is really booming and unemployment is extremely low, inflation may rise, but with labor in short supply, wages can advance more

PHILLIPS AND NAIRU: ECONOMISTS SAY
A LITTLE UNEMPLOYMENT IS A GOOD THING

The negative relationship between inflation and job growth has been plotted in the Phillips curve and similar theories. Higher unemployment is correlated with less inflation and higher inflation with lower unemployment. As a further development, economists created the non-accelerating inflation rate of unemployment (NAIRU), or the lowest rate of unemployment that can be attained without igniting general inflation. In the 1980s and 1990s some economists maintained that unemployment could not fall below 6% or even 7% without causing a pattern of accelerating inflation.

The Phillips curve and NAIRU did not always fit the historical record (the late 90s), but there is little doubt that huge unemployment rates in the early 80s were a major factor in restraining wages and prices. And there is no question that most Federal Reserve Board members believed in NAIRU and the Phillips curve. Several times in the 90s, in order to cut inflation off at the pass, the Federal Reserve raised interest rates. The effect was to slow economic growth and job creation. Above all, we should remember that there are other ways to handle inflation; the recession method is a political choice that hurts lower incomes more than upper incomes.

Sources: Bradley R. Schiller, *The Economics of Poverty and Discrimination*, 8th ed. (Upper Saddle River, N.J.: Prentice-Hall, 2001), 73–75; Jared Bernstein and Dean Baker, *The Benefits of Full Employment: When Markets Work for People* (Washington: Economic Policy Institute, 2003), 13–40; Robert Kuttner, *Everything For Sale: The Virtues and Limits of Markets* (New York: Alfred A. Knopf, 1998), 92–95.

rapidly than prices, as they did in the late 60s.[9] But there are limits to growth. Every economic boom ends in recession. That happens for many reasons, but two patterns are common. First, with high demand for people and products, price and wage inflation looms, and eventually business and government leaders see that as a problem. The Federal Reserve raises interest rates in order to cool the economy; that creates more unemployment and more poverty. That happened in the 1969–70 recession and in the 1981–82 depression. Second, in a pattern that reaches back to the nineteenth century, economic booms turn into recessions because of overinvestment and underconsumption. Investors awake to the fact that no one needs another railroad or another dot.com. As the bubble of optimism bursts, companies collapse, employees are laid off, and new investment shrinks. As incomes fall, people reduce buying, and recession spreads. Unemployment rises further, and poverty rates climb. Job and wage growth stops before it has wiped out poverty.[10]

For much of the 60s, economic growth, extended by war budgets, cured a lot of poverty, but that antipoverty cure was reaching its long-term limits. The experience of succeeding decades, in which poverty fell during periods of growth but never below 11%, suggests that growth will never last long enough to eliminate job-related poverty. (In part, growth cannot finish the job because, admittedly, some poverty is not linked to the failure of job markets but to other factors including drug addiction and bad attitudes. We lack reliable estimates of the fraction of the poor who were so addicted to crime or drugs or welfare—so damaged by bad values—that they could not seize real opportunities; but it is unlikely that they numbered more than 2 million adults, a small fraction of the poor.)[11]

In the 60s many observers had faith in growth because growth was cutting poverty, because publicized unemployment rates were low, and because poverty was seen as a marginal problem of ghetto minorities, female-headed families, and economically backward regions—not as a function of normal economic operations. In that celebratory atmosphere, poverty caused by joblessness seemed a special problem of the hard-to-hire poor.[12]

Real Unemployment Was Higher Than They Thought

But how high and how general was unemployment? Defining unemployment requires value judgments as well as scientific methods. Which people should we count as unemployed? Only those who file for unemployment compensation? All who are not working and are willing to state that they would like paid work? Should we include those who claim they would work if pay and conditions were better? Or if subsidized child care was available? Should we count only those who answered ten want ads? On the other hand, shouldn't we count as employed those who work without pay? And should we add a guess for those working in the underground economy?[13]

The methods chosen by the U.S. Department of Labor for the "official unemployment rate" tend to understate unemployment. That shows up in the department's definition of unemployment. The unemployed are those people who tell Census Bureau workers in a monthly household survey that they do not have a job but have searched for one in the past four weeks. Discouraged

TEENS FLOOD THE LABOR MARKET!

In the boom of the 1960s official unemployment rates fell for almost every group. One exception was black teens (16–17 years old). Boys' unemployment rates rose from 23% to 28% and girls' rates from 25% to 31% (white rates fell a little.) Teen unemployment rates are always high as youngsters move in and out of the labor force, but black teen rates were exceptionally high and rising. Along with discrimination, one of the problems was that these baby boomers were flooding a labor market that, even in prosperous times, could not absorb them. The population of white teens (15 to 19) was 40% larger in 1970 than in 1960; that of black teens, a whopping 62% larger. So many more teens were looking for work, and more of them could not find it.

Sources: U.S. Department of Labor, Bureau of Labor Statistics, *Handbook of Labor Statistics, 1972* (Washington: Government Printing Office, 1972), table 64, 136–38; teen population calculated from U.S. Department of Commerce, Bureau of the Census, *Historical Statistics of the United States: Colonial Times to 1970*, pt. 1 (Washington: Government Printing Office, 1975), series A123, 15–18.

workers who give up searching, perhaps because jobs are scarce, are not usually included in the monthly unemployment rates featured in government press releases. Part-time workers are counted as fully employed even if they work only one hour a week. These counting methods mean that unemployment appears lower than it is.[14]

It is true that federal agencies collected other unemployment data. When national unemployment rates averaged 3.8% in 1966, they were 6.3% for black men and 8.6% for black women. That was well known, but it did not cause social scientists to revise their opinions about the fundamental soundness of the job machine. Other danger signals received little attention. Something not much talked about was that the labor force of young people was exploding. The total population of young women, ages 20–24, grew by 50% in the 1960s. (In the 50s, the size of this age group actually shrank.) Not only did the number of young adults shoot up, but women increased their labor force participation rate, that is, the proportion of their age group with jobs or looking for jobs. Black and white young women raised their labor force participation rates to 57% (from 55% and 46%, respectively). Because of a larger population and

Table 5.1. Ghetto Subemployment in 1966

Ghetto	Subemployment Rate (%)
Roxbury (Boston)	24.2
Central Harlem (NYC)	28.6
East Harlem (NYC)	33.1
Bedford-Stuyvesant (NYC)	27.6
North Philadelphia	34.2
North Side, St. Louis	38.9
San Antonio	47.4
Mission-Fillmore (San Francisco)	24.6
Salt River Bed (Phoenix)	41.7
New Orleans	45.3

Source: William J. Spring, "Underemployment: The Measure We Refuse to Take," in Harold L. Sheppard, Bennett Harrison, and William J. Spring, eds., *The Political Economy of Public Service Employment* (Lexington, Mass.: D. C. Heath and Co., 1972), 189.

higher rates of participation, by the end of the decade, the number of young white women in the labor force had jumped by 90% and the number of young black women by 78%. A labor glut of younger workers was building up even in the prosperous 1960s. The effects would become clear in the economically troubled 70s, but not much was said about it in the 60s.[15]

One striking exception to the federal government's general underestimation of joblessness was the effort to create subemployment rates for the inner cities. Secretary of Labor Willard Wirtz, aiming to improve training programs, organized a survey of labor markets in ten ethnic ghettos. He and his staff developed a subemployment index combining four categories: first, those normally counted as unemployed (the jobless who had searched for work); second, those working part-time who wanted full-time work; third, discouraged workers and other workers who had dropped out of the count; and fourth, those who worked full-time but earned poverty-level wages. At a time when the national unemployment rate was 3.8%, subemployment rates ranged from 24.2% in Roxbury to 47.4% in San Antonio (table 5.1).

Most of the people included in the subemployment rate were trying to help themselves: the unemployed claimed to be looking for work, the part-timers were employed and wanted more hours, and the working poor were striving but poorly paid. Perhaps discouraged workers could be tagged as quitters, but it must have been easy to get discouraged in a sea of poverty and joblessness. Even allowing for the fact that some people exaggerated the effort they put into job searches, these ten labor markets registered appalling levels of subemployment.

In terms of an aggregate national picture of unemployment, it was not clear what these subemployment rates meant. The official national unemployment rate for middle-age white males was below 2% in the late 60s, so subemployment rates could be isolated as the special problem of groups facing discrimination or lacking motivation rather than viewed as symptoms of an economy that never reached full employment. Much discussion of unemployment in the 60s linked it to people without skills, those facing displacement by automation, the young, and those facing discrimination, rather than to the fact that even in growth periods there was a plentiful supply of unemployed labor. One rarely found estimates of real unemployment for the whole of the labor force or historical pieces on real unemployment over time.[16] Keynesians in the White House were riding high, delighted that economic growth was up and unemployment down. President Johnson declared: "I do not believe that recessions are inevitable." In just two years (1964–66) official national unemployment rates fell from 5.2% to 3.8%.[17]

It is asking a lot that people should use history to step outside their own era to take the long view, but the raw material was there for scholars and radicals to make a deeper analysis of unemployment. There were isolated signs of another view in the 70s. Scholars Bertram Gross and Stanley Moss constructed new estimates for 1971. I have tried to be cautious, taking only about half of their suggestions, not including part-timers who wanted full-time work and other groups but adding discouraged workers; housewives who might work if suitable jobs and reliable child-care facilities were available; a fraction of people aged 55–64 not at work, on the assumption that they had been forced into early retirement by lack of jobs; and people in training programs who were currently being counted as employed (table 5.2).

This cautious view of the Gross and Moss estimates triples the unemployment rate to 15%. Were all the additional unemployed truly unemployed? It depends on what you mean. If we agree that they were ready to work, then they were unemployed.[18]

To comprehend the full dimensions of unemployment, one could also have selected occupational sectors. It was well known that blue-collar workers had more unemployment than government workers. Over 1950–70, even using official government data, annual unemployment fell below 4% for manufacturing employees only in 1951–53 and 1966–69, that is, in wartime. Construction workers had unemployment rates of 10% or more, except in the same two war periods. Even employees in wholesale and retail trade, a white-collar area, faced unemployment of more than 4% every year except in 1951–53. Real unemployment must have been even higher.[19]

One could also study the likelihood that someone would be unemployed at

Table 5.2. Real Unemployment, 1971: Some Who Should Have Been Added to Official Estimates of the Unemployed (in Millions)

0.8	Discouraged workers
5.0	Housewives who might work if suitable jobs and reliable child care were available (1/7 of all housewives without paid jobs)
4.0	Prematurely retired (1/5 of all nonworking Americans, ages 55–64)
0.3	Fraction of those in manpower programs who wanted real jobs but were counted as employed

= 10.1 Additional unemployed

10.1 + 85.8 (standard definition of labor force) = 95.9 (revised labor force)

4.7 Officially unemployed + 10.1 (restrained Gross-Moss additions to unemployed) = 14.8 actually unemployed

14.8 ÷ 95.9 = 15.0% real unemployment (official rate was 5.7%)

Source: Data from Bertram Gross and Stanley Moss, "Real Unemployment Is Much Higher Than They Say," in Alan Gartner et al., *Public Service Employment: An Analysis of Its History, Problems and Prospects* (1973), reprinted in David Mermelstein, ed., *The Economic Crisis Reader* (New York: Vintage Books, 1975), 32–37.
Note: Gross and Moss's unrestrained conclusion was an unemployment rate of 24.6%.

some time over the year. In 1966, 36% of construction workers had some unemployment, as did 17% of retail workers. Overall, 17%, more than three times the official unemployment rate of 5.2%, were unemployed over the year. For some it might have been many months, for others just a few. But it is clear that over the year, many more than 5% of the labor force lost a job.[20]

Finally, take a longer view of history to test whether the economy normally produces full employment. If full employment means that there are always more vacancies than unemployed and that the jobs are fairly paid and accessible to the unemployed, then, argued scholar Philip Harvey, only an official unemployment rate under 2% guaranteed full employment. By that criterion, the nation never had full employment in our period (1950–2005). Even if we bend the definition of full employment upward to mean anything below 4%, we would not have room for much optimism. In the period of fifty-five years covered by this book, official annual unemployment rates for all workers fell below 4% in only two periods (1951–53 and 1966–69). Both were periods of war.[21]

A handful of government officials and liberals and leftists outside government seemed to understand the need for government to directly create jobs. But the message was often muddled and did not lead to a thorough revision of assumptions about the limits of economic growth in ending unemployment

**"THEY'VE BEEN GOING TOGETHER
FOR QUITE A WHILE."**

"They've been going together for quite a while." (From *Straight
Herblock* [Simon and Schuster, 1964]; reproduced by permission of
Herb Block Foundation)

and curing poverty. Secretary Wirtz, who generally supported direct job creation, surprisingly concluded that the extreme subemployment rates in his
ghetto study proved not that government had to create good jobs but that the
poor needed more training and rehabilitation, in other words, more War on
Poverty. Meanwhile, some War on Poverty bureaucrats and a band of unionists
and civil rights and student leaders took a new view of the job situation. In
1966, dozens of labor leaders, radicals, and liberals ranging from I. W. Abel,
president of the United Steel Workers, and Martin Luther King Jr. to Black
Power advocates Stokely Carmichael and Floyd McKissick endorsed the Freedom Budget. Along with proposals for a higher minimum wage, a guaranteed

national income for people who could not work, and more progressive taxation, authors of the Freedom Budget emphasized the need to create more jobs. They argued that unemployment was higher by a percentage point or two than the official rate of 4%; they suggested a housing program not only to rebuild structures in the urban ghettos but also to generate millions of jobs.[22] Two years later the Kerner Commission on the ghetto riots proposed that government use tax credits, subsidies, and other methods to create a million public service jobs and a million private sector jobs in three years.[23]

Unfortunately, the liberal–labor–civil rights coalition that might have helped to realize an employment program was fracturing. White workers in the North were turning against black militants, and they had long opposed residential integration. Some unions continued to resist opening their ranks to minorities. Bayard Rustin hoped for a broad coalition of liberals, minorities, white workers and their unions, and young radicals. He urged radicals to join an electoral coalition that could complete the civil rights revolution, in part by creating jobs. But the African American leadership of the civil rights movement was splitting between the softs, who emphasized integration and black–white cooperation, and the hards, who lectured on Black Power and the sins of white people. In addition, white and black radicals were disillusioned with a liberal establishment that was not moving fast enough to cure poverty and racism. Finally, disagreements over Vietnam split the liberal-left alliance.[24]

Still, liberalism on economic issues was wounded, not dead. Wisconsin senator Gaylord Nelson and Dissenting economists like Bennett Harrison argued that the subemployment index showed a shortage of work, not of workers. They pushed for government jobs and helped to create temporary public service positions under the Comprehensive Employment and Training Act. However, Nelson and his supporters were less successful in getting the Department of Labor to create an ongoing subemployment index to accompany standard unemployment reports. Officials in President Nixon's Department of Labor claimed that there was no accepted definition of subemployment and that the whole effort would cost too much.[25]

Lessons from the 60s

Job factors do not explain all kinds of poverty—for example, why an affluent person allows drugs or alcohol to drag him or her into poverty. Job factors do not address the poverty of groups like the aged or those caring for family members such as single parents of young children for whom income rather than work is often the best solution. But unemployment explains much. It speaks to the conservative charge that the poor simply need to find a job. And it speaks to the liberal faith in training programs. Neither works well if there is a labor glut.

Persisting unemployment suggested that economic growth could not go deep enough. Washington University (St. Louis) economist Hyman Minsky argued in 1965 that "tight full employment" cures a lot of poverty.[26] But the history of the U.S. economy since World War II suggests that tight full employment does not last long enough. It is cut short because output of goods and services races ahead of consumer demand or because (as in 1957–58, 1969–70, 1979–82, 1989–90, and 1999–2001) government authorities restrain spending or raise interest rates, or both, in order to dampen inflation and to protect profit. Invariably unemployment rises, and when that happens, poverty stops falling. So growth might be an effective medicine, but there will never be enough of it to cut poverty rates to near zero. When 20% of the population was poor, as in the early 60s, it was still possible with normal growth rates to pull a lot of people over the poverty lines before recession kicked in, but it takes a long period of deep growth to reach into the bottom 10–15% of the households, and growth stops before much of that happens. That is why we have not pushed poverty rates below 11% in thirty years.

The character of government spending is important, too. Minsky understood as President Johnson and his economists may not have that if government stimulus to the economy creates more demand for specialists in research and development than in road building or office work, growth will have few anti-poverty effects. If politicians wanted to cure poverty in the 60s, they should have spent more on good jobs in poor communities, as opposed simply to low-pay, part-time positions in Head Start. What was needed was big money aimed, as economist Minsky put it, "at directly employing those in the labor market who are poor, and opening up job opportunities for second earners" in their families. Minsky wanted a big government job program like the Works Progress Administration of the 1930s. He reminded skeptical colleagues that subsidized employment for the poor was just as worthy as subsidized conferences for professors. "We are rich enough to afford boondoggles for the poor as well as the affluent."[27] But government antipoverty agencies rarely created solid jobs for poor people. Economic growth, it was assumed, created jobs. Direct job creation, Stage 2 of the War on Poverty, never happened.

Prejudice and Class

Racism, sexism, and other forms of prejudice made the bigoted feel good and brought white males immediate benefits by excluding job competitors. The "isms" helped to channel women and minorities into the secondary labor market of poor pay and higher than average unemployment. Low-wage employers took advantage of discrimination and the glut of workers in low-wage labor markets by paying women and minorities less. Government efforts against discrimination shrank the low-wage sector by opening up better jobs to the victims of discrimination, but they could not eliminate that sector. White males, including those in trade unions, resisted affirmative job policies. And in the 70s, job growth would lag behind labor force growth, and low-wage jobs would increase more rapidly than high-wage jobs.[28]

In the 60s Americans began to talk about, legislate, and litigate around gender and ethnic inequalities. In later years, some of those efforts were repelled by judges and politicians, but people's awareness of these kinds of injustice remained high. Not so with class. Americans have not talked much about economic class since the 1930s. Yet even if all gender, race, and similar bigotries were eliminated, there would still be oppressive economic inequalities, significant unemployment, and much poverty. Ending gender and race discrimination would not eliminate unemployment and poverty problems; class issues would stand out more.[29]

More realistic definitions of unemployment (and higher poverty lines) might have provided intellectual support to a broader constituency for fixing low-income and job problems. Even with roomier definitions of unemployment and poverty, minorities would still have had higher than average rates, but there would have been more whites in the distressed population. The racialization of poverty in the media and in popular attitudes over the course of the 60s might have been moderated.

The problems of women and ethnic and racial minorities should not have been completely subsumed under the common problems of working people, but common problems should have received more attention. "The people" or "the working class" or the "economic majority" were all those who were not big business owners or managers or high-paid professional and sales workers; they were not affluent and were often at risk of job loss or other economic emergency. This was a very large group—about two-thirds of the population.[30] It had common interests in reforms to alleviate insecurity about jobs and health care. Western European nations were doing more to confront those afflictions. But Americans allowed themselves to be divided. Craft unionists sought job security by excluding minorities rather than expanding the welfare state. Divisions among neighbors seemed more important than class divisions. Sometimes people identified with the rich man on the hill rather than with the neighbor who could not afford to fix his leaky roof. People had little sense of causal relationships between low wages for some and riches for others. Social policy stayed relatively backward, despite specific advances in the 60s.

part three

Toward a War

on the Poor:

The 70s and 80s

chapter six

THE POLITICS OF POVERTY AND WELFARE IN THE 70S
From Nixon to Carter

Despite a backlash against racial liberalism, liberal Democrats in Congress and radicals in the streets were still able to make things happen in the early 1970s. Furthermore, although his inclinations were conservative, President Richard Nixon proposed radical improvements in the welfare system. Over the decade, however, the initiative shifted from people who wanted to improve government programs to those who wanted to cut government. Indeed, even as capitalism stumbled in the 70s, conservatives deflected blame from business to government. The welfare state, it was argued, wrecked families and stymied economic growth.

In some ways, the success of conservatism is a puzzle. Conservatism and resistance to the welfare state are associated with the Republican Party, and it looked like Nixon's Watergate resignation would discredit Republicanism. Furthermore, Republicans Nixon (1969–74) and Gerald Ford (1974–77), not liberal Democrats, held the presidency during 1973–75, the worst depression since the 1930s. And Democrats won elections on these issues. But depression and Watergate allowed victories that were too easy. The economic crisis of the 1970s energized conservatives and business leaders more than it did liberals and unions. Unions lost members, and more white workers voted for conservative Democrats and Republicans.[1] While liberalism lived on, there was no vigorous national movement on the left to offset the developing power of conservatism.

As deindustrialization spread, few Democrats—and few union leaders for that matter—did much to save manufacturing jobs. Democrats became cautious or conservative. California's Democratic governor Jerry Brown jumped on the antigovernment bandwagon. So did President Carter (1977–81).

Worse, Carter's failure to curb inflation and unemployment helped conservatives. As one economic crisis followed another, more people accepted the conservative argument that government was to blame.

The Vietnam disaster and race issues were helping to rebuild the Republican Party, but just as important—and less rarely noted—were the limits of liberalism's consensus economics. Finding political answers to the problems of the 1970s—rising imports, factory shutdowns, and high inflation and unemployment at the same time—was not easy when solutions that helped workers could alienate business. But not finding solutions meant leaving the field wide open to conservatives and harsh corporate practices.

The Poor Demand a Living

What Americans called welfare—Aid to Families with Dependent Children (AFDC)—began in 1935 as a section of the Social Security Act. A state-federal system, it aimed to keep widows at home to care for their children. Initially it was a small program, but World War II, southern racism, and the increased mechanization of southern agriculture drove millions of African Americans and poor whites from country to city and south to north. In the 40s, 50s, and 60s, Cleveland, Detroit, and Chicago received thousands of new black residents, almost every one of them poor. At first and despite surging numbers of impoverished residents and high urban unemployment, welfare rolls climbed slowly.[2] Still, politicians and welfare officials feared budget problems, and as more broken families were headed not by white widows but by young black women, conservative attacks on welfare escalated.[3]

Despite the negatives surrounding the welfare issue, one of the most effective political efforts of poor people in the 60s involved the battle for higher benefits and courtesy by welfare officials. By 1966 agitation for welfare rights led to national organization. Professors Frances Fox Piven and Richard Cloward thought that a movement to flood the welfare rolls would not only improve people's lives right away but also create budget pressures for a national guaranteed income. They pitched the idea to George Wiley, onetime chemistry professor at Syracuse University. After a year of preparatory meetings, the National Welfare Rights Organization was founded in August 1967 with Wiley as executive director.[4]

In the short run, the organization registered big successes. By August 1968 fifty groups of protesters were shaking up New York City's welfare offices. They marched, sat in, and sometimes slept in. They won millions of dollars in supplemental monthly grants for furniture and clothes. But welfare authorities held on, and later in 1968 both Massachusetts and New York state authorities

Johnnie Tillmon addressing a Mother's Day March on Washington in 1968 or 1969. George Wiley sits directly behind her, on the left. Ethel Kennedy looks on. (Courtesy of Wisconsin Historical Society, WHi-8771)

implemented a flat $100-a-year special grant; this was a sharp cut, and it deflated welfare rights activism.

Still, more people applied for welfare, and more of those who applied received aid. While the number of families on the rolls grew by 17% in the 50s, it jumped by 107% in the 60s.[5] By the time Nixon became president in January 1969, state officials were demanding more federal money. This was what Piven and Cloward had hoped for.[6]

Although the War on Poverty had been sold as an alternative to welfare, welfare rights activism was a model of what some planners wanted from community action, namely, poor people's organization to make local social services more accessible. Even without the War on Poverty, welfare rights activism would have been energized by the civil rights movement. But, as it turned out, federally funded organizations were involved in agitation and information efforts; neighborhood service centers raised people's consciousness about their rights. Hundreds of Volunteers in Service to America (VISTA) workers were organizers for welfare rights groups. And through the Legal Services programs, lawyers won court decisions to loosen restrictions on welfare.[7]

MAKING POVERTY POINTS CONCRETE

Welfare rights demonstrators were inventive. In Cleveland 200 protesters held a department store buy-in; they selected everything children needed for school and instructed the store manager to bill the Department of Welfare. In California they invited officials and their spouses to a banquet where they served only beans. In Philadelphia, Roxanne Jones targeted department stores that refused credit to poor women. The protesters had support from middle-class Friends of Welfare Rights who marched into the store and turned in their credit cards. Meanwhile, demonstrators tied up traffic outside. It did not take long for store management to become more sensitive and offer credit to low-income customers.

Sources: Richard A. Cloward and Frances Fox Piven, *The Politics of Turmoil: Essays on Poverty, Race, and the Urban Crisis* (New York: Pantheon Books, 1974), 130; Nick Kotz and Mary Lynn Kotz, *A Passion for Equality: George Wiley and the Movement* (New York: W. W. Norton and Co., 1979), 233–37.

Framing the Poverty Issue: Welfare and Wages

President Johnson had sold the War on Poverty not as a handout but as a way to prepare people for the job market. In this way, Johnson tried to maintain public support for liberal programs, but he was doing nothing to educate people about the shortage of good jobs that forced people onto welfare. The Family Assistance Plan (FAP) implied that the economy normally generated poverty, through unemployment and low wages, even among couple-headed and working families. Once in place, FAP might have helped to reorient attitudes about work and welfare, moving the United States closer to the Western European model.

In public discussion, three major claims were made about the welfare system. First, the welfare rolls were exploding, and the states wanted more funding. Second, welfare caused family breakdown; it supported a black "matriarchy," and the absence of male models meant children with poor work habits and even a propensity to crime. This was the view of Moynihan and of many Americans. Third, liberals believed that the welfare process degraded recipients, penalized work recipients, and did not cure poverty.[8] Families rarely received more than $2,000 in annual AFDC payments; in Mississippi it was $660 a year. The federal poverty line for a family of four in 1969 was $3,743.[9]

It was not much heard that people were on welfare because the economy did not create enough decent jobs, but members of the Nixon administration understood the point. Moynihan admitted that if good jobs were plentiful, fewer people would be on welfare. Secretary of Labor George Shultz admitted to a congressional committee that "our economy has lots of jobs that pay low wages." But Shultz and Moynihan did not launch a campaign to lift wages. The Republican administration, as Shultz put it, was not "going to be remaking the economy" with welfare reform. "We have to relate to the labor market. We can only put people in the jobs that exist."[10] But in some areas FAP might lift wage levels. In the South, even the $1,600 offered by FAP would allow domestics and laborers to reject very low wages. Georgia representative Phillip Landrum worried that "there's not going to be anybody left to roll these wheelbarrows and press these shirts."[11] But elsewhere, employers and conservatives liked FAP because it did not impinge on employer power in labor markets the way minimum wage laws and unions did.[12] Employers could still pay poverty-level wages, and government would add FAP payments.

Nixon Proposes a Guaranteed Income

When Nixon was inaugurated in January 1969, no one could have predicted that he would propose a reform that expanded a welfare program. Nixon was a leading anticommunist in the 40s and 50s. Eisenhower's vice president in the 50s, he was defeated for the presidency by John Kennedy in 1960. When he lost the California gubernatorial election in 1962, he told reporters that he was finished, but he won the presidency in 1968. During the campaign, Nixon claimed to have a secret plan to end the war in Vietnam. For people who resented the civil rights and other radical movements of the 60s, he promised to slow desegregation and trim the War on Poverty. For those fed up with urban riots, Nixon and his running mate, Spiro Agnew, promised law and order.

Later Agnew would leave office when accused of accepting bribes and evading income taxes, and Watergate forced Nixon to resign the presidency in August 1974. But that was in the future. For the present, the administration was sending mixed signals on the antipoverty front. Nixon closed dozens of Job Corps Centers; moved Head Start from the Office of Economic Opportunity to the Department of Health, Education, and Welfare; and eliminated the Community Action Program. On the other hand, the administration got Congress to exempt 2 million poor people from federal taxes, proposed extending unemployment insurance to more workers including some farmworkers, and urged more spending on food stamps. These things could help the poor.[13]

But something more spectacular was in the works. There were still plenty of liberals in Congress and plenty of liberals and radicals active outside Congress. The environmental movement was picking up steam; antiwar activists were still able to get hundreds of thousands of students to demonstrate in the early 70s; and the women's movement was growing.[14] There were also moderates and liberals in the Nixon administration. Some were Democrats like Moynihan. Others represented a still lively group of liberal Republicans, for the Republican Party had not yet become as hostile to social programs for the poor as it would be later. It had a liberal wing that included New York's Nelson Rockefeller and California's Robert Finch, Nixon's secretary of health, education and welfare.

Nixon himself was a nondogmatic conservative who cared more about foreign affairs and reelection than domestic social programs. He hoped to attract more white working-class voters to the Republican Party by slowing desegregation efforts, but in some areas he seemed like a liberal. His administration proposed the Environmental Protection Agency and signed work safety laws. Spending lavishly to pump up the economy for his reelection bid, Nixon declared that he was a Keynesian, a label previously applied to big-spending liberals. To fight inflation, Nixon imposed wage and price controls, which conservative free marketeers hated. Party building and electoral calculation made Nixon act like a liberal.

Despite these bows in the liberal direction, it was a surprise when word leaked out that Nixon would propose a guaranteed income. A handful of Democrats had pushed the guaranteed income as a way to end poverty, but during the 1968 campaign, Nixon doubted that he could support it. Yet on August 8, 1969, on national television, he presented the Family Assistance Plan for poor American families. The president denied that FAP was a guaranteed income, for it would include work requirements, but to a large degree FAP assured a family of four that had no other cash income a total of $1,600 a year.[15]

Why did a Republican with traditional social values propose a liberalization of welfare? One reason was the influence of liberals in government. Early in the Nixon administration, two holdover Democrats, Worth Bateman, deputy assistant secretary of health, education and welfare, and James Lyday, economist in the War on Poverty's Office of Economic Opportunity, proposed a guaranteed income and one that would include the working poor. Secretary Finch, who hoped to give the administration a progressive tone, Finch's deputy John

Veneman, and Moynihan, White House domestic policy adviser, became generals of the guaranteed-income army. Opposing them were Vice President Agnew, who doubted the plan would win liberals or conservatives, economist Arthur Burns, and Burns's very conservative assistant, Martin Anderson, who bombarded Nixon with claims that a guaranteed income would erode the American work ethic. In the end Nixon chose FAP. Why?[16]

One pressure was the funding problem. Welfare rights pressure had vastly expanded welfare expenditures, and local officials were demanding more federal aid. Nixon and Agnew could have taken the low road to harangue lazy welfare mothers, but that might have stirred social disorder, and it would have looked mean.

The crisis could have been met in other ways, but simply increasing federal funding for AFDC would not have made a media splash. Moynihan urged Nixon to do something big to embarrass the liberals. He encouraged the president to follow Britain's nineteenth-century prime minister Benjamin Disraeli, to see himself as a conservative who fixed things that the liberals had made a mess of. Some historians believe that Nixon hoped that FAP would win white working-class Democrats to the Republican Party. But FAP seemed like welfare, and that normally alienated white workers. Precisely because they understood this, FAP enthusiasts in the administration joked about hiding FAP under the name "Christian Working Man's Anti-Communist National Defense Rivers and Harbors Act of 1969." The truth seems to be that Nixon was convinced that welfare needed repair, that he was intrigued by the possibility of doing better than liberals and of eliminating welfare officials, and that he thought he *might* gain votes with FAP. When he decided that FAP was a political liability, he dropped it, and that was partly responsible for its final defeat.[17]

The path to FAP was eased when the administration found ways to frame it as a conservative program. A guaranteed income did not look conservative, but supporters emphasized that FAP, unlike AFDC, would support working poor and couple-headed families. Also, the administration made FAP look like a minimalist alternative to busybody welfare liberalism that had produced "a bureaucratic monstrosity, cumbersome, unresponsive, ineffective," "a colossal failure," a "huge monster" that was bankrupting governments and splintering families.[18] The Family Assistance Plan would mean less government and, Moynihan promised, no more social workers, a group that Nixon detested. Moynihan also told Nixon that if FAP passed he would be able to say that during his presidency "poverty was abolished in America."[19] These were wild exaggerations, but they appealed to Nixon.

The Family Assistance Plan had support from business, civil rights, and intellectual leaders. Thirteen hundred economists backed it, as did officials at Xerox, Inland Steel, Mobil Oil, and the New York Stock Exchange. Businessman Ben Heineman, director of President Johnson's Commission on Income Maintenance Programs, favored a guaranteed income.[20] The idea also had the authority of conservative economist Milton Friedman behind it. Most conservatives were social Darwinists who hated government assistance to the poor. Friedman was also a social Darwinist, but in the 50s he had proposed a guaranteed income in form of a negative income tax (if your income was low enough, government paid you) in order to eliminate government programs like job training, minimum wage laws, and welfare that interfered with the free market. Friedman's authority legitimized Nixon's contention that FAP was not liberal.[21]

Was a Guaranteed Income a Good Idea?: The Pros and Cons of FAP

The first good principle of the Family Assistance Plan was that no family with children would be extremely poor. The federal government promised to pay $500 for the first two family members and $300 for each of the rest. A four-member family would receive $1,600 a year. By spending some of its dollars on food stamps, the family could push its purchasing power over $2,000.[22]

That was about half the poverty line for a family of four. Viewed that way, FAP did not look like much, but it was a departure for U.S. social policy. In fact, by adding working families and couple-headed families and by lifting payments in the poor states, FAP would double the rolls to 20 million and increase spending by $3 billion.[23]

The Family Assistance Plan had other progressive elements. First, although states already had the option of giving welfare to families with an unemployed father, the typical AFDC family had no adult male. Under FAP it would be normal for government to support whole families.[24] Second, FAP would support the working poor, which was not common in AFDC. This element bolstered Nixon's claim that FAP emphasized work. Third, FAP would make income maintenance for prime-age families mainly a federal responsibility with national standards. Aid to Families with Dependent Children was partly financed by federal contributions, but state and local governments set benefit levels, often at brutally low levels. The Family Assistance Plan said no family should be extremely poor, whether black or white, northern or southern. The benefit levels initially proposed for FAP were low, but FAP might have created a new constituency to support benefit hikes. Social Security had done so.[25]

The Family Assistance Plan would be a boon to southern blacks, two-thirds of whom would get benefits. Many would gain a little freedom from employer threats that they should not vote if they wanted to keep their jobs. But also, in comparison with welfare, the FAP population would have more male-headed families, more working families, and more whites. This might make it politically stronger.[26] An additional, and more profound, aspect of FAP was that it took the focus off the character of recipients. It blended workers and non-workers into one group whose common problem was too little income, not bad attitudes. This aspect of FAP could have lessened the scapegoating of welfare mothers.[27]

Those were positive features of FAP. It also had plenty of negatives. For one thing, FAP included no automatic annual inflation adjustment; as soon as it passed, its purchasing power would begin to fall. For another, FAP offered nothing to single adults and couples without children. Perhaps it seemed prudent to limit aid to families with children, but childless adults were poor, too.

With respect to work requirements, FAP included both stick and carrot. As to the stick, a family head who refused to work or train would lose $300, but no one knew whether this would be enforced. As to the carrot, FAP aimed to preserve work incentives. A family of four that began with the $1,600 grant would lose none of the grant for the first $720 earned and only 50 cents for each dollar of the next $3,200 earned, until the grant was gone.[28]

Worst of all, FAP would not cure much poverty. Moynihan claimed that FAP would abolish poverty for dependent children and the working poor, but he was wrong.[29] The poverty line for a family of four was $3,743 (1969); families relying only on FAP would not get near that. Families that had one person earning the minimum wage ($1.60) for 2,000 hours a year grossed $3,200 without FAP and $3,560 with allowable FAP benefits. The Family Assistance Plan would rescue millions from extreme poverty, but it would lift few people over the poverty lines.

Probably the best way to have cured poverty would have been to raise FAP amounts for those out of the labor force and make work more attractive and more effective at fighting poverty by creating high-wage jobs for those wanting work. But in the meantime, FAP was a positive step, especially from a Republican administration. We know what happened without FAP. The after-inflation value of AFDC payments sank. The numbers of working poor grew. And the urban poor were demonized as a dangerous underclass.

The way that FAP was sold to Congress and the public echoed the way the War on Poverty was sold—as a hand up, not a handout. It would have been better, although politically more difficult, had the proponents of both programs acknowledged that many occupations were not paid at all or poorly but were socially valuable. The nature of work, earnings, and social obligation could have been debated. Certainly there were lots of important unpaid jobs in America. Parenting was one. Opponents of welfare did not think that parenting by poor people merited government assistance; others believed that all caretakers and perhaps even serious poets deserved a guaranteed income. But Nixon was not a hippie, and FAP was about as far as he could go. Big questions about economic justice, jobs and pay, and people's social obligations were usually suppressed as the Nixon team sold FAP as a conservative policy. In public Nixon denied that FAP was a guaranteed income. In private he knew better. Moynihan pushed FAP precisely because it was a guaranteed income, and he thought it would be more effective and less intrusive than other antipoverty programs.[30] America had a four-year debate about FAP, but not often about the philosophy of guaranteed incomes. The Family Assistance Program was an effort to sneak through a guaranteed income by emphasizing work requirements. That was not the most profound approach, but it seemed practical. And it almost worked.

Who Zapped FAP?

The immediate response to Nixon's FAP was encouraging. Newspaper editorials were supportive, as were citizens' letters to the White House. A Gallup poll showed 65% for and 20% against. The League of Women Voters and the U.S. Catholic Conference approved. The U.S. Chamber of Commerce opposed FAP, as it opposed most expansions of the welfare state, but the National Association of Manufacturers applauded the "opportunity to end the cycle of welfare dependency."[31] Political labels did not predict where people stood on FAP.

Liberal organizations did not give FAP the support it deserved. Unionists feared that FAP would subsidize sweatshop employers by making it easier for low-wage workers to get by. George Meany, president of the AFL-CIO, maintained that a higher minimum wage was better antipoverty medicine. Union leaders wanted guarantees that people in work training programs would be paid the minimum wage, and they wanted government-created jobs.[32] Another hole in the expected army of liberal supporters came in an attack by George Wiley and Johnnie Tillmon of the National Welfare Rights Organization. They were angry that poor people had not been consulted, and they thought that the $1,600 minimum was far too low; government figures showed that a family needed $5,500 for the basics. The Family Assistance Plan, they charged, was "anti-poor and anti-Black," "a flagrant example of institutional racism."[33]

In the early months of congressional debate Wiley's organization opposed, and the AFL-CIO waffled. The House of Representatives approved FAP 243 to 155 on April 16, 1970. Republican moderates, liberals, and party loyalists supported FAP; California's Phillip Burton organized Democratic liberals in favor, 67 to 1. Five of eight black representatives voted for FAP. The Family Assistance Plan looked like a liberal program, and liberal Democrats in the House supported it.[34]

In the Senate Finance Committee, where hearings began on April 29, 1970, conservatives were better prepared than liberals. Chair Russell Long, a conservative Democrat from Louisiana, argued that FAP would not repair welfare abuse. Delaware Republican John Williams claimed that under FAP a family in Chicago earning only $720 a year from work could end up with $6,128 counting FAP money, food stamps, Medicaid, and public housing assistance, while a family earning $5,560 from work with no FAP and only a public housing subsidy would end up with $6,109 after taxes. In other words, the family that earned $5,560 at work would end up with $19 less than the family that earned only $720 at work.[35]

It was to be expected that conservatives on the Senate Finance Committee would tear into FAP, but what about liberal Democrats like Eugene McCarthy and Fred Harris? Nixon seemed to renege on the promise that current welfare recipients in high-payment states would not lose anything under FAP, and this galvanized Wiley and his associates.[36] For public consumption, Wiley and Tillmon denounced FAP as an "act of political repression." Off the record, Wiley proposed practical alternatives to FAP that preserved existing benefits and included a timetable for reaching higher guaranteed minimums, but Senator Long refused to let Wiley speak to his committee. The liberal Common Cause proposed a meeting with the administration but refused to invite members of the National Welfare Rights Organization because, it claimed, Wiley and the welfare mothers would wreck the meeting. The meeting never happened. Meanwhile, McCarthy found a room in the Senate Office Building for a People's Hearing on FAP. Excluded from any role in almost a year of planning, poor women, most of them African American, vented. One mother announced that she wanted "the kind of jobs that pay $10,000 or $20,000." Women with jobs reportedly deluged Congress with letters asking why they had to work while welfare mothers did not, but key Senate liberals went along with the National Welfare Rights Organization.[37] On November 20, 1970, the Senate Finance Committee voted 10 to 6 against FAP. Welfare rights leader Wiley told the press he was pleased. "It's a big win."[38]

6 Yes	10 No
Russell B. Long (D-Louisiana)	John J. Willams (R-Delaware)
Abraham A. Ribicoff (D-Connecticut)	Carl T. Curtis (R-Nebraska)
J. W. Fulbright (D-Arkansas)	Paul J. Fannin (R-Arizona)
Wallace F. Bennett (R-Utah)	Clifford P. Hansen (R-Wyoming)
Len B. Jordan (R-Idaho)	Harry F. Byrd (D-Virginia)
Jack Miller (R-Iowa)	Herman E. Talmadge (D-Georgia)
	Eugene J. McCarthy (D-Minnesota)
	Fred R. Harris (D-Oklahoma)
	Albert Gore (D-Tennessee)
	Clinton B. Anderson (D-New Mexico)

In this first phase, liberal Democrats helped defeat FAP. Four of the no votes were Republicans, voting against their president, but the last four Democratic noes and the absent Vance Hartke (D-Indiana) were liberals or moderates who would ordinarily have voted for something like FAP. A switch of three votes would have sent FAP to the full Senate for a vote. Why did Liberals vote no? Some thought FAP payments were too low; some refused on principle to help Nixon. Also, the AFL-CIO, a Democratic constituent, was not offering much support, and an organization of welfare recipients, the National Welfare Rights Organization, opposed FAP.

In retrospect, some in the welfare rights movement believed that the organization had not been strong enough to have a major impact. Tim Sampson, who worked in its national office in Washington, believed that "we did not have the power to kill FAP," and activist scholars Piven and Cloward seemed to agree. But had the National Welfare Rights Organization endorsed FAP, Senators McCarthy, Harris, Anderson, and perhaps even Gore (whom Nixon had helped defeat in his reelection bid) might have voted for FAP.[39] Whether FAP would have been approved by the full Senate is another question, but Wiley and his people had influenced liberal Democrats to help defeat FAP in the first round.

Whether the National Welfare Rights Organization did the right thing can be debated. The annual amount of $1,600 was pitifully small. The Family Assistance Plan would have helped millions of desperately poor Americans, especially in the South, but at times it appeared that payments in high-benefit states might be reduced. If the National Welfare Rights Organization were a lobbying agent for northern recipients, it may have acted correctly. And if FAP, once passed, could never be improved, perhaps Wiley was right. But if the

National Welfare Rights Organization wanted to represent all of America's poor and if FAP was a foot in the door for later improvements, then it blundered. (On the other side, congressional conservatives, who had been known to call welfare mothers "brood mares," were guilty of more than tactical errors.)[40]

The administration did not work much with poor people or with Congress the second time around. The House voted 234 to 187 to keep FAP as a part of a big income bill that was approved 288 to 132 on June 22, 1971. The following year, Democratic senator Abraham Ribicoff, searching for a compromise that could pass in the Senate, raised the basic FAP grant to $2,600, set it to rise to $3,000 over several years, and guaranteed that no one would lose present benefits. This was a good compromise, but the National Welfare Rights Organization led a "Children's March for Survival" to the Washington Monument, linking Ribicoff with Nixon, Long, and Representative Wilbur Mills as a gang of villains out "to starve children, destroy families [and] force women into slavery." The organization demanded a $6,500 annual income for a family of four. This was suicide, not politics, and in any case the National Welfare Rights Organization was not much of a factor any more. More important, Nixon refused to support Ribicoff. Democratic presidential hopeful George McGovern had been derided for promising a "demogrant" of $1,000 to every person in America, and Nixon had decided that attacking income programs was good politics. He was ready to sink FAP, and FAP went down in the Senate by 52 to 34. This time liberals supported FAP, 21 to 1.[41] A concerted effort from the White House to move ten mostly Republican moderates and party loyalists might have turned things around. It never came. This time Nixon, not the National Welfare Rights Organization, buried FAP. Four years of debate ended in October 1972 in defeat for an effort to recast antipoverty thought and practice.

The Welfare State Grows, 1972–1976

The Family Assistance Plan was defeated, but meanwhile, Congress and presidents substantially enlarged the social welfare state. This occurred in part because Democrats, many of them liberals, controlled every Congress in the 70s and in part because Nixon thought going along with liberal social programs was a vote winner (Social Security) or because recipients appeared to be the deserving poor (the disabled). By the end of the 70s, however, business and conservative lobbies would be well organized for resistance to unions, regulation of business, and government social programs. Liberalism was on the defensive. The following are sketches of four successful welfare state reforms and one that was stillborn. Significantly, the failure occurred in the later 70s, after conservative forces had become stronger than in the early 70s.

"THE LADIES"

George Wiley was the first executive director of the National Welfare Rights Organization, and there were other professionals like Tim Sampson on the staff. But the people who created the movement in their own communities were those whom the staff called "the ladies." There was Beulah Sanders, who had been fired from her job in the antipoverty program because of welfare rights activism. And Edith Doering, not on welfare but poor and the mother of five. She helped organize the march from Cleveland to Columbus that sparked national organization. Marian Kidd, mother of eight, fought for welfare rights and created a food-buying co-op for recipients. Jennette Washington had been a factory worker who held seven jobs in one year until recession forced her to apply for welfare. There was Shirley Dalton, a white woman living with her seven children and unemployed husband in a West Virginia hollow; she got tired of bad treatment by relief officials and with the help of a VISTA worker formed a welfare rights group.

Finally, there was Johnnie Tillmon. Tillmon, the daughter of an Arkansas sharecropper, had become an activist as a union shop steward for the laundry workers. When she had to quit work, she was ashamed to go on welfare. When she did go on the rolls, she came to so resent the midnight raids of social workers that she formed a welfare rights group in Watts's Nickerson Gardens. Soon she linked up with Sampson's California Welfare Rights Organization, and in 1966 she was nominated to attend the founding meetings of the National Welfare Rights Organization. In 1972–74 she was its paid executive director.

These women were proof against popular stereotypes about welfare. They had not been turned into lazy dependents by welfare. Many had tried the job route and been turned away. For a while at least they and the National Welfare Rights Organization did what most people thought was impossible: they organized very poor people and improved their lives. If they failed to transform the welfare system, it was more the fault of America than of "the ladies."

Source: Nick Kotz and Mary Lynn Kotz, *A Passion for Equality: George Wiley and the Movement* (New York: W. W. Norton and Co., 1979), 219–20.

Supplemental Security Income: A Guaranteed Income after All

Even as the Senate turned down FAP, it passed another part of the administration's reform package, Supplemental Security Income (SSI). Supplemental Security Income was FAP for the blind, disabled, and aged poor. It raised federal contributions and established national minimums close to federal poverty lines. Aged individuals were guaranteed $140 a month, aged couples $210 (at $2,520 a year a couple got more than a family of four under FAP). Eligibility rules were loosened, and the rolls doubled to 6.2 million people in 1974.

Why did Congress approve this guaranteed income when it shot down FAP? Lobbying groups for the aged and for states demanding fiscal relief played a role. Bureaucrats in the Social Security Administration pushed the idea. Also, Congress had its welfare attention all wrapped up in FAP, and some members did not know what they were voting for. Finally, the blind, disabled, and aged poor seemed the "deserving poor"—not to blame for their problems.[42]

Social Security: A Model American Welfare Program

The most "deserving" and politically identifiable group of the poor were the aged. In addition, Social Security seemed like an insurance policy because it was based on people's work experience and their contributions, although in fact many people received more than they contributed. Social Security was the nation's biggest income program, sending $54 billion to 30 million Americans in 1974. Benefits had been increased in 1969 (15%) and 1971 (10%), and more increases were on the way in 1972. The Nixon administration asked for a 5% increase, but Social Security administrators changed actuarial methods to predict a surplus of funds. Democratic senators McGovern and Frank Church pushed for a 20% increase, and by 82 to 4 in the Senate and 302 to 35 in the House, Congress agreed. In the same bill Congress included a procedure for automatically adjusting benefits to inflation. The improvements sailed through Congress because the agency's bureaucrats pushed them, because Social Security did not look like welfare, and because older Americans were a large voting bloc.

Social Security was not means-tested. Lots of money went to the nonpoor. That kept it from becoming a welfare program and encouraged broad support. Payment methods were simple, administrative costs were low, and there was little room to degrade recipients as in the welfare system. Of course, the program had problems. Its financing was regressive, taking a larger fraction of incomes from poor than rich. Still, low-income retirees received larger benefits relative to their former earnings than the affluent. And Social Security cured poverty. It was the main reason why only 25% and not 57% of the aged were poor in 1969 and why only 15% were poor in 1979. In contrast, government payments made little difference in the poverty rate of nonelderly female-headed families.[43]

A Negative Income Tax: The Good and the Bad of the Earned Income Tax Credit

In 1975, Congress included in a tax reduction bill a new Earned Income Tax Credit (EITC). Right-wing columnist Pat Buchanan denounced it as a liberal plot, but it was the brainchild of Louisiana's conservative senator Long, who wanted to help workers who earned little, paid no income tax, but did pay the regressive Social Security Tax. The EITC would be part of the income tax system; families that did not owe taxes could get a cash rebate. Initially, the amounts were low—a maximum of $500 in 1978. But by 2005 some eligible families received as much as $4,400 a year.

Although President Gerald Ford tried to kill the EITC in 1976 and right-wing Republicans attacked it, the EITC won support from liberals and moderates, even without a big lobby in its favor. Limited to the working poor, it did not look like welfare. The EITC even appealed to some conservatives as an alternative to raising the federal minimum wage. For that reason, one liberal critic later judged the EITC "a thoroughly bad policy" that created a "class of parasitic employers" among whom he included Wal-Mart and McDonald's. The EITC allowed employers to pay lower wages because their employees were receiving income supplements. The critic had a point. Improving wages by hiking the minimum wage and unionization might have been better. But in meantime, the EITC gave cash to those who were trying to play the game and were still poor.

The EITC was flawed. The program was not open to the childless poor, and the EITC has always rested on artificial definitions of work. Work was something one got paid for, so women's household labor did not merit an EITC when women performed it for their own families, but a mother who got paid for taking care of another woman's children might qualify as a working poor person.[44]

From "Scrooge Stamps" to a Kind of Guarantee

The United States took another step toward income security in the 1970s by improving food stamps. Congress had authorized food stamps in 1958, and John Kennedy instituted a pilot program; in 1964, the Food Stamp

Act made the program widely available. But no entity had to participate, local administrators had wide discretion in dealing with clients, and poor people had to buy the stamps. In 1969, a family with $100 in monthly income—one-third of the U.S. poverty line—had to pay $40 to get $70 worth of stamps. The poor called them "Scrooge Stamps."

In 1967 civil rights lawyer Marian Wright brought Senators Robert Kennedy and Joseph Clark face to face with dire poverty in the Mississippi Delta. In 1968 activists published *Hunger USA,* and CBS showed *Hunger in America*; each stirred concern about malnutrition. But food programs came under the influence of conservative southern congressional committee chairs who hated welfare for the poor, especially if it went to African Americans. They claimed that ignorance, not poverty, caused malnutrition. (Meanwhile they collected corporate welfare: government checks for not planting as part of federal programs to bolster agricultural prices. Mississippi senator James Eastland received $160,000 one year.)

Obsessed with Vietnam, President Johnson refused to push the fight against hunger. President Nixon hoped to sidestep the issue, but when Senator McGovern threatened to embarrass him, Nixon proposed more funding, free stamps for the very poor, and steps toward national standards and mandatory participation throughout the nation. Much of this came to pass. By 1973, 12 million people were using stamps, and funding had multiplied by a factor of eight.

Some thought the poor should get cash and decide for themselves how to spend it, but the program continued to grow. In 1980, $9 billion was being spent on 16 million Americans. Stamps had been indexed to inflation, and the program was open to whole families, childless couples, the elderly, single persons, and the working poor. As governments allowed inflation to eat into AFDC payments, stamps became a larger fraction of poor people's budgets.

Food stamps were a piece of a guaranteed income. Like Medicaid, they were typical of the limited American welfare state—serving many but not all, only in one budget area, and still carrying the stigma that clung to welfare.[45]

The Comprehensive Employment and Training Act and Humphrey-Hawkins: Missed Opportunities for Jobs

Americans prided themselves on their work ethic, and politicians railed against lazy welfare clients, but the government has not usually supplied decent jobs when private markets failed. In the 1930s, the Works Progress Administration provided an average of 2 million jobs. But that was an exception. The Employment Act of 1946 began as a jobs bill but ended without jobs.

In the postwar era, the military industrial complex offered good jobs in the federal government and government-protected industries; both conservatives and liberals liked that kind of socialism. But the poor did not get many of those jobs; and the military-industrial complex did not stimulate much public debate about the general value of direct government job creation.

Jobs in regular government positions were vital to black progress in the 60s. In the 70s government job growth slowed, the work force ballooned, and unemployment jumped. Over the decade government created a variety of job and training programs. In 1971, in the wake of recession, Congress passed and Nixon signed the Emergency Employment Act to provide a relative handful of public service jobs. It was the first direct federal jobs program since the 30s. Meanwhile, forces in Congress had been pushing to consolidate federal job and training programs that had grown up in the 60s. Nixon wanted such a program to be controlled by local governments, and he did not want direct job creation. In 1973 a compromise was reached. The federal government gathered most job and training programs for the unemployed into the Comprehensive Employment and Training Act (CETA). The programs would be administered locally, but CETA would include a small public service jobs program for the long-term unemployed.

Events soon overwhelmed CETA. The big recession of 1973–75 led Congress to add a larger public jobs program. During 1976–79, the jobs sections of CETA accounted for more than half its total expenditures. With more sophisticated political and bureaucratic infrastructures, more patience from politicians and the press, and more forceful liberal and union defense in the public arena, CETA might have grown into an efficient program with a broad impact. But local failure contributed to spectacular scandals, and it took a while for federal officials to bring them under control. Nixon had been determined to break the Department of Labor rather than let its officials learn how to run such a program, and he supported a general policy of revenue sharing that gave states and cities more authority. So the feds paid the money and took the blame while states and cities did the damage. Outright fraud was not common, but in some cities CETA was a tool of local political machines; some governments laid off regular workers to replace them with CETA workers (sometimes the same people) for no net job gain.

At its height, CETA had more than 700,000 people in public sector jobs and provided training and assistance to 1.3 million disadvantaged. The poor and minorities were generally well represented, but thanks to a 1974 antirecession jobs program, CETA also served the nonpoor jobless. Almost by accident, CETA was becoming a broad program serving both the poor and nonpoor. It could have been a model for what the War on Poverty should have been—a permanent job-and-training program serving all Americans. But scandals and opposition to the idea of serving the nonpoor led to such severe restrictions that, by 1980, more than 90% of new enrollees were poor. However humane this seemed, it eroded support and opened the door to the elimination of CETA in the first years of the Reagan administration.

It is difficult to tell how successful CETA programs were. Studies showed that the CETA experience did little for men but improved women's earnings, although the gains were small. There was anecdotal evidence of success, but most program evaluations were not reliable. Also, the demand for quick results, Nixon's push toward defederalization, and the lack of broad support for CETA made it impossible to experiment calmly over an extended period.

Jobs provided by CETA were not meant to be permanent. They were to be a transition to real employment in government or the private sector. But if the labor force was glutted, as I argue, then the nation needed regular jobs that paid well—jobs in road and dam construction, in local and national parks, in teaching and child care, in the post office, in environmental work and home insulation. Such positions helped jobholders and improved the quality of life for everyone. A proportion of new federal jobs would have had to be guaranteed for poor people, but a politically savvy program would serve "middle-class" unemployed, too, as CETA did in the mid-1970s.

In 1976 Congress almost passed something like this. The Full Employment and Balanced Growth Act, known as Humphrey-Hawkins, made 3% unemployment a national goal and included a binding offer of a government job if other methods failed. The bill won support from liberal politicians, progressive unions, and the Congressional Black Caucus, which had helped to create it, but economists and Democrats were moving rightward in response to problems of high inflation. Left-wing economists who might have given expert support to Humphrey-Hawkins remained offstage. When Democratic economist Charles Schultze suggested that Humphrey-Hawkins was inflationary, novice Democrats in Congress, fearing voter retribution, convinced congressional leaders to postpone a vote on the bill. In the choice between more jobs or less inflation, many Democrats chose less inflation.

Meanwhile, business and conservative lobbies became more aggressive; Humphrey-Hawkins was passed in 1978, but it was just rhetoric by then. Around the same time, Carter's welfare reform, which promised more than a million low-wage jobs, failed in Congress. A year later, Carter appointed Paul Volcker to run the Federal Reserve Board. There would be no program of real federal jobs. Just the opposite: in the 80s and early 90s unemployment would be government's principal tool for fighting inflation, poverty rates would climb to their highest level since 1965, and more politicians would testify that they had converted to the small-government gospel.[46]

Social Spending and Liberal and Conservative Politics in the 70s

The 70s seemed conservative, and each of three presidents became more conservative over time. Antiliberal groups improved their skill at shaping public perceptions of poverty and welfare. The liberalism that was confident in using the federal government for people in need lost vitality. By the late 70s, some liberals supported deregulation of business, and it became popular to run against the government in Washington.[47]

However, despite changes in the political weather, the welfare state flowed on. Nixon and Carter talked about cutting government, but real (after-inflation) federal social welfare spending doubled to $314 billion in 1980. After-inflation AFDC spending fell 7% over 1977–81, but food stamps and Medicaid expenditures climbed, as did those for federal disability insurance (see chapter 7), and total social welfare spending jumped from 4% (1960) to 10% (1980) of the economy. Social Security remained half the total, and the bulk of federal welfare spending was not means-tested; that is, one did not have to prove poverty to get the benefits. Some Social Security money reached the poor and cured poverty, and some kept nonpoor people from falling into poverty. Broad coverage gave programs broad popularity.[48]

In part because of the hammer blows of high inflation and three recessions (1969–70, 1973–75, 1979–80), and in part because cash benefits to the poor were limited, poverty rates stopped falling. They had fallen to their lowest levels ever at 11.1% and 11.2% in 1973 and 1974, respectively; they have never gone lower. Until 1980, government programs kept them from rising in the face of worsening economic conditions, but they could not do much more.[49] And there were big holes in the social safety net. Indicative was the fact that the U.S. infant mortality rate was only fourteenth best in the world.

Inner-city decline in the North in the 1950s and 1960s, which hurt African American arrivals from the South, was a preview of the 1970s–1980s decline of the industrial Midwest, which would hurt both black and white workers. Movements that might have pushed interracial class perspectives to unite the poor and working class against employers were weak. Unions were unprepared to resist the corporate attack on jobs and wages; remarkably little of the 60s student and antiwar movements remained as a national movement. Democratic constituencies were still divided by Vietnam, race questions, and gender issues; suburbanization and union decline weakened the party's potential as an aggressive defender of working-class Americans. One Carter aide, with some exaggeration, claimed that there was "almost total paralysis" in the labor movement, the civil rights movement, the women's groups, and even environmental groups. Liberal forces were not united, and there were few leaders to speak aggressively on unifying issues around incomes, employment, clean air, and fair play. In the crisis of the 70s, when business success meant unemployment for workers, Democrats were confused.[50]

Jimmy Carter, Democratic Liberalism, and Hard Times for the Poor

On economic issues, President Carter leaned in a conservative direction. He gave little support to unionism, and only one major new program for the poor was enacted during his term (Low-Income Energy Assistance).[51] In his 1976 campaign, Carter's promise to fix welfare played well, and the opportunity to fix what seemed irreparable attracted Carter, who considered himself a problem solver.[52] But the president demanded the impossible. He wanted higher payments to recipients (higher costs), low penalties on work earnings (higher costs), and no additional costs to taxpayers. When Joseph Califano, secretary of health, education, and welfare, told him it couldn't be done, Carter blew up: "Are you telling me that there is no way to improve the present welfare system except by spending billions of dollars? In that case, to hell with it!" But Califano wanted guaranteed incomes, and Secretary of Labor Ray Marshall wanted jobs. Califano combined the two ideas into a "monster memo." There were "three people in the world who understood it, and no one of these fully."[53]

Outlined in this memo was the Program for Better Jobs and Income (PBJI), which promised a big change. It would give all who could not work a cash grant ($4,200 for a family of four) that would replace SSI, food stamps, and AFDC. Those who could work would receive a $2,300 subsidy that diminished in steps until total income reached $8,400. (Even after inflation, this was a more generous allowance for earnings than under Nixon's FAP.) The PBJI also included 1.4 million public service jobs paying a little over the federal minimum wage.[54]

These were simple but important ideas. There would be a federal minimum income, and that would help people in welfare-stingy states. Like Nixon's FAP, the PBJI would aid low-wage workers, but it was better than FAP because aid would not be restricted to families. Also, the idea of job creation was a good one in a period when unemployment rates were quite high.

The PBJI won approval from 70% of the public and many governors. But union and welfare groups said the payments were too low and that new jobs were too few to help the 7 million unemployed. Conservatives, led by Senator Long, opposed the PBJI on principle. For reasons that are not clear, civil rights and liberal organizations offered only lukewarm support.[55]

Passing the PBJI would have been difficult under any circumstances—especially because it would add billions to social spending—but the White House made things worse by failing to energize supporters. Despite the similarities of FAP and the PBJI, Senator Moynihan did not lead the troops, and he jumped ship when the *New York Times* claimed that income-support programs caused family breakups. Early in June 1978 Californians passed Proposition 13, which slashed property taxes and frightened politicians away from new social programs. The PBJI never got out of congressional committees. A reform that included a national minimum income and aid to whole families, working families, and needy individuals failed again. It failed more badly than FAP because liberalism had become weaker in numbers and in its faith in positive government.[56]

Few mourned the passing of Carter's welfare reform. The nation and its president faced other challenges: rapid inflation (11% in 1979, 13% in 1980), a new oil crisis, and the Iranian hostage debacle. Carter's inability to manage these crises lost him the presidency in 1980. This loss, more than the failure of the PBJI, hurt the poor. Carter's successor, Ronald Reagan, would cut social programs, support the worst depression since the 30s, saddle government with huge budget deficits that stymied social reform, and poison public debate about the poor and federal programs.[57]

Carter had bad luck. He served at a time when it was difficult for Democrats to appease both capitalists and workers. But he was the Herbert Hoover of the 70s. Good leaders turn big challenges in their own favor. Carter could not do that. Early on, McGovern accused him of Republican economics and wondered which party had won the 1976 election.[58] Against inflation, Carter might have tried price controls on items that were doing the most damage (food, mortgages, energy, and health care), but he asserted: "Government cannot eliminate poverty or provide a bountiful economy or reduce inflation or save our cities or cure illiteracy or provide energy." But government had done some of these things. Why would people vote for a man who said he could not help them? Worse, Carter had turned the economy over to Volcker, whose program was to drive up unemployment. Zooming inflation, interest rates over 20%, and rising unemployment—Carter carried these burdens into his election battle with Reagan in 1980. Most of the newly unemployed were blue-collar workers, and economist Lester Thurow could find "no objective

reason why blue-collar voters should support the Carter Administration . . .
Reagan could not be worse."[59]

Advances in the welfare state came in 1970–73, under Nixon and before the
most severe economic hardships of the decade were apparent. Social Security
benefits were hiked and indexed for inflation; ssi was created to keep the aged
and disabled out of dire poverty. Welfare was almost put on a sounder basis by
including working families and whole families. A public jobs program, CETA,
was begun.

For the rest of the decade, the passage of the Earned Income Tax Credit was
the only big success. Humphrey-Hawkins failed in Congress, and political
leadership did not come to grips with unemployment and the ruination of
communities that followed capital flight and deindustrialization. The forces of
liberalism were in disarray. Union membership and voting power sagged. Liberal economic theory was stumped by the simultaneous increase of inflation
and unemployment. It looked to Carter as though he had two bad choices.
Government spending to cut unemployment would feed inflation; curing
inflation by cutting spending and raising interest rates would initially raise
inflation and raise unemployment, especially for blue-collar workers. There
was no Franklin Roosevelt to find a magical mix; nor was there a movement to
create a Roosevelt. Carter was the Hoover of his time, imprisoned by his faith
in the private sector and his inability to find new approaches to economic
crisis.

chapter seven

TOO MUCH WORK ETHIC
One Reason Poverty Rates
Stopped Falling in the 70s, and
the Stories That Were Told about It

In chapter 8 we will survey the debate between liberals and conservatives about poverty in the 70s, 80s, and 90s, and in chapter 9 we will see how the conservative counterrevolution worked with Reagan in the White House. In this chapter we sketch real economic developments in the 70s, especially in labor markets, seeking explanations for the poverty crisis of the 70s. We will see that more Americans than ever wanted jobs but that the labor market could not fully absorb them. While some commentators mourned the death of the work ethic, there were huge increases in the number of people searching for jobs. As a result, involuntary unemployment climbed.

Three Arguments about Poverty in the 70s

As mentioned in chapter 6, poverty rates stopped falling in the 1970s. They dropped to 11.1% and 11.2% in 1973 and 1974, respectively, but never fell further (figure 7.1). Why was that? There are three main explanations for the persistence of poverty in this period. The first is the conservative tale that generous government payments and liberal permissiveness in the 60s and 70s allowed people to choose to be poor enough to live off government programs or engage in a life of crime rather than work. The second explanation is a liberal jobs story, which claims that employment prospects worsened in the 70s because of global competition and deindustrialization but also because of such domestic factors as racism, population changes, and the continuing suburbanization of good jobs.[1]

Figure 7.1. U.S. Poverty Rates, 1950–1980

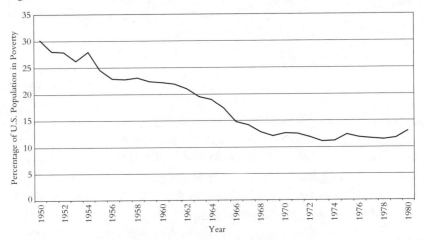

Sources: Carmen DeNavas-Walt, Bernadette D. Proctor, and Cheryl Hill Lee, U.S. Department of Commerce, Bureau of the Census, Current Population Reports, P60-229, *Income, Poverty, and Health Insurance Coverage in the United States, 2004* (Washington: Government Printing Office, 2005), table B-1; Charles Murray, *Losing Ground: American Social Policy, 1950–1980* (New York: Basic Books, 1984), 245.

Less common than the conservative tale or the jobs story is a third explanation about persisting unemployment and the necessity of government action. In this model, explained in chapter 5, economic growth will not wipe out the last chunk of job-related poverty because growth will never be long or deep enough to pull every willing worker into decently paid full-time jobs.[2] Before that happens, economic growth stops, either because business investment slows as markets become saturated or because the Federal Reserve Board, fearing wage and price inflation, raises interest rates to slow economic growth.

In this chapter I review the literature to show that the conservative story fails to explain why 30 million Americans were poor. In considering the liberal story, I sketch the economic crises that arrived in the 70s. I also analyze the labor force to show that the work ethic was alive and well in the 70s, so much so that a labor glut suppressed wages and minimized the antipoverty effects of job holding. However, I argue that special circumstances of the 1970s, such as more intense global competition, cannot alone explain the poverty situation. Story three, which claims that growth always comes up short, is also necessary.

The Conservative Explanation

One set of explanations for why poverty rates plateaued in the 1970s is that there was an underclass resistant to work and family stability and that government programs fostered bad behavior. The growing attention in the 70s to poor people's deficiencies was a mainstay of poverty studies. Moynihan had suggested in *The Negro Family* (1965) that welfare programs were generating social pathologies that had a life of their own; conservatives often made that idea their whole case. As we shall see in more detail in chapter 8, in *Losing Ground* (1984), Charles Murray maintained that liberalism fostered welfare dependence and thereby caused rather than cured poverty. It was humane, then, to cut government social programs (and taxes) and compel the poor to find jobs and rebuild their families.[3] However, many facts and arguments challenged the conservative scenario:

- Underclass alarmists pointed to surging rates of crime and teen pregnancies as evidence of social pathology, but the homicide rate among black men fell over the 70s, and so did black and white teen birth rates.
- If welfare dependence were spreading, we would expect the poor to have more babies to get more benefits, but welfare families were getting smaller.
- Following conservative logic, higher welfare benefits produced more out-of-wedlock births, but states with the highest benefits did not have the highest illegitimacy rates.[4]

Conservatives had facts on their side, too. The share of female-headed families was growing, and they raised their proportion of the poor from 30% to 36%. But most poor people were not in female-headed families and not on welfare. People in male- or couple-headed families constituted 41% of all the poor in 1979. Another 22% were elderly and nonelderly adults living alone; these people had very high poverty rates. Conservatives, the press, and politicians should have said more about low-income couple-headed families, the working poor, and individuals on their own. But they often focused on black female-headed families, whose increase fed people's anxieties about deviations from traditional morality and about the changing position of women and minorities.[5]

It was true that female-headed families were more likely to be poor than couple-headed families. Poverty, the availability of welfare benefits, lousy job markets, and changing values all contributed to the generation of poor families headed by women. But no one could demonstrate that welfare was a major cause of female-headed families or that such a family structure caused poverty. Most poor African American families headed by women had been poor *before* they became female-headed families. And most families headed by women were not below federal poverty lines; they were part of a general social trend that was not limited to poor people.[6]

Also, those who bemoaned the rise of female-headed families typically ignored the benefits when a woman escaped an abusive partner. When Gwen Johnson left a husband who was a drug addict and had beaten her, her kids were delighted: "Oh boy, now daddy can't find us."[7] Furthermore, critics often assumed that welfare mothers did not work, but 40% of them were employed. Women went on and off welfare as their marital and economic situation changed. Jesusita Novarro, mother of five, went on welfare when her first husband walked out, got off welfare when she married again, and got back on when her new husband started drinking and stopped earning. For the most part, the welfare system was not creating a large and growing class of permanently poor, permanently jobless dependents. Of 411,000 welfare (Aid to Families with Dependent Children [AFDC]) cases opened between January and March 1976, 80% were closed two years later. Nor did the welfare rolls grow sharply after the early 70s. The number on AFDC exploded from 4,396,000 in 1965 to 9,659,000 in 1970. But after that surge and despite worsening economic conditions, the rolls roughly maintained their proportion of the U.S. population at 4.8%, 5.3%, and 4.9% in 1970, 1975, and 1980, respectively. The explosion of the welfare rolls was over.[8]

Admittedly, some stayed on welfare a long time, but there is no evidence that *most* people stayed poor or used welfare in the 1970s because of the addictive qualities of welfare rather than because of real economic problems or real disabilities. A popular notion that the poverty problem consisted of black unmarried mothers who stayed on poverty for years and years was a gross distortion of welfare realities and huge distraction from the main economic problems that faced millions of poor and semipoor Americans. The fact that 20% of white working-class families in one sample used welfare in the early years of their marriage was not publicized. In fact, 25% of all families were poor during at least one year over 1969–78, and 25% of all Americans used welfare at least once.[9]

Finally, there is no evidence that people stayed in poverty longer in the 70s than in previous decades—as one would have predicted had the culture of welfare dependence strengthened. Yearly exit rates from the ranks of the poor ranged between 25% and 40% in the 70s, as they had in the 60s.[10] But if exit rates from poverty in the 70s were similar to those in the 60s when the total poverty rate fell sharply, why didn't poverty rates fall in the 70s? Perhaps something was sending more people into poverty than before.

A Liberal Jobs Story: Unusual Economic Crises and Demographic Change Kept Unemployment and Poverty High

Destructive economic changes in the 70s made more people poor. Three important economic crises were the culprits: relatively weak economic and income growth; stiffer global competition; and high inflation rates. In 1973–75 the United States experienced its worst depression since the 1930s. Unemployment reached 10%. Economic growth rates in the 70s averaged only 3% a year. Meanwhile, the U.S. position in the global marketplace eroded. As foreign competitors improved, the U.S. share of manufacturing exports dropped sharply, and Americans began to buy more from countries like Japan than these countries bought from the United States. Meanwhile, in search of cheaper labor or wider markets, corporations sent hundreds of thousands of jobs abroad. General Electric added 30,000 foreign jobs and cut 25,000 American jobs. Plant shutdowns became common.[11]

As to the third factor, inflation, for reasons having to do with Vietnam War spending and significant world events affecting oil and grain prices in the 70s, consumer prices shot up. In 1974, 1979, and 1980 prices jumped by more than 12%. Prices rose 113% over 1970–80, the biggest ten-year jump in the twentieth century.

Inflation not only eroded people's incomes; it tilted politics against curing poverty and unemployment and toward an obsession with high prices. Business lobbyists and conservatives had begun organizing in the early 70s to regain what had been lost in the 60s to unions, social movements, and environmentalists. Inflation could be harmful to the business bottom line, but, as it turned out, it was an effective political tool for uniting people against liberal government. Conservatives and business leaders argued that taxes, social programs, strong unions, and expensive regulations caused inflation and slowed economic innovation and growth. By the late 70s they were often winning this argument; some liberals came to support or accept plant shutdowns, tax cuts, and deregulation of business.[12]

A linked explanation for why poverty rates stayed high and why working poverty increased is that the potential workforce expanded more rapidly than the number of jobs. The result can be seen in this excerpt from a 1977 *Time* magazine article: "In Chicago, nearly 2,000 applicants, most of them black teenagers, lined up last month to apply for 300 jobs at a new South Side supermarket." Too few jobs, not laziness, low skills, or welfare, kept poverty rates high in the 70s and 80s.[13]

In the 70s, much was written about the decline of the work ethic, but the most striking feature of the labor force of the 1970s was the opposite. As a result of the baby boom, people crowded into the labor market. The population of those 25 to 34 years old increased by an astonishing 44% (as against 7% over 1960–69). The civilian labor force grew by 27% and more than 22 million workers in the 70s; comparable figures for the 60s were 16% and 11 million. The surge of workers in the 70s helped to put a lid on wages. While real average hourly earnings rose almost 20% in the 60s, they advanced only 2% in the 70s. The post–World War II party was over.[14]

If the first notable feature of the new labor force was the entry of the baby boomers, a second conspicuous feature was that women raised their labor force participation rate from 43% (1970) to 51% (1979). The number of women workers increased by 12 million, a figure greater than the entire population of Sweden.[15] A third trait of the labor force of the 1970s was rising immigration. In the fifties the United States gained 2.5 million immigrants; in the 70s, 7 million. Seven million newcomers affected income levels in two ways. First, many were poor. How many we may never know, but even if 2 million poor immigrants became part of the poverty totals, they constituted only one percentage point of total poverty rates that ranged between 11% and 13%. The number of immigrant poor people was a contributing factor, but not enough to explain the overall stagnation in poverty rates.[16]

There is another way that immigrants affected poverty rates: they contributed to the low-wage labor glut. Greg DeFreitas analyzed 1980 census data for metropolitan areas and found no statistically significant effects of immigrant workers on the employment and wages of native-born workers. But specific cases support another view. Immigration hurt unionization and wages in California agriculture; immigrants replaced African Americans in building services in Southern California, and immigration may have depressed the salaries of nurses. Overall, it is hard to believe that rising immigration did not dampen wage growth.[17]

Proving that a sharp influx of workers into the labor force kept wages down is not easy, but the wage numbers offer hints. Between 1970 and 1979, young women workers (ages 20–24) *increased* their labor force participation rate from 58% to 69% and saw real annual pay *fall* 7%. At the same time, older men (45–54) *reduced* their labor force participation by three percentage points, and their real pay *rose* by 10%. More workers meant lower wages, and vice versa.[18]

We know that the fraction of workers earning poverty-level wages increased between 1973 and 1979 (table 7.1). In the 70s, job growth in services and trade was almost three times (33%) as fast as in more highly paid goods production (12.7%). The category of "services" added more than 5 million workers. Here were many decent jobs but also many low-wage jobs—for example, in food services and nursing homes. Emma Rothschild concluded that the nation was

Table 7.1. Percentage of Workers Earning at or below Poverty Wages, 1973–1979

	1973	1979
White men	11.8	14.7
Black men	19.8	25.1
Hispanic men	22.4	26.6
White women	33.0	35.8
Black women	35.7	38.3
Hispanic women	41.5	49.0

Source: Data from Lawrence Mishel and Jared Bernstein, *The State of Working America, 1992–1993* (Armonk, N.Y.: Economic Policy Institute and M. E. Sharpe, 1993), 146–51.

"ever more dominated by jobs that are badly paid. . . . This most industrial of societies, this bourgeois El Dorado has in fact gone further toward a service and retail economy than any other of the largest industrial countries." Rapid growth in the labor supply made the change possible.[19]

Surprisingly, because not much was said about it at the time, work effort weakened among older men. The rate of labor force participation for men ages 55–64 fell ten points. The number of white men in that age group who were not in the labor force jumped from 1.3 to 2.4 million. I found no hostility in the media to these slackers, perhaps because they were white. On the other hand, I found little concern for them—which was unfortunate, for they were an alternative to the widespread preoccupation with welfare mothers and minority youths. These older dropouts were in the bottom 60% of incomes—those most affected by low-wage jobs, high unemployment, and plant closures, in other words, those for whom pensions or disability payments became more attractive as the job market became less attractive.[20]

While there was not much concern in the media about the living standards of adults whose connection to job markets weakened, there was concern about the cost of the Social Security Disability Insurance program, which some of them used. As we have seen in chapter 6, although welfare rolls and benefits plateaued in the 70s, the number of beneficiaries and the level of benefits grew in other social programs (Social Security, food stamps). Leading the pack for a while was the federal support program for people who were so disabled that they couldn't work. Over the decade the number of workers and their children getting disability benefits almost doubled to 4.2 million.

As the rolls expanded, politicians discussed ways to restrict access. In part, this was a bipartisan effort to control a program whose costs seemed to be soaring. But the drive to reform federal disability insurance was also part of the bourgeoning conservative movement whose captains disapproved of government income supports for people of modest and low incomes. These captains of conservatism worried that government income programs offered inducements not to work; in the long run that might mean a labor force less glutted, less obedient, and less underpaid.

The reform effort had momentum. Although the number of worker beneficiaries stopped growing in the late 70s, in 1980 Congress passed a law requiring regular three-year reviews of client eligibility. The Government Accounting Office issued a report suggesting that 20% of recipients were ineligible. These official deeds provided ammunition for the incoming conservative Reagan administration, which was determined to cut social programs. As we will see in chapter 9, the Reaganites turned what might have been a modest review into a "purge" of the rolls. The effort was so extreme that it backfired, but thousands who were kicked off the disability rolls were kept off. Meanwhile, the nation did not have a serious debate about how disability insurance could make it easier for the disabled to return to the workplace. And it did not discuss the adequacy of benefits, in part because the attackers assumed that it was because benefits were too high that people were "choosing" to live without working.[21]

In contrast to the experience of older men, most young white and black men and women were increasing their efforts to find jobs. Comparing 1970 and 1979, we can analyze selected age groups of black and white workers. It was common for conservatives to claim that the reason for black poverty was that the black poor did not want to work. But look at these facts. Among women ages 25 to 34, whites lifted their participation rates (the percentage of a population working or looking for work) from 43% to 63%, but their unemployment rate barely changed at all (from 5.3% to 5.6%). In others words, new white job searchers found enough jobs to keep their unemployment rate steady. The percentage of black women 25 to 34 in the labor force increased from 58% to 69%, but their unemployment rate rose from 8% to 11%. As black women increased their participation in the labor force, more were rejected and counted as unemployed.[22] The economy was not creating enough jobs, and the burden of the job deficit went to blacks rather than whites.

For men the pattern was more complicated. In the 25 to 34 age group, white men showed little change in their participation or unemployment rates. Black men of the same age lowered their labor force participation rate a bit (93.7% to 90.6%), but because of population increases and the desire for work, they *increased their number in the labor force from 1.2 to 1.8 million, a whopping 46% increase*. It is hard to see that the alleged work disincentives of welfare were having much effect. Many found jobs, but not at the same rate as in the past, so their unemployment rate climbed from 6.1% to 8.6%. Had they been lazy, they would have dropped out of the labor force. That would have lowered the unemployment rate, but not real poverty and unemployment.[23]

Perhaps the most troubling pattern of joblessness—and one that supplied ammunition for those attacking the welfare state and liberal permissiveness— was that black male teens (ages 16–19) experienced a sharp decline in the fraction of the age group that had jobs (figure 7.2). Why was that happening? Neither the conservative emphasis on crime and welfare nor the liberal focus on weak education and skills provides an adequate explanation. As to welfare, over the decade real welfare payments fell; presumably their allure to poor families diminished. As to education, the high school dropout rate for African Americans declined, and in some areas, such as math skills, school achievement improved. Nevertheless, complex forms of discrimination made the hiring process tough for young blacks. As more women flowed into the labor market, employers could hire a well-schooled, "well-behaved" middle-aged black or white woman ahead of a young black man with a ghetto attitude. Often black youngsters lost out not because employers' skill needs had risen but because the supply of more polished workers had grown. Ross Knight, employment director of the Richmond Urban League, maintained that "college graduates will . . . take jobs that used to go to high school graduates because that is the best they can find. Naturally the employer is going to take the higher-qualified person."[24]

It was a buyers' market. The skill demands of most jobs had not increased, but the number of educated workers had. A newspaper ad of 1971 illustrates the point: "TOPLESS DANCERS. Must have two years college. Prefer English major, languages or humanities."[25] One critic of minority hiring practices at United Airlines put it this way: "You get the feeling, they're looking for superhumans to do relatively simple jobs" Job seekers without credentials were at a disadvantage but not usually because there were so many high-tech jobs. In fact, while those with schooling earned more, the earnings advantage of college grads over high school grads fell from 35% to 20%, a result of a glut of B.A.'s. In other words, college was yielding less payback in the crowded labor markets of the 70s.[26]

Young blacks also suffered because good jobs were increasingly less likely to be found in the cities. Tom Larson showed for Los Angeles that when young blacks had access to jobs, they took them. When jobs were distant, there was more joblessness.[27] In the slums of St. Louis, 19-year-old Eddie Morris complained: "I've been to the employment office and they've got jobs there only in the suburbs and I don't have a car. It wouldn't be worth my time to pay bus fare, taxes, lunch, and stuff for a job way out in the suburbs that pays $2.65 an hour." Also, in many white suburbs, blacks simply were not wanted as employees.[28]

Figure 7.2. Employment Rates of Black and White Male Teens, 1960–1993

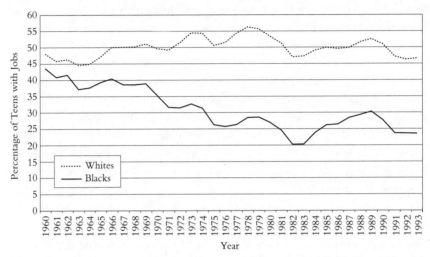

Source: *Economic Report of the President* (Washington: Government Printing Office, 1999), 375. Thanks to Tom Larson.

Since the 50s, blue-collar manufacturing jobs had been seeping out of inner cities. In some places, the decline halted in the 60s, but in the 70s things got worse almost everywhere. Chicago lost 212,000 jobs (1969–77), and its suburbs gained 220,000. New York City lost 650,000. Decline and regional shifts in manufacturing hit African Americans hard. The employment rate of young black men (ages 20 to 24) fell from 70.4% to 60.9% between 1972 and 1980; their unemployment rate—the proportion of those looking for work and not finding it—rose from 14.9% to 23.7%. Corporate ruthlessness and government inaction were undoing the gains African Americans had recently made in industry.[29]

Given these prospects, it is surprising that black male teens lowered their labor force participation rate so little, from 46% to 44% over 1972–79. Because they were baby boomers, the *number* of black male teens searching for work *rose* by 27,000. Since their employment rose only by 7,000, the net effect was 20,000 more unemployed. Their unemployment rate rose not because they stopped looking for work—in that case they would not have been counted as unemployed—but just the opposite, because they looked and did not find.[30]

By the late 70s and certainly by the mid-1980s—and except for the 1981–82 depression—moralistic ideas did more than economic facts like unemployment to shape public discourse about poverty and economic insecurity. There was plenty of information and theory for a compelling economic story to compete against the focus on drugs, crime, and welfare; it was a story of people looking for work, and often taking it, even at meager wages. It was also a story of the job seeker turned away. But this story became less common as the conservative tale about crime and welfare grabbed space on the 6 o'clock news.

The Persistence of Unemployment and Poverty

The 1970s and 1980s, with rising unemployment and job instability, were an extreme of the norm. There are usually plenty of people who want to work. That is why the conservative account is so misleading, especially about the 1970s, when people flooded the labor force. But the liberal jobs story is also misleading if it limits itself to characteristics peculiar to the 70s and 80s and assumes that robust economic growth will arrive someday to wipe out poverty.

The U.S. economy has swung from periods of more to periods of less unemployment, but except in wartime, labor surplus has been the norm. From 1960 through 1979, including the "good" 60s and the "bad" 70s, average annual unemployment for factory workers fell below 5% only three times (1966, 1968, 1969), all during the Vietnam War.[31] And, as we have seen in chapter 5, these official rates underestimate real unemployment.

The 1970s illustrate one pattern of labor gluts. Relatively weak economic growth rates and a sharp expansion of the labor force meant higher unemployment or more part-time employment. Official unemployment rates averaged less than 5% in the 50s and 60s; they averaged 6.2% in the 1970s, and actual rates were more than 10%. *Business Week* claimed that there was a "massive surge in the level of employment," but there was also more unemployment and more part-time work. While 15% of employed people were part-timers in 1969, 25% of new workers were part-timers in the 70s.[32]

Fighting inflation and aggressive efforts to rebuild profit margins came to dominate business thinking. Some employers and scholars wanted higher unemployment. "So long as the labor market can be kept relatively loose," wrote a *Fortune* analyst, "wage increases, which are the principal component of price increases, will gradually moderate." A loose labor market meant official unemployment rates of 6% or 7%. The 1960s goal of cutting unemployment to 4% was dead; the *Fortune* author claimed that "4 percent is far too low. *In fact it has been too low for the past twenty-eight years.*" Many of the jobless, it was said, were wives or teens; unemployment was only an "inconvenience" for them.[33]

Unions and even unorganized workers had done well in the 60s and early 70s, winning higher wages and better workplace protections. In the 70s employers organized to fight back. Raising unemployment was one solution to high wages and falling profit rates. Increasingly economists and business apologists talked of the "natural" rate of unemployment and the "nonaccelerating inflation rate of unemployment." What they meant was the lowest level that unemployment could reach before consumer demand and worker bargaining power ignited wage and price inflation. Over the 70s and 80s, the minimum was determined to be an unemployment rate of 6% or 7%. That policy meant that the poor and the unemployed would pay the cost of fighting inflation.

Missing the Big Picture

I have tried to demonstrate that reality offered plenty of raw material for a left-liberal analysis of poverty that focused on economic and social systems rather than welfare excess and personal flaws. Why, then, did the right-wing version win the public debate about poverty? We will answer this more fully in the next chapter, but here we note that part of the answer lies in the deeply rooted weakness of radical or socialist-liberal ideas and politics in the United States. This weakness meant an impoverished public debate. It is not that all economic problems would have been solved had Americans copied Western Europe, but Americans would have fixed *more* poverty and created a more generous society. Policy debate would have been more inclusive, focusing on the income and job problems of the majority—among whom were the poor—rather than on the defects of those on welfare. With a party or movement constantly publicizing a clear view of the economic causes of poverty and an appealing picture of the caring society, there might have been less division between Social Security recipients, whose rate of poverty fell as they garnered handsome benefit increases in the early 1970s, and welfare recipients, who suffered as inflation ate away at benefits.

Other nations had socialist and labor parties, national cultures, or trained bureaucracies—or all three—devoted to the welfare state.[34] The United States had little of any of these. The fact of a labor glut supported an economic explanation of poverty whose emphasis on the need for jobs spoke to the widely praised American work ethic. But missing or weak were mass organizations and intellectual work, scholarly and popular, that told the economic story and fostered confidence that government could act to create jobs and raise wages.

The liberal Left that existed did not make enough of its opportunities. Public opinion was flexible, opposing welfare but supporting "assistance for the poor" and government efforts to "reduce the income gap between rich and poor."[35] But too many liberal academics were worried about technical details, and too few were concerned with the big picture. Conservatives were creating foundations, think tanks, and mailing lists to get their message out. Too few liberal intellectuals used the mass media to promote big-picture solutions to poverty and unemployment.

Part of the problem was organizational. The Democratic Party as a mass organization was deteriorating in many places. The union movement declined, as deindustrialization and a failure to organize cut membership. "Why should we worry about organizing groups of people who do not want to be organized," said the AFL-CIO's George Meany. He should have been the nation's leading unionizer. Party reforms, suburbanization, and corporate contributions allowed more Democrats to be independent of party and unions. Fewer poor people voted. In short, many forces made Democrats more business-minded and more timid.[36]

On a more profound level, union and liberal "failure" reflected inability to think critically about capitalism. America's privileged global position after World War II had nourished the faith that what was good for General Motors might be good for workers. But as global competition intensified and layoffs became a corporate strategy, liberals and labor leaders did not advance an appealing alternative—for example, taxing the rich to support public investment in new companies that generated real jobs with decent wages and benefits.[37]

Four episodes and one nonevent in the 70s illustrate the feebleness of the forces for a more extensive welfare state and pro-employee policies. First was the defeat of Carter's Program for Better Jobs and Income. Second was the mutilation of the Humphrey-Hawkins bill (1978), originally requiring the federal government to lower the adult unemployment rate to 3% in four years, with government jobs if necessary. The final bill was so twisted that curing inflation, not unemployment, had become the priority.[38] Third was the appointment, by Democratic president Jimmy Carter, of Paul Volcker as head of the Federal Reserve Board. That meant more unemployment and poverty. Finally, there was the Comprehensive Employment and Training Act (CETA), which was sketched in chapter 6. For a while, the jobs part of CETA was "universalistic" program that served poor and nonpoor. If the analysis in this book is on target, then whatever CETA's flaws, it might have become a better antipoverty program, focusing on jobs and serving the whole labor force. But CETA was not well defended by liberals and labor against conservative charges of corruption and incompetence. It appears that not many liberals understood that a jobs program serving the poor and the not so poor might work. Without too much trouble, President Ronald Reagan destroyed the CETA public jobs program.[39]

Fifth—and this is the nonevent—a larger, more confident, and well-tutored labor-liberal movement might have pressured government to raise the poverty line and relabel it an economic sufficiency line, or do away with it all together. Raising the line by 25% to about half the median American family income would have increased the number of poor from 24,497,000 to 35,592,000 in

Mollie Orshansky in 1971. Orshansky, who created poverty lines in the 1960s, believed that federal officials erred in choosing the stingiest of her lines. (Courtesy of Social Security Administration Archives)

1980 and increased the poverty rate from 13% to 18.1%.[40] These additional millions, the nearly poor, had social characteristics similar to those below the existing poverty line, but the inclusion of many more whites and workers might have given the poor and nearly poor a little more political clout and eased the reluctance of the nonpoor working class to subsidize the nonworking poor. Of course raising the poverty line was politically difficult. Who would want to be president when the number of poor jumped by 10 million, even if the reason was a definitional change?

But there was a real problem with the poverty line, and it was not just that it was too low. In the world of pictures and ideas through which people and policy makers grasped reality, the poverty line built a Chinese wall between the poor and the nonpoor and encouraged people to think of the two groups as fundamentally different rather than, as was usually the case, similar people facing different opportunities and misfortunes. The poverty line, however useful as an indicator of success or failure in wiping out poverty, added to the factors isolating the poor, and in the long run that could not help them.

The rich European nations paid less attention to poverty lines and had more programs that served broad populations. It is true that governments were not always very enlightened in Western Europe in the 70s and 80s. In seven of eleven economies, unemployment benefits were cut even though unemployment increased. European leaders, right and left, accepted the unproven assumption that welfare expenditures hurt economic growth.[41] Labor and social democratic parties lost elections and cut welfare. Still, the cuts were minimal; in Sweden and Denmark, social expenditures increased in spite of late 70s victories by conservatives. Of eleven mixed economies in Europe and North America, the United States devoted the smallest proportion of gross domestic product to social programs. The average for the eleven was 28.5%; the United States remained under 21%. It is true that direct American expenditures grew rapidly over 1965–75. But despite everything, after many difficult years, other affluent nations had lower poverty rates than the United States. While the U.S. rate was 13.3% in the mid-1980s, it was only 2.8% in West Germany. Despite a troubled history in the 70s, social democracy's past success guaranteed that fewer Europeans fell into poverty during a frightening shakeout in the world economy.[42]

In America the weakness of the effort to create a welfare state that was as generous to the working-age poor as to retirees meant that many people remained poor and nearly poor. The absence of powerful liberal stories that linked economic explanations with liberal morals and values—people's right to a decent job, to health care, to good schools and services for their children—

opened the door for conservatives, who framed the debate around the failures of welfare and poor people's addiction to crime and drugs. As a result, by the late 1970s, little was in place for another view of the world, an alternative to the one that had been developing for several years and would soon be the force known as Reaganomics.

chapter eight

CUTTING POVERTY OR
CUTTING WELFARE
Conservatives Attack Liberalism

Starting in the 1970s, there was a resurgence of conservatism in many of the rich nations of Western Europe and North America. High energy prices, slow economic growth, and tougher global competition fueled the conservative counterrevolution, but so also did conservatives, who worked hard to shape public debate. Nowhere was this more true than in the United States.[1]

In the next chapter we will describe the political impact of conservative efforts to undo the New Deal–1960s welfare state. In this chapter, we focus on the world of ideas and attitudes. In the United States, the Right seemed to be winning the battle of ideas on poverty and welfare. In 1984, Owen Harries, a fellow at the conservative Heritage Foundation, asserted that conservatives determined "the spirit of the age, the prevailing notions concerning what is possible, inevitable, desirable, permissible, and unspeakable."[2] By the mid-80s, when Americans and their columnists considered poverty, they were as likely to think about drugs and welfare fraud as about unemployment.

Public opinion was not carved in stone; even in the mid-80s, after years of conservative speeches from the White House, the public supported more "assistance to the poor."[3] But while public opinion had not moved far to the right, conservatives increasingly set the agenda for public discussion. The reasons for conservative success are many. The first three have to do with background factors that made people more receptive to conservative stories.

The first background factor was rapid social change and its effect on old beliefs. The 60s counterculture threatened the work ethic. The Vietnam War was profoundly unsettling to assumptions about national goodness and power.

More wives went to work, and some demanded equality. At sea amid many conflicting currents, some people were receptive to conservative efforts to scapegoat liberalism, feminism, and the welfare state.[4]

A second factor involved reaction to government efforts to expand opportunity for minorities and the poor. Conservative writers and Republican politicians attacked antipoverty programs and affirmative action, and their ideas moved white workers from the more labor-oriented Democrats to the more business-friendly Republicans.[5]

A third and surprising boost to conservatism was the economic crisis of the 1970s: the highest unemployment rates since the 30s, along with soaring inflation. Imports rose, and hundreds of factories shut down. Conservatives worked hard to turn voter resentments away from business's failure to modernize and toward government and taxation.

These historical processes provided opportunities for action, but very important was the response of liberals, business, and conservatives. Liberal Democrats were baffled because it seemed that economic growth could not provide benefits to both capital and labor. Confusions about how to fix the economy inclined liberals to relax their support for the welfare state and regulation of business. There was still plenty of left-wing activity at a local level and with respect to national issues like pollution, but liberalism as a national force was in disarray.

Worried about low profit rates and smarting from losses to consumer activists, business groups reorganized their political and lobbying activities in the 70s and became diligent about funding right-wing attacks on social programs, progressive taxes, and regulation of business. At the workplace, capitalists increasingly took the low road: challenging unions' very right to exist, laying off workers, and exporting jobs.[6]

That brings us to the third camp. Conservatives organized and debated with increasing confidence and sophistication. The spread of conservative ideas in the 70s and 80s goes beyond questions of truth and falsity and involves fundraising, aggressive outreach, and a focus on a few big ideas. Conservatives urged business leaders to stop funding liberal professors and to start subsidizing explicitly pro-capitalist research.[7] They reformed old propaganda organizations (the American Enterprise Institute) and built new ones (the Heritage Foundation). Heritage vice president Burton Pines admitted that he was not in the business of discussing all sides of an issue. "Our role is to provide conservative public-policy makers with arguments to bolster our side." Liberal and union lobbyists were still active on Capitol Hill, but Heritage representatives wooed young congressional aides with free lunches and usable information. They sent ready-to-print opinion pieces to hundreds of papers around the nation.[8]

Perhaps because they began on the outside looking in, conservative intellectuals came to understand, as liberals did not, that they were engaged in a war, not a scholarly debate; victory depended less on facts and careful argumentation than on the ability to sell to the public a few big points. Conservative work was accessible. Liberal writing was often more technical and less focused on big ideas that resonated with large audiences.[9]

Finally, conservatives linked their attack on the welfare state (too much government) with defense of the family (against some kinds of intrusive government—for example, in the schools and the welfare system), an attack on affirmative action (too much government), and a diagnosis of what was wrong with the economy (too much government and taxation). A handful of conservatives were libertarians who believed government should not even regulate sexual behavior, but most wanted government restrictions on pornography and abortion, and conservative activists were often good at keeping the focus on what united rather than what divided them. Groups with opposing interests united against the common enemy: liberalism. Businesses whose operations were destructive of economic security and family and community stability won support from religious conservatives who claimed to treasure those things.

Conservative efforts showed success; there were more stories about blacks on drugs and Latino gangs than about the devastating impact on minorities of deindustrialization. There was not a single major book about the economics of white poverty.[10]

Historical change cannot be explained solely in terms of ideas, but books, articles, and media presentations help to determine how the world is viewed, what problems are pushed to the front, and whether poverty or welfare seems the greater evil. This chapter deals with argumentation and large ideas in books about poverty and welfare in the 70s and 80s. If conservatives changed the focus of the social policy debate, let us see whether better facts and argumentation were part of the reason.

Anderson and Wilson (1978): Less Welfare or More Jobs?

Did welfare or systems like racism and class oppression create poverty? Early works by two important authors exemplified conservative and liberal answers. Economist Martin Anderson argued in his 1978 book that the problem was welfare. When he worked for President Nixon (1969–71), Anderson fought the guaranteed income, for he was a follower of libertarian Ayn Rand, whose bulky novel *Atlas Shrugged* extolled selfishness and hatred of government.[11] Surprisingly, Anderson claimed that because of government programs poverty was "virtually non-existent in America by 1973."[12] In fact, even a person who received all available benefits in most states stayed below poverty lines. Furthermore, those lines were pathetically low. But Anderson really wanted to make a noneconomic case. He claimed that while welfare raised people out of material poverty, it destroyed their soul. At one point he expressed fear that people on welfare might become "a truly separate caste"; a bit later, he asserted that they already were "Dependent Americans." A less dogmatic scholar would have asked whether welfare really was "rapidly strangling any incentive" to work. How many people worked while on aid? How many escaped welfare quickly?[13] If people moved often between welfare and work, perhaps the reason was that family change and lousy jobs compelled them to seek aid.

In the late 70s, Anderson attacked President Carter's effort to improve welfare payments and job access because, he claimed, the bulk of new moneys would go to the nonpoor and they would stop working.[14] Carter's Program for Better Jobs and Income initially won broad public support. But there was little union, liberal, civil rights, or feminist support for the initiative. The program was probably already dying, but when Senator Russell Long distributed forty copies of Anderson's *Welfare* to senators, Congress had additional arguments to bury it.[15]

So Martin Anderson helped to sink liberal welfare reform. His book left out so much—the low level of government poverty lines, the labor glut, declining wages, and the fact that many recipients did not stay on welfare very long. *Welfare* was not a balanced, thorough piece of research; it aimed to rationalize cuts in government income supports for poor people.[16]

From the liberal camp the same year that Anderson's *Welfare* appeared came William Julius Wilson's *The Declining Significance of Race* (1978). Wilson's book was an effort to rethink class and race. Wilson argued that current discrimination in the job market had disappeared—hence the growth of the black middle class. But the black underclass, poor and frequently living in female-headed families, was also growing. This growth was due to automation and capital flight, which narrowed opportunities for low-skilled workers. Urban blacks were disproportionately unprepared for modern jobs not because of "current discrimination" but because the "accumulated disadvantages stemming from previous discrimination," such as lower levels of schooling, left them ill prepared for the new economy.[17] What this meant for policy was not clear until Wilson added a chapter to the second edition of the book. There he declared that neither black separatism nor affirmative action would bring as much progress as broad efforts to guarantee jobs like the Humphrey-Hawkins bill.[18]

The Declining Significance of Race was a more theoretical book than Anderson's *Welfare*. It appears not to have created a stir outside academic and African American journals, but there it did provoke debate. Although it won an American Sociological Association award, Black sociologists, who thought it underestimated discrimination, condemned it.[19] But it was a laudable effort to rethink race theory.[20]

The Declining Significance of Race was not crafted to appeal to opinion makers; the first edition omitted policy proposals. Also—and this was something conservatives did better—Wilson's book lacked villains, a group responsible for job loss and urban deindustrialization. Wilson mystified causation; while he tried to substitute class analysis for a race analysis, he omitted capitalists, the business class, which had decision-making powers. Wilson may have ignored them because of fuzzy conceptualization, or because of political caution: don't arouse sleeping dogs.[21] But the dogs were awake and snapping. By the late 70s, they had begun a fierce attack on unions, job security, high wages, and full employment.

Wilson's missing enemy was not merely a theoretical flaw; it was a political problem. *The Declining Significance of Race* seemed like a shrewd effort to move liberal attention from affirmative action, which fostered white resentment, to a unifying coalition of blacks and whites for more jobs. But in building a movement, it helps to have someone to organize against. The Right was learning to mobilize its troops by demonizing government and liberals. The Left may have had better facts, but it needed targets—people and organizations that harmed the poor and the working class. Were the troops likely to rally against "complex corporate bureaucracies"?[22]

Gilder, Auletta, and Piven and Cloward (1981–1982): Right, Center, and Left

About the time the presidency was being transferred from the centrist Democrat Carter to the conservative Republican Reagan, three important books on poverty appeared. One illustrated both the intellectual shortcomings and public relations success of conservative writers. A second showed how bad ideas from an apparently impartial journalist supported conservative views. A third illustrated both intellectual acuity and the probability that the Left was not connecting with big audiences.

The first work was George Gilder's *Wealth and Poverty* (1981). It echoed Anderson's attack on welfare but emphasized tax cuts. Gilder wrote the book with support from the conservative American Enterprise Institute. After a first printing of 8,000 copies, endorsements from members of the Reagan administration boosted interest, and soon there were 135,000 copies in print.[23]

George Gilder had been born into a distinguished literary family in 1939. His father was killed during World War II, and Gilder came under the care of his father's roommate at Harvard, David Rockefeller, the grandson of the oil baron. In the 60s Gilder worked for Nelson Rockefeller and coauthored a scathing attack on conservatives Barry Goldwater and Ronald Reagan, *The Party That Lost Its Head* (1966). But in the 70s he turned against liberals and feminists for destroying the family.[24]

Wealth and Poverty was a brilliant blend of opposites: business and family conservatism. Gilder helped to refurbish the reputation of business and justified its efforts to raise profits by lowering taxes; he supported conservative and business efforts to cut government regulations; and, appealing to those who yearned for male-dominated families, he attacked the welfare state as a cause of economic decline and crumbling families.

Gilder argued that men must work their way out of poverty. Biology equipped them to be providers, and marriage tamed their wild sexual instincts. "When they are providing for women and protecting them, men feel masculine and sexual"; when women become independent of men, family breakups, crime, and poverty result. Welfare is not necessary; the jobs are there for men. Like most conservative ideologues, Gilder was in denial about the reality of unemployment.[25]

Surprisingly, Gilder admitted that most poor people rejected welfare, and for all but 20% of those on the rolls, welfare was a "passing phase." Welfare was not very alluring except in one area: minority ghettos. There welfare seemed vital not because job markets were bad but because of a conspiracy, the "insidious seductions of the war on poverty and its well-paid agents." In short, welfare was foisted on urban blacks by liberal bureaucrats.[26]

Liberal government was always the villain. Like Anderson before him and Murray afterward, Gilder asserted that the welfare state encouraged people to become poor so they could live off the government; the *average* welfare family, he claimed, received $18,000 in cash and benefits in 1979. But except in areas like New York City, most welfare recipients stayed poor; a family in Bolivar County, Mississippi, receiving all benefits ended up with $2,349 a year.[27] And while people on welfare sometimes did better than low-wage workers, that was because wages were so low, not because welfare was so high. Why not lift pay rates to strengthen families?[28]

Perhaps the key element in *Wealth and Poverty* was Gilder's plea for "supply-side" tax cuts. This plan was sold as an innovation, but it was not. In the 60s, Democratic tax cuts raised business investment and people's consumption power and helped bring the lowest levels of poverty in U.S. history. The Democratic cuts increased business and consumer spending and were not so different from supply-side cuts. While supply-side cuts were supposed to increase the supply of labor and investment, there was nothing very supply-side about Gilder's proposal (or the outcomes of the Reagan tax cuts, as we shall see). There was nothing in the program to assure that tax savings went to longer workdays or job-producing investments rather than less work and more trips to Bermuda. Why, then, did Gilder and other conservatives assail Keynesian Democrats and demand-side policies?[29] The reason is that Gilder and other supply-side soldiers like Paul Craig Roberts were involved in a war on liberalism, not a scholarly discussion. A war needs enemies, and although supply-side tax cuts were not so different from what Democratic economists carried out in 1962–64, the Democratic program was part of a package of reforms, such as more spending on education, job training, and health care, that used government to aid the poor and workers. The liberal reform package was anathema to the new conservatives of the 70s and 80s. While there was little to distinguish liberal and conservative tax cuts—Democratic actions in the 60s included investment credits for business and a sharp decrease in the top income tax rate (from 90% to 65%)—the attack on Democratic tax policy and puffing up the supply-side were part of the ideological war on liberalism.[30]

Conservative foundation head Leslie Lenkowsky made a similar point: "Supply-side economics is less an economic theory than a philosophy, an ideology . . . an effort to reorient policy."[31] The tax cuts would do something very like what cuts under Kennedy and Johnson had accomplished; they would reduce business and income taxes, increase economic demand, raise federal deficits, and stimulate the economy. But supply-side was also a weapon in the war on liberal social programs. That was the real difference between liberals and conservatives, not whether tax cuts focused on demand or supply.[32]

Wealth and Poverty also provided cover for harsh business practices. Corporations used the economic crises of the 70s to demand tax cuts and cutbacks in government regulation. They attacked people's living standards, and many tried to destroy unions. Gilder provided public relations for business. His story of a beleaguered capitalism was, reviewer Michael Kinsley wrote, a bizarre "fantasy" that Gilder "should see someone about."[33] Gilder's story of the capitalist as victim of government drew attention away from the reality of the capitalist who exported millions of jobs. But Gilder warmed himself with the bizarre faith that capitalism was based on charity. "Capitalism begins with giving." Adam Smith had been wrong about the invisible hand of self-interest.[34]

Gilder linked diverse right-wing tendencies: the moral concerns of conservative voters and the economic desires of big capital. Conservatives who were anxious about changing gender roles could blame welfare and government. These conservatives could ally with businesses that wanted to limit taxes, reg-

WHAT WAS THE LAFFER CURVE?

Conservatives had traditionally opposed government social spending, especially if it created deficits. To help ease the conservative conscience about tax cuts causing deficits, supply-siders added the Laffer curve. This brainchild of University of Southern California economist Arthur Laffer began with the obvious point that very high tax rates could stifle business activity and trim tax revenues. Conversely, cutting tax rates could increase tax revenues by stimulating economic activity. This was good theory, but Laffer jumped from theory to the assumption that U.S. tax rates *were* stifling business activity and that a cut would grow business and tax revenues. In fact U.S. tax rates were low compared with those in other rich nations. But the idea was more important than the facts. The Laffer curve taught that Reagan's cuts would be painless—indeed, would increase tax revenues.

Conservatives changed their view of deficits over the 80s. Even as President Reagan attacked Democrats for causing deficits, many conservatives came to love them. The surest way to cut social programs or stop new ones was to argue that the money wasn't there. Cutting taxes not only rewarded affluent and businesses supporters; it created deficits that provided a budgetary rationale for cutting liberal programs. Conservatives came to call this tactic "starving the beast."

ulations, and employee bargaining power. Millions of people in the lower economic half would suffer from lower unemployment benefits, lower pay, and weak environmental and workplace regulation. But they might feel better having their doubts about big government and welfare validated. And they were promised a tax refund.[35]

Gilder's book was an inspiring story for conservatives; Democrats and liberals failed to inspire. In July 1979, during the second energy crisis, President Carter scolded Americans for wasteful self-indulgence, but he was unable to balance the harangue with a positive picture of a better tomorrow. Liberal scholars did no better. *The Zero-Sum Economy*(1981), by the gifted economist Lester Thurow, was poor prophecy (growth was not over) and bad public relations. Liberalism needed a program that combined attention to real problems and a positive vision. Lacking that, wavering politicians and curious voters turned to the diversions offered by Gilder and Reagan.

One did not have to be a conservative to reach conservative conclusions. It was possible to ignore the impact of faster globalization and deindustrialization and the labor glut of the 70s. Even experienced journalists ignored causes and contexts.

Surely an in-depth study of a handful of poor people would reveal the truth. Or would it? If one focused on a few troubled individuals, it was easy to conclude that poor people were losers who could not get to an interview in time or kick their drug habit. One might easily forget that *most* poor people were not psychologically damaged; they just lacked decent jobs and adequate income.

Case-study authors often seemed indifferent to whether their subjects were representative of a larger poverty population. Oscar Lewis had used a handful of families to discover that a debilitating "culture of poverty" infected millions of people around the world (chapter 2). In *A Welfare Mother* (1976), Susan Sheehan painted a grim tale of welfare dependence, drugs, and murder, but she never demonstrated that her family was typical of people on welfare.[36]

In the late 70s, it became more common for the press and politicians to offer harsh views of poor people. On August 29, 1977, *Time* magazine featured "The American Underclass," the people behind ghetto walls who "are more intractable, more socially alien and more hostile than almost anyone imagined. They are the unreachables: the American underclass." At the 1978 convention of the National Association for the Advancement of Colored People (NAACP), liberal Democratic senator Edward Kennedy warned of "the growth, rapid and insidious, of a group in our midst, perhaps more dangerous, more bereft of hope, more difficult to confront, than any for which our history has prepared us . . . a permanent underclass."[37]

The most important study of the underclass for general readers was by Ken Auletta, columnist for the *New York Daily News*. In *The Underclass* (1982), he focused on two dozen participants in a New York City supported-work program run with federal funds by the Manpower Demonstration Research Corporation. A private organization, the corporation worked in this program with former convicts, drug addicts, long-term welfare recipients, and juvenile delinquents. The Manpower Demonstration Research Corporation's experiment was not a triumph. By the end of the program only ten participants remained; of this tiny sample, welfare mothers and former drug addicts showed the best success rates. Auletta was hopeful that an intensive educational experience could improve attitudes and job prospects, but he noted that Reagan cutbacks threatened the program.[38]

Auletta thought the underclass was filled with people who had dysfunctional values; they were criminals, drifters, addicts, and welfare dependents. Just how large was the American underclass? Auletta swallowed economist Frank Levy's estimate of 9 million, that fraction of 30 million poor Americans who stayed poor five out of seven years. But like so much being said about the underclass, this was pure guesswork. That people stayed poor proved nothing about whether the causes lay in the people or the economy.[39]

Auletta had chosen his title to "get people to listen"; it was a term "that resonated." A more honest and less inflammatory title would have been *The Underclass: A Very Small Part of the Poverty Problem and Just a Chapter in a Larger Book.*[40]

Auletta claimed that to understand the underclass we needed to turn away from academic experts and study the people themselves. One strength of *The Underclass* was that Auletta helped the reader get to know his people. There was 19-year-old Timothy Wilson, on his own since the age of 13, in trouble with the law, looking for a boss who was concerned about his work and not his personal habits. Timothy was a poet and essayist and, as it turned out, a success story for the program. On the other side was William Black, trying to surmount alcoholism, illness, and fears of being rejected as a former convict. He lasted two weeks in his job at a dry cleaners before vanishing. In Appalachia Auletta found a similar mix of losers and strivers: 22-year-old Sam Clendenin, barely able to spell his own name and drunk most of the time; and Mary Sue Boggs, who used a supported-work program to escape welfare and join the ranks of the working poor.[41]

Speaking to poor people was important, but if poverty's causes were rooted in economic and political structures, why expect the poor to understand them? The causes of people's actions do not pop out of behavior and announce themselves to the observer. Explanation requires analysis about structures that shape people's options. "There is no way," anthropologist Marvin Harris put it, "that the study of capricious expressions of individual will and character can contribute to an understanding of why the scourge of hardcore poverty took root in the inner cities." Auletta's approach could not determine whether social problems were a failure of systems or of individuals, but he sided with conservatives who believed that poverty was "just one symptom of a far more pernicious and intractable malady," the breakdown of the family. Conservative *Commentary* reviewer Chester Finn congratulated Auletta for having shown how little could be done to help people escape from the underclass.[42]

In fact, Auletta had proved nothing about most poor people. Surprisingly, he had facts for a different book, *The Unemployed.* He admitted that "if there were an adequate number of jobs, members of the underclass would readily take them"; 26,200 mostly unemployed men and women had waited three hours in line in Baltimore for job applications for seventy-five entry-level jobs paying $7,000 to $11,500 in the Social Security Administration.[43] This demolished the premise of Auletta's book—an underclass too damaged to want to work. But it is doubtful that most readers noticed the jobs story; the book's title and its focus communicated that there was something so wrong with poor people that training and jobs could not help much.

While Auletta isolated a resistant population called "the underclass," Frances Fox Piven and Richard A. Cloward did the opposite in *The New Class War: Reagan's Attack on the Welfare State and Its Consequences* (1982). One a professor of political science at Boston University and the other a professor of social work at Columbia University, the authors were models of the activist scholar. Furthermore, in works like *Regulating the Poor: The Functions of Public Welfare* (1971) and *Poor People's Movements: Why They Succeed, How They Fail* (1977), they taught people to think about the welfare system not as a barometer of social generosity but as an arena of struggle and benefits as tools of social control for government and employers. Their writings reflected unflinching devotion to the cause of poor people, skepticism about the working class and trade unions, and, sometimes, an anarchistic suspicion of organizations.[44]

In *The New Class War* Piven and Cloward assumed that there was a large working class all of whose members were made of the same human stuff but some of whom were poor owing to causes outside themselves.[45] The poor were not a deviant "underclass" but a badly treated section of the working class, and one whose low wages suppressed living standards for the rest of the working class.[46] Government income programs such as unemployment insurance and welfare allowed the jobless to stay out of the labor market. That meant less competition for jobs and less downward pressure on wages. In this light, the fight to preserve unions, the fight to hold on to the jobs program in the Comprehensive Employment and Training Act (CETA), and resistance to cuts in welfare and food stamps were all part of one struggle to protect living standards. In effect Piven and Cloward were arguing for a class perspective and for a way to connect the poor and the nonpoor working class.

But the strategy that flowed from their analysis was not clear. They had little faith in the possibilities of a new labor movement that made the poor a key constituency. And, it is true, George Meany and Lane Kirkland at the AFL-CIO showed little interest in building a progressive political movement. The authors conceded that union leaders might be radicalized by conservative and corporate onslaughts, but their doubts about labor and liberalism blurred their vision. They claimed that unions had not been important to the development of the welfare state and that unions had usually ignored the electoral realm. These were debatable judgments, shaped by the dreary moderation of many unions in the 70s rather than their long-term possibilities. Since the late 30s, unionists had been the foot soldiers of Democratic Party liberalism, and labor organizations had lobbied for civil rights legislation and improvements in welfare and Social Security. And if there was no hope for white workers and trade unions, what was the political point of *The New Class War*? It is hard to see how any movement to save the welfare state could succeed without the union movement. And if not some kind of broad movement, it is hard to know what action was to come from the class analysis that linked the concerns of poor and not so poor, employed and not employed.[47]

There was also an outreach question. *Wealth and Poverty* and *The Underclass* received a fair amount of public attention; *The New Class War* apparently received less. People needed to understand the link between welfare state programs and better wages. People's view of the world was fractured: while opinion polls showed broad support for helping the poor, preserving Social Security, and opposing Reagan's favoritism to the rich, few Americans showed deep loyalty to the welfare state. In part because of racism and in part because of their idealization of self-reliance, whites had a hard time combining respect for work and respect for welfare assistance to people raising children. "Anyone who has done welfare organizing," a reviewer chided, "knows how hostile most white working- and middle-class people are to the idea of welfare. Many people will not even apply for what they deserve and are convinced that most recipients are cheats and shirkers."[48] Few Americans identified with a big "us" of welfare recipients, Social Security beneficiaries, and employees fighting company take-backs, against "them," conservative and corporate leaders. Republicans used race and welfare to detach conservative whites from the Democratic Party and to advance right-wing ideology. Piven and Cloward knew all this, but they may not have appreciated how successful conservatives were in framing public debate.

Murray and Harrington (1984): Libertarian Conservative and Liberal Socialist

Despite the scientific paraphernalia of charts, graphs, and footnotes, there was nothing academic about Charles Murray's *Losing Ground: American Social Policy, 1950–1980* (1984); every page supported Murray's attack on liberal government. Murray posed a riddle: antipoverty spending had grown in the 60s and 70s, but poverty rates had stopped falling, and crime rates had risen. Murray answered the riddle with the claim that liberal policies caused poverty.

Murray had not always been a government hater. He served in the Peace Corps in Thailand in the late 60s. After earning a PH.D. in political science at the Massachusetts Institute of Technology in 1974, he spent seven years evaluating federally subsidized programs in urban education and delinquency prevention. Eventually he decided that government social programs were inherently flawed, and he assailed the War on Poverty in *Safety Nets and the Truly Needy* (1982), a pamphlet funded by the Heritage Foundation. The conservative Manhattan Institute for Policy Research raised $125,000 from right-wing foundations for the completion and marketing of *Losing Ground*. The institute distributed 700 copies to academics, journalists, and public officials all over the world and assigned a publicist to handle Murray's appearances. Conservative idea brokers knew they had a winner and spent freely to make sure their author reached opinion makers. *Losing Ground* sold 30,000 hardbound copies and launched Murray as an authority on poverty and welfare. He became a media star, and his book was the subject of dozens of reviews and newspaper columns. *Losing Ground* was a boon to conservatives; it encouraged them to believe that someone had "proved" the case against welfare and other liberal programs.[49]

Murray argued that liberalism caused poverty, family breakup, and illegitimacy. It did so, first, because liberals were permissive about crime and welfare and, second, because generous programs lured people into qualifying themselves as poor to live off the government in relative ease.[50]

Almost as soon as *Losing Ground* appeared in the fall of 1984, liberals attacked and conservatives counterattacked. Gilder slandered the attackers as intellectually disabled and effeminate,[51] but critics found real flaws in *Losing Ground*. Moynihan asserted that Murray "has not proved anything," and certainly he was selective in his use of evidence. When it supported his bias (income subsidies weakened work effort), he accepted social science research; when it did not (no statistical correlation between welfare and out-of-wedlock births), he ignored it.[52] Christopher Jencks demonstrated that most social indicators for poor people had not gone bad when Great Society programs kicked in. Robert Greenstein of the liberal Center on Budget and Policy Priorities noted that most poor people were not on welfare, so how did welfare cause their poverty? If most female-headed households were not poor, was having a female head of a household a cause of poverty? The real value of welfare payments had fallen for a decade, making it less attractive to be poor, but poverty had not declined.[53]

It is also easy now to point out that *Losing Ground* was cut off from global realities. First, the social democracies of Western Europe that provided more generous government payments had *less* illegitimacy, *less* crime, and *much less* poverty than the United States. Second, global economic change was destroying American communities, in part because corporations, enjoying the market freedom Murray wanted for them, were free to close even profitable plants and send jobs abroad.[54]

Missing from Murray's tale was the real labor market. So many people entered the workforce as to cause a wage-depressing labor glut and higher unemployment, but Murray focused on the declining proportion of young black men working or looking for work. Murray blamed liberalism, which, he said, made it permissible not to work, but a better explanation was that huge unemployment rates (40% in 1978) discouraged African American youths from looking for work. Murray, like many conservatives, did not take unemployment very seriously.[55]

Murray's libertarianism may have been too extreme for the Reaganites, as Murray later recalled.[56] But *Losing Ground* encouraged conservative, corporate, and Reaganite efforts to limit the welfare state and cut worker protections. Murray, Anderson, and Gilder deflected blame from an increasingly nasty capitalism to liberal government. Murray's book was not fair and balanced, and it was not really "conservative," if that meant to discuss all the forces that threatened the family, neighborhood institutions, and individual security. But one-half of American conservatism was not very conservative at all; it was extreme laissez-faire economics, a version of social Darwinism.

Murray's book acquired a dazzling mystique. Columnist Meg Greenfield noticed that even though its scholarship was questioned, when someone argued for more government programs, he or she would be " 'Charles Murrayed,' and that would be the end of the argument. The simple invocation of the book's existence" was taken as an adequate rebuttal.[57] Murray's success was due in part to conservatives in the White House and Congress; they pounded away at welfare and affirmative action. *Losing Ground* also benefited from a strong marketing apparatus. But Murray deserves credit. *Losing Ground* was a work of sharply etched arguments. Although each was supported with notes and other academic tools, the book was easy to read. It was a model of scholarship in the service of a political agenda.

What did the Left have to put up against it? There was Michael Harrington, the author of *The Other America* (1962), discussed in chapter 2. Harrington's *The New American Poverty* (1984) appeared in the same year as *Losing Ground*. Unlike *The Other America*, this book faced a hostile government. A member of Reagan's hunger task force claimed that hunger was not a problem; "as we look at the problems of our blacks, all we have to do is look at our sports page to see who are the best nourished in the country."[58]

Despite Reaganism, public opinion still supported assistance to the poor. Moreover, workers were being shaken by plant closures and, in 1981–82, the worst depression since the 30s. Official poverty rates jumped from 11.4% to

15.2% (1978 to 1983). It was obvious that massive economic change, not changes in people's attitudes, was causing more poverty and unemployment, even among the once comfortable working and middle classes.[59]

Harrington showed that poverty came in many shapes and sizes, from the welfare mother to the jobless steel worker. By covering a variety of poverties, *The New American Poverty* was more useful than *Losing Ground*. But Harrington's book lacked a driving theme to grab the reader.[60] Worse, the book targeted no enemy. There was not much politics in *The New American Poverty*. Harrington urged a program of full employment, which would help the poor and millions of others, but he pulled his punches by claiming that many business leaders wanted full employment, too. In fact, many had come to accept high unemployment as essential to their domination of the workforce.

The sharpest sections of *The New American Poverty* were about the underclass. Against the notion of a criminal or lazy underclass coddled by liberal social programs, Harrington argued that economic processes like deindustrialization lopped off the bottom of the occupational ladder, condemning people to poverty. As Harrington noted, the recession and other big economic events, not welfare policy, added 8 million people to the poverty population over 1979–82; Volcker and Reagan, using unemployment to fight inflation and trimming government job-training programs, were pushing people into poverty.[61]

Here is where a left-wing Charles Murray would have soared: Reaganomics and pro-business economics in the 70s and 80s meant more poverty and more family disorganization; that was immoral. Why didn't Harrington summon the troops to do battle against enemies who wanted to return workers to the social Darwinian jungle? I think there were two reasons. First, it was not easy for Harrington to be severe with anyone. He was, remarked Thomas Palmer of the *Boston Globe*, "the gentlest of beings" who "rarely speaks harshly."[62] Second, Harrington probably lacked faith that the troops were there, in the Democratic Party or elsewhere. Liberals in Congress fought Reagan cutbacks, but some went along with tax cuts that limited social programs.[63] Whatever Harrington's motives, *The New American Poverty* did not capture the public imagination the way *Losing Ground* did. It could not match nasty stories about the underclass. One reason was the lack of a big story of the caring community working through its government against those who wanted more unemployment.

Mead and Wilson (1986–1987): Any Jobs or More and Better Jobs?

In this section we contrast the Right and the Left on the jobs issue. Lawrence Mead believed that any job was good for people's character; William

Wilson thought that a shortage of good jobs caused poverty and social disorganization among urban blacks.

Mead, associate professor of politics at New York University, published *Beyond Entitlement: The Social Obligation of Citizenship* in 1986. He believed that respect for hard work and authority was on the wane. He claimed that the reasons were twofold: the "sociological" mentality by which liberals and black activists blamed society rather than the poor, and government programs that required nothing of recipients. Only a more demanding government could rebuild the disabled superegos of members of the underclass.[64]

There was much of interest in Mead's book,[65] but on poverty and unemployment, it was, as reviewer Michael Sosin put it, "a rather cavalier examination of the issues."[66] It ignored a lot of questions. Of the people who worked their way off welfare, how many remained poor? No answer. Mead seemed less concerned to cure poverty than to instill obedience and work discipline.[67]

And he was selective. Although Mead claimed to be neither conservative nor liberal, his positions bolstered business conservatism. If work really was so important, why not raise the minimum wage or encourage unions for low-wage workers? These actions would make jobs more attractive. But Mead followed mainstream economists and business preferences to assume that people got paid what they were worth; allegedly wage increases for the poor would raise their pay above their skill and productivity contribution, and that would be wrong. As I argue in chapters 4 and 10, these assumptions were dubious.

Mead's book appeared to wrestle with a profound question. Why were Americans less disciplined than in the past? Why, to use Mead's prejudicial phrase, had "personal dysfunctions" like unemployment, low SAT scores, and welfare use increased? One good answer for the first and third was that a bad economy created more unemployment and more low-wage jobs. Mead's answer was that the liberal welfare state enticed people to avoid work.

If Mead had really wanted to deal with the decline of work discipline and do it without scapegoating the poor, he could have asked whether all adults should be required to engage in paid work. Did that include those who lived primarily from investments? Did it include affluent mothers who stayed home to care for their children? Should all mothers be forced to go to work for pay, or only those who were unlucky enough to be born poor and thus dependent on low-wage jobs and men with poor economic prospects?

There was a second distortion in Mead's book. Was it liberal social policy that eroded people's obedience to authority? Or government leaders who lied about Vietnam and Watergate and corporate executives who shuttered profitable factories? Which eroded the work ethic more: welfare or the flood of advertising urging people to buy now and pay later? In the end, Mead's book was not about the decline of discipline; it was about the behavior of one group that conservatives did not seem to like. It aimed to impose sacrifice on poor Americans. In effect, *Beyond Entitlement* was simply a "new strategy for preserving a pool of cheap, docile labor."[68]

Hinting at the power of the conservative model, University of Chicago sociologist William Julius Wilson prominently featured the scourge of crime and family disorganization among poor blacks in *The Truly Disadvantaged: The Inner City, the Underclass, and Public Policy* (1987), but he subordinated those issues to the economics of unemployment. As we have seen, his first major book, *The Declining Significance of Race* (1978), irked readers for underestimating racism. *The Truly Disadvantaged* also underplayed racial discrimination, but it was more reader-friendly and included a program.[69]

The Truly Disadvantaged was not only an alternative to Murray and Mead but a critique of 1960s liberalism. Wilson argued that planners of the War on Poverty had been foolish to focus on the deficiencies of the poor rather than defects in the socioeconomic structure. When both civil rights laws and government training programs failed to reverse the catastrophic decline of America's ghettos, liberals were at sea. This failure of liberalism was one reason that conservatives were winning the policy debate. Another, Wilson claimed, was that because of the flap over the Moynihan report, liberals, fearful of being called racists, avoided research on the social pathologies of the black urban underclass.[70] But there was liberal research on ghetto dysfunctions. What was lacking was a big book about social and economic problems in and outside the ghetto linked to a compelling economic program and political strategy. Was *The Truly Disadvantaged* that book?

Wilson was most concerned about high black male unemployment as a cause of female-headed families. Although Wilson identified himself as a social democratic proponent of an expanded welfare state and his emphasis on government action for full employment and training programs placed him on the left, his preference for a father-centered family looked conservative. There were good arguments that a two-parent family was an easier way to raise children, but short of police-state action to maintain marriages, millions of children would continue to be raised outside such families. Why not deal with the economic problem, for example, of low pay for women workers? Why not support policies that "enable people to sustain whatever sorts of living arrangements they find most congenial?"[71]

Although he used underclass rhetoric, Wilson rejected the idea that people were trapped in the underclass by a culture that perpetuated itself regardless of job prospects. While he included much about crime and broken families, he connected them not to welfare but to joblessness. In fact, *The Truly Disadvantaged* was loaded with graphs and tables on the declining ratio of employed marriageable black men to black women. Joblessness was rising, and the ratio was falling; the result was more female-headed families and more social disorganization.[72]

At times Wilson implied that fixing unemployment might not be so hard, but even if people wanted job programs—and opinion surveys showed some support—could the party, media, and money system that was American politics deliver?[73] A majority had supported the Humphrey-Hawkins full employment bill, but that was gutted. A majority favored Carter's plan to add jobs and income to the welfare system, and that never even reached a vote in Congress. What were the political prospects for more jobs?[74]

The Truly Disadvantaged was more readable than *The Declining Significance of Race*; it was clear about solutions. It was more focused than Harrington's *The New American Poverty*, in part because Wilson studied one group of poor people, urban blacks. It probably underestimated the continuing force of racism,[75] but *The Truly Disadvantaged* was a strong answer to the right wing's preoccupation with bad government programs and bad values. It could have been more popular in language and organization, but it had a big-picture focus on unemployment that fit important facts and tapped into the vaunted American work ethic.

Moynihan, Moyers, and Other Liberals (1986–1988): The Contagion of Conservative Ideas

Harrington and Wilson did not win the public debate; the latter half of the 1980s saw a flood of regressive opinions in the media about poor people. Those opinions can be summed up briefly: the poverty question is not about people with inadequate income, it is not about stingy government compensators for market failures, and it is not about the economic system's generation of poverty and unemployment. It is about crime, drugs, liberal permissiveness, welfare dependence, and black people with bad attitudes.

There was no active demand from the populace to end welfare, but it appeared that way from right-wing publications. A team of twenty authors working for the conservative American Enterprise Institute stretched the truth when they called their collection *The New Consensus on Family and Welfare: A Community of Self-Reliance* (1987), and it was dishonest to claim that they represented "a broad spectrum of philosophies"; most were right-wingers like Murray and Mead.[76] But these authors were on to something; more nonconservatives were focusing on fixing welfare rather than ending poverty.

The New Consensus authors claimed that the welfare state and liberal permissiveness encouraged bad behavior, which in turn caused poverty and underclass dysfunctions. They ignored capitalism, which was always missing from the conservative list of institutions that encouraged self-indulgence and eroded community feelings. Terms like "deindustrialization," "unemployment," and "multinational corporations" never appeared.[77] *The New Consensus* writers alleged that people in high-poverty areas were "unusually resistant to economic growth." They claimed that family breakups and out-of-wedlock births caused poverty, but they admitted that half of poor white children lived with both parents, a fact that raised doubt about the conservative precept that broken families caused poverty.[78] *The New Consensus* authors admitted that the behaviorally damaged "portion of the poverty population is not large, compared with the total number of the poor." Why, then, focus on a tiny minority? A charitable explanation is that conservatives wanted to help the neediest. More likely, the worst cases could be linked to moral failings, and that connection fit the conservative propaganda model.[79]

Liberalism survived in public opinion, but conservative views, like those in *The New Consensus*, were spreading rapidly. From a search of three major newspapers and three national news magazines, sociologist Herbert Gans discovered that items on the underclass had multiplied from a handful in the mid-1970s to more than one hundred by the late 1980s. Not every piece emphasized poor people's bad values, but underclass stories spread in the 80s, and they often emphasized that the poor themselves, not economic factors, caused poverty.[80]

An indication of the growing power of right-wing paradigms was the way that some liberals agreed that a criminal and socially deviant black underclass was the problem to focus on. One example was Wilson's *The Truly Disadvantaged*, which accepted conservative rhetoric, even if for liberal goals.[81] Another instance was Pete Hamill's "America's Black Underclass: Can It Be Saved?" Hamill, a well-known New York journalist who described himself as "a man of the Left," equated the entire population of 9 million poor blacks with an underclass trapped by drugs, alcohol, disease, dependency, and crime. This underclass was "the single most dangerous fact of ordinary life in the United States."[82] This was a wild generalization. It showed how liberalism had slipped to the right.

Another example was Daniel Moynihan. Once champion of Nixon's guaranteed income, the senator offered little support in the late 70s for Carter's version of the same.[83] In the Godkin Lectures of 1985, *Family and Nation* (first published in 1986), Moynihan argued for government policies to support the two-parent family. The federal government should expand its efforts to chase down delinquent fathers; it should raise income tax exemptions so that people weren't being taxed into poverty.[84] These were, arguably, positive reforms, but

CONSERVATIVE ASSUMPTIONS ON POVERTY, WELFARE, AND ECONOMICS IN THE 70S AND 80S

1. Business is good (except for the liberal media), business leaders are good, and markets are efficient. (Missing is the view of older conservatisms that business and modern technology are disruptive of tradition and community.)

2. Economic classes, no; cultural class conflict, yes. Everyone can rise, and there is no conflict between capitalists and workers. There is a conflict between good Americans and the liberal media elite. (Conservative attacks on the liberal elite give conservatism a populist tinge.)

3. Unemployment is a choice. Everyone can find a job. However, many conservative economists (and some liberals, too) believe that monetary authorities must take action to keep unemployment high in order to fight wage and price inflation.

4. Labor markets work smoothly and without discrimination. Unless unions and governments interfere, people are paid what they are worth. (Many mainstream economists agree with this.)

5A. Poverty is often a choice. Neither capitalism nor discrimination causes poverty. Get a job, marry, and stay married; that will pull you out of poverty. The working poor are on the way to a better life.

5B. Variant. There is market-caused poverty, but government programs have solved it by giving people money. Unfortunately, these programs do not build strong families. The latter are more important than curing material poverty.

5C. Variant. The poor are not inherently bad, but they lack middle-class values. Generous government programs encourage bad values. Tough love, in the form of limiting welfare access and harsh work requirements, can build proper values about work and family.

6. Liberal government interferes with choice, hard work, investment, and innovation. Taxes are bad because they take from people what is rightfully theirs. (In this respect conservatives are extreme individualists, lacking a sense of a community of interests, incomes, and resources. They assume that every person has earned every dollar he or she possesses.)

7. Welfare programs for the poor split families, undermine men's

authority, and erode the will to work. (That generous European social programs are associated with less social dysfunction is ignored.)

8. The traditional male-headed family is best. It's what God and nature intended. Father-absent families cause juvenile delinquency, higher school dropout rates, and poverty. However, governments should not assure even the male head an adequate family wage because that interferes with market efficiencies and business needs. Anyway, markets pay people what they are worth.

they barely scratched the surface of an economy that left a fourth of its population poor and nearly poor. But the economy was absent from Moynihan's lectures. Moynihan had become convinced that welfare caused family breakup and broken families caused economic failure.[85]

Perhaps he was right, but as Moynihan remarked of Murray's proofs, "How do we know? Causality in the social sciences is elusive."[86] Most telling about Moynihan's move to the right was that he said little about labor markets. Moynihan's *The Negro Family* (1965), for all its flaws, paid attention to unemployment as a cause of poverty and social disorganization. Twenty years later, unemployment had all but disappeared.[87] Why not create good jobs? In the midst of the Reagan recovery in 1985, real unemployment was still more than 10%; the 80s had the worst economy for low-wage workers since the Great Depression.[88] But Moynihan had drifted too far to the right to speak for the unemployed poor. He was lining up for welfare reform, and that could mean shoving people into low-wage labor markets.

Another well-known liberal who seemed to surrender to conservative ideas was Bill Moyers. Moyers had served as deputy director of the Peace Corps, as President Johnson's special assistant for Great Society legislation (1963–65), and then as presidential press secretary (1965–67). He grew disillusioned about Vietnam and departed in 1967. Still a young man, he turned *Newsday* into an award-winning newspaper. Later his work with Public Television and CBS brought accolades for *Bill Moyers' Journal* and *Joseph Campbell and the Power of Myth*.[89]

In a 1982 CBS report, *People like Us*, Moyers attacked Reagan for program cuts that harmed helpless Americans, but in 1986 Moyers presented a CBS documentary on the black underclass, *The Vanishing Family: Crisis in Black America*. It was a study of welfare culture and unmarried families in Newark.

Some of Moyers's subjects looked wildly irresponsible. A central character named Tim validated his manhood by impregnating women while he lived off their welfare checks. He and his girlfriends seemed proof that welfare was a social disaster.

But Moyers said little about causes—for example, the seepage of good jobs from urban ghettos. And he said nothing about poor whites or about class. There was no acknowledgment that welfare mothers were having fewer children or that many welfare families left the rolls quickly. Moyers could have questioned whether Tim was typical of poor blacks. And it was possible to study the impact of harsh economic change, especially the deindustrialization of the rust belt, on black and white poor and working-class families. Documentaries that did so, such as *The Business of America* (1984), did not receive as much attention as Moyers's presentation.[90]

Men like Tim were real, and a rising proportion of black children were reported to be fatherless. And it was true that African American teens had high pregnancy rates. But why? Other rich nations offered more government benefits, and their teens had lower pregnancy rates. Even in America birth rates among black and white teens were falling, not rising. School achievement may have been rising, too. Drug use by nonpoor whites involved many more people than drug use by minority poor. The point is not that black leaders should not have preached responsible behavior—Jesse Jackson was doing it—but rather that the viewer needed to see how racism and economic crisis restricted people's choices.[91]

Moyers's irresponsible characters did exist, but not in a vacuum, without economic and social context and causation. Without the bigger picture, *Vanishing Family* scapegoated black poor people and government programs. In effect, Moyers was supplying ammunition to conservatives like Murray and Gilder who wanted to tear down the welfare state.[92]

Few Americans knew *The Business of America* (1984), a documentary about the shutdown of the Homestead, Pennsylvania, steel mill, and the lines at the food bank of once highly paid steel workers, black and white. Many people understood parts of what was happening to the economy, but they lacked stories to connect the dots of plant shutdowns, conservative attacks on minority poor, and business power.

Although liberal organizations and Democrats limited Reagan's attack on social programs, conservatives had many victories in the 80s: not one increase in the federal minimum wage between New Year's 1981 and April 1990; a fall in the purchasing power of welfare benefits; no comprehensive health care program while the numbers of uninsured climbed; the demonization of unions as wages fell; and the passage of the Family Support Act of 1988, to push people off welfare without lifting wages.

Although conservatives were able to keep the focus on welfare and crime,[93] areas in which people had conservative inclinations, public opinion remained liberal in many areas. It is true that a majority of people surveyed, beginning in the late 70s, wanted tax cuts, were losing confidence in government, and opposed special programs for blacks and "welfare." But the public also wanted to preserve most social welfare programs; supported Social Security, Medicare, and Supplemental Security Income; and was willing to be taxed more to help poor people. In 1976–78, business and conservative lobbies mauled the Humphrey-Hawkins jobs bill, but 70% of the people agreed that government should guarantee that every person who wanted to work had a job. Those who thought we were spending too much on welfare reached 60% in 1976–80, but the percentage fell to the low 40s for most of the Reagan years (1982–88). In the mid-1980s, 65% of people surveyed were satisfied paying taxes to support welfare for the poor. Those who thought we were spending too much on the poor fell to 7% in 1988.[94] Thomas Ferguson and Joel Rogers concluded that there was "no right turn in public opinion corresponding to the right turn in public policy." On six of seven major social programs, Congress was more conservative than the public.[95] Conservatives framed public debate without transforming public opinion.

I have tried to show that conservative success was not due to superior research and argumentation. The works of Anderson, Gilder, Mead, and Murray were flawed. Each author assumed that jobs were plentiful, that jobs cured poverty, and that government programs discouraged work. None examined the labor glut of the 1970s, the work effort of poor people, or the middle-class values of people on welfare. None admitted that generous European programs did not precipitate the bad consequences they found in the United States. Most of all, conservatives were never forthright about the way capitalism undermined communities and families. Yet if conservative intellectual work was not more scholarly, more balanced, or more truthful than liberal thought, it was more focused; it was armed for battle; it was more accessible to wider audiences than liberal work; and it touched hot buttons on individual responsibility and race.[96]

Conservatives blasted the media for liberal bias, and the media moved to the right. In any case, network anchors and national journalists may have been liberal on issues like abortion, but on taxes, trade, and Social Security, they were more conservative than the general public. Lavishly paid, they ignored the widening gap between the affluent and poor. Perhaps too, left-wing messages —for example, that poverty caused street crime—did not play on television as well as the picture of a black or Latino crime suspect; certainly the media devoted more attention to minority street crime than to white-collar crime by white people.[97]

Conservatives overcame their greatest handicap, obedience to business interests; their tax program was Robin Hood in reverse: take from the poor and working class and give to the rich. Meanwhile, although they fought Reagan, liberal Democrats did not usually offer a forthright critique of capitalism or a unifying populist message that blended work and welfare, family and freedom. Segments of the party once had a class perspective, defending the people against the rich and corporations, but there was not much of that left.

Why weren't liberals more effective? Race, a changing political base, and liberal ambiguity about capitalism were important reasons. Race certainly was a factor, but it was not insurmountable. William Wilson and Thomas and Mary Edsall claim that liberal intellectuals lost debates and Democrats lost elections because, fearing to be labeled racist, they were "reluctant to discuss openly or, in some instances, even to acknowledge the sharp increase in social pathologies in ghetto communities." Certainly, Democratic support of civil rights sent whites to the Republican Party. But there were liberal books and speeches on the association between race and poverty, crime, and female-headed families.[98] What was missing was not more emphasis on ghetto crime but liberal explanations and solutions conveyed with feeling and imagination. The facts were there. As corporations deserted their communities, the image of the big bad capitalist could play as well as the minority drug dealer. There were economic stories that explained crime, unemployment, poverty, and the corporate destruction of 3 million manufacturing jobs over 1980–82. And there were ways to create good jobs.[99] But the economic crises of the 70s and 80s were not severe enough to create a 30s-like radicalization of the Democratic Party and liberalism. Unions declined, and so did their public influence. More Democrats took corporate money and were less willing to criticize business.

Finally, most liberals were at heart middle-of-the roaders, in favor of capitalism but also in favor of social reform and business regulation. That was not enough to end poverty and unemployment; nor was it a fighting credo for troubled times. Conservative publicists and intellectuals pushed boldly for markets free of regulation and welfare programs. Liberals did not provide much of a counterstory of "how markets suffer from imperfections that can prevent the creation of public goods," including the end of poverty. In part that was because the experts, liberal as well as conservative economists, had blind faith in competitive markets. But there was also an imbalance in the political agenda of the foundations. While conservative foundations and think tanks subsidized extreme scholarship attacking liberalism and government, there were no equally "affluent liberal foundations devoted to propagating the idea that poverty is mainly the fault of the economy." The Rockefeller Foundation, once thought to be part of the liberal establishment, funded research about the underclass, but it did not intentionally fund studies showing that capitalism itself caused poverty. Often debate ranged between far right positions supported by the Heritage, Olin, and Scaife foundations and fuzzy centrist positions supported by the Rockefeller and Ford foundations.[100]

The liberal confusion was profound. Economic growth in the 50s and 60s allowed liberal reform without threatening much the power of big business and the rich. Liberalism had aimed to grow the economy and humanize it. Growth gave poor people jobs and income, without taking from the rich. But in the 70s, growth slowed, and capitalist success seemed to require mass layoffs. Liberal axioms were crumbling. It was hard to promise workers legislation against plant closings and capitalists a free market to do what they wanted with capital. To escape confusion, liberals could move to the right and praise free markets (neoliberalism) or to the left and admit that free markets generated poverty and unemployment and required an expanded welfare state and progressive taxes for social justice. Many wavered.[101]

A new radical liberalism was possible. Parts of it were already in place (Social Security, Supplemental Security Income, Medicare), but an appealing morality tale of government that nourished a secure and cooperative populace was not. A not too radical departure might have looked like this. Capitalist markets excel at developing products and improving production, but they are prone to recession, and, without government compensations, they accentuate inequalities, generate unemployment and poverty, and fail to provide vital goods at reasonable costs (housing, health care, clean air). Markets make life risky for millions, and through the business usurpation of ever more domestic functions (recreation, food preparation) they erode local sources of creativity and community. A just society requires a large social support state like the ones in Western Europe. Its achievement would be a moral victory, charity writ large, as people taxed themselves and the rich to assure that no one was poor and all had a chance at a decent job.[102]

Liberal politicians and intellectuals were not doing much to create this kind of narrative. While people supported the welfare state, their support was sometimes thin, not only for welfare itself but for food stamps and even unemployment insurance. Piven and Cloward claimed that there had been a transformation of popular understanding, a new "moral economy of the welfare state," but if a new value system existed, it was selective, and people were easily swayed by conservative claims.[103]

The Left needed to publicize big-picture economic explanations of unem-

ployment, poverty, and inequality. It needed to preach the idea that government could embody communal values, neighborhood aid on a national scale. It
had to teach, as Piven and Cloward taught, that government income supports
not only paid the bills in hard times but empowered the economic majority by
giving people alternatives to taking the first available job.

chapter nine

REAGAN, REAGANOMICS,
AND THE AMERICAN POOR,
1980–1992

When Ronald Reagan took office as president in January 1981, Americans had been living with economic crises for a decade. They had endured high food prices and long lines for expensive gas. Unemployment and poverty were on the rise, and wages had been sinking for eight years. Meanwhile, some white people were fed up with what they saw as special privileges for black Americans; others, like George Gilder, hoped to restore male-dominated families by cutting welfare. It looked like a good time for conservatives.

Conservative ideas would get a boost, but they would also face a trial. The Reaganites planned nothing less than the reversal of five decades of liberalism. In the 1930s, Americans had built the foundations of the liberal welfare state. Unemployment rates of 25% and mass movements convinced politicians that private markets had failed and that government action was necessary to protect the unemployed, the poor, and the aged; to nurture unions; and to end the depression. On these foundations liberals like Lyndon Johnson and pragmatists like Richard Nixon added civil rights laws, environmental regulations, and more income supports. Their actions assumed that private markets were imperfect and that government action was necessary for justice and efficiency.

Conservatives like Reagan, on the other hand, assumed that in domestic matters government was guilty until proven innocent. Government regulation raised the cost of doing business; income programs encouraged people to avoid work. High taxation cut investment and profits and caused people to work less. Complete laissez-faire was impossible, but extremely limited government intervention on welfare issues, such as we had in the 1920s, would promote investment and profits and reduce poverty and inflation. This conservative credo was essentially social Darwinism. The competitive struggle for survival advanced economic goals, and the survival of the fittest rewarded the talented. Or so the theory went. How much it would be implemented under Reagan and whether it would work out for most Americans remained to be seen.

An Actor and His Image

Who was the man who led this radical attack on five decades of liberalism? Born in Tampico, Illinois, in 1911, Reagan had a rough childhood, but in 1937 he made a screen test that led to a contract with Warner Brothers. Reagan appeared in numerous films in the 40s, including memorable pictures like *Kings Row* (1942) and *Knute Rockne—All American* (1940). As his movie career faded in the 50s, he turned to television. He was also a union activist in the Screen Actors Guild, which he served as president (1947–52, 1959). As the Cold War turned icier, the once liberal Reagan moved to the right, out of anticommunism and self-interest. He was angry about the progressive income tax, which, he claimed, meant that it did not pay for him to make more than four movies a year.[1]

Reagan helped to run the Hollywood blacklist and worked as an informant for the FBI. By 1954 he was hosting General Electric's drama series on television and lecturing around the country against communism, government regulation, and Social Security. Later he won two terms as governor of California (1967–75). At every opportunity he assailed young radicals, welfare, and the War on Poverty; but a pragmatic conservative, he allowed state spending to double, signed a liberal abortion bill, and worked with the legislature to add higher benefits as well as work requirements to welfare.[2]

In 1980, President Carter's failure to solve stagflation and his inability to rescue seventy-one hostages from Iranian militants gave Reagan a huge victory in the electoral college (489 to 49). Most alarming to labor leaders, Reagan won more than half of all white union members and their families. Republicans took control of the Senate for the first time in three decades. Democrats were at sea. Some concluded not that they needed a better economic program but that Reagan was the future and "they had better get on board." Although the election was more a vote against Carter than a vote for conservatism, the Reaganites "pretended [they] had a mandate that was very much larger than it was." Congressional Democrats "lost the power to set the national political agenda."[3]

President Reagan branded the Soviet Union the evil empire and won huge increases in military spending, but he learned to work with Mikhail Gorbachev to end the Cold War. He allowed his aides to violate congressional prohibitions on aid to the anticommunist contras in Nicaragua. When this and information about trading missiles for hostages with Iran broke in 1986, Reagan claimed that he could not remember.

Reagan filled people's hunger for a successful president. Colorado representative Pat Schroeder dubbed him the Teflon president because nothing bad stuck to him. Bill Moyers remarked that Americans did not elect "this guy because he knows how many barrels of oil are in Alaska. We elected him because we want to feel good." People opposed Reagan's economic policies, but they yearned for a strong president, after four failures in a row.[4] Americans knew that Reagan favored the rich, but they still liked him. Although Democrats gained seats in the Senate and held on to the House in 1984, Reagan captured forty-nine of fifty states.[5]

Part of Reagan's success was a matter of public relations, as was some of the conservative revolution. Reagan cut federal aid to education, and the public opposed him, but he spoke for excellence in education, and public opinion turned in his favor. Reporter Leslie Stahl of CBS did a feature contrasting Reagan's effort to cut federal aid to the handicapped with his attendance at the Handicapped Olympics. Reagan's advisers liked the piece. Haven't you figured out, they asked Stahl, "the picture always overrides what you say?" Although some reporters criticized social program cuts, especially during the depression of 1981–82, voters liked the good Reagan, and reporters usually went along.[6]

It was not all image. The affluent class and business conservatives favored Reagan because he promised them more money and more control over employees. Social Darwinists and economic conservatives had high hopes. Men fed up with feminism, whites resentful of minorities, and people who hated welfare expected that Reagan would do something for them.[7]

Reaganomics: The General Program

Prices jumped 28% between December 1978 and December 1980. Corporate profits had been weak for years, the nation's share of world trade was slipping, and twice in the 70s oil producers restricted production and threatened access to cheap energy.

There were other problems. Economists worried about sluggish productivity growth. Business lobbyists complained of a capital shortage and promised that lower business taxes would fuel investment in new technology; that would improve productivity and tame prices. A Democratic-controlled Congress lowered corporate taxes in 1978, but business wanted more.[8]

High inflation was sparked by Vietnam War spending and energy problems, but Paul Volcker at the Federal Reserve decided that it should be reversed by raising unemployment, in order to check wage growth and consumption demand. During Carter's last years, Volcker drove up interest rates—the prime rate hit 20%—"to create a deep recession, to break inflation, and with it, to crush the last traces of labor militancy."[9]

In this season of gloom, Reagan arrived with a positive message: freedom from government and taxation. The Reaganites proposed to cut government regulations and social programs; they promised "supply-side" tax cuts to modernize business and cut prices. More quietly, they urged that the Federal Reserve restrict money supply growth; that meant more of what it was doing. Some Reaganites believed that tax cuts would boost the economy even while Volcker was restricting the amount of money in circulation. They claimed—and some of them believed—that inflation could be solved without raising unemployment and that a credit crunch would not increase joblessness. It sounded like magic. Before joining the ticket, George Bush called it "voodoo economics."[10] But it was just a conservative delusion, one part Gilder, one part Milton Friedman.

The Truth about Supply-Side Economics

The tax-cut campaign had been building in the 70s. In 1980 the *Wall Street Journal's* Jude Wanniski, economist Arthur Laffer, and Republican representative Jack Kemp converted Reagan. The supply-siders maintained that if tax rates were cut, people would work more because they got to keep more of their earnings and business would have more money for cost-cutting technology and job creation. In fact, there was no evidence that taxes were stopping people from working and investing, but tax cuts were conservative dogma, and they appealed to voters.

Tax cuts to stimulate the economy were nothing new, but the public relations effort behind the Reagan tax program displayed novelties. There was Laffer's claim that if the United States lowered tax rates, government would collect more money because there would be more economic activity.[11] Also, supply-siders insisted that while Democratic tax cuts boosted consumption demand, Republicans would fix production. Along with tax cuts for business, the supply-siders believed that cutting personal income tax rates on the rich was key to building savings for investment. But to sell the program everyone had to get a little cut. Budget director David Stockman called the whole tax package a Trojan horse to get tax cuts for the wealthy. As it turned out, those who paid marginal rates of 51%–70% on the highest portion of their unearned income received an immediate cut to 50%; general income tax rates would be lowered by 5%, 10%, and 10% over three years. The lower half of the population would receive 16% of the dollar savings and the top half 84%.[12]

Supply-siders promised that benefits would trickle down, but there was no guarantee that savings would not flow to foreign investment, job-cutting mergers, or the purchase of old master paintings. As it turned out, there was nothing supply-side about recovery from the depression of 1981–82; it was led by government and consumer demand. The savings rate did not improve over the 80s, and real investment showed no effects of an enlarged pool of savings. But after-tax profits jumped. They were declining at 1.3% a year in the 70s (1973–80); now they grew by 12.2% a year (1980–86). Along with the tax cuts, business lobbyists won investment credits and the option to sell unused tax breaks. In this area, Democrats vied with Republicans to please the lobbyists. Stockman recalled: "The hogs were really feeding. The greed level . . . just got out of control."[13] The tax cuts meant that businesses and prosperous individuals kept more of their money, but whether that repaired economic fundamentals remained to be seen.

While tax breaks made business more profitable, the combination of huge tax cuts and massive increases in military spending meant that the deficit gap between federal revenues and federal spending widened. Reagan promised to eliminate deficits by 1984, but they surged to $200 billion a year. Wall Street was worried that government borrowing for the deficits would drive up interest rates. In 1982, Congress repealed some of the more outrageous tax breaks of the previous year and raised taxes on gas, cigarettes, air travel, and phone calls.[14]

In the 30s, Keynes had urged deficit spending to solve the depression; that is what finally happened during World War II, and deficit spending was promoting economic recovery by 1983. Government disbursed hundreds of billions of dollars it had not removed from taxpayers' pockets. But many conservatives claimed to hate deficits, and they defined themselves against Keynes, whom they associated with liberalism. So they were not frank about the Keynesian sources of the Reagan recovery. Reagan attacked the deficits, which he caused and which were rescuing the nation from the worst depression since the 30s. It was surreal. And meanwhile, some conservatives discovered that big deficits were a marvelous excuse for cutting social programs and refusing new ones.[15]

Direct Attack: Making More Unemployment and Making It Hurt More

The depression of 1981–82 made millions jobless and was the government's main weapon against inflation. But a second part of the campaign was also important. Cuts in food stamps, disability insurance, unemployment in-surance, and other support programs flowed from many motives including antigovernment dogma, but also from the view that unemployment had to be more painful if people were to be driven to accept low-wage jobs. The idea that more unemployment would cut wages and thereby solve inflation was traditional textbook economics. The notion that social programs should be cut to make unemployment harder to endure was a new emphasis.

The crises of the 70s and anemic profit rates had left some economists and business leaders ready to support recession. *Fortune* magazine argued that higher unemployment would be necessary to cut wages and inflation. Former Federal Reserve chair Arthur Burns judged that recession might be the best way to restore profit rates. In 1976 Reagan asserted that we had not been able to reduce government debt and inflation because "no politician can stand up to an increase in unemployment"; if high unemployment became necessary to stop inflation, Reagan was confident that Americans would "be able to bear the burden."[16]

Not much of this was heard in the 1980 campaign or the first months of the Reagan presidency. Reagan, Stockman, and the supply-siders hoped that cuts in taxes, regulations, and social programs would encourage an economic boom without monetary growth and inflation; they thought that "the monetary brakes [could] be applied without affecting real economic growth." When Beryl Sprinkel in the Treasury Department mentioned that cutting money growth might cut economic growth, Stockman turned a deaf ear. Supply-siders stayed a while longer in their fantasy world.[17]

But by the last quarter of 1982, the unemployment rate reached 10.7%; it was 20% for black workers. About 25% of the labor force experienced a bout of unemployment that year; that was the closest we ever came to the depression of the 30s.[18] Because inflation rates were high and the Reagan tax cuts might cause big deficits that fueled inflation, Volcker thought he had to create a giant recession to curb wage and price increases. Even before Reaganomics Volcker had been clear that "the standard of living of the average American has to decline," and his main strategy was to cut wage increases. He kept a little card in his pocket with the latest union wage settlements; he was using unemployment to cripple the unions.[19]

Once the slump was under way and supply-side delusions evaporated, Presi-dent Reagan supported recession. In December 1981, he admitted that high unemployment was tragic, but his press secretary, Larry Speakes, told reporters: "This is the price you have to pay for bringing down inflation." In private meetings, Reagan never once urged Volcker to let up. Although Reagan had promised voters less unemployment, he now supported more. He had never

JOB SEEKERS FAR OUTNUMBER JOB VACANCIES

Conservatives all but denied the reality of unemployment. Reagan pointed to the want ads to prove that anyone could get a job. But many serious studies comparing job seekers and job openings led researchers to these conclusions: there were more unemployed than vacancies; most jobs filled rapidly; and poor people were excluded from many of the jobs offered by lack of training, experience, and other factors. Professor Katherine Abraham estimated that in the 70s the unemployment rate was four or five times the job vacancy rate.

Sources: John Pease and Lee Martin, "Want Ads and Jobs for the Poor: A Glaring Mismatch," *Sociological Forum* 12 (December 1997): 545–64; Katherine G. Abraham, "Structural/Frictional vs. Deficient Demand Unemployment: Some New Evidence," *American Economic Review* 73 (September 1983): 708–24; Herbert E. Meyer, "Jobs and Want Ads: A Look behind the Words," *Fortune*, November 20, 1978, 88–90, 94, 96.

taken unemployment very seriously, and now he had a story to make him feel good: the nation had been on a binge for thirty years; recession was the painful process of sobering up. In the spring of 1982, Stockman told the U.S. Chamber of Commerce that bankruptcies and high unemployment were "all part of the cure, not the problem." Economic adviser Martin Feldstein said that recession was the way to get inflation down, and it might take five or six years to reduce unemployment to 6%, which he considered full employment.[20]

No one in the administration proposed more assistance to help the jobless get through the recession. Just the opposite. Reagan worked to cut unemployment benefits and eligibility. In 1980, 50% of the unemployed received benefits; in 1988, only 32%. Stockman convinced Congress not to provide health benefits for the unemployed, and Reagan got Congress to cut to 29,000 (from 532,000 in 1980) the number of people getting aid because their jobs were lost to imports. To add insult to injury, while denouncing taxation, Reagan proposed on Thanksgiving Day, 1982, to tax unemployment benefits. This was one of Feldstein's weapons to force the unemployed back to work. It looked mean and was put on hold; but it later became law.[21]

Making unemployment more painful forced people back into the labor market and dampened wage growth. Employers liked that. Perhaps that is why in 1983 and 1984 a majority of executives thought the president's program was working and should continue even if it brought more unemployment and more bankruptcies.[22] Employers also liked another effort to make employees more insecure. In August 1981 Reagan fired air traffic controllers. They were striking in violation of federal labor law, but the real point of the firing was not the legal issue but an example of toughness against unions and for striker replacement.

Unemployment, too, was doing antiunion work; union (and often Democratic) strongholds in steel and auto were pummeled by imports.[23] Even in the mid-80s recovery, union contracts called for annual wage increases of only 1% or 2%. The Reaganites had no reindustrialization policy; they let depression, high energy prices, and imports destroy high-wage blue-collar jobs. Union membership fell from 23.2% of the labor force in 1980 to 17% in 1988.[24]

Additionally, the administration added 400,000 public service workers to the jobless pool. In 1978–79, the Comprehensive Employment and Training Act (CETA) had been providing 750,000 federally subsidized government jobs to the poor and unemployed. That number was halved by Carter, and Reagan's first budget eliminated the program. That meant more people looking for work and more downward pressure on pay levels.[25]

Business leaders and their lobbying groups opposed adequate unemployment insurance and government job programs. They were in tune with the administration and conservative ideologues. Reagan's favorite author, George Gilder, argued that government job programs robbed the poor of the essential insight that they simply had to work harder. Business organizations sought to limit workers' alternatives to accepting a job, no matter the conditions or pay, by eliminating government jobs and income programs. Yet as unemployment surged to the highest level since the 30s, conservatives and business leaders worried about looking callous. Pushed by Indiana senator Dan Quayle, Congress and the administration supported the Job Partnership Training Act, a poorly funded, business-controlled program. It was not a plan to solve joblessness but a public relations effort.[26]

Overall, the Reagan-Volcker program was a mixture of realism, fantasy, and deception. There were disagreements among conservatives on deficits and monetary growth. But in its broad outcomes, the Reagan-Volcker program amounted to a unified campaign, a class war to solve inflation and low profits at the expense of poor and working-class Americans. In the long run, if the trickle down created a powerful river of high-wage jobs, the conservative campaign might seem ethical. But the strategies employed by Volcker, the Reaganauts, and business leaders, along with big economic events, were restructuring labor markets for the long term toward less job security and weaker employee bargaining power.

Drastic Action on the Disabled

Social Security Disability Insurance paid $15.4 billion to about 4 million disabled Americans in the late 70s. The disability rolls had ballooned as eligibility standards were loosened and unemployment rates rose. In 1980, Congress authorized the Social Security Administration to begin regular reviews of eligibility, and the Reagan administration, philosophically committed to cut social programs, took up the cause with a vengeance. Initially, 500,000 people were dropped from the program, but the effort turned into a public relations disaster. Severely handicapped people were being pushed off the rolls; several people committed suicide, and others succumbed to heart attacks. The facts were bad enough, but politicians and the press helped things along, accentuating the negative. Various levels of review including the federal courts resisted Social Security Administration decisions, and Congress voted unanimously to limit the Reagan administration's effort to force the disabled back to work. But thousands of people thrown off stayed off, and entry was made more difficult. The number of beneficiaries had been cut and did not again reach the 1977–80 level until 1989.[27]

Fixing Social Security

The political weight of Social Security recipients was large and focused, and that made it difficult for conservatives to eliminate Social Security. Thirty-six million households received old age and survivors' benefits every month from one agency. Meanwhile Social Security helped to cut the poverty rate for the elderly to 16% in 1980; it might have been 50% without the program.[28]

Extreme conservatives were always looking to cut Social Security, and they thought they had a chance in the early 80s. Social Security faced a short-term funding problem. Benefit increases and inflation indexing in the 70s raised spending as inflation soared; high unemployment cut revenues. The perception of crisis might, Stockman said, "permit the politicians to make it look like they're doing something *for* the beneficiary population when they're doing something *to* it which they normally wouldn't have the courage to undertake."[29]

At the same time, Stockman had a giant budget problem; contrary to Laffer's prediction, the Reagan tax cuts would not stimulate enough growth to raise sufficient revenues to offset the deficits created by the cuts. Federal debt would soar, and conservatism would look bad. Since Social Security was part of the federal budget, one way to cut deficits was to cut Social Security expenditures. And aside from the deficit crisis, cutting a social program appealed to the conservatives in the White House.

Stockman and Reagan first tried to trim early retirement benefits, but that created a political firestorm, and the Senate turned them down 96 to 0. Then Stockman tried to sneak into the budget a cut in general benefits, but the Democratic Speaker of the House, Tip O'Neill, led the fight to stop that. As public opinion swung sharply against Reagan on Social Security, the president appointed an independent commission to fix the program. Chaired by conservative economist Alan Greenspan and including Republican senator Robert Dole and Democrat Daniel Moynihan and former Social Security head Robert Ball, the commission had trouble finding a workable compromise. But a secret group of nine (five commissioners including Ball and Moynihan and four presidential advisers including Stockman) worked out a deal. The compromise of 1983 increased taxes on the self-employed, sped up previously legislated payroll tax increases, delayed cost-of-living adjustments for six months, required new federal employees to enter the system, and, in a provision added by Congress, set the normal retirement age to rise to 67. A low-income retiree in 2030 would get only 51% of his or her average earnings, while in 1985 the same worker would receive 64% of his or her average wage.[30]

The funding crisis was fixed; by 2006 the Social Security trust fund had trillions of dollars in reserves.[31] Perhaps more important, the principles of Social Security had been preserved under a conservative administration on a crusade to cut government social programs. The turnabout came to pass in part because liberals and the public hammered Reagan and Stockman in their first efforts to cut Social Security. The Republicans lost twenty-six House seats in the November 1982 elections; Senator Dole thought half of the losses were due to missteps on Social Security. A pragmatic conservative who cared more about defense spending and tax cuts than about eliminating Social Security, Reagan saw which way the parade was going and jumped on the bandwagon, even if he could not carry congressional right-wingers along. He was soon taking credit for the automatic cost-of-living raises that came to Social Security beneficiaries. The congressional bill that saved the system, Reagan said, "demonstrates for all time our nation's ironclad commitment to Social Security." Reagan reaffirmed "Roosevelt's commitment that Social Security must always provide a secure and stable base so that older Americans may live in dignity." Tip O'Neill, a caretaker of the Roosevelt legacy, could not have put it better. The nation's largest social program and one of its best antipoverty programs had "escaped the Reagan revolution largely unscathed." Because it had broad support, a very conservative administration had been forced to help save it.[32]

Welfare and Welfare Reform

The Reagan administration did not have a mandate to cut federal social programs, but there was one program that voters disliked almost as much as conservatives did: Aid to Families with Dependent Children (AFDC), popularly known as welfare. The number of families on welfare climbed 40% in the 70s, but since the size of welfare families shrank, the number of people on the rolls increased only by 10%, despite hard economic times. Still, 11 million people on welfare were far too many for some.[33]

Attacking women and children on welfare seemed easy at first. In the first budget, Reagan removed 500,000 families from the rolls, in part by eliminating provisions that allowed working recipients to retain partial benefits.[34] The states, which oversaw welfare, got stingier, so even as unemployment climbed and the number of poor jumped by 9 million (1979–83), the number on AFDC changed little. Meanwhile, a million children were dropped from school lunch programs. The number of food stamp recipients was cut by 5%. The administration engineered a 12% decline in the number of elderly and disabled people on Medicaid.[35] Reagan claimed that private charities could fill in, but the head of his own Task Force on Private Sector Initiatives, C. William Verity, admitted that "such a complete shift of responsibilities is out of the question. . . . The gap remains."[36]

There were still enough liberal Democrats to fight further cuts in social welfare programs, and they were often able to win moderates to their cause after the Volcker-Reagan recession worsened in the fall of 1981. Democrats increased their seats in the House by twenty-six in the 1982 election, and Congress was able to raise the gas tax for job creation and to pass a $4.9 billion public works program. In the mid-80s, Congress liberalized food stamp eligibility, and by the end of the Bush years, stamp expenditures were twice what they had been in the early 1980s. Reagan tried to cut nutritional subsidies to pregnant and lactating women and poor infants and children, but Congress increased spending for the programs.[37]

Despite Reagan's reelection victory in 1984, Democrats kept control of the House and gained in the Senate in 1984. But conservatives did not relax their drumbeat against aid to the poor. Murray's *Losing Ground* appeared in 1984. Anxieties about street crime and the underclass spread. In his 1986 State of the Union message, Reagan urged an end to welfare dependency.[38]

Many streams flowed into welfare reform. Voters did not like their taxes going to lazy people. Especially as millions of mothers went to work, it seemed unfair to pay some women to stay home. Also, as more women worked and more families splintered, there was interest in addressing child-care issues and

LABEL AND MEANING: WELFARE

Most Americans used the term "welfare" in a narrow, negative way: welfare did not include an array of government programs, from unemployment insurance and health care to Social Security and child-care programs, as it did in Western Europe. Rather, it was the name of bad programs for the undeserving poor. People in other affluent nations weren't as likely to distinguish between good and bad welfare. They usually had bigger welfare states and less poverty.

low rates of child support from absent fathers. In 1981, Reagan pushed mandatory workfare. Congress turned him down, but he won welfare cuts and more room for states to experiment with work programs. Governors formed a bipartisan reform commission headed by Mike Castle of Delaware and Bill Clinton of Arkansas. Some observers found a new consensus for workfare, but there were disagreements.[39] Conservative Republicans and Democrats wanted people off the rolls; they had no qualms about flooding the labor market and depressing wages; they had no problem compelling low-income mothers to leave their children for the workplace. Liberals wanted jobs, training, and child care, but some of them accepted the idea that welfare caused poverty.

At an opportune moment in 1987 the Manpower Demonstration Research Corporation reported that welfare-to-work experiments yielded more work and income. The governors were elated. No one cautioned that many of the women were still on welfare or still poor. The reform process of 1986–88 was not about truth; it was about cutting welfare, and the new research supported cuts. The Senate passed the Family Support Act of 1988 by a vote of 96 to 1, the House by 347 to 53. Reagan signed it in October.[40]

The Family Support Act looked like the first major reform of AFDC. But what had the reformers achieved? First, there were improvements in the collection of child-support payments and a requirement that women identify the fathers of their children as a condition of getting welfare. Second, in a victory for liberals, all states had to implement welfare for couple-headed families (AFDC–Unemployed Parent program [AFDC-UP]); the program had previously been optional. Third, the reform promised transitional programs: child care, education, and job search or training. Job Opportunities and Basic Skills Training, neatly summarized in the acronym JOBS, would let states design their own programs and provided an extra year of Medicaid and child care for families moving from welfare to work. Finally, the states were required to move people into jobs.[41]

Senator Moynihan thought that by the year 2000 the Family Support Act would be having a big impact, but in historian Michael Katz's phrase, the law was the "illusion of welfare reform." It did nothing to make welfare mothers less poor, and it did little to prepare women for jobs that would lift them out of poverty. Many states began training programs without allocating matching funds, and so they received no federal money. The welfare-to-work element of Family Support flopped.[42]

If welfare reform was a flop, people benefited a little more from quieter efforts to help the working poor. The Reaganites did not believe that government had "a responsibility to supplement the income of the working poor." While they talked a lot about the value of work, they refused to lend a helping hand. They allowed the after-inflation value of the Earned Income Tax Credit (EITC) for working poor families to fall, and they eliminated the incentive that allowed welfare recipients to keep without loss of benefits the first $30 and a third of the rest of their earnings each month.[43] But conservative Democrats and Republicans worried about the appearance of unfairness and went along with liberal efforts. In the 1986 Tax Reform Act, 6 million poor people were removed from the tax rolls, and the EITC was raised and indexed to inflation. Four years later, under President Bush, the EITC was expanded again. By 1990, the number of working poor families getting the EITC had jumped from 7 million in 1980 to 11.3 million, and EITC expenditures had tripled to $7 billion.[44]

What Wasn't Repaired in the Economy and What Was

In the early 80s, the economic majority was given a painful bloodletting. Volcker, Reagan, and stronger corporations were the surgeons. When it was over, the patients were supposed to be healthier, but as with the ancient cure of taking blood, the Reagan operation was a kind of quackery. Patients paid their bill, and the surgeons were better off, but the patients who lived came away with permanent disabilities.

Economic recovery began in 1983. Fearing financial collapse at home and abroad, Volcker made credit cheaper. Military spending increases kicked in. Meanwhile, inflation rates had fallen from 13.5% in 1980 to 3.2% in 1983. That was the biggest success of Reaganomics.[45] But it had little to do with supply-side theory and much to do with policies that hurt millions of Americans. Inflation rates fell for several reasons, but one of the most important was that the Volcker-Reagan recession shrank markets, forcing businesses to cut prices, and it shrank employment, forcing workers to cut wage demands.[46] An old-

Boiler plant built for Republic Steel in Youngstown, Ohio, in the early 1950s and destroyed by LTV Steel in 1989. (Photograph by Alexander Chytra; courtesy of Ohio Historical Society and Youngstown Historical Center of Industry and Labor)

fashioned depression and a high dollar that made imports cheap, not supply-side tax cuts, cut inflation rates.

Economic fundamentals were not mended. Confounding supply-side promises, personal and business savings rates fell to historic lows, and new business investment in plant and equipment per worker was the same in the early 80s as in the late 70s. There was no long-term improvement in productivity rates or economic growth rates.[47] Deficit financing promoted the economic recovery, but the borrowed funds did not repair roads and schools or stimulate high-wage jobs for poor and low-income workers.

Reaganomics and the Lower Half: A Balance Sheet

For some Americans, the economy was back on track in the mid-80s. Profits and executive pay were rising. Plant closings yielded bonuses for executives. Shrinkage was the corporate version of Reaganomics: pain to workers and communities but gain for profit statements. Average after-inflation wages, which had climbed 60% over 1947–73, fell 15% in the next fifteen years. People who had once given to their church and the United Way now "had to accept food from them. That hurts."[48] The Reagan recovery was something new: wages stayed low and poverty stayed high. In the 80s, 70% of total growth in family incomes went to the top 1% of the families. With the bulk of tax cuts going to businesses and the affluent and with the bulk of social program cuts and unemployment going to the bottom, it was not surprising that income inequality widened.[49]

If all personal income in America were divided equally among all families, each fifth of the families would receive 20% of the income pie. In the 80s, the poorest fifth of the families saw its share of all income fall from 4.5% to 3.7%, while the richest fifth saw its share increase from 47.4% to 51.8%.[50] Although it could be argued that some at the top had valuable skills and some at the bottom had none, much of the increased inequality and falling wages came even as average educational and skill levels were rising and had more to do with the political and economic power of those at the top than with the defects of those at the bottom.[51]

A clever person observed that "a rising tide lifts all boats," but in the 80s "the rising tide lifted the yachts; the rowboats foundered." Growth in the 80s did not perform its antipoverty work well. Every year had higher poverty rates than the worst year in the 1970s.[52]

Policy and economic conditions affected social groups differently. In 1991 the child poverty rate hit 46% for blacks and 40% for Hispanics. It was much less for whites, but still 17%. As adult unemployment climbed, so did the rates of divorce, suicide, and domestic abuse. Reaganites lectured people on family values, but their policies engendered more poverty and unemployment, which harmed family stability. As a counselor in Peoria, Illinois, home of downsizing Caterpillar, put it: "You have a lot of depressed dads, and they have to take it on someone, and a lot of them are taking it out on kids."[53]

The incidence of poverty for retirees, whose support programs had not been hit too hard by the administration, continued to fall and was soon close to the average for the whole population. But unsettling population changes, globalization, and harsh corporate policies confronted working-age Americans. Reagan policies accentuated the trend. The result was more low-wage jobs. Over 1979–89, the percentage of full-time, year-round workers earning poverty-level wages rose for non-Hispanic whites from 15% to 19%, for blacks from 25% to 33%, and for Hispanics from 27% to 38%. Economic expansions usually lifted wages; now, there were more working poor. Average family incomes increased a bit only because family members were putting in more hours at work.[54]

Unemployment rates fell over the 80s as the economy recovered, but they stayed at higher levels than were normal in good times. In 1988, a conservative columnist claimed that the United States faced a "severe labor shortage," but in most places shortages meant that employers did not want to raise pay to attract workers. Officially, unemployment had fallen from 9.7% in 1982 to 5.5% in 1988, but real rates were much higher. Policy makers feared that low unemployment would send wages and prices up again, and full employment was redefined as 6% or 7% unemployment. Ideology conquered facts. During so-called full employment, millions could find only part-time work, and millions dropped out of the unemployment numbers.[55] Black unemployment was still 12% in 1988. But depression eased, and conservatives stayed upbeat. A Reaganite was not joking when he emphasized that the failure to get full employment had not hurt blacks *worse* than whites. After all, while white teen unemployment fell from 16% to 13%, black teen unemployment fell by a larger percentage, from 39% to 31%![56]

The Underclass—A Diverting Morality Play

Despite the Democratic comeback in Congress, conservatives kept their view of poverty in the news. Their story said that the generosity of liberal social programs and liberal permissiveness on crime spawned an underclass of unwed mothers on welfare and murderous gangsters. Nothing was said about global economic change, urban deindustrialization, and depression-level unemployment. In the *New Republic*, Morton Kondracke alleged that "it is universally accepted that black poverty is heavily the result of family breakdown." It was not universally accepted, but liberal Democrats, despite victories in the mid-80s, weren't doing much to challenge such ideas.[57]

There certainly were race-correlated social problems. Indexes of inner-city crime had soared, and the crack cocaine epidemic broke out in the mid-1980s. Black young men were ten times as likely to die as a result of homicide as their white counterparts. A majority of black babies were born to single mothers. The jails were jammed with people of color. But it is remarkable how little was said about harmful economic policies.

Race was politically useful. If bad outcomes could be colored black or brown, more whites ignored the economic forces hammering all workers and blamed minorities, welfare mothers, and drug abusers. People supported the high-profile government war on drugs in low-income communities.

There were facts for a different story. In some cities the unemployment rate was 60%, and the impact of business closures was obvious. Half of all black male workers in heavy manufacturing in the Great Lakes region lost their jobs over 1979–84. Minority men and women with low levels of schooling were not doing well, but the white-black income gap lengthened the most among college graduates, rising from 3% to 16% in favor of whites.[58]

The poverty rate for blacks hit 36% in 1983; the white rate was only 11%. That still meant almost 20 million white poor. Big economic forces destroyed black and white lives; it was much worse for blacks, and racism impeded a unified political response.[59] There was ample evidence that most poor able-bodied adults, black or white, wanted to work. Gilbert Maxwell had ten years at a Georgia shrimp factory. He had worked his way up to a job with the cleanup crew, in which he earned $10,800 a year; he was advancing but still $3,400 below the poverty line. Kenneth Jones had been laid off from a white-collar position at Amtrak that paid $30,000; he spent his days at a Baltimore job center where he was told he had too much experience. Most of the poor, wrote one reporter, want to work. "Most share the dreams of an industrious nation. . . . They are people like us, their poverty the icy curve on a hazardous road."[60]

Public debate and public opinion moved on different tracks. Despite conservative victories in the media, by two to one Americans rejected the view that the poor were poor because of defects in intelligence or character. By two to one, they thought Reagan favored the rich and mistreated the poor. They supported more spending on the poor, even to the point of accepting a 1% federal sales tax to finance the effort, but they were skeptical about government's ability to make a difference.[61] Not much was said about government success stories. Medicaid and Medicare brought health care to millions; Head Start gave poor children a boost; Social Security converted the elderly from one of the poorest to one of the least poor groups; survivor benefits softened the blow of a death in the family. These were positive outcomes of citizens using government for mutual aid.

But the story of the caring society was not being well told, and conservatives kept up their bombardment of liberal government programs. As one liberal put it, "There has been some real poisoning of the atmosphere in recent years in a cynical way to convince the public that nothing works."[62] Incisive examinations of the Reagan experiment showed up in magazines and newspapers, but fewer Americans got their news from newspapers; more turned to television, a source that was unlikely to provide expert commentary.

The Homeless Poor

In the early 1980s Americans noticed more people living on the streets, and these new homeless did not fit the stereotype of the 50s and 60s: an older alcoholic man on skid row. There were more young families and more young men. Almost half were African American.

Rising homelessness was a worldwide phenomenon, and the European welfare states did not solve it.[63] But the debate in America was not about which country had more homeless; it was about how many homeless there were and what caused people to fall into desperate poverty.

The homeless were hard to count. A journalist estimated that 5,000 people lived in tunnels under New York City. Official surveys would not locate these people. Homeless advocate Mitch Snyder claimed that 2 million or 3 million Americans were homeless, but he later admitted to ABC's Ted Koppel that he had made up the numbers. The Department of Housing and Urban Development collected several estimates from large cities, picked the middle number in each, and announced in 1984 that there were between 250,000 and 300,000 homeless. Scholar Christopher Jencks estimated that there were 350,000 homeless in one week of March 1987. This was less than 1% of the total U.S. population, but more than 1% of the population would be homeless at some point in their lives.[64]

The homeless population had begun to grow in the 70s, it jumped in the 80s, and its composition changed. It included fewer older white males and more families, more young adults, more blacks, and possibly more veterans; perhaps a third were mentally ill.[65] For some people in this last group homelessness caused mental illness. Others, however, were mentally ill persons who might once have lived in state institutions but, since a variety of new policies that began in the late 1950s, were living on the streets. Removing people from ineffective and sometimes dangerous asylums was the good part of deinstitutionalization, but the promised system of halfway houses and social services for the deinstitutionalized fell short of the need. On top of that, local officials and the Reagan White House resisted efforts to simplify application procedures for disability and other funds; the procedures were daunting even for the sane.[66] The nation's treatment of the mentally ill ranks as one of the nastiest episodes in our recent history. Did these people merit poverty?

Why other people became homeless was a matter of debate. It was comforting to think that through drug and alcohol abuse, and because of the inability to get along with family and friends, the homeless willfully cut themselves off from society. And it is true that half the homeless admitted that they abused alcohol or used illegal drugs. For some people abuse caused the descent into poverty; for others poverty caused the descent into drugs. Often substance abuse was part of a cluster of social and economic difficulties that struck at the poor and weak and left them homeless. The affluent abused drugs and alcohol, too, but rarely lost their jobs or homes.

Personal and family problems played a role. Spousal abuse caused poor female-headed families. Misfortune shattered the lives of people in the mainstream. One family with five children lost everything in a fire, including the husband's work tools, which he had purchased over the years one tool at a time.

A Miami woman got a throat disease that wiped out family savings and destroyed her marriage. Another woman sank into a paralyzing depression when her mother died. Better government programs, including government-supported health care for all, might have kept these people off the streets.[67]

Many of the homeless were like Walter Bannister, who needed a decent job. Bannister slept in shelters and on a children's playground and attended business college during the day. He had veterans' benefits and a Pell grant to pay his tuition, but he was cut from his $228 monthly relief check—illegally it turned out—when a clerk claimed that he had been late for an appointment. He was not mentally ill. He had a high school degree. But he could not find a regular job. He sold his blood and worked odd jobs to get by.[68]

Bannister's story shows the imprint of government policies that contributed to homelessness. Officials from the White House down to the local welfare office tried to cut programs rather than to help people. The Los Angeles County Grand Jury concluded that the county "aimed to terminate from public assistance as many people as possible for as long as possible, thus keeping down costs."[69] In addition, governments connived in a system that could not supply regular work at livable wages to millions of willing workers. Over 1978–83, the numbers in poverty increased 44%. Unemployment stayed high. Poverty and homelessness were the price that the nation's poor were forced to pay to cut inflation and rebuild profit rates. As there were soup lines and homeless encampments called Hoovervilles in the 30s, so there were more homeless in the depression of the 80s. In the 30s, the president expanded aid to the poor and homeless; in the 80s, the president cut programs for the poor.[70]

Government could have been there when family, friends, and private organizations were not. Without savings or money from friends, poor people lost their private living space, and that made it harder to stay clean and get a job. Without a job or with a low-wage job, it was hard to accumulate the first and last months' rent and a security deposit.[71]

If low incomes were the demand side, the inadequate supply of affordable housing was the supply side. The free enterprise system created too many low-pay jobs and too few low-income housing units. It was more profitable for developers to build fancy condominiums than affordable apartments. Through federal urban renewal programs that cleared "slums," government helped developers demolish low-income housing. Half of all single-room occupancy units were demolished in the 70s, including 89% of those in New York City. This added to the housing crunch. Some poor families were paying as much as half their income in rent.[72]

Americans were told horror stories about government housing projects, but public housing was often better than the alternatives. In New York City there were 175,000 public housing units and 200,000 names on the waiting list. Shortages and politics led to bizarre outcomes. New York welfare officials required that homeless welfare families search for housing at rents below $245 a month. To house people until they found such dwellings the city paid up to $2,000 a month at welfare hotels.[73]

Reagan policies did not start the housing crisis, but the Reaganites supported depression, lower incomes, and reductions in social programs, so people could afford less. There were still hundreds of thousands of homeless even as the economy moved through a long expansion. Many of the homeless were employed or had recently been employed. And because of Reagan's big cuts in long-term spending on public housing programs, the housing situation was not likely to get better.[74]

Government has the tools to ease the problem. The mentally ill and people needing drug rehabilitation services can be served. For the rest, shelters are a way station but no substitute for a home; they lack privacy and safety and usually eject the homeless during the day. To redress the shortage of affordable housing, two areas need reform. The homeless problem is first a poverty problem. Joblessness, low wages, and racial and gender discrimination have to be addressed. Second, governments can expand the supply of affordable housing by spending more on rental subsidies and incentives to nonprofit builders. Where nothing else works, they can build and rehabilitate housing.[75]

There is plenty of money to fix these problems, but most of the gains of economic growth in the 1980s and 1990s went to the richest fraction of the population. Tax cuts in 2001–3 assured that even more would go to the very top. The United States can have several million extremely rich people, or it can have less poverty and homelessness. It cannot have both.

A Reagan Harvest: Bush, Recession, and Riots

The presidential election of 1988, which pitted Reagan's vice president, George Bush, against the Democratic governor of Massachusetts, Michael Dukakis, was about the missing liberal story. The Republican strategy ignored the damage wrought by Reaganomics and painted Dukakis with negatives on race, crime, and patriotism. Dukakis responded weakly; until it was too late he said little about economic issues that could have mobilized voters. He was routed.[76]

President Bush seemed uninterested in domestic policy. While his agile handling of the end of the Cold War and his military success against Iraq were applauded, he had little to say about people's economic struggles.[77] This silence was bad enough in light of long-term problems of poverty and stagnating incomes; it was worse when recession began in the summer of 1990. Bush's treasury secretary, Nicholas Brady, asserted: "I don't think it's the end of the world even if we have a recession. We'll pull out of it again. No big deal."[78]

Recessions are inevitable. The precise combination of causes for this one is not certain, but among the factors were the Federal Reserve's obsession with wage and price inflation, the dependence of the Reagan boom on debt, corporate ruthlessness in cutting jobs, and restricted low-income purchasing power.[79] In part, then, the 1990–91 recession sprang from the warped policies of the 80s.

But it also illustrated one theme of this book: growth periods are halted before they wipe out poverty. In 1987–88 first-year wage increases in major union contracts were only 2%, but consumer prices were rising by more than 4%, and some people worried about labor shortages. Head of the Federal Reserve Alan Greenspan reacted by raising interest rates in order to slow economic growth. That meant more unemployment and poverty.[80]

One of Greenspan's predecessors quipped that it was the Federal Reserve's job "to take away the punch bowl just as the party gets going." Greenspan may have been trying for a "soft landing"—slow rather than no growth—but he went too far. Economic growth limped along at 1.8% in 1990 and declined in 1991. The Reagan expansion ended before it had produced permanent success against high poverty rates.[81]

Soon Greenspan changed hats to fight recession, but other factors kept it going. Corporate, federal, and personal debt levels had reached record highs. Large debt had once fueled economic growth, but now it made business and consumers hypersensitive about bad news. As unemployment jumped, the recession snowballed. In 1990, 600,000 families declared bankruptcy. After deregulation, savings institutions and commercial banks had made bad loans and bad investments. Some institutions collapsed; others were reluctant to lend. Bankers invested not in loans to local businesses but in government bonds with higher long-term interest rates.[82]

Corporate America had learned a new game in the 80s: cut the workforce to the bone; shut not only unprofitable plants but those that were not highly profitable. Executives used the recession to clean house. In December 1991, General Motors announced it would close twenty-one plants and then awarded bonuses to its executives. Money that could have gone for modernization instead widened the income gap. This time many people who lost their jobs were managers, professionals, and technicians; workers in the banking industry were hard hit. Even IBM, once proud bastion of job security, laid off thousands. In the euphemism of the day, these workers were not fired; they were downsized.[83]

The poor and nearly poor could barely purchase essentials, so they could not raise their consumption to boost a sagging economy. In the 80s, the explosion of debt had compensated for inadequate incomes and buying power at the bottom, but debtors were reaching their limits. Federal debt was also huge. The Keynesian deficit route out of recession was unlikely, since annual deficits were already approaching a record $300 billion in 1992; Wall Street wanted to bring the deficits down, not raise them.[84]

The recession of 1990–92 caused more poverty. Poverty rates stopped falling at 12.8% in 1989, and the 1993 rate of 15.1% matched the worst of the 1980s rates. The number of unemployed jumped by 3 million (1989–93) and the number on welfare by the same number.[85]

Minority joblessness was part of the explanation for the worst civil unrest of the century, the Los Angeles riots of 1992. In 1991 Los Angeles police officers had been videotaped beating African American Rodney King; on April 29, 1992, four officers on trial for the beating were acquitted. That night south central Los Angeles exploded in a riot of window smashing, shoplifting, beatings of people driving through the area, and hundreds of spectacular fires. It was a stunning comment on twelve years of conservatism. Bush blamed gangs and Johnson's War on Poverty; Vice President Dan Quayle blamed a television character, Murphy Brown, whose decision to have a child on her own, he claimed, mocked fatherhood.[86]

The causes of the explosion were many, but the important ones involved race and racism and economics and poverty. Police brutality was key, and it had not begun with Rodney King. In seven years, the Los Angeles Police Department, using choke holds, killed sixteen people, most of them African Americans. The verdict in the Rodney King case seemed to condone police brutality. The decision struck hard at respectable working-class and middle-class blacks in Los Angeles, at people who were following the rules. The riot surged first not in the poorest areas but in lower-middle-income neighborhoods, some with many homeowners.[87]

The ethnic mix in Los Angeles was changing. Prior to the riots, a Korean shop owner shot a black girl, Latasha Harlins, in the back of the head and received no jail time. Rioters took aim at Korean-owned businesses. Blacks were feeling competition also from Latinos, who seemed usefully docile to employers. But in the riots, Latinos were not timid; more of them were arrested than blacks.[88]

If the riots did not begin in the poorest neighborhoods, they spread there quickly. The Reagan boom had not done much for south Los Angeles; the Bush recession made things worse. Officially, minority unemployment in south Los Angeles was 15%, and that figure omitted thousands who had dropped out of the statistics.[89] Over 1978–89, 200,000 manufacturing jobs evaporated. There was construction and job growth downtown and on the west side, but poverty rates in south Los Angeles exceeded 30%, twice the national average. Job creation and youth programs were being replaced by a new war on the poor: California's prison population soared by 400% to 106,000 (1980–92). Two-thirds of the inmates were black or Hispanic.[90]

The kindling of years of economic and police brutality was lit on the evening of April 29, 1992. In three days of burning and looting, 58 people lost their lives, and 2,500 were injured; 16,000 were arrested. The nation watched on live TV as whites driving through the area were beaten and as fire after fire flared to the skies. In the end it took the Los Angeles Police, county sheriffs, highway patrol officers, and the National Guard to restore order.[91]

The Reagan-Volcker depression of the early 80s, along with a strong dollar and falling energy prices, tamed inflation, and the economy began to grow again. But even in recovery, poverty rates stayed high, and so did unemployment. Reagan promised a renewal of community and patriotic pride, but his policies supported deindustrialization, and that made ghost towns.

In the long run, Reagan conservatives wanted to eliminate most of the social welfare state, and they had some success. Aid to the unemployed and people on welfare was trimmed. Public housing programs were sharply cut, and public employment under the Comprehensive Employment and Training Act was eliminated. Along with higher unemployment rates, social program cuts like these made life more insecure for many people. But much remained: Social Security's fundamentals were preserved, and the Earned Income Tax Credit for the working poor was upgraded in 1986.

Perhaps the most enduring services Reagan rendered to the right-wing crusade against programs for low- and middle-income Americans were these: he made it easier for people in power to speak disparagingly of the poor and unemployed; and his tax cuts created huge budget deficits that were used against liberals who thought of creating new social programs.

If the Reagan effort to chip away at the welfare state was only partially successful, so too was the Reagan economic boom. Growth was fueled by record levels of federal, corporate, and personal debt; that did not seem like conservativism. And much of the debt did not finance better bridges or a better trained, more committed workforce; it supported huge increases in military spending, upper-class incomes, and business mergers. Accumulated federal debt rose from $1 trillion to $4 trillion, but there was no yield in lower poverty rates, higher wages, higher savings rates, and higher productivity. Reaganism meant more profits, not more parks; more fast-food joints, not more factories.[92]

Most Americans were paying the same total tax rates in 1992 as in 1980. The poorest 20% enjoyed a 10% cut, thanks not to Reaganomics but to 1986 and 1990 reforms. The richest 1% were the only Americans to register permanent gains from Reagan's tax cuts. Their rates were still 19% lower in the early 1990s, despite take-backs in 1986 and 1990. This outcome of Reaganomics was not a mistake; Reagan aimed to increase upper-class incomes, as part of trickle-down economics and because of the belief that rich people like himself merited every dollar of their income.[93]

The Reagan-Volcker cold-bath method of depression and benefit cuts was not the only way to cure inflation. There were a dozen alternatives, including targeted tax cuts to modernize industry, softer Volcker methods, tax breaks for employees who accepted lower-than-inflation wage increases, and controls on energy and home prices. A program that was kinder to low-income Americans would have been popular with voters. But such a program did not fit the conservative view of the world: less government, more self-reliance, more rewards for the rich.

Reaganomics was not the expression of the odd beliefs of one man or even of a small group. There was delusion, contradiction, and deception in Reaganomics, but consistent goals and outcomes ran through it and its partner, the Volcker depression: reduce inflation and restore business dominance and profits and do it by cutting government social programs, raising unemployment and poverty, and increasing upper-class and corporate incomes. Not all the players understood all the implications of the economic program, but most were clear about the essentials; Volcker, Reagan, and Stockman by the end of the first year and Feldstein all along—they all believed that conservative solutions required pain for those at the bottom and rewards for those at the top.

The conservative ideological barrage and liberal disarray; Reagan's attacks on unions, worker protections, and social welfare programs; tax cuts that favored the rich; the worst depression since the 30s; and a jobless recovery in the early 90s—all these had profound effects. They shifted the balance of economic power farther toward employers and away from employees, toward the rich and away from the poor and working class. Whether Reagan policies and harsh economic trends would not only give Democrats political victories but goad them to reinvent liberalism and learn to shape the terms of political debate might soon become clear.

part four

The Poor You

Will Always Have

with You—If You Don't

Do the Right Thing:

1993–Present

chapter ten

STAYING POOR IN
THE CLINTON BOOM
Welfare Reform, the Nearby Labor Force,
and the Limits of the Work Ethic

Why, forty years after the War on Poverty, does the United States still have more than 30 million poor people? Why does the United States usually have the highest poverty rate among the rich nations? Part of the answer is that economic growth does not wipe out unemployment and poverty. But that is only half the answer. Other nations start out with as much unemployment and poverty, but they offer more money and services to those people who are left behind. That is why they have less poverty.

In the 90s two mainstream solutions to poverty were put to the test. The first ended entitlement to welfare benefits; the second was a booming economy. Both conservatives and liberals had long believed that growth was an effective method for solving poverty. Also, the conservative political surge of the 80s and mid-90s had won more politicians to the cause of trimming welfare. The 1996 repeal of the sixty-year-old welfare system represented a climax in the successful drive of conservatives to target the welfare poor as a source of social disorganization and economic lag.

What was the outcome of economic expansion and welfare shrinkage? Average wages increased and poverty rates fell in the late 90s. However, although welfare rolls declined sharply, most people who left welfare stayed poor. Poverty rates did not decline as much as expected in a booming economy; they fell from 15.1% (1993) to 11.3% (2000), a welcome contrast to the 80s but no lower than in the 1970s (see figure A.2 in appendix 1). And the poor were poorer; only 30% of them fell below *half* the poverty line in 1975, but 41% did in 1997.[1]

The poverty figures are even more shocking when we recall that they were based on the already low federal poverty line. A family of four with $18,000 in the 90s was not poor by federal standards, but it is easy to see that an urban family paying rent of $700 or $800 a month might feel that it was.[2] In 1998 a line of $21,000, just a bit more realistic, would have meant 46 million poor people, or 17% of all Americans and 40% of young children.[3] These large numbers show the reality of poverty behind the Clinton boom and welfare reform.

Why weren't the long economic boom and welfare reform more successful? What happened to people who left welfare? Why didn't economic growth reduce poverty as fast as it had in the 50s and 60s? The answer to these questions is the subject of this chapter.

Some people claim that the poor lack skills; more will be said on that later. Others assert that the poor are warped by underclass values that encourage crime and welfare dependence. But the underclass theory applies only to a tiny fraction of the poverty population. The real problem is rather that, first, a labor glut keeps millions without steady work and suppresses the pay rates of those with jobs; second, because of the limits of American liberalism and the success of conservatives in the 70s and 80s, governments allow too many of the benefits of income growth to flow to the rich and too few to the economic majority; and third, the American welfare state does not adequately compensate for market failures.[4]

As a result of the high inflation rates of the 70s and of the rightward shift of political debate, politicians allowed the Federal Reserve and Wall Street to manage the business cycle; economists developed theories to rationalize high unemployment, and people in power felt moral fighting inflation with more poverty and unemployment. Financial markets, complained economist Gordon Richards of the National Association of Manufacturers, "have a pathological fear of growth."[5] It was widely believed, and not just by conservatives, that if official unemployment rates fell below 6%, wages and inflation would skyrocket.

It did not work out that way in the late 90s. Give credit to Federal Reserve chair Greenspan for allowing unemployment to fall below what economic theory dictated. But we should also remember that he raised interest rates frequently and harmfully in 1994–95 and 1999–2000. His professed goal was to fight inflation, but there was little inflation on the horizon, and it can be argued that Greenspan's real goal was to maintain sufficient unemployment to weaken labor's bargaining power against employers.

In the very late 90s, the Federal Reserve Board reversed its slowdown strategy when other factors sent the economy into a tailspin. An excess of shopping malls and dot.coms led to a falling stock market and rising unemployment.

(The terrorist attacks of September 11, 2001, were just the final blow to the economy.) The outcome fit a pattern: whether by Federal Reserve Board action or the normal business cycle, recession always arrives to raise unemployment and poverty. Growth eventually undermines itself as an antipoverty strategy; high wages incite the Federal Reserve to stifle economic growth, which is supposed to be curing poverty.[6]

Other rich capitalist economies have inflation and unemployment problems, but most have parties and programs to offset the ill effects of capitalist labor markets. Compensators include labor and socialist parties, progressive taxation, effective unions, generous income supports, and extensive social services. In the Netherlands, for example, workers receive unemployment benefits for up to five years, a National Assistance Act assures everyone a minimum income, and, in a measure that is both trivial and indicative of an advanced welfare state, the Dutch government offers the poor a small "Fun Things" subsidy for such activities as joining a music group or sports club.[7] In the United States in the 80s and 90s, some support programs were improved (the Earned Income Tax Credit) or initiated (health insurance for poor children), but as unions and liberalism weakened, the real minimum wage fell, unemployment insurance coverage shrank, welfare became more limited and punitive, and tax policy often endorsed income inequality.

It's about Equality and Taxes, not Skills

Among rich market economies, the United States has one of the largest per capita outputs, but it also has one of the largest gaps between rich and poor. There is plenty to go around, but more of it goes around in Europe than in America.[8] Because of labor gluts, weaker unions, and a low minimum wage, average wages did not take off until the late 1990s (figure 10.1). At the same time, executive pay jumped from 85 times to 326 times average pay between 1990 and 1997. Most of the gains from economic growth were being skimmed off at the top. The sums involved were immense. It used to be argued that if we redistributed the wealth and incomes of the very rich to those with low incomes, the latter would not get much because there were so many of them and so few of the rich. But it is clear now that a lot of poverty can be solved by correcting the extremely unequal distribution of income and wealth. If we had redistributed into jobs or income just 42.5% of *one year's (1997 to 1998) increase* in the net worth of the 400 richest Americans, that $48.4 billion would have lifted 30 million Americans above the poverty line or provided assets for their long-term advancement. In 1977–99, nine-tenths of the growth in the income pie went to the top 1% of the households. It's true that the rich pay a

Figure 10.1. Real Average Hourly Earnings of Production and Nonsupervisory Private Nonagricultural Workers, 1961–2001

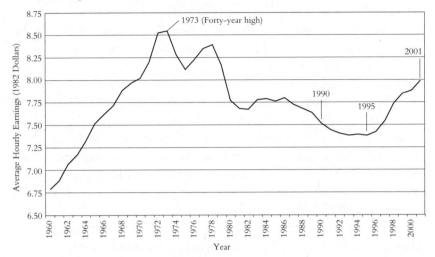

Source: *Economic Report of the President* (Washington: Government Printing Office, 2002), table B47, at <www.gpoaccess.gov/eop/tables02.html>.

larger share of federal taxes than the poor and middle groups, but there has been so much income inequality to begin with that real *after-tax* incomes doubled for the top 5% and tripled for the top 1% (1979–2000). Taxation did little to offset huge inequalities in the economy.[9]

The main arguments of this chapter are that welfare reform has been a failure and that economic growth won't wipe out even job-related poverty. Part of the argument should now be familiar. Despite periods of lower unemployment, the United States has millions of ready workers. Substantial unemployment is the norm, and periods of low unemployment are interrupted by recession and higher unemployment. Government can solve the problem by doing more to avoid recession or by compensating victims more generously. Each solution requires a new politics.

Against my interpretation, there is an alternative, popular among not only conservatives but also liberals and centrists like Bill Clinton and his first secretary of labor, Robert Reich. People have low incomes because they lack training and skills. It seems common sense that some people have good writing and speaking skills and thus succeed as journalists and teachers and preachers. We know that Michael Jordan was a very talented basketball player and very well paid. We know that on average people with more formal schooling earn more than those with less. And we were told in the 90s that those who had high-tech training would make out the best.[10]

The skills-and-education argument tells us about Jordan and physicists, but not why so many Americans are poor and nearly poor.[11] Consider these propositions:

1. Many positions require what can be learned quickly on the job, not specific skills that people bring to the job.

2. The 90s showed that when the economy grows very rapidly, there are plenty of jobs that the less skilled can do. Economist Jeff Madrick, noting the late 90s rise in wages for low-income workers, argued that "so-called unskilled workers can handle their new jobs."[12] But there has to be sustained demand for workers to force employers to raise low-level wages.

3. There are plenty of reasons to improve our schools, such as inspiring more intelligent citizenship and enriching people's lives, but lifting people's educational and skill levels won't necessarily increase the number of high-wage, high-skill jobs in the economy. In the 70s and 90s there was a glut of educated labor; the wages of new college graduates fell 7% over 1989–97. In 1997 new engineers and scientists were earning 11% and 8% less than their counterparts in 1989. Between three-quarters and two-thirds of new jobs will not require a college diploma. Recently Frederick Pryor and David Schaffer found an excess of educated workers falling down the occupational ladder into less skilled jobs, driving out less educated workers who were perfectly fit for those jobs. Others have pointed out that the big winners in the 90s were not scientists and tech workers but doctors, lawyers, sales representatives, brokers, and managers.[13]

4. A worker with more skills will not find a better job if the jobs aren't there. A participant in one training program upgraded her skills, but the main result was that she could use MapQuest to get directions to the houses she cleaned twelve hours a day, seven days a week.[14]

5. It is a dogma of free marketeers and most economists that people get paid what they are worth. But the reality is that many political, social, and economic factors affect employee compensation. Women and minorities are often paid less than others making the same contribution. Part of executive pay has to do not with managerial skill but with the cozy relationship between boards of directors and managers; it is easy to cite examples of chief executives who failed miserably but walked away with huge bonuses and severance packages.[15] Another example of the disconnection: the share of child-care workers with more than a high school degree jumped from 18% to 42% (1984–97), but real wages declined.[16] Finally, it is not self-evident that those who know how to sweep the halls or take care of our children must be paid little for their hard work or even that they are not skilled.

The widespread problem of low pay in the United States will not be fixed mainly by raising the average level of education and training. In fact, raising this level may intensify the game of musical chairs for good jobs. We need better incomes for the poor who cannot work for pay; for millions of others, we need, to rephrase a Spike Lee movie title, More Better Jobs.

Compensators and Targeted Policies: Clinton's Fair Record

Before we examine welfare reform and the labor market, we will take a look at whether President Clinton supported specific measures to assist the poor. Clinton was the product of a rightward move among Democrats in response to Reagan's victories for conservatism. To recapture Reagan Democrats, the Democratic Leadership Council disparaged government social programs and praised market solutions. Clinton asserted that the days of big government were over, and he promised to reform welfare. Nevertheless, he was enough of a liberal to support a variety of reforms that involved government aid to poor people.[17]

Clinton's effort to reform health care in 1993 was a mishmash of liberal and business ideas, and it was a public relations failure. However, in 1997 he supported the Children's Health Insurance Program created by Ted Kennedy and Orrin Hatch to expand health care for poor children.[18] He supported an increase in the federal minimum wage to $5.15 (1997); that helped the working poor a bit, although the new minimum was still 30% below its purchasing power of the late 60s and not enough to lift many families over the poverty line. Local "living wage" ordinances that set pay rates at $7 to $10 an hour were more likely to do that; they involved difficult campaigns in hundreds of cities. By the early 2000s, living wage ordinances covered no more than 100,000 workers. No one in the Clinton administration took a prominent role in supporting the living wage movement.[19]

Clinton's first effort on taxes was progressive. In 1993, rates were raised for the top fifth and especially the top 1% of taxpayers (some of these increases were rescinded in the Taxpayer Relief Act of 1997). One motive was budget balancing to assure Wall Street that deficits were under control. Clinton also supported a major expansion of the Earned Income Tax Credit that increased the number of covered working poor families from 14 million to 20 million.[20] This was part of Clinton's antipoverty strategy, and it meant that a low-wage breadwinner with two or more dependents, forced off welfare by welfare reform, could combine minimum wage earnings ($10,000 for almost a full year of full-time work) with several thousand federal dollars. The total amount of money would fall short of supplying the family's needs, but the worker might

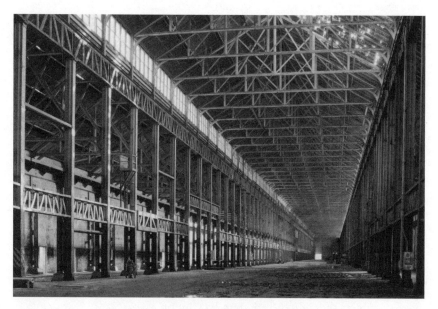

Bethlehem Steel, Bethlehem, Pennsylvania, 2006. Steelmaking facilities were shut down in Bethlehem in the mid-1990s during the Clinton boom. (Copyright Shaun O'Boyle, 2006, oboylephoto.com; all rights reserved)

rise above the official poverty line for a family of three ($13,133 in 1998). The president's economists claimed that Earned Income Tax Credit lifted 4.3 million Americans out of poverty in 1997, about twice as many as in 1993.[21] Finally, Clinton deflected conservative calls for privatizing Social Security, possibly saving millions from falling into poverty in later years, for Social Security has lifted the elderly from being one of the poorest to one of the least poor social groups.[22]

Overall, Clinton's efforts were better than Reagan's hostility to poor people, but they were not an outstanding record for a president who was elected because voters were anxious about low wages and high medical costs. The failure of health care reform in 1993 meant continued insecurity for 42 million Americans, many of them workers who lacked any health insurance, private or public.[23] Also, Clinton did nothing to reverse one of the most important poverty policies of the 80s and 90s: locking up young men from low-income backgrounds. Furthermore, although he won many union votes, Clinton offered little but rhetoric to encourage unionization and to defend labor standards as he pushed unregulated global capitalism and allowed job flight. He championed free trade agreements, such as the North American Free Trade Agreement, one goal of which was to keep prices and wages down. One economist concluded that Clinton had done "virtually nothing to advance the interests of organized labor or working people more generally." To some degree Clinton accepted the Wall Street model. While most workers see "stagnating wages and job insecurity as the scourge of the labor market, [in] the Wall Street Model . . . rising imports, stagnant wages, and job insecurity are said to be peculiarly good for the economy. . . . Even President Clinton's Council of Economic Advisors . . . bought into a logic that suggests the United States needs to keep 7 to 8 million people unemployed in order to keep the economy healthy."[24]

While Clinton seemed more compassionate toward the poor than Reagan, the effects on poor people of each man's two-term presidency were not as different as we might expect. Reagan cut welfare programs; Clinton agreed to end the federal welfare entitlement. Poverty rates averaged 13.3% during Clinton's terms (1993–2000) and 14.1% during Reagan's presidency (1981–88). However, although there were still 31 million poor in 2000, Clinton had cut the poverty numbers by almost 7 million, Reagan by only 2.7 million. Things were moving in the right direction under Clinton.[25]

Welfare Repeal: Ignoring Lousy Jobs

Whatever sound and compassionate reasons there were for welfare reform, they were not the main ones in play when Aid to Families with Dependent Children (AFDC) was repealed in August 1996. Conservatives had been trying for years to get rid of AFDC. The 1996 law showed that they had won, for it reflected the views of Reagan and Murray that poverty was not a matter of low wages and unemployment; of class, race, and gender inequality; and of a stingy welfare state. Rather, poverty stemmed from cultural or social flaws, chiefly, a weak work ethic and absent fathers, both of which were encouraged by the welfare system. By the mid-90s most Republican politicians and many Democrats had come to agree with the conservative analysis.

In the debate about reform, welfare's negative effects were exaggerated, and complications were ignored. It did not matter that the average size of welfare families was shrinking (in contrast to the notion that recipients had babies to get more benefits) or that millions cycled on and off the rolls as the job market rose and fell (in contrast to the idea that people were psychologically hooked on welfare, regardless of economic conditions).[26] Critics of welfare ignored the fact that millions of workers were poor and that most poor people were not on welfare. But especially for conservatives, facts were not pertinent, and the goal was not to solve poverty; it was to penalize people in nontraditional family situations and, above all, to get people off welfare. During congressional debate, Florida's John Mica compared welfare recipients to wild animals and held up a sign that read: "Don't Feed the Alligators."[27] Conservatives would judge welfare reform a success if every poor person "had exactly as much money after as before reform" as long as they did not get all or most of it from taxpayers.[28] Meanwhile, moderates like President Clinton, who signed the Personal Responsibility and Work Opportunity Reconciliation Act (PRWORA) in August 1996, accepted much of the conservative analysis but with a liberal twist. They believed that government should enforce desired behaviors in the welfare poor, but they hoped that a combination of work and government programs (tax credits, food stamps, and a higher minimum wage) would lead people to self-sufficiency and prosperity.

Under the 1996 law, welfare's name was changed from Aid to Families with Dependent Children to Temporary Assistance for Needy Families (TANF). No family could get federal welfare dollars for more than five years over a lifetime. States were given capped block grants and direct control of their welfare systems, and they could limit welfare to fewer than five years. States were required to push recipients off welfare and into the workforce, regardless of training or mental health and child-care issues. The law limited the access of recent legal immigrants to welfare, food stamps, and disability payments. It cut support for disabled children. There were no provisions for increased funding during recessions.[29]

Soon it appeared that the goal of ejecting people from the rolls was a huge success. The national numbers fell by half and in Wisconsin by 90%. Some people who left welfare felt better about themselves because they were working. In one survey of those who left, 69% said life was better. But 69% said they were barely making ends meet.[30]

Welfare reform was failing in three significant ways. First, little was done to repair the problems that limited poor people's success in the world. The philosophy underlying reform was "work first." People were pushed into jobs, any jobs; training and general education were deemphasized, so poor women's long-term ability to compete for good jobs was slighted. By the middle of 1999, Los Angeles County had only 150 people in its federally funded training program; thousands were eligible.[31] Second, to the extent that poor people were trapped in mental illness, drug addiction, alcoholism, abusive relationships, or physical and psychological disabilities, welfare reform failed. These problems were common among long-term recipients who were supposed to be the main target of welfare reform, but welfare reform did little to address them.[32] Third, and most important, welfare reform did not solve poverty. A fair number of people who left welfare found jobs, but they lost welfare benefits, rent supplements, and, eventually, Medicaid; they faced new transportation, child-care, and clothing costs; and they worked at jobs that paid poverty-level wages. Contrary to conservative claims, most had not escaped dependency; they needed food stamps, tax credits, and help from friends and family to get by. Poverty itself was the real dependency.[33]

In the late 1990s average wages started to grow, and official unemployment fell. Robust economic growth made it easier for people to find jobs. However, poverty rates fell slowly, and most people who left welfare were about as poor as they had been on welfare. Here is a selection of evidence from a variety of studies.[34]

- The average incomes of the poorest 20% of female-headed families with children fell $580 between 1995 and 1997, largely as a result of cuts in government cash and food assistance.[35]
- One 1999 sample of people who left the rolls over 1995–97 showed that a fifth were without work, a working spouse, or government disability support, almost a third had returned to welfare, and the rest were working at low-wage jobs that paid $6.61 an hour and $1,149 a month.[36]
- A 1998 Illinois survey of people leaving welfare from mid-1997 though December 1998 found 64% living in poverty.[37]
- Welfare reform in the state of Wisconsin may have won Governor Tommy Thompson a position as George W. Bush's secretary of health and human services, but in the first three years of "Wisconsin Works," one-fourth of former welfare recipients were back on the rolls, and half of those at work were poor. When recession arrived in 2001, unemployment rose to 7.6% in Milwaukee, and Wisconsin's welfare rolls jumped by 25% in less than a year. One scholarly report claimed that there were seven job seekers for every job in Milwaukee's core, but Wisconsin officials refused aid to people who were laid off.[38]
- In September 2001, Secretary Thompson boasted that welfare reform had "helped unprecedented numbers of people on welfare to become self-supporting," but he was telling stories, not truths. Over 1995–2000 the poorest 40% of single mothers increased their annual earnings by only $2,300 and their disposable income by only $292 because they lost welfare and other benefits.[39]
- A Michigan sample of people on welfare in 1997 showed that six years later the percentage with jobs paying above-poverty-level wages had increased but 70% still had no jobs or had jobs paying poverty-level wages.[40]
- Of people in Los Angeles County's welfare-to-work program who entered the labor force at some point in 1998–2001, half had no earnings in 2001, and of those who had earnings in any quarter, the average was just over the poverty line. Most were still poor.[41]

- A fair summary of the condition of people who left welfare would be this one: 40% were unemployed and not on welfare; about half of these, 20%, were poor; 30% were employed and poor; 30% were employed and not poor.[42]

This looked like a 50% poverty rate, but welfare reformers wanted to believe that leaving welfare meant being self-sufficient. They omitted mention of the fact that people who left welfare were scraping by only with the aid of such government programs as food stamps and the Earned Income Tax Credit and handouts from friends and charities. In the winter of the prosperous year of 1998–99, Milwaukee's homeless shelters ran out of room. A year later in San Diego more of the homeless were single-parent families than in earlier years, and there was not enough space for them in local shelters. In 1998, the number of Americans working full-time year-round but still living in poverty rose by 20%, or by 459,000 people. This was not a large fraction of the population, but that it was rising in a period of prosperity was startling.[43]

Negative facts got into the newspapers and think tank reports, but they did not seem to change the big story in the media. The view that "any job is a good job" was a line that had been pushed by Lawrence Mead and other conservatives in the 80s and 90s. Most dogmatic in defining the poverty problem this way was a company that developed and evaluated welfare-to-work programs, the Manpower Demonstration Research Corporation. The corporation's writers bent over backward to make the work-first approach look successful, and journalists did not peel away its public relations cover. The corporation disseminated a rosy appraisal of Los Angeles County's Greater Avenues for Independence (GAIN) program but downplayed the fact that although people in the GAIN program did better than those in the control group, who left welfare without special assistance (annual earnings of $4,000 and $3,200, respectively), neither group was doing well. The Manpower writers also raved about the Minnesota Family Investment Program begun in 1994; its creators hoped to solve poverty and welfare dependence by allowing participants to keep more benefits after they started working. The results were positive but disappointing. More people in the Minnesota group worked after three years than in the AFDC control group (50% versus 37%), and their earnings were higher. But on an annualized basis the difference was between totals of $3,820 and $3,116, that is, $704, and the total amounts were miserable. The Minnesota Family Investment Program, like GAIN, did little to solve poverty, but politicians, evaluators, and journalists clung to the dogma that work saved.[44]

For many of them welfare reform was not about solving poverty; it was about getting people off the public rolls and under market discipline.[45] And it was effective in that respect. This central objective of welfare reform was "successful" in part because there was a good economy in which jobs appeared to be plentiful. Furthermore, welfare clients were politically isolated because of the triumph of conservative ideas about welfare and because the idea of paying mothers to stay home looked unfair when many nonpoor mothers were at work. So it was easy to fix welfare: kick people off the rolls and keep them off. Thirty states and many cities had diversion programs and other impediments, some of them illegal, that shut people out of welfare. New York City, Milwaukee, Mississippi, and Idaho were leaders in the field. South Carolina officials ejected families from welfare for trivial errors, such as being late for a class or an appointment. Hundreds of thousands were sanctioned off welfare.[46]

By the early 2000s millions of people who would once have been poor on welfare were poor off welfare. More poor female-heads of household were working but still poor. Little had been done to fix the low-wage problem, and despite all the hype about a high-tech society, the economy continued to generate millions of low-wage jobs.[47] There were few potent liberal voices arguing that the nation should reform the low-wage labor markets as well as income-support programs. Conservative political success in the 80s had frightened Democrats; reforming welfare without doing much to fix low-wage jobs was a sign of the waning power of liberalism. Despite occasional rhetoric from both parties in the late 90s about a second hike in the minimum wage, nothing happened.

The Nearby Labor Force: Why Job-Based Poverty Won't Go Away

Economic growth has been America's preferred method of solving poverty; it is politically easier than taking from the rich and giving to the poor. A rising tide is supposed to lift all boats. And it worked in the 1950s and 1960s when a fortunate mix of government policy, international power, and spending surges from two hot wars and a long Cold War slashed poverty rates. Thereafter, except for the later 1990s, growth no longer had the same effect. Early in the decade there was talk of the jobless recovery, and poverty rates did not fall until 1994 and then only slowly (see figure A.2 in appendix 1). Poverty expert Rebecca Blank claimed that there was less demand for unskilled workers, but I believe the problem was bigger.[48] It is true that those with fewer "skills" and educational credentials earned less, but if one morning everyone with a high school diploma had magically earned a college degree, the number of better jobs would not increase much; average pay for people with college degrees would fall. Low-wage poverty is a symptom of the general state of the whole workforce, which still earns at levels below those of the 70s (figure 10.1).

The reasons for generally poor wage performance in the 80s and much of the 90s involve a workforce traumatized by decades of layoffs and insecurity, a persistent labor surplus, and continuing weakness in unions and wage laws. What follows in this section recapitulates briefly an earlier exposition of why high-wage periods are rare and why they will not be long and deep enough to solve poverty. Analyzing the links between poverty, work, and economic growth is also a way to judge the record of the Clinton years. As a campaigner, Clinton had promised public investment, infrastructure repair, support for skill improvement, and job creation. In *Putting People First* he had proposed spending $50 billion a year for four years in these areas. But Greenspan, deficit conservatives in Congress, and Wall Street advisers convinced Clinton to set aside his economic stimulus plan. He had hoped, he told the people on February 15, 1993, "to invest in your future by creating jobs, expanding education, reforming health care. . . . But I can't—because the deficit has increased so much beyond my earlier estimates." So the administration pulled out all the stops to pass, without Republican votes, a plan to reduce the deficit by raising taxes and cutting spending. In effect, Clinton cleaned up the mess left by Reagan; he pampered Wall Street and Greenspan in the hope that the Fed chair would keep interest rates low and thus encourage economic growth.[49]

Perhaps in the long run Wall Street, Main Street, and Skid Row had common interests. Were low-income Americans the beneficiaries of solid growth? As it turned out, economic growth rates were good, although sluggish at first. In the first six years of Clinton's presidency, real gross domestic product, a common measure of economic growth, increased by a total of 25%, not as good a percentage as in the Kennedy-Johnson administration's first six years (36%) but better than in equivalent periods under Reagan (22%) and Eisenhower (17.5%).[50] In the late 90s, official unemployment rates fell to less than 5%, well below predictions. Tighter labor markets lifted pay rates in the late 90s, even for low-wage workers. But most workers had a long way to go after two decades of lousy job markets and sliding wages (figure 10.1). In 1999 the share of all jobs paying poverty-level wages was still 26.8%; it had been only 23.7% in 1979.[51]

For much of the 90s, employers tried everything before increasing wages. They offered new employees free transportation, tuition subsidies, shopping discounts, and softball fields before they increased pay. Frank L. Salizzoni, chief executive at H&R Block, claimed, "We have not been pressured to raise wages because of the labor shortage." Even when employers had to increase pay to attract workers, they did not go far. When Sprint lost operators to better jobs, the company had to increase hourly pay only from $7 to $8.25 to get replacements. That 18% increase left some Sprint workers below the family poverty line.[52]

Given the slow reaction of wages, it would have taken a very long boom to lift the bottom, and the lifting had just begun when Greenspan started raising interest rates in the summer of 1999 to slow the economy. Since certain groups started farther back, ending their poverty required an economic boom that continued for a much longer time. It is true that jobs had grown by 7.5% for blacks and 14% for Latinos, faster than for whites. By the late 90s, reported unemployment rates for these groups were at their lowest level since data were first collected in 1972. But they still remained higher, at 8.1% and 5.8%, respectively, than the rates for whites, and now recession increased minority jobless rates rapidly; by November 2001 official black rates were 10.1% and Latino rates 7.6% (the national rate for all groups was 5.7%).[53] And these rates understated real unemployment.

Most workers had seen a long-term wage decline from the mid-70s to the mid-90s. The median real hourly wage of male workers fell 9.1% over 1979–89, fell again by 6.5% over 1989–95, and then increased by 5.5% over 1995–99. The last was good news, but not enough to offset previous losses. High school graduates with no college education experienced a real wage decline of 15% over 1979–95; things turned around for them in the latter part of the Clinton boom (1995–99), when their wage rates rose 4.4%. But they had not climbed back to earlier wage peaks.[54]

What was wrong? The late 90s economy grew rapidly. But a longer and deeper boom was needed to bring wages back to 70s levels and to push poverty rates down to 10% or 9% or 8%. Full employment and real labor shortages over a long period could have done it. But there was no shortage of workers. "We seem to keep finding the bodies to hire," remarked Bradford DeLong, an economist at the University of California, Berkeley.[55]

Surprisingly, the workforce did not grow very rapidly. The civilian labor force increased by 11% in the 90s, well below increases of 16% in the 1960s and 1980s and 27% in the 1970s. In part, slow growth reflected demographic factors, for the adult population had not expanded very fast (10%). But also for much of the 90s, demand for labor grew slowly, too, and offset the benefits of fewer labor market entrants. The percentage of adults participating in the labor force changed only a little, rising from 66.5% to 67.1% (1990–99), a slight decline for men almost offsetting a small increase for women. Labor demand was not so robust until the later 90s.[56]

In the 80s and early 90s, the poverty-curing effects of economic growth were blunted for several reasons. For one thing, workers were traumatized. More joblessness, less job security, more globalization, and weaker social programs over two decades made employees cautious about fighting for their interests. Also, for most sectors, there were more than enough workers. In short, a workforce weakened by unemployment and job instability and a glut of workers gave power to employers and made for low wages and poverty.[57]

The rest of this section elaborates on these two general areas. As to the first, workers' anxieties reflected reality. While official unemployment rates were low, layoffs continued at a high rate.[58] In the 70s, 67% of all workers stayed with one employer at least nine years; in the 80s, only 52%. The percentage of workers who lost their jobs in the early years of the Clinton recovery (1993–95) was 11.4%, almost as high as in the worst depression since the 30s (12.3% over 1981–83).[59] Even Clinton's economists admitted in 1999 that "job displacement remains relatively high given today's low unemployment rates." Because of rising global competition, job flight, and a corporate strategy of lean production, layoffs became the "Strategy of First Resort." A sampling of the press in 1998 found almost forty announcements that giant corporations like Exxon, Packard Bell, Boeing, and Raytheon were each laying off thousands of workers. This was in the midst of an economic boom. Adding to job anxieties was the fact that only a third of the unemployed were receiving unemployment insurance.[60]

Also making employees nervous was the growth of the contingent labor force. For example, people counted as temporary workers had expanded by a factor of ten since 1973; by the turn of the century, they constituted 2.5% of the labor force. This was a tiny fraction, but as economist Paul Osterman noted, "regular employees are well aware of contingent employment within their organization and the implicit threat it entails."[61] Other threats were common, too. Labor expert Kate Bronfenbrenner found that more than half the firms she surveyed fought unionization by threatening to shut down U.S. operations. And many jobs were moved to Mexico, China, and India.[62]

These things made workers less aggressive and glad to have a job. But the economic force that most depressed employee bargaining power—what made people's feelings of insecurity real—was the fact that the potential labor force was much larger than official data showed and unemployment was much higher than widely used official rates. While the federal government's most highly publicized model of the labor force includes people who are at work and those who are actively looking for work, there also is a large group of workers in what I call the nearby labor force. It is because this nearby labor force was outside the official one that unemployment appeared low, and it is because its members were ready to work that wages did not rise or poverty fall as much as they should have in a long period of economic growth and falling unemployment rates.[63]

It is not possible to quantify with mathematical precision the true size of the labor force and the level of real unemployment in the 1990s. In fact, in recent years federal agencies and economists have become more confused about what is happening to the job market.[64] But we can list groups that are not included in the officially unemployed, people who are underemployed, and people who seem distant from the labor force but affect employee bargaining power. The total is large enough to limit wage growth and poverty cures.

1. First, we mention people officially counted as unemployed. These are people who have searched for work in the weeks preceding the monthly unemployment survey. They made up about 6% of the labor force in the mid-90s and 4% by the late 90s. With only this group counted, the unemployment problem appeared to be solved by the late 90s. Many economists think that 4% is virtual full employment, for it includes mainly people moving from job to job.

2. To the standard count of the unemployed we add part-time workers who want full-time work and who can be considered partially unemployed. There were almost 5 million of them in 1995.[65]

3. Hundreds of thousands and sometimes millions of Americans are "discouraged" workers who want to work but have given up looking and are not counted as unemployed. When the categories of involuntary part-timers (2) and discouraged workers (3) are included, the national unemployment rate is often double the official rate, about 8% in the late 90s.[66]

4. In a category involving some duplication with other categories, millions of people are always about to be available for new jobs because rapid "downsizing" is eliminating their old ones. In 1993–94, 6.5 million employees had their jobs wiped out; of those, by 1996 about 1.5 million had not found new jobs and 500,000 were only working part-time. Some downsized workers stopped looking for work, and some were probably not counted as discouraged or unemployed workers.[67]

5. Some of the urban poor including millions of women being pushed off welfare were added to the labor force in the late 90s. Coming from outside the labor force, they were another ready supply of labor, especially for less-skilled jobs.

6. The number of immigrants flowing into the labor force stayed high. They constituted 80% of the labor force in California agriculture and a large presence in hotel and food services, construction, and janitorial work. Many immigrants inhabited an underground economy where both those who were employed and those who were unemployed and underemployed were undercounted. Undoubtedly, government statisticians missed a lot of employment, but they also missed a lot of unemployment.

7. There were 18 million Americans ages 65–74 who were not in hospitals or nursing homes; only 3 million had jobs. A Harris poll found that 4 million older Americans wanted jobs. As pension coverage shrank, more elders sought employment.

8. The male segment of the prison population equaled 2.3% of the potential male labor force. Many were in prison because of dim employment prospects. Had half of them been out of prison, they would have added a point to the unemployment rates.

9. In a better economy, several hundred thousand homeless adults would be in the labor force, with jobs or counted as unemployed.

10. The number of nonelderly adults leaving the workforce to get federal disability payments doubled over 1984–2000; some were low-skilled workers who chose disability payments rather than low pay or unemployment. With better labor markets, they would have been working or looking for work.

11. There were uncounted scientists, engineers, and technical workers who were dismissed because they required company training to adapt their skills to new jobs or were being paid more than employers wanted to pay. Instead of paying for training, employers used a special immigration program (H-1B) to import cheaper workers. In an almost surreal illustration of how government helped to disemploy people and glut the labor market, H-1B immigration continued even when the high-tech sector sank and layoffs soared.

12. Some temporary workers were not counted as unemployed when they were between jobs, and possibly millions of "independent contractors," often downsized professionals, were unemployed or underemployed but too proud to admit it.

13. Here is an example not of hidden unemployment but of an expandable workforce. To compensate for slow wage growth or fearful of losing their jobs, employees raised their hours of work in the 90s by an amount about equal to an increase in the labor force of 4%.

14. Finally, the American labor force was now integrated into the global labor force, not only by immigration but by the ease with which companies sent work abroad. Nations with huge populations and staggering unemployment rates like India and China functioned as an adjunct to the U.S. labor force.[68]

It is impossible to add all these factors in a precise way for a perfect measure of unemployment. But these additions to the unemployment rate suggest an accordion-like labor force, expanding now at the top and now at the bottom as the music of demand directed. The effect of this nearby labor force was equivalent to having an unemployment rate of 10% or more.

The existence of a huge but submerged force of potential workers alongside the official one has been described by a handful of other scholars. In the mid-90s, economist Lester Thurow found an "enormous sea of unemployment and underemployment," a third of the workforce looking for jobs or more hours. In 1999 Marc-Andre Pigeon and L. Randall Wray argued that the Clinton boom was not so hot; if labor markets had really been good, perhaps 15 million more people, many without college education, would have been drawn into the labor force and pulled up the job ladder. Economist Timothy Bartik estimated that there was a shortage of 8 million jobs for low-skill workers in the late 80s. Katherine Newman and her associates found that there were fourteen applicants for every fast food job in Harlem.[69] In light of these estimates and my own, it is realistic to think that unemployment in the late 90s was above 10% rather than below 5%. If so, we have part of the explanation for why, in the year 2000, at the end of the longest economic expansion in U.S. history, a tenth of the population was still officially poor, another tenth was nearly poor, and the average worker's wage was still below what it had been in the 70s.[70]

Here we have studied the unemployment story for the good times of the mid- to late 90s. But as good times got better and wages increased for several years in a row, the monetary authorities at the Federal Reserve raised interest rates six times in twelve months (1999–2000) to slow economic growth. Fearing higher prices and wages, the government agency tried to halt the economic expansion that, according to many conservatives and some liberals, was the way to solve poverty. More jobs and rising wages did cure poverty, but they were, paradoxically, the signal that growth had to be curbed. In other words, growth undermined itself as a poverty cure. High demand for workers and rising wages became the warning bell that lower profits and inflationary pressures might be on the way. Recession was the way to avert or ameliorate the bad events that loomed in economic projections.

Other Nations Compensate for Market Weakness

Conservatives and moderates have promised something they won't deliver. They claim that work is the salvation of the poor; they repealed welfare and opposed more generous unemployment benefits. But they will not admit that economic growth never runs long enough to cure unemployment and job-related poverty.

Since growth stops before unemployment is erased, and since many busi-

Table 10.1. Relative Poverty Rates before and after Government Programs, 1991

Country	Before Taxes and Transfer Payments	After Taxes and Transfer Payments
Australia	21.3%	6.4%
Belgium	23.9	2.2
Canada	21.6	5.6
Denmark	23.9	3.5
Finland	9.8	2.3
France	27.5	4.8
Germany	14.1	2.4
Ireland	25.8	4.7
Italy	21.8	5.0
Netherlands	20.5	4.3
Norway	9.3	1.7
Sweden	20.6	3.8
Switzerland	12.8	4.3
United Kingdom	25.7	5.3
United States	21.0	11.7

Source: Data from Lane Kenworthy, "Do Social-Welfare Policies Reduce Poverty?: A Cross-National Assessment," Working Paper No. 188, Luxembourg Income Study, 1998, table 3; used by permission of author.

Note: Poverty rate is the percentage of people in households with incomes (adjusted for household size) below 40% of median household incomes in each country.

nesses run a lean-and-mean policy of job and wage cuts rather than job enrichment, more good jobs for low- and middle-income Americans must come from government. But even if we think that the right kind of government employment will expand in some utopian future, the working poor need immediate improvements in the minimum wage and the Earned Income Tax Credit, guaranteed health and child care, and more powerful living wage and union movements.

American capitalism does not initially produce more poverty, but American governments offer fewer income supports to help the poor than every one of fourteen other rich nations. The results are clear in table 10.1.[71] When government programs are not factored in (left column), the United States does not have the highest poverty rate, but once the impact of government programs is included, it does. By the calculations of Timothy Smeeding and his colleagues, government programs cut poverty by 37% in the United States, but by 83% in Holland and 87% in Sweden. If American elites cannot manage the economy without significant unemployment, they ought to do more to compensate people who suffer most. But they won't do so voluntarily. Without a new politics the United States will continue to have the highest poverty rate of all the rich nations.[72]

Is the U.S. Welfare State Really Backward?

I argue that one reason the United States has a lot of poor people is that government social programs are too few or too weak to fully counteract the negative impact of social and economic factors, such as unemployment, health emergencies, and family problems.[73] The advanced welfare states of Western Europe and elsewhere do better. But there are credible arguments against mine. One is that through their government Americans encourage and subsidize private welfare spending on a large scale. Another is that funding shortages and the conservative revolution of recent decades compelled even the generous European welfare states to cut back. In short, the U.S. and the European models may not be so different any more.

In fact, government-induced or subsidized items such as employer pensions and health plans cost the U.S. government in foregone taxes (or "tax expenditures") several hundred billion dollars a year. When all private welfare expenditures that are supported by tax loopholes, subsidies, and government mandates or regulations are added to direct government social welfare expenditures, the United States jumps from dead last in social spending to the midpoint among eleven rich Western nations.[74]

Does that mean that the U.S. welfare regime is pretty much the same as the European model? It does not. One piece of evidence (table 10.1) shows that other advanced nations spend more to cure poverty.[75] And that fits with the fact that American tax breaks for private welfare spending disproportionately benefit the affluent. The average tax-break subsidy in 1998 for private health insurance was $71 for families with less than $15,000 annual income and $2,357 for families with $100,000 or more. In part because of the home mortgage interest deduction, housing subsidies were seven times as high for people earning more than $50,000 as for those earning less than $10,000.[76]

On another issue of convergence, it is true that the affluent welfare states have begun to introduce market mechanisms into their systems or have pared social programs. But, to take one example, even after almost three decades of government under the extremely conservative Margaret Thatcher and the backtracking Laborite Tony Blair, there have been cuts but "no serious erosion of universal social security" in Britain.[77] In Germany, years of agitation by employers and conservatives have yielded only small changes. Recently, the long-term unemployed were required to move to less generous welfare support. But welfare supplied $420 a month per adult and $240 for each child under 14, free rent and utilities, and no time limit on benefits. In the United States unemployment insurance normally runs out after twenty-six weeks, and welfare payments are low in many states, all but nonexistent in others, and stingy or nonexistent for male adults.[78]

Perhaps the most powerful contrasts between the American and the European model, after poverty rates, involve medical care and the welfare ethos. As to the former, the United States—government and private sector—spends much more per capita than any European nation but does not have the best health record. In Europe there may be wait lists for procedures, but in France and Italy, for example, medical benefits are still generous and effectively universal, available to immigrants as well as others. Moreover, French and Italian authorities have controlled medical costs more successfully than Americans. That is part of the reason that three times as much is spent on each American as on each Italian yet more than 40 million Americans are uninsured. Above all, in most of the rich welfare-state nations people have a feeling of security. They are not likely to omit health care or proper drugs because they have no insurance. They are not likely to be pushed into bankruptcy by loss of job-based insurance and a medical emergency, as happens in the United States.[79]

Finally, there is the matter of the idea system or the culture surrounding social welfare programs. In the United States, where a third of social benefits are private, tax breaks for private social programs are rarely debated openly. In addition, some people consider tax breaks for welfare programs (private health insurance, for example) not breaks at all. The government is simply letting people keep what is theirs anyway. Both points contribute to popular confusion about the welfare state and about how much income an individual deserves. They foster resentment toward recipients of some kinds of welfare while the resenter accepts other kinds of help. The popular welfare state ethos is rather selective (strong for Social Security, weak for "welfare" itself, and wavering on unemployment insurance). People are not informed about whom government aid is benefiting the most or about the true costs of various social programs. These confusions add to mystification about social obligations and the ownership of society's common resources.[80]

chapter eleven

BUSH AND BEYOND
On Solving and Not Solving Poverty

Government policy in the early 2000s was a good example of how not to cure poverty and unemployment. Events of those years showed that private markets and a government policy favoring the affluent failed the people. It does not have to be that way. Other rich nations have social programs that are more generous and that help parents work if they want to. The problem is not that Americans don't want to work at something useful and or that they don't want stable social relationships; it is that the economy cannot supply the jobs people need and that government policy does too little to help those who combine family and jobs, those who stay home, and those who want to work and are still poor.

Bush's Jobless Recovery

The most important economic event of the George W. Bush presidency was a recession, the first in a decade. The Bush administration did not cause the recession, but it did little to counteract it; the result was few new jobs and more poverty. The recession began in March 2001, six months before the terrorist attacks on the World Trade Center. The background causes included, first, efforts by Alan Greenspan, who, fearing tight labor markets and rising wages and prices, escalated interest rates to slow economic growth, and, second, the deflation of the 1990s bubble of overbuilding in telecommunications and commercial structures. The downturn was the normal outcome of political and economic decision making that fuels booms and busts. However, the harsh effects of the recession were not normal or necessary.[1]

The recession meant that total output and jobs declined. Output growth soon resumed, but job growth did not. The peak unemployment rate of 6.3% in June 2003 was not particularly high, but the statistic was misleading. An unusually large number of people gave up the search for work and were not counted as unemployed. Real unemployment was probably 10%. Manufacturing lost 3 million jobs, many of them forever. A larger fraction of new jobs was going to older Americans and to immigrants, which was fine for them but hard on young people and the native-born middle-aged jobless; black workers were especially hard hit by the recession.[2]

Total job growth in Bush's first term was zero, the worst record since Herbert Hoover. Normally a recession slides into rapid job creation, and that is necessary not only to wipe out recession losses but also to add millions of new jobs for an expanding labor force. As the country came out of an earlier recession, 8 million jobs were added in Clinton's first term. Under Bush, instead of adding the 5 million jobs necessary to keep up with population growth, there was virtually no net job growth.[3]

It is not clear why this recovery took so long to begin creating jobs. In part the explanation has to do with the corporate gospel of lean-and-mean employment policy. Big layoffs are now common even in prosperous times. Managers squeeze more out of their existing workforces, and Wall Street likes the effect on the bottom line.[4] For the citizenry as a whole, however, this is a vicious circle. Job loss limits income growth, and that limits spending and economic recovery—which in turn limits job growth. Over time employment recovers, but because of a second factor, it limped along this time. As in the early 90s, in 2004 Greenspan was worried about inflation, and he began to raise interest rates in order to chill economic growth. This was long before jobs had returned to their 2000 level.

A third exacerbating factor was that the Bush administration did little to stimulate job creation. Policy was warped by Republican-led tax cuts for business and the rich. Rates were cut on dividends and inheritances, neither of which had much to do with job stimulation. Tax cuts rewarded investment in machinery rather than people. Instead of tax cuts for the least needy, government should have spent on roads, parks, and schools; assisted states with troubled budgets; expanded and enriched preschool programs; improved unemployment benefits; and enlarged tax cuts and credits for middle- and low-income consumers, for they spend more of their refunds in job-creating ways. But fiscal policy under President Bush and his fellow Republicans favored the very rich. The Congressional Budget Office estimated that one-third of the tax cuts went to the top 1% of income holders; these millionaires averaged $78,460 in tax cuts. The richest 257,000 taxpayers were handed an aggregate tax cut bigger than that given the lowest 85 million taxpayers.[5] Furthermore, most of the cuts were welfare for the rich, not economic stimulus. In fiscal 2003, according to the Office of Tax Policy Research at the University of Michigan, two-thirds of the tax-cut dollars were saved or used to pay down debt; they were not put into play to fuel economic growth.[6] Finally, government financed the cuts by more federal borrowing, and that would eventually be paid for by higher taxes, benefit cuts in Social Security and Medicare, or both. When gains from tax cuts and losses from program cuts are totaled, the bottom four-fifths of the households lose, and the poor lose the most.[7]

Poverty: Some Results of Bush Policies

The recession and the feeble job recovery meant more unemployed and more poor. Wage rates held up for a little while but soon dipped. Average real weekly pay for full-time workers was lower in early 2006 than it had been in early 2001.[8] As income growth faded and as more people lost their jobs, more became homeless. By New Year's 2002, evictions were surging in the Midwest and East. Poverty inched up each year from 11.3% of the population in 2000 to 12.7% in 2004. Enough people for a good-sized country, 37 million Americans, were poor.[9]

In some areas government was helping a little more, in others quite a bit less. On the positive side, more low-income Americans were removed from the income tax rolls. On the negative side, the federal minimum wage was stuck at $5.15. Meanwhile, as the employer-based health system unraveled, an additional 5.2 million Americans (comparing 2003 with 2000) were found to lack health insurance. Things would have been worse had it not been for the expansion of the state-federal Children's Health Insurance Program. Still, with 45 million uninsured, the system was cracking, and little was being done to fix it.[10]

At times federal officials seemed callous in their determination to make the poor and unemployed suffer from economic events and bad government policy. First, the president and Congress allowed extended unemployment benefits to lapse in December 2003, even though job creation was sluggish and the duration of unemployment had lengthened. A record number of people exhausted their unemployment benefits in the first half of 2004. Second, leading Republicans continued to boast about the success of welfare reform, even as half the people leaving welfare stayed poor or became poorer. Poverty rates for children and female-headed families—the primary clientele for Temporary Assistance for Needy Families (TANF)—climbed, but the number of families on the TANF rolls fell by 500,000 (1999–2003). In other words, more people were poor, but fewer received cash assistance.[11]

Some Democrats were out of touch with economic reality and the disappointing outcomes of welfare reform, but conservative Republicans seemed willingly blind to what was happening. Although the job market was lousy and tax cuts did little to fix it, Bush and Secretary of Health and Human Services Thompson wanted to make TANF more punitive: they hoped to spend millions of dollars pressuring women to marry, they wanted to push women into the workforce more rapidly, and they aimed to make it harder for poor women to get the schooling that helped them compete for jobs. (As of late 2005, these more draconian policies had not been put into effect because Bush could not get a majority in the Senate to go along.)[12]

Pushing the work ethic made antiwelfare dogma appealing to some, but conservatives were able to get away without doing anything to create or improve jobs, in part because of a successful thirty-year propaganda war that explained poverty as the result of government permissiveness and poor people's bad attitudes. They were successful in tying a conservative attack on welfare to their idea of the work ethic. But they were able to do so also because there was not much of an opposition party to articulate a different view of the world.

While it is true that Republicans controlled Congress and the White House and thus could often get their way, there were many issues on which the populace could be roused against the Republicans' nineteenth-century view of wealth and poverty. Bush and his cronies made a mess of the postwar occupation of Iraq; they did little to encourage job creation; they bungled the introduction of the Medicare Drug plan, forcing many states to step in with subsidies for the poor; and they made the United States almost alone among rich Western nations in showing official contempt for scientific estimates about the effects of global warming.

Above all, administration officials were indifferent and incompetent in the wake of the massive hurricane that struck the Gulf Coast on the morning of August 29, 2005. Local authorities failed miserably, too, but the federal government, with vast resources, failed to act in a timely manner to assure that people were evacuated from the storm that everyone knew was coming. Some pundits argued that politicians who had long been proud to fight against government aid to the poor had acted just about as expected in the first days of the crisis. It was obvious that the people who suffered most were those who had for decades been left behind: poor and black. The nation learned that 28% of New Orleans population was poor and 84% of those were black. For a few weeks, poverty was back on the agenda, and some liberals talked about the opportunity for new programs. But not much was made of the moment. The rebuilding effort along the Gulf Coast was a mess, and in January 2006, the U.S. House Representatives passed a budget that cut aid to the poor by $40 billion over five years. It did so in part to free up money for tax cuts to the rich. Liberals and the Left missed an opportunity to publicize a more humane view of the world than is broadcast from the White House. There will be many more opportunities. And a new movement to end poverty and economic insecurity needs a positive program.[13]

What Needs to Be Done

The United States is not Europe, but we can learn from social programs in Western European nations that have virtually eliminated poverty. Many social programs are open to all, unlike some in the United States that target and degrade the poor. A good new antipoverty program would be a program that is good for the nonpoor, too. Economic reality itself is moving in this direction: working and middle-class Americans have a little more in common with the poor than they had in the 50s and 60s. They are now more likely to be laid off, to lose their health insurance, and to be forced into bankruptcy. There are signs, too, that people are ready to tackle economic issues and set other issues to the side; for example, 78% of voters claimed to care more about fighting poverty than about fighting gay marriage.[14] The following list outlines what can be done to fix the economy, erase poverty, and help people achieve their dreams. Much of it seems like pie in the sky, but it is more practical than urging more tax cuts and nastier welfare policies, neither of which cure poverty or the jobs crisis.

1. *Use government tools to stimulate job creation.* As this book has argued, there is almost always a shortage of jobs in the United States and always a shortage of good jobs. Fiscal and monetary policy should emphasize creating good jobs for middle- and low-income people, even at the risk of a little more inflation. And instead of fighting inflation by means of recessions that punish the lower half by raising unemployment and poverty rates, specific causes of inflation in health care and energy prices should be attacked directly. Members of the Federal Reserve Board and all politicians need a workshop in how to distinguish between upper-class interests and the national interest. Slow or no economic growth is a form of inflation control that attacks the weakest. If inflation is a problem, control profits. If oil prices surge, attack those. Remember, too, that rising wages need not be inflationary if worker productivity is rising and if owners share the benefits of increased efficiency. Real wages for the majority of workers are lower than in the 1970s, despite significant increases in output per hour.

2. *Create good government jobs.* Government should not devise elaborate job-training schemes, especially those disconnected from real jobs. The research shows that most such programs bring few benefits. Access to college should be

eased to improve people's general skills and sense of well-being; job-specific training programs should normally involve on-the-job training for real jobs.[15]

In part because economic authorities will never allow macroeconomic policy to run fast and long enough to create all the jobs we need, the federal government should expand its own labor force. For decades government jobs have been an important avenue of success for the poor and nearly poor, especially among minorities, but that effect has waned recently, in part because of the conservative assault on government. Governments should do more to create permanent jobs that provide useful services and pay decently (protecting our national parks, running after-school programs at neighborhood parks, delivering the mail, building schools, insulating buildings, manufacturing solar cells, caring for our children, acting as teaching aides). The private sector is subverting the American dream; there is less job mobility today than in the 70s. Few Bush supporters admit it, but all net job growth was in government employment from January 2000 to May 2005. Honesty requires that we acknowledge the failure of the private sector and create civilian-sector government jobs.[16]

3. *Lift the low-wage job market.* In 2004, there were 47 million full-time workers earning under $10 an hour.[17] The federal minimum wage should be raised from $5.15 to $10 an hour. That would still leave some families in poverty, but it would be a substantial increase. Annual increases should be tied to growth in national income. Communities should resist the invasion of big box stores like Wal-Mart that pay their employees poorly, encourage them to use public welfare, drive worldwide wages down, ruin small businesses, and drain dollars out of local communities and into the pockets of billionaires. (Five of the ten richest Americans are Wal-Mart owners.) Unionization should be made easier, and penalties for violating workers' rights should be enforced. And it seems unlikely that some of the suggestions in this list will be effective if imports from nations that pay extremely low wages continually undercut American wages. There must be limits on low-wage imports; nations that keep their currencies and prices artificially low should be penalized.

4. *Avoid scapegoating immigrants.* Since many people who immigrated to the United States were poor when they arrived, heavy immigration raised poverty rates. In 2000, immigrants had a poverty rate of 17.8%, and that of recent immigrants was 22.4%. The rate for the native-born was only 10.2%. Since the overall poverty rate in 2000 was 11.3%, it appears that immigrants added about a point to the poverty rate.[18]

There are several ways to assess the economic impact of immigration. As discussed in chapters 7 and 10, heavy immigration adds to the labor glut in America. Although immigration stimulates job creation, there are more immigrants than new jobs, so immigration adds to the labor surplus, making for lower wages and more poverty.

But estimating the total economic impact of immigration is difficult. Scholars disagree. George Borjas and Lawrence Katz of Harvard once claimed that, from 1980 to 2000, illegal Mexican immigration cut the average wages of high school dropouts by 8.2%. Other scholars found no such effect. Borjas and Katz later concluded that the wage impact was about 5% and that it fell most heavily on low-income workers of African American and Hispanic backgrounds. The impact on the whole labor force was not severe. Many impact studies did not take into account that with less immigration and higher wages more businesses would have fled the country. Katz himself gave a balanced summation of how to understand the role of immigration in the wage stagnation of the past thirty years: illegal immigration reinforced "adverse trends for the least advantaged, but there are much stronger trends operating over the last twenty-five years."[19]

The flood of immigrants was just one of many factors that included a fierce corporate attack on wages, unions, and labor standards; the decline of the minimum wage and contraction of unemployment insurance; the successful conservative effort to control tax policy and widen income inequality; and, finally, the failure of business and government to create or hold on to good jobs. Ironically, heavy immigration, by keeping wages down, may have slowed just a bit the export of capital and jobs.

Immigration, then, is a complex factor, helping to dampen wage growth but possibly saving jobs. All in all, its effect on poverty is dwarfed by other factors. Much poverty has nothing to do with immigration; it is unlikely, for example, that immigration explains much of the long history of high poverty rates in Detroit and New Orleans.

Immigration can make unionization more difficult, and in specific local occupations, immigrants have pushed out native-born workers—for example, in janitorial services in Los Angeles, But political institutions and organizing energy are vital. California is a good example. With a huge immigrant population, it is nevertheless one of a handful of states in which the unionized share of the labor force has grown in recent years. Or compare Ohio and Nevada. In Ohio, where there is little illegal immigration, the median wage of high school dropouts is almost 20% below the same wage in Nevada. Nevada has more illegal immigrants but is highly unionized.[20]

What is the solution to the "immigration problem?" A 1986 reform promoted amnesty for illegal immigrants and promised to punish employers who hired them—a promise that was not fulfilled. Twenty years later, in 2006, immigration reform was again on the table, although divisions among Republicans threatened to derail it.

For the antipoverty forces it makes sense to frame the issue around how to solve poverty rather than how to fix immigration. Draconian restrictions on immigration will not fix much poverty. Furthermore, the cost of totally "closing" our borders would be high in terms of money and national ideals. It would sharpen tensions with Mexico and with Latinos in the United States. Furthermore, people with a sense of history have to feel uneasy about keeping or kicking out Mexican immigrants when they remember that the United States snatched much of the Southwest from Mexico in the 1840s.

Guest worker programs, used in the 1940s and 1950s and proposed by the president in 2006, involve a kind of indentured servitude; the guests usually cannot move toward citizenship, form unions, or protest too loudly. In any case, why do we need a guest worker program? It is true that there are labor shortages in some occupations at some times, but usually the claim of a labor shortage means that employers do not want to pay adequate wages. It is interesting that big farmers, a pretty conservative bunch, do not believe in free market economics when it comes to their own workers.

Some people who claim to be worried about our borders and about the plight of workers hate unions, fight against raising the minimum wage, and support tax breaks for Wal-Mart billionaires. If those who want to close the borders support unionization and a higher minimum wage, we might believe that they really cared about "the American worker."

Instead of guaranteeing a low-wage labor force, government and other institutions should do everything possible to create better-paying jobs. Cheap imports made under bad conditions ought to pay a penalty at our borders. Imports from China or Germany should be penalized if they are manufactured by severely underpaid workers

On a broader level, the antipoverty forces have to strive to get people to think of themselves not mainly as individual consumers without moral and social ties to other people but as members of a large group of employees, including those at stores like Wal-Mart and those in Bangladesh who make the products that end up on the shelves at Wal-Mart. Low prices are not a magic trick performed by Wal-Mart executives. They are squeezed out of the wages of store workers and foreign factory workers; they are sucked out of benefit packages until there is not much benefit left.

In some cases, higher wages need not mean higher prices for the consumer. If worker productivity rises, prices should not have to. And for some products employee compensation is not a large part of the final price. By one estimate a 40% increase in the hourly wage of $8.83 paid to farmworkers would cost the average household $9 a year.[21] Even if the cost was a little more, many buyers might want business to pay a fair wage because that is the moral position and because people who live in poverty in an affluent, democratic society are not fully a part of that society.

5. *Do more to support the unemployed.* Unemployment insurance should be expanded in coverage and in duration, especially during job droughts like the early 2000s. States should be required to cover part-time workers. The United States pays less to fewer unemployed for shorter periods than other rich nations.[22] If conservatives revere work, they should do more to help people who have worked and want to work; the jobless should not suffer so much for nasty government policy and harsh economic events.

6. *Strengthen Social Security; don't privatize it.* Social Security has been one of our most effective government antipoverty programs. In late 2005, Bush tried to begin privatizing the system, but he failed. Privatization of the system would bankrupt its finances and risk throwing tens of millions of Americans into poverty. It would come at a time when private pensions are in decline.

There are two problems for Social Security. First, although there is nothing inherently wrong with federal budget deficits if they produce jobs and income for the millions, today's deficits are being financed in part by loans from the Social Security Trust Fund. President Bush has raised the question of whether the government will repay what is owed to the Trust Fund. One wonders if he would make the same point about federal obligations to foreign and domestic bankers. Second, even if the federal government repays its loans, there may be a demographic D-day for Social Security. As baby boomers retire and labor force growth slows, Social Security *may* not be able to pay full benefits. (D-day could be in the 2040s, or later, or, with good growth in jobs and wages, never. Social Security trustees' projections have been too pessimistic in recent years.) If there is a problem, it can be fixed with a package of modest reforms, such as raising the amount of income subject to Social Security taxation and taxing unearned income. The economics of the solution are simple, and the politics could be too. There is anxiety about Social Security, stoked by privatizers, but there is wide support for saving and improving the system.

7. *Create one government health insurance program for everyone.* The employer-based health insurance system is eroding; people without insurance use emergency rooms, and that practice is bankrupting many institutions. There must be a federally run system open to all and including price controls on drugs and services. A system that allows the healthy and the affluent to bow out will be financially unsound and will set itself up for attacks from welfare bashers. Insurance works if everyone is included; the healthy subsidize the sick, and that is the point.[23]

8. *Expand the Earned Income Tax Credit.* The EITC should be enriched and extended to more people.

9. *Rethink poverty lines.* Poverty lines should be raised or reconceptualized. In 2004, a family of four with $20,000 a year was not considered poor, but it should have been. There will be debate about whether the line should be raised to $25,000 or $35,000 or to 50% of the median family income, but it should be raised to give a more accurate idea of how many people are in trouble and to expand the political base for antipoverty action. No president wants to see the number of poor people jump during his administration, so this reform might require an agreement between incoming and outgoing presidents. But there would have to be a great deal of debate and political pressure to get to that point. A better approach would be to eliminate poverty lines and emphasize comprehensive efforts to help not just the very poor but middle- to low-income Americans. We could still learn every year how many people fall below specified income levels, but the poor might seem less different, and we would not congratulate ourselves when families crawl over the poverty line and into semipoverty.[24]

10. *Enforce equal opportunity for good jobs and income for women and minorities.* Economic growth alone will not bring enough permanent progress for women and ethnic minorities. Affirmative action targets are often the only way to assure that there really is equal opportunity rather than just rhetoric about it.

11. *Protect affordable education.* College degrees and college-level vocational programs are associated with income gains. The current welfare system should be replaced, but until it is, more rather than less college work should be counted toward work requirements for welfare recipients. And if politicians really believe that education is the road to success, they should do more to make college free. We are moving in the opposite direction. As it becomes harder for low-income people to afford college, equal opportunity is compromised.[25]

At the other end of the school channel, there is new evidence that investment in early childhood education may pay off in later years. Expanded pre-school programs, including a more richly funded Head Start, will not end poverty or solve the job shortage, but they could make the competition a bit more equal among races and classes.[26]

12. *Move toward a more progressive tax system.* Recent tax cuts that favor the rich should be reversed or allowed to lapse. Inequality matters. In 2003 the bottom 20% of the households collectively took in 3.4% of all income; the top 20% took 50%, or fifteen times as much.[27] Most of the tax cuts passed in the early 2000s accentuated income inequalities, and they served no useful social or economic purpose. The estate tax, which affects the affluent few, should be fully restored. (The flat tax and national sales tax would allow the rich to pay less and would increase taxes on the poor and working class.) On the plus side, there have been changes in the tax code that lifted tax burdens from people

with low incomes. We need more of that. Social Security reform might eliminate taxes on low-income workers. Parts of the tax system are mildly equalizing, but many recent cuts have gone in the opposite direction and should be reversed.

13. *Start planning for an American minimum income.* We have some of this in food stamps, which are available to most poor people, and in Supplemental Security Income, which provides an income floor for disabled and elderly Americans. It seems like pie in the sky today, but for the long run we need to think about a guaranteed minimum income. People deserve income because they are human beings, whether or not they are working, whether or not they are working at jobs that pay, and even if they look dirty and smell bad. Also, a guaranteed minimum might be one way to reward people who are now taking care of relatives and friends for free. It would provide support for college students who are on their own. Its implementation should go hand in hand with a reconsideration of what life is all about. Should everyone be working as much as possible? Should we have more things or more time? How about time for roses and poetry?

14. *Increase pay rates so that people can work less.* Surveys show that most people want more time for family and leisure, even if that means less pay, but American jobs and incomes are not family-friendly. We need a less unequal distribution of wages and salaries so that workers in the middle class and below can get by on shorter workweeks. We have much more total income than we had in 1938, when federal hours legislation was passed, but we have less income equality, and we have not changed our assumption that the standard workweek is forty hours. Higher pay and fewer hours could be a good thing for people.[28]

15. *Scrap our current welfare program, Temporary Assistance for Needy Families (TANF).* Even before we get a minimum income for all, our current welfare program, Temporary Assistance for Needy Families, should be scrapped. It has been a flop as an antipoverty program. In many states, monthly payments are under $200, and authorities strive to keep people off the rolls. Defenders of TANF are dishonest about the antipoverty success of low-wage work. Policy for single mothers ought not to be focused on how tough welfare agencies can be or how many recipients are forced into marriage but on making it easier for parents to work without neglecting their children. We need better jobs, paid family leave, and more public support for child care. In Sweden and Finland such programs exist and are aimed at the general population rather than just the poor; those two countries have higher rates of work, lower poverty rates for single parents, and higher rates of children growing up with two parents. Some Americans who hate government programs will never support these programs, but a majority will; they help everyone who is struggling to balance work and family.[29]

In October 2004, union members of UNITE HERE, employed at the Fairmont Hotel in San Francisco, wait to find out if they are going back to work after a two-week strike. (Photograph by David Bacon)

16. *Do more to support affordable housing.* Government should do more to subsidize and stimulate nonprofit builders of low-income housing, especially where the average wage is not enough to afford decent housing. For the homeless, placing people in real housing, with social services nearby, has been found to be the best solution.

17. *Challenge conservatives on unions and the working poor.* Those conservatives who worship the private sector and talk big about work and family values might ask companies to play fair with unions. Many businesses have found that it is cheap to violate laws against firing union members and organizers. When privatizers learn that simply asking businesses to be nice does not work, they can support labor law reform that levels the playing field between management and labor. They can support obligatory card check unionization, which would require employers to bargain with the union when a majority of employees have signed union cards. They can raise penalties for violations of labor law and see that labor laws are enforced. These reforms will not happen soon, conservatives won't support them, and unionization does not depend on them. But these reforms can be part of a long-range antipoverty program. Unionization raises wages and reduces the number of people who work and are poor.

Politics and Vision

None of these reforms will happen without political conflict. Most solutions to poverty involve disagreements about political fundamentals, especially the role of government; erasing poverty will not come merely from warm feelings about the downtrodden or appeals to the good-heartedness of the rich. Charles Dickens is dead. We need a new politics, and that means national movements separate from but involved in national parties. Extreme conservatives have taken over the Republican Party. Perhaps people who want to cure poverty and soften economic inequality ought to make a real effort to take over the Democratic Party, from the bottom up. In the early 60s, some activists hoped for a realignment of the parties—all the conservatives in the Republican Party and all the liberals in the Democratic Party. The Republican side of things worked out, but conservative success scared many Democrats, moving them rightward. On economic issues we now have a right-wing Republican Party with a handful of moderates and a centrist Democratic Party with a handful of old-time liberals. Whether the Democratic Party can be unchained from corporate contributions and whether millions of low-income Americans who vote infrequently or not at all can be brought to the polls will be discovered only by trying. Currently, 40% of the poor vote, compared with 74% of the investor class.[30] There are organizations like the Association of Community Organizations for Reform Now (ACORN) doing good work in communities across the nation, but we also need a national party that speaks to the needs of people with low incomes and for national solutions to many poverty and unemployment problems that are national.

There is a constituency for a more generous social policy; millions of people can be detached from conservative dogmas that are economically hurtful to them. Realizing such a policy will take an attractive alternative to the conservative view that seems to lack compassion and generosity toward the poor and is energized not only by sincere moral positions but by a crazy hostility to using government for social justice. People understand the failures of Bush conservatism in the Katrina fiasco. A compassionate left-liberal view has much to recommend it, but it requires more institutions—such as think tanks and unions and community organizations—to broadcast it. And it must be broadcast in attractive ways. In the end people may find that this world view is truly conservative, not only in its respect for positive government and for communities and relationships that work and endure but also in its faith that our natural resources, our labor force, our economic output, and our governments are public goods that should belong to us all.

UNEMPLOYMENT, POVERTY, EARNINGS, AND HOUSEHOLD STRUCTURE

Figure A.1. Annual Official Civilian Unemployment Rate and Author's Estimate of Real Rate, 1959–2005

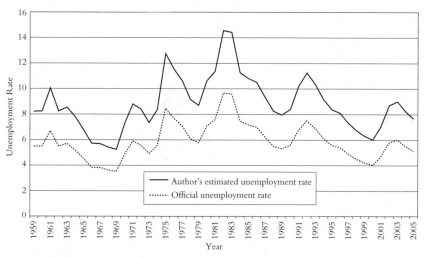

Source: Official data from *Economic Report of the President* (Washington: Government Printing Office, 2006), table B-42, at <www.gpoaccess.gov/eop/tables06.html#erp2>. Author's real rate is 150% of official rate, a deliberately conservative estimate based on information in chapter 5.

Figure A.2. U.S. Poverty Rates, 1950–2004

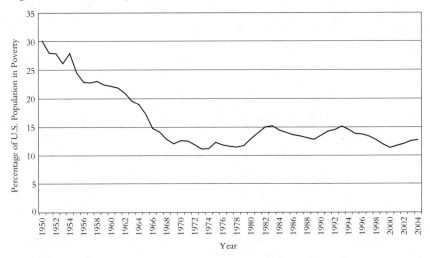

Sources: Carmen DeNavas-Walt, Bernadette D. Proctor, and Cheryl Hill Lee, U.S. Department of Commerce, Bureau of the Census, Current Population Reports, P60-229, *Income, Poverty, and Health Insurance Coverage in the United States, 2004* (Washington: Government Printing Office, 2005), table B-1; Charles Murray, *Losing Ground: American Social Policy, 1950–1980* (New York: Basic Books, 1984), 245.

Figure A.3. Real Weekly Earnings of Production and Nonsupervisory Workers in the Private Sector, 1964–2005

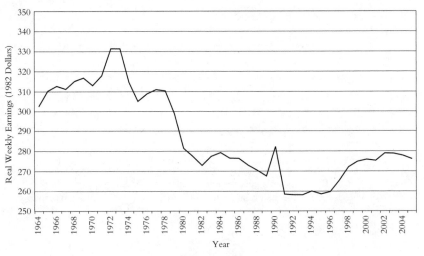

Source: *Economic Report of the President* (Washington: Government Printing Office, 2006), table B-47, at <www.gpoaccess.gov/eop/tables06.html#erp2>.

Figure A.4. Percentage of Poor by Household Type, 1959, 1979, 1998

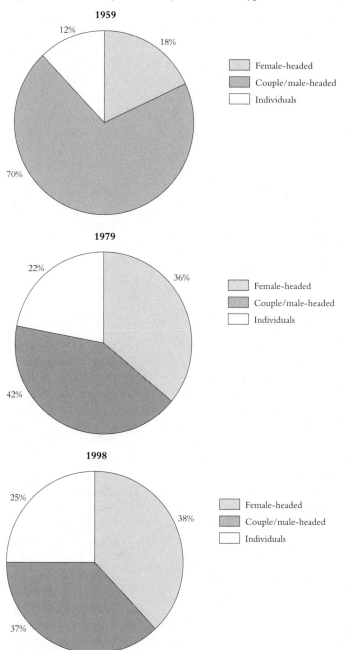

1959

12%

18%

70%

☐ Female-headed
■ Couple/male-headed
☐ Individuals

1979

22%

36%

42%

☐ Female-headed
■ Couple/male-headed
☐ Individuals

1998

25%

38%

37%

☐ Female-headed
■ Couple/male-headed
☐ Individuals

Source: Gary Burtless and Timothy M. Smeeding, "The Level, Trend, and Composition of Poverty," in Sheldon H. Danziger and Robert H. Haveman, eds., *Understanding Poverty* (New York: Russell Sage Foundation; Cambridge, Mass.: Harvard University Press, 2001), 62.

APPENDIX TWO

GROUPS OFTEN LEFT OUT OF ANTIPOVERTY DISCUSSIONS IN THE 60S AND TODAY

Snapshot 1: Rural Poverty—Not Much Policy

Most scholarly attention in the 60s and 70s focused on the urban poor, but in 1970 half of the poor lived outside metropolitan areas.[1] Federal programs looked urban, but most were available in rural areas. This was the case with the Child Development Group of Mississippi, which provided Head Start programs for rural blacks (chapter 3). Volunteers in Service to America (VISTA) workers went into mining areas and Native American reservations, and the Job Corps attracted youngsters from town and country. California Rural Legal Assistance served the poor in agricultural areas.

Still, it must be said that the people who created the War on Poverty never decided how to approach the problem of rural poverty. Should the rural poor be encouraged to migrate to the cities, or should they get help to stay where they were? The nation's planners and political leaders did not have long-range policies for the development of the countryside and the preservation of regional cultures. The problem of rural poverty received attention, but it was easier to ignore than urban poverty. Often the rural poor solved the problem by moving to metropolitan areas.[2]

Snapshot 2: How Many of the Poor Were Sick or Disabled?

Of all Americans counted as poor in 1970, half were under 14 or over 64. Of the 12,272,000 who were 14–64 years old, 1,208,000 (almost 10%) were listed as ill or disabled. Surprisingly, in 1966 nearly one-sixth of the labor force was disabled for longer than six months. Disabilities and illness caused some poverty by making success in the workplace more difficult. But the reverse was also true; poverty caused illness and disability. Poor people often had bad nutrition, lacked access to medical care, and were subject to environmental and workplace dangers that did not afflict the middle class. Illness and disability helped to make some people poor, but poverty also led to more illness and injury. Causation was a two-way street.[3]

Snapshot 3: Singletons

Individuals on their own were included in government poverty rates, but except for teens, they were often less studied than families, and they were some times badly treated in government programs. They had an extremely high poverty rate, about 44% in the early 1960s.[4] Some were homeless and uncounted. Single adults were not eligible for welfare, and local relief programs were stingy. They deserve more scholarly and political attention.

NOTES

Abbreviations

EWP	U.S. Senate, Committee on Labor and Public Welfare, Subcommittee on Employment, Manpower and Poverty, *Examination of the War on Poverty*, 90th Cong., 1st sess., May 10 and 11, 1967
HLS, 1972	U.S. Department of Labor, Bureau of Labor Statistics, *Handbook of Labor Statistics, 1972* (Washington: Government Printing Office, 1972)
HLS, 1980	U.S. Department of Labor, Bureau of Labor Statistics, *Handbook of Labor Statistics, 1980* (Washington: Government Printing Office, 1980)
HLS, 1983	U.S. Department of Labor, Bureau of Labor Statistics, *Handbook of Labor Statistics, 1983* (Washington: Government Printing Office, 1983)
HS	U.S. Department of Commerce, Bureau of the Census, *Historical Statistics of the United States: Colonial Times to 1970*, pt. 1 (Washington: Government Printing Office, 1975)
HT	Executive Office of the President of the United States, Office of Management and Budget, *Historical Tables: Budget of the United States Government, Fiscal Year 1997* (Washington: Government Printing Office, 1996)
Jacobs, *Handbook*	Eva E. Jacobs, ed., *Handbook of U.S. Labor Statistics: Employment, Earnings, Prices, Productivity and Other Labor Data*, 3rd ed. (Lanham, Md.: Bernan Press, 1999)
NF	U.S. Department of Labor, Office of Policy Planning and Research, *The Negro Family: The Case for National Action* (1965), reprinted in Lee Rainwater and William L. Yancey, *The Moynihan Report and the Politics of Controversy* (Cambridge, Mass.: MIT Press, 1967), 41–124; all citations are to the Rainwater and Yancey reprint

Pechman interview	Walter Heller, Kermit Gordon, James Tobin, Gardner Ackley, and Paul Samuelson, recorded interview by Joseph Pechman, August 1, 1964, Oral History Program, John F. Kennedy Library, Boston
Poverty, 1998	U.S. Department of Commerce, Bureau of the Census, Current Population Reports, series P60-207, *Poverty in the United States, 1998* (Washington: Government Printing Office, 1999)
SA, 1981	U.S. Department of Commerce, Bureau of the Census, *Statistical Abstract of the United States, 1981* (Washington: Government Printing Office, 1981)
SA, 1992	U.S. Department of Commerce, Bureau of the Census, *Statistical Abstract of the United States, 1992* (Washington: Government Printing Office, 1992)
Unemployment Hearings, pt. 4	U.S. Senate, *Unemployment Problems, Hearings before the Special Committee on Unemployment Problems*, 86th Cong., 1st sess., pt. 4, November 19 and 20 and December 17, 1959
Unemployment Hearings, pt. 7	U.S. Senate, *Unemployment Problems, Hearings before the Special Committee on Unemployment Problems*, 86th Cong., 1st sess., pt. 7, December 1, 2, 3, and 4, 1959

Introduction

1. Seth Rockman, *Welfare Reform in the Early Republic: A Brief History with Documents* (Boston: St. Martin's, 2003), 1–20, 148–53.

2. There is more discussion of poverty lines throughout this book. Chapter 2 discusses their origins, and chapters 7 and 11 argue that they are too low.

3. Economic Policy Institute, *Job Watch Bulletin*, May 6, 2005, at <www.epinet.org>.

4. Aaron Donovan, "For Many, Sliding into Poverty Takes Only a Few Missed Paychecks," *New York Times*, November 16, 2001, A30; Peter G. Gosselin, "How Just a Handful of Setbacks Sent the Ryans Tumbling out of Prosperity," *Los Angeles Times*, December 30, 2004, A1, A18–A19.

Chapter One

1. Lawrence S. Wittner, *Cold War America: From Hiroshima to Watergate*, expanded ed.(New York: Holt, Rinehart and Winston, 1978), 111–40, esp. 122; Douglas T. Miller and Marion Nowak, *The Fifties: The Way We Really Were* (Garden City, N.Y.: Doubleday, 1977), esp. 105–21. For another positive view, Alan Ehrenhalt, *The Lost City: The Forgotten Virtues of Community in America* (New York: Basic Books, 1995).

2. James T. Patterson, *America's Struggle against Poverty, 1900–1980* (Cambridge, Mass.: Harvard University Press, 1981), 78–96, offers a brief treatment of the 50s.

3. Gross domestic product data from U.S. Department of Commerce, Bureau of Economic Analysis, at <http://www.bea.doc.gov/bea/dn/gdplev.htm>. Also, Frank

Levy, *Dollars and Dreams: The Changing American Income Distribution* (New York: Russell Sage Foundation, 1987), 47, 56, 66. Median family size grew from 3.54 to 3.67; the increase was less than expected in a baby boom. See *HS*, 41.

4. *HS*, 130–31, 132.

5. Ibid., 173. These are pre-inflation earnings for 1950–60. Prices rose about 23%.

6. Unless otherwise stated, in this book poverty rates are based on the federal government's official poverty lines. There are lines to fit a variety of family structures and sizes, but most commonly cited is the line for a family of two parents and two children under 18. In 2004 such a family with more than $19,157 a year was not, officially, poor. Government agencies use the lines to estimate the size of the poverty population and the poverty rate. The lines are the basis for figure A.2, and they are discussed in several chapters and in the profile of Mollie Orshansky in chapter 2. The U.S. Census Bureau publishes its annual study of the previous year's poverty in August. It is available at <www.census.gov>.

7. Mark J. Stern, "Poverty and the Life-Cycle, 1940–1960," *Journal of Social History* 24 (Spring 1991): 530, table 6; Christine Ross, Sheldon Danziger, and Eugene Smolensky, *The Level and Trend of Poverty, 1939–1979*, Discussion Paper #790-85 (Madison, Wis.: Institute for Research on Poverty, 1985).

8. Robert J. Lampman, *The Low Income Population and Economic Growth*, Study Paper No. 12, prepared for the Joint Economic Committee, 86th Cong., 1st sess. (Washington: Government Printing Office, 1959), 14, 23, 32; Mark J. Stern, "Poverty and Family Composition since 1940," in Michael B. Katz, ed., *The "Underclass" Debate: Views from History* (Princeton, N.J.: Princeton University Press, 1993), 220–53; Stern, "Poverty and Life-Cycle," esp. 527; Levy, *Dollars and Dreams*, 132–41.

9. William L. O'Neill, *American High: The Years of Confidence, 1945–1960* (New York: Free Press, 1989), esp. 9–32, and Charles C. Alexander, *Holding the Line: The Eisenhower Era, 1952–1961* (Bloomington: Indiana University Press, 1976), 31, 41–42. Alexander claims that the private sector created only one-tenth of the new jobs, while government, education, and nonprofits created the rest (107). I found no evidence for that, but governments were creating civilian jobs at a faster rate than the private sector. *HS*, 137–39.

10. Government payments can make people less poor without lifting them above the lines. On the fraction of poor people's incomes supplied by government, Nan L. Maxwell, *Income Inequality in the United States, 1947–1985* (New York: Greenwood Press, 1990), 87.

11. Patterson, *America's Struggle against Poverty, 1900–1980*, 87.

12. Welfare numbers under "Temporary Assistance for Needy Families (TANF), 1936–1999," at <http://www.acf.dhhs.gov/news/stats/3697.htm>, accessed June 21, 2000. Caretaker grants—money for the mothers—were added in 1950, but the name change from ADC to AFDC did not occur until the Public Welfare Amendments of 1962; Christopher Green, *Negative Taxes and the Poverty Problem* (Washington: Brookings Institution, 1967), 16–17. Transfer payments are those made to individuals in return for which no service or goods are provided. Payments to people in the military or computer vendors are not transfers. Social Security and welfare payments are. Some

of Green's figures include private transfers, probably a small proportion of all transfers. Patterson, *America's Struggle against Poverty, 1900–1980*, 85–86; *HS*, 356; Stern, "Poverty and Family Composition since 1940," 237; Staff of the Subcommittee on Low Income Families (Sparkman Committee), Joint Committee on the Economic Report, 84th Cong., 1st sess., *Characteristics of the Low-Income Population and Related Federal Programs* (Washington: Government Printing Office, 1955); U.S. Department of Health, Education, and Welfare [HEW], Welfare Administration, Bureau of Family Services, Division of Program Statistics and Analysis, *Characteristics of Families Receiving Aid to Families with Dependent Children, November–December 1961* (1963), table 38. The states failed to live up to their own standards; see Ellen J. Perkins, "Unmet Need in Public Assistance," *Social Security Bulletin*, April 1960, 3–11. The HEW survey found that welfare families had $320 beyond their grants, not enough to lift many of them out of poverty. Ross, Danziger, and Smolensky, *Level and Trend of Poverty*, tables 3 and 5 (on pp. 11 and 14) show that, for example, for nonwhite women ages 25–64, nonearned income cut the poverty rate from 75.2% to 71.5%.

13. *HS*, 132. On benefit changes, Martha Derthick, *Policymaking for Social Security* (Washington: Brookings Institution, 1979), 274–80, and Edward D. Berkowitz, *America's Welfare State: From Roosevelt to Reagan* (Baltimore: Johns Hopkins University Press, 1991), 55–65. Average monthly payments are in *HS*, 350, H-233. I estimated poverty lines using U.S. Department of Commerce, Bureau of the Census, Current Population Reports series P-60, no. 168, *Money Income and Poverty Status in the United States, 1989* (Washington: Government Printing Office, 1990), 86, and price indexes in U.S. Department of Labor, Bureau of Labor Statistics, *CPI: Detailed Report, Data for December 1997* (Washington: Government Printing Office, 1997), 76–77. Lenore A. Epstein, "Money Income of Aged Persons: A 10-Year Review, 1948–1958," *Social Security Bulletin*, June 1959, 3–11, and Epstein, "Income of the Aged in 1962: First Findings of the 1963 Survey of the Aged," *Social Security Bulletin*, March 1964, 11. Ida Merriam (cited in Mollie Orshansky, "Recounting the Poor—A Five-Year Review," *Social Security Bulletin*, April 1966, 89), estimated that in 1965 35% of Social Security recipients were still poor; 38% were lifted out of poverty by Social Security; and 27% had not been poor to begin with.

14. Patterson, *America's Struggle against Poverty, 1900–1980*, 85–86. Paul Peterson was wrong that the American welfare state was stagnant in the 1950s. See Paul Peterson, "The Urban Underclass and the Poverty Paradox," in Christopher Jencks and Paul Peterson, eds., *The Urban Underclass* (Washington: Brookings Institution, 1991), 3–27, esp. 12.

15. On percentages of national income going to AFDC and Social Security, Christopher Jencks, *Rethinking Social Policy: Race, Poverty, and the Underclass* (New York: Harper Perennial, 1993), 77. See also *Unemployment Hearings*, pt. 4, 1619, which shows that in Illinois AFDC benefits were lower than those for old-age assistance, assistance to the blind, and even general assistance.

16. Victor R. Fuchs, "Redefining Poverty and Redistributing Income," *Public Interest*, Summer 1967, 89–94, reprinted in Robert E. Will and Harold G. Vatter, eds., *Poverty in Affluence: The Social, Political and Economic Dimensions of Poverty in the United*

States, 2nd ed. (New York: Harcourt, Brace and World, 1970), 14–18; Gabriel Kolko, *Wealth and Power in America: An Analysis of Social Class and Income Distribution* (New York: Praeger, 1962), 14, table 1. Wittner, *Cold War America*, 78, for wealth data.

17. Godfrey Hodgson, *America in Our Time: From World War II to Nixon—What Happened and Why* (New York: Vintage Books, 1978), 67–98; Alexander, *Holding the Line*, 148–58; Miller and Nowak, *The Fifties*, 105–24; Robert Heilbroner, "Who Are the American Poor?," *Atlantic Monthly*, June 1950, 27–33.

18. David Riesman and Nathan Glazer, "The Intellectuals and the Discontented Classes" (1955), in Daniel Bell, ed., *The Radical Right* (Garden City, N.Y.: Doubleday, 1964), 108; Nisbet quoted in Patterson, *America's Struggle against Poverty, 1900–1980*, 85.

19. Richard Pells, *The Liberal Mind in a Conservative Age* (1985), excerpted in Michael S. Mayer, ed., *The Eisenhower Presidency and the 1950s* (Boston: Houghton Mifflin, 1998), 157–72; Alice O'Connor, *Poverty Knowledge: Social Science, Social Policy, and the Poor in Twentieth-Century U.S. History* (Princeton, N.J.: Princeton University Press, 2001), 3–123, on the lack of attention to economic class in poverty studies; and Daniel Horowitz, ed., *American Social Classes in the 1950s: Selections from Vance Packard's "The Status Seekers"* (New York: St. Martin's Press, 1995), esp. 1–7, 15, 23–25, 32–33. A study that did pay attention to workers was Ely Chinoy, *Automobile Workers and the American Dream* (1955; Boston: Beacon Press, 1965).

20. Patterson, *America's Struggle against Poverty, 1900–1980*, 94–95.

21. Helen Hill Miller, "Today's 'One Third of a Nation,' " *New Republic*, November 17, 1958, 13–15; Leo Egan, "State Poverty Study Urged by Governor," *New York Times*, February 1, 1956, 1, 10 (for first quotation); "Text of Governor Harriman's Message Outlining 1958 Program to State Legislature," *New York Times*, January 9, 1958, 23–26 (for second quotation); editorial, "Attack on Poverty," *New York Times*, February 4, 1956, 18. The next governor, Nelson Rockefeller, eliminated Harriman's antipoverty initiatives in 1959.

22. The Joint Committee on the Economic Report was later renamed the Joint Economic Committee. Among the publications of the Sparkman Committee: Staff of the Subcommittee on Low Income Families, Joint Committee on the Economic Report, 81st Cong., 2nd sess., *Low-Income Families and Economic Stability: Materials on the Problem of Low-Income Families* (Washington: Government Printing Office, 1950), and the previously cited *Characteristics of the Low-Income Population* (1955).

23. Conference Group of Nine National Voluntary Organizations Convened by the National Social Welfare Assembly, *Making Ends Meet on Less than $2,000 a Year (Case Studies of 100 Low-Income Families)*, Communication to the Joint Committee on the Economic Report, U.S. Senate, 82nd Cong., 2nd sess. (Washington: Government Printing Office, 1952), 4–5.

24. Maurice Isserman, *The Other American: The Life of Michael Harrington* (New York: Public Affairs, 2000), 156–82.

25. James L. Sundquist, *Politics and Policy: The Eisenhower, Kennedy and Johnson Years* (Washington: Brookings Institution, 1968), 118–20.

26. *HS*, 716, 848 on vehicle sales, and 135, D94, on unemployment.

27. Sundquist, *Politics and Policy*, 57–83; *Unemployment Hearings*, pt. 4, 1323, 1663–78, 1691–1757. Along the same lines, Senator Hubert Humphrey of Minnesota introduced a proposal for a Youth Conservation Corps in 1957.

28. Sundquist, *Politics and Policy*, 77–82, and *Unemployment Hearings*, pt. 4.

29. Harold L. Sheppard, Louis A. Ferman, and Seymour Faber, *Too Old to Work—Too Young to Retire: A Case Study of a Permanent Plant Shutdown*, U.S. Senate, 86th Cong., 1st sess., Special Committee on Unemployment Problems (Washington: Government Printing Office, 1960).

30. Quoted in Sundquist, *Politics and Policy*, 81. The complete testimony is in *Unemployment Hearings*, pt. 7, 2732–33. See also 1808.

31. Goldwater is quoted from a 1956 Senate debate, in Sundquist, *Politics and Policy*, 65. The sharp decline of coal-mining jobs occurred in southern Illinois over 1949–59; see *Unemployment Hearings*, pt. 4, 1571–77.

32. John Kenneth Galbraith, *The Affluent Society* (Boston: Mentor Books, 1958), 199.

33. Ibid., 258, 250.

34. Ibid., 252–54.

35. Isserman, *Other American*, 179–80; Harvey Swados, "Myth of the Happy Worker," *The Nation*, August 17, 1957, reprinted in Eileen Boris and Nelson Lichtenstein, eds., *Major Problems in the History of American Workers*, 2nd ed. (Boston: D. C. Heath and Co., 2003), 2–7. Galbraith could have learned from the Sparkman Committee and the Conference Group of Nine National Voluntary Organizations Convened by the National Social Welfare Assembly, *Making Ends Meet on Less than $2,000 a Year*. It may be relevant to his exaggeration of affluence that in 1955 the salary for full professors at Harvard, where Galbraith worked, was $13,000, three times the median American family income. See Seymour E. Harris, *The Economics of Harvard* (New York: McGraw-Hill, 1970), 147.

36. Alice Mary O'Connor, "From Lower Class to Underclass: The Poor in American Social Science, 1930–1970" (Ph.D. diss., Johns Hopkins University, 1991), 328.

37. Raymond Moley, "Vanishing Proletariat," *Newsweek*, January 19, 1959, 92. Arthur Schlesinger Jr., "Where Does the Liberal Go from Here?" *New York Times Magazine*, August 4, 1957, sec. 6; "Eggheads and Politics: Galbraith and Schlesinger Reply to Leon Keyserling," *New Republic*, November 10, 1958, 14–15.

38. "Leon Keyserling on Economic Expansion," *New Republic*, November 17, 1958, 16–17. Also Leon Keyserling, "Eggheads and Politics," *New Republic*, October 27, 1958, 13–17; Arthur Schlesinger Jr., "Death Wish of the Democrats," *New Republic*, September 15, 1958, 7–8; Leon Keyserling, *Poverty and Deprivation in the U.S.: The Plight of Two-Fifths of a Nation* (Washington: Conference on Economic Progress, 1962), 11, 26, 36, 61, 75. On Keyserling, Irving Bernstein, *Turbulent Years: A History of the American Worker, 1933–1941* (Boston: Houghton Mifflin, 1971), 186, 323; Iwan W. Morgan, *Eisenhower versus "The Spenders": The Eisenhower Administration, the Democrats and the Budget, 1953–60* (New York: St. Martin's Press, 1990), 28–29, 42–48; Leslie Wayne, "Leon Keyserling, Economic Aide to Truman, Dies," *New York Times*, August 11, 1987, D22.

39. Lampman, *Low Income Population and Economic Growth*, esp. 14, 23, 31. Using 1960s thresholds, the poverty rate had fallen to 22.8% in 1957.

40. Lampman (in ibid.) concluded that 70% of the poor had at least one handicap, but he also showed that 50% of the nonpoor population had one or more handicaps.

41. Ibid., 24–28, 4–5, 31–32; O'Connor, *Poverty Knowledge*, 152–54, 157.

42. About 3% of Americans moved to a new state each year in the 1950s. The farm population, on average poorer than the nonfarm population, fell over 1950–54 by 4 million, or 17.5%; over 1954–58 by 1.9 million, or 9.9%; and over 1958–62 by 2.8 million, or 16.4%. See *HS*, 96 (C87 divided by C81 = percentage of change).

43. Ibid., 380, H609, H617.

44. Lowell E. Gallaway, "Labor Mobility, Resource Allocation, and Structural Unemployment," *American Economic Review* 53 (September 1953): 694–716; Yale Brozen and the Chamber of Commerce of the United States, *Employment and Unemployment: The Problem of the 1960s* (1961), excerpted in Stanley Lebergott, ed., *Men without Work: The Economics of Unemployment* (Englewood Cliffs, N.J.: Prentice-Hall, 1964), 94–104.

45. *HLS, 1972*, 168, 332–33; also Albert Rees, "Discussion," in Arthur M. Ross, ed., *Unemployment and the American Economy* (New York: John Wiley and Sons, 1964), 135–36.

46. John Ross is quoted in Sundquist, *Politics and Policy*, 82. His complete testimony is in *Unemployment Hearings*, pt. 7 (December 1, 1959), 2801–16. Few experts acknowledged that there might be more skilled workers than skilled jobs, but an exception was on 1434. An advocate of the stue position was Thomas B. Curtis, *87 Million Jobs: A Dynamic Program to End Unemployment* (New York: Duell, Sloan, and Pearce, 1962); the author was a Republican representative from Missouri. See also N. J. Simler, "Long-Term Unemployment, the Structural Hypothesis, and Public Policy," *American Economic Review* 54 (December 1964): 986–87; Walter Heller, "The Administration's Fiscal Policy," in Ross, *Unemployment and the American Economy*, 93–115, esp. 104; and Seymour L. Wolfbein, "The First Year of the Manpower Act," in Ross, *Unemployment and the American Economy*, 54–70, esp. 59. The definition of vacancies was fluid, and employers sometimes inflated estimates of their needs to flood the labor market, as in California agriculture. See Garth L. Mangum and John Walsh, *A Decade of Manpower Development Training* (Salt Lake City, Utah: Olympus Publishing Co., 1973), 93–99.

47. Sheppard, Ferman, and Faber, *Too Old to Work*. See also U.S. Department of Labor, Bureau of Labor Statistics, for Joint Economic Committee, *The Extent and Nature of Frictional Unemployment*, 86th Cong., 1st sess. (Washington: Government Printing Office, 1959), 64–69, which showed a slight increase in structural unemployment in the goods-producing sector between 1948 and 1956.

48. Subcommittee on Economic Statistics of the Joint Economic Committee (James W. Knowles), *Higher Unemployment Rates, 1957–60: Structural Transformation or Inadequate Demand*, 87th Cong., 1st sess. (Washington: Government Printing Office, 1961), 38. Albert Szymanski, "Trends in the American Class Structure," *Socialist Revolution* 2 (July–August 1972): 107, shows that between 1950 and 1960 the number of manual workers was stable but as a share of all workers fell from 41.1% to 36.1%.

49. Jacobs, *Handbook*, 163. Harold G. Vatter, *The U.S. Economy in the 1950s: An Economic History* (New York: W. W. Norton and Co., 1963), 54; Alan Batchelder, "Poverty: The Special Case of the Negro," in Will and Vatter, *Poverty in Affluence*, 81–87; manufacturing laborer positions fell by 20% between 1950 and 1960. Charles C. Killingsworth, "Negroes in a Changing Labor Market," in Arthur M. Ross and Herbert Hill, eds., *Employment, Race, and Poverty* (New York: Harcourt, Brace and World, 1967), 49–75, esp. 66, for estimates that 1 million manufacturing jobs were lost over 1953–65.

50. George Haberman, president of the Wisconsin State AFL-CIO, claimed that "the day of the unskilled worker is near an end," in *Unemployment Hearings*, pt. 4, 1437.

51. Batchelder, "Poverty the Special Case of the Negro"; Levy, *Dollars and Dreams*, 106, 78, 112–15; John F. Kain, "Housing Segregation, Negro Employment, and Metropolitan Decentralization," *Quarterly Journal of Economics* 82 (May 1968): 175–97; Thomas J. Sugrue, "The Structures of Urban Poverty: The Reorganization of Space and Work in Three Periods of American History," in Katz, *"Underclass" Debate*, 103–5, 110–14; Daniel R. Fusfeld and Timothy Bates, *The Political Economy of the Urban Ghetto* (Carbondale: Southern Illinois University Press, 1984), 262–63 n. 22, 117–21.

52. Sugrue, "Structures of Urban Poverty," 103–5, 110–14; Kolko, *Wealth and Power in America*, 73; Kenneth T. Jackson, *Crabgrass Frontier: The Suburbanization of the United States* (New York: Oxford University Press, 1985), 190–305; Levy, *Dollars and Dreams*, 113.

53. *HS*, 135. David W. Rasmussen, "A Note on the Relative Income of Nonwhite Men, 1948–1964," *Quarterly Journal of Economics* 84 (February 1970): 168–72.

54. The average median incomes of black families as a percentage of white families were 52.3% in 1947–50, 55.2% in 1950–55, 53.2% in 1955–60, 54.2% in 1960–65, 59.8% in 1965–70, and 60% in 1970–75. Calculated from Dorothy K. Newman et al., *Protest, Politics, and Prosperity: Black Americans and White Institutions, 1940–1975* (New York: Pantheon Books, 1978), 269. See also U.S. Department of Commerce, Bureau of the Census, Current Population Report, series P-60, no. 85, *Consumer Income: Money Income in 1971 of Families and Persons in the United States* (Washington: Government Printing Office, 1972), 31, on the share of blacks with very low incomes.

55. As quoted in Sundquist, *Politics and Policy*, 58. Many at the *Unemployment Hearings* and many politicians, such as Senator Hubert Humphrey of Minnesota, had no trouble urging both aggregate and structural measures.

56. On Eisenhower and civil rights, William H. Chafe, *The Unfinished Journey: America since World War II*, 2nd ed. (New York: Oxford University Press, 1991), 153–57, and Alexander, *Holding the Line*, 197, 201.

57. Lowell E. Gallaway, "The Foundations of the 'War on Poverty,'" *American Economic Review* 55 (March 1965): 122–31, plots correlations between falling unemployment, poverty rates, and rising family incomes.

58. Keyserling, *Poverty and Deprivation*, 75. Growth data from the U.S. Department of Commerce, Bureau of Economic Analysis, "Gross Domestic Product, in Current Dollars and in Chained (1996) Dollars," at <http://www.bea.doc.gov/bea/dn/gdplev

.htm>. The site's name is the same except that "doc" has been removed. After-inflation changes are done in terms of 2000 dollars. Recession dates in Robert Aaron Gordon, *Economic Instability and Growth: The American Record* (New York: Harper and Row, 1974), 108–36. See also *HS*, 224, F4, and Vatter, *U.S. Economy in the 1950s*, 7–8.

59. Vatter, *U.S. Economy in the 1950s*, 113, 149, 198, 204, 283. The United Mine Workers and the International Longshoremen's and Warehousemen's Union agreed to job-reducing productivity changes; the United Steel Workers, on the other hand, waged a bitter strike in 1959 to preserve work rules.

60. Ibid., 46, 87, 103, 146–48, 175, chart on 110, and 282–94; Gordon, *Economic Instability and Growth*, 127–28; Simler, "Long-Term Unemployment." On the security-conscious postwar generation, John P. Sisk, "Security First," *Commonweal*, August 19, 1949, 458–60. Real per capita consumption expenditures were 8.6% higher in 1954 than they had been in 1949; in 1959 they were 11.6% higher than in 1954. Calculated from total consumption divided by population—from *HS*, 317, 8—and adjusted for price changes, using U.S. Department of Labor, Bureau of Labor Statistics, *CPI—Detailed Report*.

61. Paul A. Baran and Paul M. Sweezy, *Monopoly Capital: An Essay on the American Economic and Social Order* (New York: Monthly Review Press, 1968).

62. "Battle behind the Budget Battle: Is Red Ink a Tonic or a Poison?," *Time*, March 16, 1959, 22–23.

63. Keyserling, *Poverty and Deprivation*, 82; Sundquist, *Politics and Policy*, 13–34; Morgan, *Eisenhower versus "The Spenders,"* 29, 42–43, and passim.

64. "The Economy: Good News for Bad," *Time*, February 24, 1958, 13–14, and "Putting the Brakes on Inflation" *U.S. News & World Report*, June 15, 1959, 46, 56, 58. *HS*, 230, series F 66–69. Defense amounts are in current dollars. After inflation, government purchases of goods and services fell over 1954–59. Senator Hubert Humphrey, in *Unemployment Hearings*, pt. 4, 1334–35, claimed in 1959 that interest rates were at their highest levels since 1933. Edwin Dickens, "U.S. Monetary Policy in the 1950s: A Radical Political Economic Approach," *Review of Radical Political Economics* 27 (December 1995): 83–111, argues that the Federal Reserve used tight money and recession to cut union wage demands. The budget for fiscal 1959 had a deficit of more than $12 billion, but that came from the need to respond to Sputnik and from falling revenues rather than from Keynesian action. See Alexander, *Holding the Line*, 219–20, and *HT*, 23.

65. Morgan, *Eisenhower versus "The Spenders,"* 120–21, and 24–48, which sets out the Democratic position; Sundquist, *Politics and Policy*, 13–15, 19–29, 42, 46, 60–73 on the politics of inflation and growth. Senator Sparkman did finally get the president to sign a bill for housing loans.

66. Morgan, *Eisenhower versus "The Spenders,"* 14, 21, 74, 99–126, 134–38, 154–61, 179–80; Robert Lekachman, *The Age of Keynes* (New York: McGraw-Hill, 1975), 220–24, 257. For alternatives to the Eisenhower-Martin approach to inflation, see Morgan, *Eisenhower versus "The Spenders,"* 41; Vatter, *U.S. Economy in the 1950s*, 121–36; Leon H. Keyserling, *Growth with Less Inflation or More Inflation without Growth?* (Wash-

ington: Conference on Economic Progress, 1970); and W. Robert Brazelton, *Designing U.S. Economic Policy: An Analytical Biography of Leon H. Keyserling* (New York: Palgrave, 2001), 83–92. On rising prices in the recession, *Unemployment Hearings*, pt. 4, 1334. Democrats, even liberals, were divided as to how best to stimulate the economy. Some preferred budget deficits; others wanted monetary easing. See Morgan, *Eisenhower versus "The Spenders,"* 24–48, 103, 117, 137, and University of Minnesota economist Edward Coen, *Unemployment Hearings*, pt. 4, 1527–34.

Chapter Two

1. See, for example, the 1964 *Economic Report of the President*, in Herman P. Miller, ed. *Poverty American Style* (Belmont, Calif.: Wadsworth Publishing Co., 1966), 92–106. The sum of $3,000 for a family of four in 1964 was close to what would soon become the poverty line. It had about the same purchasing power that $19,500 had in 2006.

2. "Poverty U.S.A.," *Newsweek*, February 17, 1964, 19–38.

3. Kennedy's inaugural address is in Paul F. Boller and Ronald Story, eds., *A More Perfect Union: Documents in U.S. History*, 2nd ed. (Boston: Houghton Mifflin, 1988), 2:239–41; Carl M. Brauer, "Kennedy, Johnson, and the War on Poverty," *Journal of American History* 69 (June 1982): 119; Arthur M. Schlesinger Jr., *A Thousand Days: John F. Kennedy in the White House* (Boston: Houghton Mifflin, 1965), 1006; "Needed: More Jobs," *Time*, December 19, 1960, 77. On West Virginia, see Pechman interview, 86; on the New Frontier, Irwin Unger, *The Best of Intentions: The Triumph and Failure of the Great Society under Kennedy, Johnson, and Nixon* (New York: Doubleday, 1996), 23.

4. Gertrude Schaffner Goldberg and Sheila D. Collins, *Washington's New Poor Law: Welfare Reform and the Roads Not Taken—1935 to the Present* (New York: Apex Press, 2001), 75–78; Edward D. Berkowitz, *America's Welfare State: From Roosevelt to Reagan* (Baltimore: Johns Hopkins University Press, 1991), 91–115; James T. Patterson, *America's Struggle against Poverty in the Twentieth Century* (Cambridge, Mass.: Harvard University Press, 2000), 122–31. Walter I. Trattner, *From Poor Law to Welfare State: A History of Social Welfare in America*, 5th ed. (New York: Free Press, 1994), 321–22.

5. James L. Sundquist, *Politics and Policy: The Eisenhower, Kennedy, and Johnson Years* (Washington: Brookings Institution, 1968), 66–85, and Allen J. Matusow, *The Unraveling of America: A History of Liberalism in the 1960s* (New York: Harper Torchbooks, 1984), 100–102.

6. Matusow, *Unraveling of America*, 103–5. Kennedy also signed an Accelerated Public Works program for depressed areas and a minimum wage increase to $1.25. Also a food stamp program was implemented.

7. Judith Russell, *Economics, Bureaucracy, and Race: How Keynesians Misguided the War on Poverty* (New York: Columbia University Press, 2004), and Gary Mucciaroni, *The Political Failure of Employment Policy, 1945–1982* (1990; Pittsburgh: University of Pittsburgh Press, 1992).

8. Sundquist, *Politics and Policy*, 31–52; Matusow, *Unraveling of America*, 52–53; and Pechman interview, 197–98, 204, 243–59, 425–34.

9. Matusow, *Unraveling of America*, esp. 53, and Unger, *Best of Intentions*, 31–34.

10. Sundquist, *Politics and Policy*, 112, quoting Heller's speech of March 25, 1965. Heller told the president that poverty associated with minorities, widowhood, and old age might be harder to overcome "than the more generalized poverty of earlier generations." Quoted in Brauer, "Kennedy, Johnson, and the War on Poverty," 102–3.

11. Matusow, *Unraveling of America*, 119–20; Frances Fox Piven and Richard A. Cloward, *Regulating the Poor: The Functions of Public Welfare* (1971; New York: Vintage Books, 1972), 248–282; Unger, *Best of Intentions*, 49–53. Not long after, planner Adam Yarmolinsky denied that the War on Poverty was a response to civil rights agitation, but later he agreed with Piven that the poverty program was a response to profound social movements; he just did not like what he thought was a Marxist idea of government responding to "an upsurge of revolt of the masses." Yarmolinsky, "The Beginnings of OEO," in James L. Sundquist, ed., *On Fighting Poverty: Perspectives from Experience* (New York: Basic Books, 1969), 42, 49. Also, Michael B. Katz, *The Undeserving Poor: From the War on Poverty to the War on Welfare* (1989; New York: Pantheon Books, 1990), 85–87, and Nicholas Lemann, *The Promised Land: The Great Black Migration and How It Changed America* (New York: Vintage Books, 1992), 156. In the spring and summer of 1963, Kennedy knew that there were riots and militant civil rights demonstrations (Matusow, *Unraveling of America*, 90–93, 115–20; Lemann, *Promised Land*, 150, 126–27). Civil rights and antipoverty programs were, in part, administration responses.

12. Peter Marris and Martin Rein, *Dilemmas of Social Reform: Poverty and Community Action in the United States*, 2nd ed. (Chicago: University of Chicago Press, 1982), 45, 53.

13. Quotation from Henry Street proposal in Joseph H. Helfgot, *Professional Reforming: Mobilization for Youth and the Failure of Social Science* (Lexington, Mass.: Heath Lexington Books, 1981), 19–28.

14. Daniel Knapp and Kenneth Polk, *Scouting the War on Poverty: Social Reform Politics in the Kennedy Administration* (Lexington, Mass.: Heath Lexington Books, 1971), 27. Richard A. Cloward and Lloyd E. Ohlin, *Delinquency and Opportunity: A Theory of Delinquent Gangs* (Glencoe, Ill.: Free Press, 1960).

15. But see Cloward and Ohlin, *Delinquency and Opportunity*, 97–103, on economic barriers to educational opportunity in poor communities.

16. "A Proposal for the Prevention and Control of Delinquency by Expanding Opportunities: A Demonstration Project Conceived and Developed by Mobilization for Youth," typescript, New York, December 9, 1961, iv.

17. Ibid., 54, 96–97.

18. Helfgot, *Professional Reforming* 48–49, 52–60, agrees that over time leaders of the Mobilization for Youth "discovered that it had little power to alter an opportunity structure" (53) that was controlled by powerful external forces. It is also possible that they were alert to what might get funded and kept their ideas vaguer than their beliefs. See also Matusow, *Unraveling of America*, 112–13; "Proposal for Prevention," 71, 50–51, 90–95; Frank Levy, *Dollars and Dreams: The Changing American Income Distribution* (New York: Russell Sage Foundation, 1987), 112–15.

19. Sundquist, *Politics and Policy*, 120, 124, 134. Within a week of his election,

Kennedy ordered David Hackett to organize the delinquency effort; this suggests a priority. One catalyst was Eunice Shriver, the president's sister (Lemann, *Promised Land*, 124–25). She had worked on a delinquency project in the Justice Department in 1947. See James Gilbert, *A Cycle of Outrage: America's Reaction to the Juvenile Delinquent in the 1950s* (New York: Oxford University Press, 1986), 33–53, 127–42, and Helfgot, *Professional Reforming* 33, 43.

20. Knapp and Polk, *Scouting the War on Poverty*, 109–11; Helfgot, *Professional Reforming* 70–74, 81–84. The shift toward aggressive, community-based actions was also happening elsewhere. One project of Students for a Democratic Society ran a roughly parallel course over 1962–64.

21. Gabriel Kolko, *Wealth and Power in America: An Analysis of Social Class and Income Distribution* (New York: Praeger, 1962); Leon Keyserling, *Poverty and Deprivation in the U.S.: The Plight of Two-Fifths of a Nation* (Washington: Conference on Economic Progress, 1962); Michael Harrington, *The Other America: Poverty in the United States* (1962; New York: Penguin Books, 1981); Herman Miller, "Is the Income Gap Closed? 'No!,' " *New York Times Magazine*, November 11, 1962, 50, 52, 54, 58; Dwight Macdonald, "Our Invisible Poor," *New Yorker*, January 16, 1963, 82–132; Harry M. Caudill, *Night Comes to the Cumberlands: A Biography of a Depressed Area* (Boston: Little, Brown, 1963); Homer Bigart, "Kentucky Miners: A Grim Winter," *New York Times*, October 21, 1963, III, 1, 79; and Mollie Orshansky, "Children of the Poor," *Social Security Bulletin*, July 1963, 3–13.

22. Maurice Isserman, *The Other American: The Life of Michael Harrington* (New York: Public Affairs, 2000), and Michael Harrington, *Toward a Democratic Left: A Radical Program for a New Majority* (New York: Macmillan, 1968).

23. Harrington, *Other America*, 189, 177.

24. Quotations from Oscar Lewis, *The Children of Sanchez: Autobiography of a Mexican Family* (New York: Vintage Books, 1963), xxiv–xxv. See also Oscar Lewis, *Five Families: Mexican Case Studies in the Culture of Poverty* (New York: Mentor Books, 1959), esp. 15–31. Among the commentaries on Lewis's concept is Alice O'Connor, *Poverty Knowledge: Social Science, Social Policy, and the Poor in Twentieth-Century U.S. History* (Princeton, N.J.: Princeton University Press, 2001), 117–23. In a review of *The Children of Sanchez*, Harrington emphasized that the poor were less deranged in Mexico, where poverty was more normal than in white America. See *Commonweal*, November 16, 1961, 214–15. Lewis listed seventy traits associated with poverty culture in *La Vida: A Puerto Rican Family in the Culture of Poverty, San Juan and New York* (New York: Vintage Books, 1966), xliv–xlv, li–lii. See also Elizabeth Herzog, "Some Assumptions about the Poor," *Social Service Review* 137 (December 1963): 389–402.

25. Harrington, *Other America*, 2, 10, 11, 14, 18, 25–26, 70, 81, 83, 145–46, 152, 166–67, 169, 174, 199. A critique is William Ryan, *Blaming the Victim*, rev. ed. (New York: Vintage Books, 1976), 117–41. Isserman, *Other American*, 216, claims that Harrington used the idea of the culture of poverty only as a synonym for poverty, but I think he often used it in Lewis's sense, to mean a world in which the poor were slightly deranged. However, it is doubtful that Harrington deeply believed in the concept, for it

was absent from the 1971 introduction and the 1981 afterword to Harrington, *Other America*.

26. How do we know that most of the poor were not imprisoned in a dysfunctional culture? For one thing, there was movement in and out of poverty. Planners knew little of this until the 1965 *Economic Report of the President* (Washington: Government Printing Office, 1965), 163–65, which concluded that between 1962 and 1963 70% of the same families stayed poor. That was a 30% change every year and over time a big turnover. But the authors concluded that the poor were "a largely unchanging group of families." Assumptions were more powerful than evidence.

27. S. M. Miller, Frank Riessman, and Arthur A. Seagull, "Poverty and Self-Indulgence: A Critique of the Non-Deferred Gratification Pattern," in Louis A. Ferman, Joyce L. Kornbluh, and Alan Haber, eds., *Poverty in America* (Ann Arbor: University of Michigan Press, 1965), 285–302.

28. Kolko, *Wealth and Power in America*, 129.

29. Kolko's book was discussed in Macdonald's *New Yorker* review of *The Other America*, but his name does not appear in the index of Gillette's collection of oral histories; Harrington's does. See Michael L. Gillette, *Launching the War on Poverty: An Oral History* (New York: Twayne Publishers, 1996), 402–4.

30. Isserman, *Other American*, 208; Unger, *Best of Intentions*, 66.

31. Brauer, "Kennedy, Johnson, and the War on Poverty," 102–3.

32. William H. Chafe, *The Unfinished Journey: America since World War II*, 4th ed. (New York: Oxford University Press, 1999), 215–16.

33. Bigart, "Kentucky Miners," and Sundquist, *Politics and Policy*, 163.

34. Lyndon Johnson, *The Vantage Point: Perspectives on the Presidency, 1963–1968* (New York: Holt, Rinehart and Winston, 1971), 71; Sundquist, *Politics and Policy*, 136–37, for the quotation; Lemann, *Promised Land*, 131, 142–43; Brauer, "Kennedy, Johnson, and the War on Poverty"; Marris and Rein, *Dilemmas of Social Reform* 256–57.

35. This and the latter part of the preceding paragraph based on three memoranda: David L. Hackett to Walter Heller, November 6, 1963; Hackett to the Attorney General, November 6, 1963, copies in supplementary materials for Brandeis Conference on Poverty and Urban Policy, May 16–17, 1973, John F. Kennedy Library, Boston; and Hackett to Attorney General (copies to Heller and Capron), December 2, 1965, microfilm roll #37, Walter Heller Personal Papers, John F. Kennedy Library, Boston. See also Matusow, *Unraveling of America*, 116–22; Lemann, *Promised Land*, 133; and Sundquist, *Politics and Policy*, 138.

36. Current news about community action should have alarmed politicians. In 1963, Ohlin and Cloward's Mobilization for Youth was being investigated by the FBI, and on August 16, 1964, just as the War on Poverty was born, this headline appeared in the *New York Daily News*: "Youth Agency Eyed for Reds." See Helfgot, *Professional Reforming*, 69, 90–105; Matusow, *Unraveling of America*, 262–65; Sundquist, *Politics and Policy*, 138–39; and Lemann, *Promised Land*, 143.

37. Matusow, *Unraveling of America*, 123. Johnson claimed in *Vantage Point*, 73–75, that he could not sell a small program to Congress. For the budget message, *Public Papers*

of the Presidents of the United States: Lyndon B. Johnson, 1963–1964, bk. 1 (Washington: Government Printing Office, 1965), 175–95.

38. Lemann, Promised Land, 145–48, quotation on 148; Sundquist, Politics and Policy, 142–43; Sar A. Levitan, The Great Society's Poor Law: A New Approach to Poverty (Baltimore: Johns Hopkins University Press, 1969), 26–31; Matusow, Unraveling of America, 124.

39. Isserman, Other American, 211–12, 218, and Michael Harrington, "The Politics of Poverty," in Irving Howe, ed., The Radical Papers (Garden City, N.Y.: Doubleday, 1966), 125–47.

40. Yarmolinsky, "Beginnings of OEO," 38–39; Sundquist, 52; Matusow, Unraveling of America, 56, 239–40. Lemann, Promised Land, 154, alone claims that the AFL-CIO opposed the jobs programs. It is true that the AFL-CIO came to oppose the Area Redevelopment program for subsidizing runaway shops, but it did not oppose Accelerated Public Works. See Irving Bernstein, Promises Kept: John F. Kennedy's New Frontier (New York: Oxford University Press, 1993), 177–79. Union attitudes depended in part on whether government-created jobs replaced union jobs. The union position can be seen either as narrowly selfish or as a reasonable effort to preserve jobs that paid above the poverty line.

41. Lemann, Promised Land, 131, Brauer, "Kennedy, Johnson, and the War on Poverty," 107–8.

42. Lemann, Promised Land, 149–50. Reacting to a proposal for a guaranteed annual income, Labor Secretary Wirtz told the United Auto Workers that no one owed anyone a living; society owed everyone only the right to work. David R. Jones, "Johnson Urges Restraint on Pay in Talk to U.A.W.," New York Times, March 24, 1964, I, 1, 19.

43. Economists' quotations from the 1964 Economic Report of the President, in Miller, Poverty American Style, 102–3. See also Yarmolinsky, "Beginnings of OEO," 49. Shriver's presentation to Congress on March 17, 1964, is in The War on Poverty: Economic Opportunity Act of 1964: A Compilation of Materials Relevant to S. 2642, prepared for the Senate Select Subcommittee on Poverty (Washington: Government Printing Office, 1964), esp. 35–36, 43. For more on the culture of poverty, Orshansky, "Children of the Poor," 13.

44. Johnson, Vantage Point, 77–78, Sundquist, Politics and Policy, 147 n. 81; Lemann, Promised Land, 156–57. William C. Selover, "The View from Capitol Hill: Harassment and Survival," in Sundquist, On Fighting Poverty, 158–87.

45. Tower-Goldwater statement, in Miller, Poverty American Style, 235–46; Yarmolinsky, "Beginnings of OEO," 47; Sundquist, 147–48; Selover, "View from Capitol Hill," 164.

46. Jill Quadagno and Catherine Forbes, "The Welfare State and the Cultural Reproduction of Gender: Making Good Girls and Boys in the Job Corps," Social Problems 42 (May 1995): 171–90.

47. Unger, Best of Intentions, 179, 183; Levitan, Great Society's Poor Law, 173.

48. Matusow, Unraveling of America, 115–18; Lemann, Promised Land, 121–29, 149–

52; and for the quotation, Levitan, *Great Society's Poor Law*, 110. Boone had been trained in the Chicago school of sociology, engaged in prison and gang research, and worked at the Ford Foundation. Other sources for this and preceding paragraph are Shriver's presentation to Congress, March 17, 1964, in *War on Poverty* (see n. 42 above), 52; Yarmolinsky, "Beginnings of OEO," 49, 51 n. 2; and Sanford Kravitz, "The Community Action Program—Past, Present, and Its Future?," in Sundquist, *On Fighting Poverty*, 52–69. On existing programs that already included at least the idea of democratic participation, Robb K. Burlage, "Appalachia: The Heart of the Matter," from *New University Thought* (1964), reprinted in Ferman, Kornbluh, and Haber, *Poverty in America*, 470–81; and Piven and Cloward, *Regulating the Poor*, 266 n. 18.

49. Yarmolinsky, "Beginnings of OEO," 35, cited a solid body of experience in community action, but there was little to prove it could solve poverty. Some advocates equated the *existence* of organizations with their *effectiveness*. On the absence of minorities in the planning process, Daniel P. Moynihan, "The Professors and the Poor," in Moynihan, ed., *On Understanding Poverty: Perspectives from the Social Sciences* (New York: Basic Books, 1969), 14–15.

50. Lillian Rubin, "Maximum Feasible Participation: The Origins, Implications, and Present Status," *Poverty and Human Resources Abstracts* 2 (November–December 1967): 5–18, esp. 9, with Rubin's emphasis.

51. Wickenden's January 4, 1964, letter, quoted in Lemann, *Promised Land*, 144.

52. Isserman, *Other American*, 216.

53. Levitan, *Great Society's Poor Law*, is a useful guide to most OEO programs.

54. The 1964 *Economic Report of the President*, 106, in Miller, *Poverty American Style*.

55. Nancy A. Naples, *Grassroots Warriors: Activist Mothering, Community Work, and the War on Poverty* (New York: Routledge, 1998); Diana Pearce, "Welfare Is Not for Women: Why the War on Poverty Cannot Conquer the Feminization of Poverty," in Linda Gordon, ed., *Women, the State, and Welfare* (Madison: University of Wisconsin Press, 1990), 265–79; Henry M. Levin, "A Decade of Policy Developments in Improving Education and Training for Low-Income Populations," in Robert H. Haveman, ed., *A Decade of Federal Antipoverty Programs: Achievements, Failures, and Lessons* (New York: Academic Press, 1977), 123–88, esp. 143–45, 171, 179; and Robert A. Levine, *The Poor Ye Need Not Have with You: Lessons from the War on Poverty* (Cambridge, Mass.: MIT Press, 1970), 35, 67, 79, 130–31, 214.

56. And this woman lived in New York City, which had relatively high benefits.

57. There is more on poor people's connection to jobs in the following chapter.

58. See Levitan, *Great Society's Poor Law*, 207–13, on how government agencies lagged on family planning.

59. Phrase quoted from antipoverty expert Paul Ylvisaker, in Levitan, *Great Society's Poor Law*, 91.

60. Johnson's statement to Doris Kearns, in John A. Andrew III, *Lyndon Johnson and the Great Society* (Chicago: Ivan R. Dee, 1998), 84. See also, in the same book, 51, 84, 195, 199.

61. Lampman, "One-fifth of a Nation," *Challenge*, April 1964, reprinted in Walter

Fogel and Archie Kleingartner, eds., *Contemporary Labor Issues* (Belmont, Calif.: Wadsworth Publishing Co., 1966), 112–17, quotation on 115.

62. Stanley L. Friedlander, *Unemployment in the Urban Core: An Analysis of Thirty Cities with Policy Recommendations* (New York: Praeger, 1972), 149.

63. Barry Bluestone, "The Poor Who Have Jobs," *Dissent*, September–October 1968, 411.

64. William J. Spring, "Underemployment: The Measure We Refuse to Take," in Harold L. Sheppard, Bennett Harrison, and William J. Spring, eds., *The Political Economy of Public Service Employment* (Lexington, Mass.: D. C. Heath and Co., 1972), 193.

65. In *Toward a Democratic Left* Harrington argued that corporate planning hid behind laissez-faire ideology. Martin Gilens, *Why Americans Hate Welfare: Race, Media, and the Politics of Antipoverty Policy* (1999; Chicago: University of Chicago Press, 2000), shows that there has been support for many social programs, but that because of race and other factors, Americans don't like "welfare" and are stingy toward the unemployed.

Chapter Three

1. Michael Harrington, *The New American Poverty* (1984; New York: Penguin Books, 1985), 21. For other viewpoints, Irwin Unger, *The Best of Intentions: The Triumph and Failure of the Great Society under Kennedy, Johnson, and Nixon* (New York: Doubleday, 1996), 350–60, and Michael B. Katz, *The Undeserving Poor: From the War on Poverty to the War on Welfare* (1989; New York: Pantheon Books, 1990), 79–80, 113–14.

2. Margaret Weir, *Politics and Jobs: The Boundaries of Employment Policy in the United States* (1992; Princeton, N.J.: Princeton University Press, 1993), 62–86.

3. Henry M. Levin, "A Decade of Policy Developments in Improving Education and Training for Low-Income Populations," in Robert H. Haveman, ed., *A Decade of Federal Antipoverty Programs: Achievements, Failures, and Lessons* (New York: Academic Press, 1977), 179. Daniel Friedlander, David H. Greenberg, and Philip K. Robins, "Evaluating Government Training Programs for the Economically Disadvantaged," *Journal of Economic Literature* 35 (December 1997): 1809–55, conclude that the programs did not make "substantial inroads in reducing poverty, income inequality, or welfare use."

4. Allen J. Matusow, *The Unraveling of America: A History of Liberalism in the 1960s* (New York: Harper Torchbooks, 1984), 104; Garth L. Mangum and John Walsh, *A Decade of Manpower Development Training* (Salt Lake City, Utah: Olympus Publishing Co., 1973).

5. Mangum and Walsh, *Decade of Manpower Development Training*, 22–35, 41–44, quotation on 47, emphasis in original. The difficulty of getting consistent evaluations was a blow to the confidence of liberal intellectuals that they could design and evaluate successful programs. See Peter Marris and Martin Rein, *Dilemmas of Social Reform: Poverty and Community Action in the United States*, 2nd ed. (Chicago: University of Chicago Press, 1982), and Alice O'Connor, *Poverty Knowledge: Social Science, Social Policy, and the Poor in Twentieth-Century U.S. History* (Princeton, N.J.: Princeton University Press, 2001). See also Levin, "Decade of Policy Developments," 176–78; Charles

Brecher, *The Impact of Federal Antipoverty Policies* (New York: Praeger, 1973), 26–33, 59–65; Laurie J. Bassi and Orley Ashenfelter, "The Effect of Direct Job Creation and Training Programs on Low-Skilled Workers," in Sheldon H. Danziger and Daniel H. Weinberg, eds., *Fighting Poverty: What Works and What Doesn't* (Cambridge, Mass.: Harvard University Press, 1986), 140. Another problem was creaming; those who entered training programs were often a self-selected group of the highly motivated.

6. Levin, "Decade of Policy Developments," 168–70, 178; Mangum and Walsh, *Decade of Manpower Development Training* 17–41. On the partial displacement of existing workers by newly trained workers, Timothy J. Bartik, *Jobs for the Poor: Can Labor Demand Help?* (New York: Russell Sage Foundation, and Kalamazoo, Mich.: W. W. Upjohn Institute for Employment Research, 2001), 69–111.

7. On the U.S. Employment Service, Greenleigh Associates, Inc., *Opening the Doors: Job Training Programs: A Report to the Committee on Administration of Training Programs* (Washington: Government Printing Office, 1968), 11.

8. Quoted in ibid., 61. In theory, a highly trained workforce could win wage increases without causing inflation because productivity would rise. Since the monetary authorities would not, under these circumstances, have to create a recession to cut inflation, job growth would be preserved. But rising education and skills might not bring higher wages if unions were weak and workers plentiful. Mangum and Walsh, *Decade of Manpower Development Training* 116.

9. Matusow, *Unraveling of America*, 237.

10. The President's Task Force on Manpower, *One Third of a Nation: A Report on Young Men Found Unqualified for Military Service* (Washington, 1964), and Godfrey Hodgson, *The Gentleman from New York: Daniel Patrick Moynihan* (Boston: Houghton Mifflin, 2000), 82.

11. Sar A. Levitan, *The Great Society's Poor Law: A New Approach to Poverty* (Baltimore: Johns Hopkins University Press, 1969), 273–306, and Matusow, *Unraveling of America*, 237–40.

12. "The Administration: 'My Neighbor Needs Me,' " *Time*, March 5, 1965, 21.

13. Unger, *Best of Intentions*, 175.

14. Ibid., 179.

15. Stanley Lebergott, "Unemployment: A Perspective," in Lebergott, ed., *Men without Work: The Economics of Unemployment* (Englewood Cliffs, N.J.: Prentice-Hall, 1964), 1–53, esp. 40–41, made the point that corporate America trained thousands of employees every day. Perhaps so, but many poor youngsters were not even getting a foot in the corporate door, and Job Corps might help them do so.

16. Robert Weisbrot, *Freedom Bound: A History of America's Civil Rights Movement* (New York: Plume, 1991), 165; John Bainbridge, "The Job Corps," *New Yorker*, May 21, 1966, reprinted in Gerald Leinwand, ed., *Poverty and the Poor* (New York: Washington Square Press, 1968), 129–39.

17. Levin, "Decade of Policy Developments," 171–72; Robert A. Levine, *The Poor Ye Need Not Have with You: Lessons from the War on Poverty* (Cambridge, Mass.: MIT Press, 1970), 121–28; Levitan, *Great Society's Poor Law*, 285.

18. Levitan, *Great Society's Poor Law*, 306; Sar A. Levitan and Benjamin H. Johnston, *The Job Corps: A Social Experiment That Works* (Baltimore: Johns Hopkins University Press, 1975), 42–43, 71; David Sullivan, "Labor's Role in the War on Poverty," *AFL-CIO American Federationist*, April 1966, 10–11; David Wellman, "Putting-On the Poverty Program," *Steps* 1, no. 2 (1967): 51–66, reprinted in David M. Gordon, ed., *Problems in Political Economy: An Urban Perspective*, 2nd ed. (Lexington, Mass.: D. C. Heath and Co., 1977), 120–28; Charles E. Silberman and the Editors of *Fortune*, *The Myths of Automation* (New York: Harper and Row, 1966), 124–25.

19. Herman P. Miller, "Changes in the Number and Composition of the Poor," in Margaret S. Gordon, ed., *Poverty in America* (Berkeley: University of California, 1965), 86–87.

20. Blacks constituted about 44% of all families on welfare in 1961. Most welfare families were headed by women. Of 1,039,000 welfare families in 1965, perhaps 400,00 to 450,000 were headed by black women. See Robert H. Mugge, "Aid to Families with Dependent Children: Initial Findings of the 1961 Report on the Characteristics of Recipients," *Social Security Bulletin*, March 1963, 3–15, esp. 4; U.S. Department of Labor, Wage and Labor Standards Administration, *1969 Handbook on Women Workers* (Washington: Government Printing Office, 1969), 137–39; O'Connor, *Poverty Knowledge*, 202–6; and chapter 4 in the present volume, on Moynihan.

21. For subemployment, William J. Spring, "Underemployment: The Measure We Refuse to Take," in Harold L. Sheppard, Bennett Harrison, and William J. Spring, eds., *The Political Economy of Public Service Employment* (Lexington, Mass.: D. C. Heath and Co., 1972), 189, and chapter 5 in the present volume.

22. Sheldon H. Danziger, Robert H. Haveman, and Robert D. Plotnick, "Antipoverty Policy: Effects on the Poor and the Nonpoor," in Danziger and Weinberg, *Fighting Poverty*, 70.

23. The Kerner Commission on the riots of 1967 recommended the creation of 2 million jobs. See Gareth Davies, *From Opportunity to Entitlement: The Transformation and Decline of Great Society Liberalism* (Lawrence: University Press of Kansas, 1996), 203–8.

24. Martin Gilens, *Why Americans Hate Welfare: Race, Media, and the Politics of Antipoverty Policy* (1999; Chicago: University of Chicago Press, 2000), 116–21.

25. Edward Zigler and Susan Muenchow, *Head Start: The Inside Story of America's Most Successful Educational Experiment* (New York: Basic Books, 1992), 4–5. Lisbeth B. Schorr with Daniel Schorr, *Within Our Reach: Breaking the Cycle of Disadvantage* (New York: Anchor Books, 1989), 184–92.

26. Zigler and Muenchow, *Head Start*, 3, 10–19, and 27 for the quoted phrase from Johnson; Schorr and Schorr, *Within Our Reach*, 184–86, 191; Unger, *Best of Intentions*, 186; Levitan, *Great Society's Poor Law*, 135–37.

27. Zigler and Muenchow, *Head Start*, 7, 35, 15, 99–122, and quotation on 43.

28. Ibid., 21–25; there were 6-year-olds in the summer program, but most students in the regular year program were 4 and 5 years old. Levitan, *Great Society's Poor Law*, 140.

29. Zigler and Muenchow, *Head Start*, 28–37, 44; Unger, *Best of Intentions*, 187–88; Levin, "Decade of Policy Developments," 132. Later, when many of these teachers

went back to regular jobs, there was a Head Start teacher shortage, a problem exacerbated by low pay.

30. Zigler and Muenchow, *Head Start*, 42–47, 51–52, 58; Levitan, *Great Society's Poor Law*, 150, 158–60.

31. Zigler and Muenchow, *Head Start*, 56–80; Unger, *Best of Intentions*, 233. Coleman included the first summer of Head Start in his evaluation, but in any case his study cast doubt on all forms of compensatory education. The report is James S. Coleman et al., *Equality of Educational Opportunity* (Washington: U.S. Department of Health, Education, and Welfare, 1966), and it is cited in Zigler and Muenchow, *Head Start*, 59–60.

32. Zigler and Muenchow, *Head Start*, 169–72, 192; Schorr and Schorr, *Within Our Reach*, 192–94; Levin, "Decade of Policy Developments," 151–55; Matusow, *Unraveling of America*, 266.

33. Zigler and Muenchow, *Head Start*, 40–55; Levitan, *Great Society's Poor Law*, 148, 163. On the lack of rigor in the High/Scope method used in some Head Start centers, Richard Lee Colvin, "Head Start, Some Say, Isn't Helping Kids Catch Up," *Los Angeles Times*, June 17, 2001, A1, A24–A25.

34. Zigler and Muenchow, *Head Start*, 83, 105–16, 23; Unger, *Best of Intentions*, 360. The 30,000 figure is for fiscal year 1968, cited in Levitan, *Great Society's Poor Law*, 142. See Levitan's whole section, 133–63.

35. John Dittmer, *Local People: The Struggle for Civil Rights in Mississippi* (Urbana: University of Illinois Press, 1994), 371; Polly Greenberg, *The Devil Has Slippery Shoes: A Biased Biography of the Child Development Group of Mississippi, a Story of Maximum Feasible Parent Participation* (Washington: Youth Policy Institute, 1990), 199, 354, 364, 377, 387–88, 398–99, 408, 426, 437, and 80 for the quotation from Governor Paul Johnson. Also, Nicholas Lemann, *The Promised Land: The Great Black Migration and How It Changed America* (New York: Vintage Books, 1992), 323–27; Robert Coles, *Migrants, Sharecroppers, Mountaineers*, vol. 2 of *Children of Crisis* (Boston: Little, Brown, 1971), 553–67; Pat Watters, "Mississippi: Children and Politics," *Dissent*, May–June 1967, 293–310, reprinted in Jeremy Larner and Irving Howe, eds., *Poverty: Views from the Left* (New York: William Morrow and Co., 1968), 221–44. According to Kay Mills, *Something Better for My Children* (New York: Plume, 1998), 65, the CDGM lacked receipts for only $26,000 of $1,500,000. Dittmer, *Local People*, 372, claimed that only 1% of CDGM expenditures were in doubt.

36. Carter quoting Shriver in Dittmer, *Local People*, 376, 380–81.

37. Greenberg, 22, 45, 61–62, 76–77, 98–100, 118, 152–53, 639, and 3 for the quotation. Final quotation is from "Say It Isn't So, Sargent Shriver," *New York Times*, October 19, 1966, 35.

38. Greenberg, 224, 259–65, 304–11, 427–57, 601–66, 674–81, 778–93, 801; Zigler and Muenchow, *Head Start*, 84, 102, 171–91. Since much of the South was still a one-party system, conservative, often racist, Democrats won reelection time and again and, as a result, controlled many congressional committees.

39. Dittmer, *Local People*, 365–66, 377, 384–88.

40. Robert Kennedy's testimony quoted in Matusow, *Unraveling of America*, 126. See

also Daniel Patrick Moynihan, *Maximum Feasible Misunderstanding: Community Action in the War on Poverty* (New York: Free Press, 1969), and Adam Walinsky review in the *New York Times*, February 2, 1969, reprinted in Harold L. Sheppard, ed., *Poverty and Wealth in America* (Chicago: Quadrangle Books, 1970), 263–71.

41. Quotation from Robert Halpern, *Rebuilding the Inner City: A History of Neighborhood Initiatives to Address Poverty in the United States* (New York: Columbia University Press, 1995), 117. See also Weir, *Politics and Jobs*, 78. Large corporations did not even steer job offers to community action agencies under a Concentrated Employment Program.

42. Matusow, *Unraveling of America*, esp. 244, 265; Unger, *Best of Intentions*, 151; Levitan, *Great Society's Poor Law*, 109–12; Sanford Kravitz and Ferne K. Kolodner, "Community Action: Where Has It Been? Where Will It Go?," in *Poverty and Human Resources Abstract* 4, no. 4 (1969): 9–17.

43. David Greenstone and Paul Peterson, *Race and Authority in Urban Politics: Community Participation and the War on Poverty* (New York: Russell Sage Foundation, 1973). Other agencies run by local establishments were in Philadelphia, Atlanta, Pittsburgh, Rochester, and Cleveland. See Stephen M. Rose, "Community Action Programs: The Relationship between Initial Conception of the Poverty Problem, Derived Intervention Strategy, and Program Implementation" (Ph.D. diss., Brandeis University, 1970).

44. Mobilization for Youth would still do fruitful work for welfare rights. See Martha F. Davis, *Brutal Need: Lawyers and the Welfare Rights Movement, 1960–1973* (New Haven, Conn.: Yale University Press, 1993), 26–39, 86–98, and Matusow, *Unraveling of America*, 263.

45. On the Mobilization for Youth and Syracuse, Matusow, *Unraveling of America*, 248, 262–65, and Unger, *Best of Intentions*, 154. See also Sanford D. Horwitt, *Let Them Call Me Rebel: Saul Alinsky, His Life and Legacy* (New York: Vintage Books, 1992).

46. Maurice Isserman, *The Other American: The Life of Michael Harrington* (New York: Public Affairs, 2000), 214.

47. Jill Quadagno, *The Color of Welfare: How Racism Undermined the War on Poverty* (1994; New York: Oxford University Press, 1996), 47–52, and Video Series by Henry Hampton et al., *America's War on Poverty*, pt. 2, *City of Promise* (Boston: Blackside, 1995). The Newark events occurred under Model Cities. See also Greenstone and Peterson, *Race and Authority in Urban Politics*; Halpern, *Rebuilding the Inner City*, 116; Murray Seidler, "Some Participant Observer Reflections on Detroit's Community Action Program," *Urban Affairs Quarterly* 5 (December 1969): 183–205; and Neil Gilbert, *Clients or Constituents* (San Francisco: Jossey-Bass, 1970), quotation from 162.

48. Matusow, *Unraveling of America*, 257–62. Unger, *Best of Intentions*, 162, claims that 80% of funds went for salaries in one community action agency, Harlem Youth Opportunities Unlimited–Associated Community Teams.

49. Levitan, *Great Society's Poor Law*, 129; Kravitz and Kolodner, "Community Action," 15; Ralph M. Kramer, *Participation of the Poor: Comparative Community Case Studies in the War on Poverty* (Englewood Cliffs, N.J.: Prentice-Hall, 1969), 210–11, 231; Frances Fox Piven and Richard A. Cloward, *Regulating the Poor: The Functions of Public*

Welfare (1971; New York: Vintage Books, 1972), 274–75 n. 37; Nancy A. Naples, *Grassroots Warriors: Activist Mothering, Community Work, and the War on Poverty* (New York: Routledge, 1998).

50. Matusow, *Unraveling of America*, 265–66; Kravitz and Kolodner, "Community Action," 15; Levitan, *Great Society's Poor Law*, 116, 128–29. Rose, "Community Action Programs," shows that very few of his twenty sample agencies directly operated service programs like Head Start.

51. Matusow, *Unraveling of America*, 267–68. See also William C. Selover, "The View from Capitol Hill: Harassment and Survival," in James L. Sundquist, ed., *On Fighting Poverty: Perspectives from Experience* (New York: Basic Books, 1969), 177–79, and Selover, "U.S. Poor Gain Foothold in Local Programs," *Christian Science Monitor*, August 2, 1966, 10.

52. Matusow, *Unraveling of America*, 251, 269–70; only nineteen local governments used the Green amendment to seize control. See also Levitan, *Great Society's Poor Law*, 113–15; Selover, "View from Capitol Hill," 172–73, 182; and Kramer, *Participation of the Poor*, 189 n. 3.

53. Halpern, *Rebuilding the Inner City*, 118–24; Unger, *Best of Intentions*, 221–33, 332–35.

54. On TWO, Lemann, *Promised Land*, 98–103, 122–23, 152, 234, 246–50. David F. Selvin, "The Rise of the Farm Workers Union," *American Federationist*, May 1967, 1–5. Farmworkers did not even have protection of federal labor laws.

55. Lemann, *Promised Land*, 122–23; Douglass Cater, "The Politics of Poverty," in Chaim Isaac Waxman, ed., *Poverty: Power and Politics* (New York: Grosset and Dunlap, 1968), 110.

56. Matusow, *Unraveling of America*, 268; Marris and Rein, *Dilemmas of Social Reform*, 265–67; Sanford Kravitz, "The Community Action Program—Past, Present, and Its Future?," in Sundquist, *On Fighting Poverty*, 52–69, esp. 66–67; Kramer, *Participation of the Poor*, esp. 228–31, 260–73.

57. For this and preceding paragraph, Levitan, *Great Society's Poor Law*, 177–89; Matusow, *Unraveling of America*, 266–68; Unger, *Best of Intentions*, 180–83; Ellen Jane Hollingsworth (and responses by Earl Johnson Jr. and Edward Sparer), "Ten Years of Legal Services for the Poor," in Haveman, *Decade of Federal Antipoverty Programs*, 285–327; Edgar S. Cahn and Jean C. Cahn, "The War on Poverty: A Civilian Perspective," *Yale Law Journal* 73 (July 1964): 1317–52; and Katz, *Undeserving Poor*, 107.

58. Jerome Carlin quoted in Halpern, *Rebuilding the Inner City*, 118. Defenders of guaranteed incomes included John Rawls. See Katz, *Undeserving Poor*, 111–12; Davies, *From Opportunity to Entitlement*, and chapter 6 in the present volume.

59. Sparer quoted in Haveman, *Decade of Federal Antipoverty Programs*, 326–27.

60. *Poverty, 1998*, B-2; Charles Murray, *Losing Ground: American Social Policy, 1950–1980* (New York: Basic Books, 1984), 245.

61. John E. Schwarz, *America's Hidden Success: A Reassessment of Public Policy from Kennedy to Reagan*, rev. ed. (New York: W. W. Norton and Co., 1988), 25; Levitan, *Great Society's Poor Law*, 309.

62. Wellman, "Putting-On the Poverty Program."

63. Robert D. Plotnick and Felicity Skidmore, *Progress against Poverty: A Review of the 1964–1974 Decade* (New York: Academic Press, 1975), 112; Danziger, Haveman, and Plotnick, "Antipoverty Policy," 54. These estimates include only cash transfers. The percentage points of decline in the text indicate not the *total* impact of growth or transfers but only the additional effect for the stated years. Federal payments were already, by 1965, lifting a third of the poor out of poverty; by 1970, just a bit more. See Plotnick and Skidmore, *Progress against Poverty*, 138–40.

64. *Poverty, 1998*, B-2; Plotnick and Skidmore, *Progress against Poverty*, 113, 145, 148, 153, 162.

65. Plotnick and Skidmore, *Progress against Poverty*, 89, 114; *Poverty, 1998*, B-2; Christine Ross, Sheldon Danziger, Eugene Smolensky, *The Level and Trend of Poverty, 1939–1979*, Discussion Paper #790–85 (Madison, Wis.: Institute for Research on Poverty 1985), table 16. I rounded the percentages.

66. Weir, *Politics and Jobs*, 90; *Report of the National Advisory Commission on Civil Disorders* (New York: Bantam Books, 1968), 251–65.

67. Schwarz, *America's Hidden Success*, 29, 35–36; John A. Andrew III, *Lyndon Johnson and the Great Society* (Chicago: Ivan R. Dee, 1998), 17, 66, 71, on "the crowded generation." On glutted labor markets, chapters 5, 7, and 10 in the present volume. Some argue that female-headed families were not increasing as fast as it seemed; they had just come out of the closet. See Frances Fox Piven and Richard A. Cloward, "The Contemporary Relief Debate," in Fred Block, Richard A. Cloward, Barbara Ehrenreich, and Frances Fox Piven, *The Mean Season: The Attack on the Welfare State* (New York: Pantheon Books, 1987), 53–57.

68. "Hard Times for Black America," *Dollars & Sense*, April 1986, 5–7; William Julius Wilson, *The Truly Disadvantaged: The Inner City, the Underclass, and Public Policy* (1987; Chicago: University of Chicago Press, 1990), 81–106.

69. *Poverty, 1998*, B-1 for this and for the numbers in preceding paragraph.

70. Henry Aaron, quoted in Weir, *Politics and Jobs*, 69. See also Robert Dallek, *Flawed Giant: Lyndon Johnson and His Times, 1961–1973* (New York: Oxford University Press, 1998), 74–80, 107–11; Lemann, *Promised Land*, 131.

71. Unger, *Best of Intentions*, 84, 359; Hugh Heclo, "The Political Foundations of Antipoverty Policy," in Danziger and Weinberg, *Fighting Poverty*, 331. On the limits of War on Poverty training, *EWP*, pt. 11, 3467, 3469 for the quoted phrase, and Wellman, "Putting-On the Poverty Program." On what Johnson might have done, Charles Noble, *Welfare As We Knew It: A Political History of the American Welfare State* (New York: Oxford University Press, 1997), 93–104.

72. Dallek, *Flawed Giant*, 330, 334.

73. Matusow, *Unraveling of America*, 250–51; Davies, *From Opportunity to Entitlement* 75–104, 173–74; Martin Luther King Jr., *Where Do We Go from Here: Chaos or Community?* (New York: Harper and Row, 1967), 162–66; Tom Wicker, "In the Nation: The Right to Income," *New York Times*, December 24, 1967, E9; Robert B. Semple Jr., "U.S. Finds Only 1% on Welfare Lists Are Employable," *New York Times*, April 20,

1967, 1, 30; *EWP*, pt. 1, 132–133, 232, 233, 236; Levine, *Poor Ye Need Not Have with You*, 192–212; Unger, *Best of Intentions*, 287–92.

74. Unger, *Best of Intentions*, 293–94; Levine, *Poor Ye Need Not Have with You*, 86–87, 110–16, 212–13; Weir, *Politics and Jobs*, 93; Brecher, *Impact of Federal Antipoverty Policies*, 59–69.

75. See Jacob S. Hacker, *The Divided Welfare State: The Battle over Public and Private Social Benefits in the United States* (Cambridge: Cambridge University Press, 2002); Christopher Howard, *The Hidden Welfare State: Tax Expenditures and Social Policy in the United States* (Princeton, N.J.: Princeton University Press, 1997), e.g., 28–32, 106.

76. Isserman, *Other American*, 307; Plotnick and Skidmore, *Progress against Poverty*, 63–75; and Bruce J. Schulman, *Lyndon B. Johnson and American Liberalism: A Brief Biography with Documents* (Boston: St. Martin's Press, Bedford Books, 1995), 101–2.

77. Heclo, "Political Foundations of Antipoverty Policy," 319, 326–32.

78. Laurence E. Lynn Jr., "A Decade of Policy Developments in the Income-Maintenance System," in Haveman, *Decade of Federal Antipoverty Programs*, 92–93; Plotnick and Skidmore, *Progress against Poverty*, 187–88; Alan Brinkley, *The End of Reform: New Deal Liberalism in Recession and War* (New York: Vintage Books, 1996); Nelson Lichtenstein, "American Trade Unions and the 'Labor Question,'" in Century Foundation, *What's Next for Organized Labor* (New York: Century Foundation Press, 1999), 82–87. Robert H. Zeiger, *American Workers, American Unions*, 2nd ed. (Baltimore: Johns Hopkins University Press, 1994), 137–92; Quadagno, *Color of Welfare*, 76. Walter Reuther's United Auto Workers supported civil rights and antipoverty movements. But on poverty and class issues, United Auto Workers' union leaders seemed to confess their own failure when union official Brendan Sexton argued that workers who had been made jobless by the collapse of Studebaker lacked leadership and could not be organized the way the urban poor could in their communities. So there could be no community of interest between the urban poor and the deindustrialized jobless, not because the underclass was disorganized but because union members were. See Kevin Boyle, *The UAW and the Heyday of American Liberalism, 1945–1968* (Ithaca, N.Y.: Cornell University Press, 1995), 191.

79. Robert S. McElvaine, *The Great Depression: America, 1929–1941* (New York: Times Books, 1993), xxiii–xxix.

Chapter Four

1. On the United States, Germany, and the Netherlands, Robert E. Goodin, Bruce Headey, Ruud Muffles, and Henk-Jan Dirven, *The Real Worlds of Welfare Capitalism* (Cambridge: Cambridge University Press, 2000); on different poverty levels, Benjamin Friedman, "What Is Poverty," *New York Review of Books*, November 21, 2002, 58–59; on health care, John-Thor Dahlburg and Richard Boudreaux, "Europe's Rx for Health," *Los Angeles Times*, October 21, 2000, A1, A14.

2. Nelson Lichtenstein, "From Corporatism to Collective Bargaining: Organized Labor and the Eclipse of Social Democracy in the Postwar Era," in Steve Fraser and

Gary Gerstle, eds., *The Rise and Fall of the New Deal Order, 1930–1980* (Princeton, N.J.: Princeton University Press, 1989), 122–52; Robert S. McElvaine, *The Great Depression: America, 1929–1941* (New York: Times Books, 1993), 310–11; Robert C. Lieberman, *Shifting the Color Line: Race and the American Welfare State* (1998; Cambridge, Mass.: Harvard University Press, 2001).

3. Peter B. Levy, *The New Left and Labor in the 1960s* (Urbana: University of Illinois Press, 1994).

4. Johnson's Howard speech, in Lee Rainwater and William L. Yancey, *The Moynihan Report and the Politics of Controversy* (Cambridge, Mass.: MIT Press, 1967), 126.

5. Gareth Davies, *From Opportunity to Entitlement: The Transformation and Decline of Great Society Liberalism* (Lawrence: University Press of Kansas, 1996), 99–115.

6. Tom Hayden, "The Politics of the 'Movement,'" in Irving Howe, ed., *The Radical Papers* (Garden City, N.Y.: Doubleday, 1966).

7. Bayard Rustin, "From Protest to Politics: The Future of the Civil Rights Movement," *Commentary*, February 1965, reprinted in Howe, *Radical Papers*, 347–61, quotation on 355–56; Michael Harrington, "The Politics of Poverty," 124–47, in Howe, *Radical Papers*; and Levy, *New Left and Labor*. See also Michael Harrington, *Toward a Democratic Left: A Radical Program for a New Majority* (New York: Macmillan, 1968), which lacks a sustained argument for why white workers should join a radicalized Democratic Party, and Taylor E. Dark, *The Unions and the Democrats: An Enduring Alliance*, updated ed. (Ithaca, N.Y.: Cornell University Press, 2001), 47–98, 137. Reuther aimed to liberalize the Democratic Party, backed New Left and antipoverty organizations, and was a bridge between old labor and new radicals.

8. *NF.*

9. Jacob Weisberg, "For the Sake of Argument," *New York Times Magazine*, November 2, 2000, 48–53, 68–69, 102, 104, is insightful on this.

10. Later it was common also to hear that the continuation of high levels of black poverty and crime proved that Moynihan had been right.

11. Godfrey Hodgson, *The Gentleman from New York: Daniel Patrick Moynihan* (Boston: Houghton Mifflin, 2000); Jacob Heilbrun, "The Moynihan Engima," *American Prospect*, July–August 1997, 18–24; Peter Steinfels, *The Neoconservatives: The Men Who Are Changing America's Politics* (New York: Touchstone Books, 1980), 69, 108–60, 248–72.

12. Daniel Patrick Moynihan, "Where Liberals Went Wrong," in Melvin R. Laird, ed., *Republican Papers* (New York: Praeger, 1968), 129–42; Godfrey Hodgson, *The World Turned Upside Down: A History of the Conservative Ascendancy in America* (Boston: Houghton Mifflin, 1996), 128–57. Steinfels, *Neoconservatives*, 294, suggests that neoconservatism was at first a liberal effort to reform liberalism but later became conservative and risked becoming simply "the legitimating and lubricating ideology of an oligarchic America where decisions are made by corporate elites."

13. Quoted words and phrases from *NF*, 43, 51.

14. Ibid., 54–55, 52–53, 64, 103–4, 107–8, 58 for the quoted phrase.

15. Ibid., 51, 76, 81–91, 122. See also Moynihan, "Employment, Income, and the

Ordeal of the Black Family," *Daedelus*, May 1965, reprinted in Talcott Parsons and Kenneth B. Clark, eds., *The Negro American* (Boston: Beacon Press, 1966), 134–59.

16. *NF*, 58–59, 93.

17. *The Negro Family* was marked "for official use only," and until the summer of 1965, there were one hundred copies, all for internal government use. Rainwater and Yancey, *Moynihan Report*, 26, 137–38.

18. Hodgson, *Gentleman from New York*, 117–18. Rainwater and Yancey, *Moynihan Report*, 26–29, 135–41, and 200 for the McKissick quotation. Ryan is quoted from "Savage Discovery: The Moynihan Report," *The Nation*, November 22, 1965, as reprinted in Rainwater and Yancey, *Moynihan Report*, 458. Moynihan had not quite blamed poor blacks for their plight, although some columnists thought so.

19. Rainwater and Yancey, *Moynihan Report*, 10–13, 17, 193, 247.

20. Ibid., 407.

21. Moynihan, "The President and the Negro: The Moment Lost," *Commentary*, February 1967, as quoted in Stephen Steinberg, *Turning Back: The Retreat from Racial Justice in American Thought and Policy* (Boston: Beacon Press, 1995), 121–22.

22. Rainwater and Yancey, *Moynihan Report*, 29, and *NF*, 71; Moynihan, "Employment, Income, and the Ordeal of the Black Family," 150.

23. Moynihan, quoted in Rainwater and Yancey, *Moynihan Report*, 20–21; See also *NF*, 66–69.

24. Perhaps black unemployment seemed to fall not because black men found jobs but because, not finding them, they dropped out of the labor force. In *The Politics of a Guaranteed Income: The Nixon Administration and the Family Assistance Plan* (New York: Vintage Books, 1973), Moynihan mentioned eligibility issues (84). See also Rainwater and Yancey, *Moynihan Report*, 476n. Moynihan's "The Crises in Welfare," *Public Interest*, Winter 1968, 3–29, is a less alarmist program focusing on unemployment, income, and discrimination rather than fixing the family. On declining labor force participation, Charles C. Killingsworth, "The Continuing Labor Market Twist," *Monthly Labor Review* 91 (September 1968): 12–17.

25. See Sut Jhally and Justin Lewis, *Enlightened Racism: The Cosby Show, Audiences, and the Myth of the American Dream* (Boulder, Colo.: Westview Press, 1992), for example, 70, 134.

26. Quoted in Steinberg, *Turning Back*, 117. See also Moynihan's broadening conceptions in "The Crises in Welfare," esp. 24–25, and "Three Problems in Combatting Poverty," in Margaret S. Gordon, ed., *Poverty in America* (Berkeley: University of California, 1965), 51–53.

27. Also on poverty and family structure, "Hard Times for Black America," *Dollars & Sense*, April 1986, 5–7, and Mary Jo Bane, "Household Composition and Poverty," in Sheldon H. Danziger and Daniel H. Weinberg, eds., *Fighting Poverty: What Works and What Doesn't* (Cambridge, Mass.: Harvard University Press, 1986), 208–31.

28. Rainwater and Yancey, *Moynihan Report*, n. 313, and Moynihan, "Crises in Welfare."

29. *NF*, 54–55, 52–53, 64, 103–4, 107–8. Steinfels, *Neoconservatives*, 130, notes that

Moynihan ignored positive responses to his report. Moynihan's book on the War on Poverty, *Maximum Feasible Misunderstanding: Community Action in the War on Poverty* (New York: Free Press, 1969), was, in part, revenge on the liberals but did not mention the flap around *The Negro Family*.

30. Michael B. Katz, *The Undeserving Poor: From the War on Poverty to the War on Welfare* (1989; New York: Pantheon Books, 1990), 29 for the quotation; William Julius Wilson, *The Truly Disadvantaged: The Inner City, the Underclass, and Public Policy* (Chicago: University of Chicago Press, 1987), 4–9. Studies of "the culture of poverty" include Elliot Liebow, *Tally's Corner* (1967); Rainwater, *Behind Ghetto Walls* (1970); Joyce Ladner, *Tomorrow's Tomorrow* (1971); Sidney Wilhelm, *Who Needs the Negro?* (1970); Douglas Glasgow, *The Black Underclass* (1980); Carol Stack, *All Our Kin* (1974); and Herbert Gutman, *The Black Family in Slavery and Freedom* (1976). See also Steinberg, *Turning Back*, 81.

31. Exceptions were Andrew Levison, *The Working-Class Majority* (New York: Penguin Books, 1975), and the Sextons, discussed later in this chapter.

32. Quoted in Alice O'Connor, *Poverty Knowledge: Social Science, Social Policy, and the Poor in Twentieth-Century America* (Princeton, N.J.: Princeton University Press, 2001), 209.

33. David Wellman, "Putting-On the Poverty Program," *Steps* 1, no. 2 (1967): 51–66, reprinted in David M. Gordon, ed., *Problems in Political Economy: An Urban Perspective*, 2nd ed. (Lexington, Mass.: D. C. Heath and Co., 1977), 120–28.

34. William J. Spring, "Underemployment: The Measure We Refuse to Take," in Harold L. Sheppard, Bennett Harrison, and William J. Spring, eds., *The Political Economy of Public Service Employment* (Lexington, Mass.: D. C. Heath and Co., 1972), 190.

35. I found no book-length study of radical economics in the 60s and 70s, but see David A. Spencer, "The Demise of Radical Political Economics?: An Essay on the Evolution of a Theory of Capitalist Production," *Cambridge Journal of Economics* 24 (2000): 543–64; Michael Reich, "Radical Economics: Successes and Failures," in Fred Moseley, ed., *Heterodox Economic Theories: True or False?* (Aldershot, England: Edward Elgar, 1995), 45–70; James B. Rebitzer, "Radical Political Economy and the Economics of Labor Markets," *Journal of Economic Literature* 31 (September 1993): 1394–1434; William T. Dickens and Kevin Lang, "Labor Market Segmentation Theory: Reconsidering the Evidence," in William Darity Jr., ed., *Labor Economics: Problems in Analyzing Labor Markets* (Boston: Kluwer Academic Publishers, 1993), 141–80.

36. Barry F. Bluestone, "Economic Theory, Economic Reality, and the Fate of the Poor," 117–128, in Sheppard, Harrison, and Spring, *Political Economy of Public Service Employment*, and Bluestone, "The Poor Who Have Jobs," *Dissent*, September–October 1968, 410–19; Howard M. Wachtel and Charles Betsey, "The Determinants of 'Working Poverty,'" in Sheppard, Harrison, and Spring, *Political Economy of Public Service Employment*, 77–83; David M. Gordon, *Theories of Poverty and Underemployment* (Lexington, Mass.: D. C. Heath and Co., 1972), 28–29, 92, on the lack of proof for marginal productivity. For summaries of conventional wisdom, Bennett Harrison, *Education, Training, and the Urban Ghetto* (Baltimore: Johns Hopkins University Press, 1972), 8–12, 32–38.

37. Bluestone, "Poor Who Have Jobs," 413–14; Wachtel and Betsey, "Determinants of 'Working Poverty.'"

38. Ivar Berg, "Education and Work," in Sheppard, Harrison, and Spring, *Political Economy of Public Service Employment*, 208–14, quotation on 211; Berg, *Education and Jobs: The Great Training Robbery* (Boston: Beacon Press, 1971); editors' commentary, Sheppard, Harrison, and Spring, *Political Economy of Public Service Employment*, 199–208; Harrison, *Education, Training, and the Urban Ghetto*, 92–93. Two radical works engaged the skills issue directly. Harry Braverman, *Labor and Monopoly Capital: The Degradation of Work in the Twentieth Century* (New York: Monthly Review Press, 1974), esp. 424–49, and Samuel Bowles and Herbert Gintis, *Schooling in Capitalist America: Educational Reform and the Contradictions of Economic Life* (New York: Basic Books, 1977).

39. Gordon, *Theories of Poverty and Underemployment*, 43–52; Harrison, *Education, Training, and the Urban Ghetto*, 97–116. More schooling yielded higher pay for whites but not for blacks, even if they worked in the suburbs.

40. Suggesting that dysfunctional ghetto culture had sources independent of the labor market were Peter B. Doeringer et al., *Low-Income Labor Markets and Urban Manpower Programs: A Critical Assessment* (Washington: U.S. Department of Labor–Manpower Administration, 1972), 9, and Gordon, *Theories of Poverty and Underemployment*, 43–81. Arguing that unstable labor markets created a culture of poverty were Bluestone, "Poor Who Have Jobs," and Elliot Liebow, *Tally's Corner: A Study of Negro Streetcorner Men* (Boston: Little, Brown, 1967), in which p. 212 is the source of the quotation.

41. Bluestone, "Poor Who Have Jobs," 411.

42. Spring, "Underemployment," 193.

43. Wachtel and Betsey, "Determinants of 'Working Poverty,'" 77; Bluestone, "Poor Who Have Jobs"; Liebow, *Tally's Corner*; and Dawn Day Wachtel, *The Working Poor* (Washington: Clearinghouse for Federal Scientific and Technical Information, 1965). Sometimes low-income people had no trouble finding jobs, but they could not find good jobs. See Doeringer et al., *Low-Income Labor Markets*, 32.

44. Wachtel, *Working Poor*, and Howard M. Wachtel, "Looking at Poverty from a Radical Perspective," *Review of Radical Political Economics* 3 (Summer 1971), in Gordon, *Problems in Political Economy*, 307–12.

45. Pete Hamill, "The Revolt of the White Lower-Middle Class," *New York Magazine*, April 14, 1969, reprinted in Louise Kapp Howe, ed., *The White Majority: Between Poverty and Affluence* (New York: Random House, 1970), 10–22; Richard Parker, *The Myth of the Middle Class* (New York: Harper Colophon Books, 1974), 14–15, 134–52; Patricia Cayo Sexton and Brendan Sexton, *Blue Collars and Hard Hats: The Working Class and the Future of American Politics* (New York: Random House, 1971), 31–32; and, a bit later, Levison, *Working-Class Majority*, and Lillian Breslow Rubin, *Worlds of Pain: Life in the Working-Class Family* (New York: Basic Books, 1976).

46. Thomas Byrne Edsall and Mary D. Edsall, *Chain Reaction: The Impact of Race, Rights, and Taxes on American Politics* (New York: W. W. Norton and Co., 1991). Gordon, *Theories of Poverty and Underemployment*, 46–47, 94, 112, 118–20; Harrison,

Education, Training, and the Urban Ghetto; Doeringer et al., *Low-Income Labor Markets*; Bluestone, "Poor Who Have Jobs," and Bluestone, "Low-Wage Industries and the Working Poor," *Poverty and Human Resources Abstracts* 3 (March–April 1968): 1–14.

47. Levy, *New Left and Labor*, 102–27.

48. The first issue of *Dollars & Sense* was November 1974; Editorial Board, "Revised Statement of Editorial Policy for the *RRPE*," *Review of Radical Political Economics* 6 (Spring 1974): ii–iv.

49. Quotation from "What the Marxists See in the Recession," *Business Week*, June 23, 1975, 86–87.

50. Bowles and Gintis, *Schooling in Capitalist America*; Braverman, esp. his chapter "The Structure of the Working Class and Its Reserve Armies" in *Labor and Monopoly Capital*. See also Paul A. Baran and Paul M. Sweezy, *Monopoly Capital: An Essay on the American Economic and Social Order* (New York: Monthly Review Press, 1966), 285–289, and Howard M. Wachtel, "Capitalism and Poverty in America: Paradox or Contradiction"; Barry F. Bluestone, "Capitalism and Poverty in America: A Discussion"; and David M. Gordon, "American Poverty: Functions, Mechanism, and Contradictions," all in *Monthly Review* 24 (June 1972): 51–79.

51. Reich, *Radical Economics*, 58–59. Gordon (*Theories of Poverty and Underemployment*) is a Dissenter underestimating unemployment. Dissenters who emphasized the role of aggregate unemployment in class conflict included authors in Sheppard, Harrison, and Spring, *Political Economy of Public Service Employment*, and also Raford Boddy and James Crotty, "Wage-Push and Working-Class Power: A Reply to Howard Sherman," *Monthly Review* 10 (March 1976): 35–43.

52. Nicholas von Hoffman, "Nixon Isn't a Very Good Marxist," *Washington Post*, August 13, 1971, B1, B11.

53. As quoted in David M. Gordon, *Fat and Mean: The Corporate Squeeze of Working Americans and the Myth of Managerial "Downsizing"* (New York: Free Press, 1996), 66.

54. State and local taxes in 1965 intensified inequality, taking 25% of the income of people earning less than $2,000 but only 7% from those earning more than $15,000. See Parker, *Myth of the Middle Class*, 143–44, 177–79.

55. O'Connor, *Poverty Knowledge*, shows that scholarship on poverty became more narrowly technical in the 70s.

56. David J. Garrow, *Bearing the Cross: Martin Luther King, Jr., and the Southern Christian Leadership Conference* (New York: Vintage Books, 1988), 431–624, and Richard D. Kahlenberg, *The Remedy: Class, Race, and Affirmative Action* (New York: A New Republic Book, Basic Books, 1996), xiii–xvii, 183–209.

57. "Yorty Says Jobs Are Solution to Many Problems of the Slums," *New York Times*, December 24, 1967, 37.

58. Levy, *New Left and Labor*, 192. Edsall and Edsall, *Chain Reaction*.

59. Martin Gilens, *Why Americans Hate Welfare: Race, Media, and the Politics of Antipoverty Policy* (1999; Chicago: University of Chicago Press, 2000), 102–53.

60. Margaret Weir, *Politics and Jobs: The Boundaries of Employment Policy in the United States* (1992; Princeton, N.J.: Princeton University Press, 1993), 69.

61. Gertrude Schaffner Goldberg and Sheila D. Collins, *Washington's New Poor Law: Welfare Reform and the Roads Not Taken—1935 to the Present* (New York: Apex Press, 2001), 122–23.

62. See chapter 8 in the present volume and Carl Ginsberg, *Race and the Media: The Enduring Life of the Moynihan Report* (New York: Institute for Media Analysis, 1989).

Chapter Five

1. See chapter 10 in the present volume and Robert Pollin, "Class Conflict and the 'Natural Rate of Unemployment,'" *Challenge* 42 (November–December 1999): 103–11, accessed at <www.proquest.com> on August 17, 2003.

2. Bradley R. Schiller, *The Economics of Poverty and Discrimination*, 8th ed. (Upper Saddle River, N.J.: Prentice-Hall, 2001), 49–71, 242–57, 278–85, and *Freedom Budget for All Americans: Budgeting Our Resources, 1966–1975, to Achieve "Freedom from Want"* (1966), reprinted in *EWP*, pt. 1, 407–505. For more on skills, see chapters 4, 7, and 10 in the present volume and Samuel Bowles and Herbert Gintis, *Schooling in Capitalist America: Educational Reform and the Contradictions of Economic Life* (New York: Basic Books, 1977).

3. *HLS, 1972*, 221.

4. Paul Osterman, "Gains from Growth?: The Impact of Full Employment on Poverty in Boston," in Christopher Jencks and Paul E. Peterson, eds., *The Urban Underclass* (Washington: Brookings Institution, 1991), 122–34; Richard B. Freeman, "The Rising Tide Lifts . . . ?," in Sheldon H. Danziger and Robert H. Haveman, eds., *Understanding Poverty* (New York: Russell Sage Foundation; Cambridge, Mass.: Harvard University Press, 2001), 97–126; Schiller, *Economics of Poverty and Discrimination*, 68–70, 245; Jacob Heilbrun, "Sacrificing Workers in the War on Inflation," *Los Angeles Times*, May 28, 2000, M1, M6.

5. Mollie Orshansky, "Counting the Poor: Another Look at the Poverty Profile," *Social Security Bulletin*, January 1965, reprinted in Orshansky, *The Measure of Poverty: Technical Paper I*, (Washington: U.S. Department of Health, Education, and Welfare, n.d [probably 1976]), 16–43, especially tables 2, 3, and 8.

6. Ibid., 18–19, and Schiller, *Economics of Poverty and Discrimination*, 61.

7. *Freedom Budget for All Americans*, 29, for quotations. See also Howard M. Wachtel, "Looking at Poverty from a Radical Perspective," *Review of Radical Political Economics* 3 (Summer 1971), reprinted in David M. Gordon, ed., *Problems in Political Economy: An Urban Perspective*, 2nd ed. (Lexington, Mass.: D. C. Heath and Co., 1977), 307–12.

8. Howard M. Wachtel and Charles Betsey, "The Determinants of 'Working Poverty,'" in Harold L. Sheppard, Bennett Harrison, and William J. Spring, eds., *The Political Economy of Public Service Employment* (Lexington, Mass.: D. C. Heath and Co., 1972), 77–83. Schiller, *Economics of Poverty and Discrimination*, 64–65, demolishes claims made in the late 60s that there were lots of job vacancies.

9. On wages outpacing inflation, see Frank Stricker, "The Wages of Inflation: Workers' Earnings in the World War I Era," *Mid-America* 63 (April–July 1981): 93–105, and

Jared Bernstein and Dean Baker, *The Benefits of Full Employment: When Markets Work for People* (Washington: Economic Policy Institute, 2003), 41–63.

10. Businesses don't like the loss of revenues in recessions, but they don't like wage increases, either. Usually the Federal Reserve does what it conceives in its conservative way is best for the long-range health of businesses, even if most companies don't like the temporary slide in economic activity.

11. Research on the underclass is slippery. Erol R. Ricketts and Isabel V. Sawhill, "Defining and Measuring the Underclass," *Journal of Policy Analysis and Management* 7 (Winter 1988): 316–25, estimated that 2.5 million lived in underclass areas with high concentrations of female-headed and welfare families, high school dropouts, and chronically jobless males, but they said nothing about people's attitudes, the key to underclass theory. If one's husband dies or flees, one does not necessarily become mired in bad attitudes that make one dysfunctional.

12. In the 1960s, the draft and rising college enrollments cut unemployment by 0.5 of a percentage point. A decision to define people in manpower training programs as employed cut the rate by 0.4 of a point. A more rigid requirement for job searches lowered unemployment by about 0.2 of a point. Charles C. Killingsworth, "Changes in the Definition of Aggregate Unemployment," in Sheppard, Harrison, and Spring, *Political Economy of Public Service Employment*, 169–74, and Killingsworth, "The Continuing Labor Market Twist," *Monthly Labor Review* 91 (September 1968): 12–17.

13. The underground economy was probably less than 10% of the total economy in 2000. Some commentators assume that omitting the underground economy omits only employed workers—thus giving too dark a picture—but it omits also the unemployed and subemployed; Stanley L. Friedlander, *Unemployment in the Urban Core: An Analysis of Thirty Cities with Policy Recommendations* (New York: Praeger, 1972), 113–14, 186–89, thought that people engaged in illegal activities might tell surveyors they were employed to avoid suspicion about the source of their income. See also Friedrich Schneider, "The Size of Shadow Economies in 145 Countries from 1999 to 2003," and R. T. Naylor, "The Rise and Fall of the Underground Economy," both in *Brown Journal of World Affairs* 11 (Winter/Spring 2005), 113–43.

14. On government methods, William K. Stevens, "Those Statistics on the Nation's Unemployed Do Not Come Easily," *New York Times*, November 24, 1974, reprinted in David Mermelstein, ed., *The Economic Crisis Reader* (New York: Vintage Books, 1975), 28–31, and U.S. Department of Labor, Bureau of Labor Statistics, *How the Government Measures Unemployment*, Report 418 (Washington: Government Printing Office, 1973). Also, Thomas F. Dernberg, "The Behavior of Unemployment: 1967–1969," in Sheppard, Harrison, and Spring, *Political Economy of Public Service Employment*, 175–86. The jobless recovery of the early 2000s stimulated reporters and economists to remark on how unemployment was higher than official monthly rates. See David Streitfeld, "Jobless Count Skips Millions," *Los Angeles Times*, December 29, 2003, A1, A16–A17. Also, the Bureau of Labor Statistics and the press began to highlight data from 400,000 businesses. This "payroll" estimate led to conclusions that were often wildly different from those of the household survey that generated unemployment statistics.

15. *HLS, 1980*, table 4, 14–15; *HS*, series 124, 15; *HLS, 1972*, table 4, 34–35, 129. The unemployment rates of 20- to 24-year-old women fell for a while in the 60s boom, despite potential overcrowding. The white rate fell from 7.2% in 1960 to 5.3% in 1966 but then rose to 8.5% in 1971. The black rate fell from 15.3% in 1960 to 12% in 1969 and then shot up to 17.3% in 1971. See *HLS, 1972*, table 64, 136–39. For women ages 25–34, unemployment rates fell in the 60s, but the rate for black women in the same group was 8.4% in 1968, a recession level and twice the black male rate and five times the white male rate (1.7%). Data from *HLS, 1972*, table 64, 136–39.

16. A Marxist statement, by a professor of biology, that accelerating automation was returning capitalism to a normal state of high unemployment after a period of prosperity was Hyman Lumer, *Poverty: Its Roots and Its Future* (New York: International Publishers, 1965), 29–35, 72–74.

17. "The Economy: Bill Martin's Red Flag," *Time*, June 11, 1965, 83.

18. See also William Spring, Bennett Harrison, and Thomas Vietorisz, "In Much of the Inner City 60% Don't Earn Enough for a Decent Standard of Living," *New York Times Magazine*, November 5, 1972, 42–60, and Editors, "Capitalism and Unemployment," *Monthly Review* 27 (June 1975): 1–14.

19. Jacobs, *Handbook*, 113.

20. Friedlander, *Unemployment in the Urban Core*, 30.

21. See Jacobs, *Handbook*, 92, and Philip Harvey, *Securing the Right to Employment: Social Welfare Policy and the Unemployed in the United States* (Princeton, N.J.: Princeton University Press, 1989), 12–16. The official unemployment rate has fallen below 2% six times since 1890 (*HS*, 135).

22. The Freedom Budget was the brainchild of A. Philip Randolph, head of the Sleeping Car Porters Union and a veteran civil rights activist, and Bayard Rustin. Much of the text and graphics came from economist Leon Keyserling. See Helene Slessarev, *The Betrayal of the Urban Poor* (Philadelphia: Temple University Press, 1997), 48–51.

23. *Report of the National Advisory Commission on Civil Disorders* (New York: Bantam Books, 1968), 413–24.

24. Bayard Rustin, "From Protest to Politics: The Future of the Civil Rights Movement," *Commentary*, February 1965, reprinted in Irving Howe, ed., *The Radical Papers* (Garden City, N.Y.: Doubleday, 1966), 347–61.

25. Margaret Weir, *Politics and Jobs: The Boundaries of Employment Policy in the United States* (1992; Princeton, N.J.: Princeton University Press, 1993), 120–21; chapters 4 and 6 in the present volume; and Spring, Harrison, and Vietorisz, "In Much of the Inner City," 42.

26. Hyman Minsky, "The Role of Employment Policy," in Margaret S. Gordon, ed., *Poverty in America* (Berkeley: University of California, 1965), 175–200.

27. Ibid., 190, 195–96, 200. Minsky also urged government wage subsidies to avoid wage-push inflation. See also Dawn Day Wachtel, *The Working Poor* (Washington: Clearinghouse for Federal Scientific and Technical Information, 1965), 73–75.

28. Slessarev, *Betrayal of the Urban Poor*. Bennett Harrison, *Education, Training, and the Urban Ghetto* (Baltimore: Johns Hopkins University Press, 1972), 119–21, found that

ending occupational racism would cut low-schooled white incomes 6% to 9%. On employer discrimination in the secondary labor market, David M. Gordon, *Theories of Poverty and Underemployment* (Lexington, Mass.: D. C. Heath and Co., 1972), 46–47, and Daniel R. Fusfeld and Timothy Bates, *The Political Economy of the Urban Ghetto* (Carbondale: Southern Illinois University Press, 1984), 171–90.

29. Without other discriminations, schools would be more important in channeling people while giving the sorting process a meritocratic justification. See Bowles and Gintis, *Schooling in Capitalist America,* and Leonard Goodwin, *Do the Poor Want to Work?: A Social-Psychological Study of Work Orientations* (Washington: Brookings Institution, 1972), 173 n. 11.

30. Harry Braverman, *Labor and Monopoly Capital: The Degradation of Work in the Twentieth Century* (New York: Monthly Review Press, 1974), 377–80. If only families were considered, Braverman's working class would have included incomes of zero to $7,999 in 1963 (*HLS, 1972*, 394). The latter was about $50,000 in 2005 dollars.

Chapter Six

1. Charles Noble, *Welfare As We Knew It: A Political History of the American Welfare State* (New York: Oxford University Press, 1997), 113–19, and Thomas Ferguson and Joel Rogers, *Right Turn: The Decline of the Democrats and the Future of American Politics* (New York: Hill and Wang, 1986), 78–114.

2. Frances Fox Piven and Richard A. Cloward, *Regulating the Poor: The Functions of Public Welfare* (1971; New York: Vintage Books, 1972), 123–247 and appendix, table 1, and Piven and Cloward, *Poor People's Movements: Why They Succeed, How They Fail* (1977; New York: Vintage Books, 1979), 203, 211.

3. Edward D. Berkowitz, *America's Welfare State: From Roosevelt to Reagan* (Baltimore: Johns Hopkins University Press, 1991), 100–105.

4. Piven and Cloward, *Poor People's Movements*, 264–359, and Richard A. Cloward and Frances Fox Piven, "A Strategy to End Poverty," *The Nation*, May 2, 1966, reprinted in Cloward and Piven, *The Politics of Turmoil: Essays on Poverty, Race, and the Urban Crisis* (New York: Pantheon Books, 1974), 89–106. Also, Nick Kotz and Mary Lynn Kotz, *A Passion for Equality: George Wiley and the Movement* (New York: W. W. Norton and Co., 1979), 181–217. Wylie wanted his to be an interracial organization (Kotz and Kotz, *Passion for Equality*, 208–9, 222).

5. Piven and Cloward, *Regulating the Poor*, appendix, table 1.

6. Kotz and Kotz, *Passion for Equality*, 233; Martha F. Davis, *Brutal Need: Lawyers and the Welfare Rights Movement, 1960–1973* (New Haven, Conn.: Yale University Press, 1993), 55; Cloward and Piven, "Strategy to End Poverty." On the white working class, see Cloward and Piven, "Workers and Welfare: The Poor against Themselves," *The Nation*, November 25, 1968, reprinted in Cloward and Piven, *Politics of Turmoil*, 141–50.

7. Davis, *Brutal Need*, 40–55; Piven and Cloward, *Regulating the Poor*, 329; chapter 3 in the present volume.

8. M. Kenneth Bowler, *The Nixon Guaranteed Income Proposal: Substance and Process in*

Policy Change (Cambridge, Mass.: Ballinger Publishing Co., 1974), has a slightly different list on 24.

9. U.S. Department of Commerce, Bureau of the Census, Statistical Abstract of the United States, 1972 (Washington: Government Printing Office, 1972), 302; Cloward and Piven, Politics of Turmoil, 128; and President's Commission on Income Maintenance Programs, Poverty amid Plenty: The American Paradox (Washington: Government Printing Office, 1969), 114–26.

10. Daniel P. Moynihan, The Politics of a Guaranteed Income: The Nixon Administration and the Family Assistance Plan (New York: Vintage Books, 1973), 81, 44. Shultz's testimony of October 16, 1969, quoted in Barry Bluestone, William M. Murphy, and Mary Stevenson, Low Wages and the Working Poor (Ann Arbor: Institute of Labor and Industrial Relations, University of Michigan and Wayne State University, 1973), 14. Shultz worried that there was not enough incentive to work under the first FAP proposals. See Moynihan, Politics of a Guaranteed Income, 186–88, 202, and A. James Reichley, Conservatives in an Age of Change: The Nixon and Ford Administrations (Washington: Brookings Institution, 1981), 140–41.

11. Quoted in Jill Quadagno, The Color of Welfare: How Racism Undermined the War on Poverty (1994; New York: Oxford University Press, 1996), 130.

12. The federal minimum wage was $1.60, or about $3,300 a year. See SA, 1981, 408.

13. Moynihan, Politics of a Guaranteed Income, 114–16.

14. For background, Thomas Byrne Edsall and Mary D. Edsall, Chain Reaction: The Impact of Race, Rights, and Taxes on American Politics (New York: W. W. Norton and Co., 1991); Ferguson and Rogers, Right Turn; and John B. Judis, The Paradox of American Democracy: Elites, Special Interests, and the Betrayal of Public Trust (New York: Pantheon Books, 2000).

15. Moynihan, Politics of a Guaranteed Income, 67, 181–83nn, 217–35nn. On August 7, according to Moynihan, Nixon said he did not "care a damn" about the work requirement; it was there to sell the guaranteed income; see ibid., 218, 220. Robert Nathan, quoted in Peter Steinfels, The Neoconservatives: The Men Who Are Changing America's Politics (New York: Touchstone Books, 1980), 256, claimed that Nixon took the work requirement seriously.

16. Reichley, Conservatives in an Age of Change, 130–34; Vincent J. Burke and Vee Burke, Nixon's Good Deed: Welfare Reform (New York: Columbia University Press, 1974), 41–44. Nixon's welfare task force suggested increased federal contributions and a uniform national floor of $40 per person per month ($1,920 a year for a family of four). It also suggested that welfare and assistance to the blind, aged, and disabled be federalized; see Burke and Burke, Nixon's Good Deed, 65–77. Reichley, Conservatives in an Age of Change, 142–143, lists nine reasons why the administration took up FAP and none include electoral considerations. Other treatments include Moynihan, Politics of a Guaranteed Income, 17–235; Burke and Burke, Nixon's Good Deed, 1–125, 142; Bowler, Nixon Guaranteed Income Proposal, 58–69; Reichley, Conservatives in an Age of Change, 130–61; and Alice O'Connor, "The False Dawn of Poor Law Reform: Nixon, Carter, and the Quest for a Guaranteed Income," Journal of Policy History 10 (Winter 1998): 99–129.

17. For quotation, Burke and Burke, *Nixon's Good Deed*, 59. See too Godfrey Hodgson, *The Gentleman from New York: Daniel Patrick Moynihan* (Boston: Houghton Mifflin, 2000); and Michael A. Genovese, *The Nixon Presidency: Power and Politics in Turbulent Times* (New York: Greenwood Press, 1990), 80. On electoral calculations, Quadagno, *Color of Welfare*, 122–23, 133–34; Gareth Davies, *From Opportunity to Entitlement: The Transformation and Decline of Great Society Liberalism* (Lawrence: University Press of Kansas, 1996), 216–19. Jefferson Cowie, "Nixon's Class Struggle: Romancing the New Right Worker, 1969–1973," *Labor History* 43 (August 2002): 257–83, suggests that election strategy was still in formation in 1969–70 and does not mention FAP.

18. Quotation from Nixon's August 8, 1969, speech, in Moynihan, *Politics of a Guaranteed Income*, 220. Prior to the introduction of FAP, a Gallup poll claimed that the public opposed guaranteed incomes two to one; Reichley, *Conservatives in an Age of Change*, 135, 171–72.

19. Burke and Burke, *Nixon's Good Deed*, 65.

20. Moynihan, *Politics of a Guaranteed Income*, 56; Burke and Burke, *Nixon's Good Deed*, 62; Bowler, *Nixon Guaranteed Income Proposal*, 61–62; Quadagno, *Color of Welfare*, 121.

21. Burke and Burke, *Nixon's Good Deed*, 78–79. Milton Friedman, *Capitalism and Freedom* (Chicago: University of Chicago Press, 1962), 190–95; Reichley, *Conservatives in an Age of Change*, 135. See also Bowler, *Nixon Guaranteed Income Proposal*, 66, and Robert Theobald, *Free Men and Free Markets* (New York: Doubleday, 1965).

22. Bowler, *Nixon Guaranteed Income Proposal*, 25. On food stamps, Nick Kotz, *Let Them Eat Promises: The Politics of Hunger in America* (New York: Doubleday, 1971), 247, 251. How did planners arrive at the $1,600 FAP figure? They estimated that anything over $1,700 would be too expensive and anything below $1,500 would not offer much relief to beleaguered state and local welfare funds. See Bowler, *Nixon Guaranteed Income Proposal*, 46, 55–56.

23. Bowler, *Nixon Guaranteed Income Proposal*, 35.

24. Ibid. Gus Tyler claimed that an employed father could still increase family income by deserting and having his family go on FAP. But one could have argued that FAP gave people economic reasons to stay together, since it offered income supplements to whole families. See Gus Tyler, "The Politics of Pat Moynihan," *New Leader*, April 2, 1973, reprinted in Lewis A. Coser and Irving Howe, eds., *The New Conservatives: A Critique from the Left* (New York: Quadrangle/New York Times, 1977), 181–92.

25. The Family Assistance Plan is one issue that does not support Bruce J. Schulman's view that Nixon always sought to turn social programs back to the states. See Bruce J. Schulman, *The Seventies: The Great Shift in American Culture, Society, and Politics* (New York: Free Press, 2001), 23–52.

26. Quadagno, *Color of Welfare*, 128–30; Bowler, *Nixon Guaranteed Income Proposal*, 36–37. Another positive aspect was that national standards would lessen whatever magnet effect there was to high-benefit northern and western states.

27. Bowler, *Nixon Guaranteed Income Proposal*, 29–30.

28. Ibid., 29–31.

29. Ibid., 48.

30. Tyler, "Politics of Pat Moynihan," 186. Nixon and Finch claimed that because FAP had work requirements it was not a guaranteed income, but FAP guaranteed something even to families with a willful nonworker.

31. Burke and Burke, *Nixon's Good Deed*, 125, 130, and 131 for the quotation; Quadagno, *Color of Welfare*, 131–33; and Moynihan, *Politics of a Guaranteed Income*, 250–70.

32. Burke and Burke, *Nixon's Good Deed*, 139–45; Reichley, *Conservatives in an Age of Change*, 144; Quadagno, *Color of Welfare*, 132; Moynihan, *Politics of a Guaranteed Income*, 270–77. After the House passed FAP, Nixon agreed to include the creation of 200,000 jobs, paying at least 75% of the minimum wage. That should have won AFL-CIO support in the Senate, but the details of this are fuzzy in Burke and Burke, *Nixon's Good Deed*, and Moynihan, *Politics of a Guaranteed Income*. See also Vincent Burke, "Nixon's Family Assistance Plan Killed by Senate Finance Panel," *Los Angeles Times*, November 21, 1970, 1, 12. The public employee union, the American Federation of State, County, and Municipal Employees (AFSCME), opposed FAP because it threatened the jobs of its social worker members.

33. As quoted in Irwin Unger, *The Best of Intentions: The Triumph and Failure of the Great Society under Kennedy, Johnson, and Nixon* (New York: Doubleday, 1996), 319. To most commentators $5,500 seemed large; it was equivalent in purchasing power to about $29,000 in 2006.

34. Reichley, *Conservatives in an Age of Change*, 90, 145; Unger, *Best of Intentions*, 322; Burke, "Nixon's Family Assistance Plan Killed," 172.

35. Burke, "Nixon's Family Assistance Plan Killed," 154–157.

36. Health, Education, and Welfare Secretary Elliot Richardson cut FAP payment schedules to fix the problems that Senator Williams had brought to light, but at one point he agreed to grandfather in the changes to protect current recipients. Still the National Welfare Rights Organization (NWRO) was alarmed. Exactly who would have lost in the Richardson reforms was not certain, but 90,000 unemployed or partially employed parents were one target. Family Assistance Plan revisions also raised the penalty from $300 to $500 if the head of household refused work or training. On the plus side FAP added federally subsidized health insurance for the working poor, so that people would not stay out of work to preserve Medicaid benefits. See David A. Rochefort, "Responding to the New Dependency: The Family Assistance Plan of 1969," in Donald T. Critchlow and Ellis W. Hawley, eds., *Poverty and Public Policy in Modern America* (Chicago: Dorsey Press, 1989), 291–303, esp. 297–98; Quadagno, *Color of Welfare*, 127, 222 n. 54; Reichley, *Conservatives in an Age of Change*, 448; Burke and Burke, *Nixon's Good Deed*, 157 and 160n; Moynihan, *Politics of a Guaranteed Income*, 507–9; Kotz and Kotz, *Passion for Equality*, 269–71.

37. Unger, *Best of Intentions*, 324–25; Moynihan, *Politics of a Guaranteed Income*, 532. In a press release on November 10, 1970, Wiley asked only for $2,464, conceded the elimination of food stamps, but demanded guarantees for current recipients and a plan to get to higher minimums in the future. See Kotz and Kotz, *Passion for Equality*, 269–

72, 275. Attacks on liberals for defeating FAP are Joan Hoff, *Nixon Reconsidered* (New York: Basic Books, 1994), 122–37, and David Whitman, "Liberal Rhetoric and the Welfare Underclass," *Society* 21 (November–December 1983): 63–69.

38. Reichley, *Conservatives in an Age of Change*, 148; Unger, *Best of Intentions*, 325 for quotation. And see two reports by Warren Weaver Jr. in the *New York Times*, "President Losing Welfare Support," November 20, 1970, 1, 30, and "Welfare Reform Is Again Rejected by Senate Panel," November 21, 1970, 1, 18.

39. On the NWRO's lack of impact, Piven and Cloward, *Poor People's Movements*, 346, and Tim Sampson, conversation with author, Portland, Oregon, May 4, 2001. See also the editorial "Welfare Reform in Jeopardy," *New York Times*, November 21, 1970, 30, and Weaver, "Welfare Reform Is Again Rejected by Senate Panel." The AFL-CIO did not push liberals to support FAP at this stage, but later it supported Ribicoff's compromise (Burke and Burke, *Nixon's Good Deed*, 180n).

40. Bowler believes that FAP was "radical departure" (*Nixon Guaranteed Income Proposal*, 29–30). One Nixon official claimed that had Wiley supported FAP, more in Congress would have rejected it. See Kotz and Kotz, *Passion for Equality*, 233, 251, 276, 285–87; Davis, *Brutal Need*, 53. Piven and Cloward, *Poor People's Movements*, 333, 347; Quadagno, *Color of Welfare*, 121; Davis, *Brutal Need*, 139.

41. Reichley, *Conservatives in an Age of Change*, 150–51, shows that Republican "progressives" voted for the Ribicoff plan 7 to 0 and Democratic liberals 14 to 1. Kotz and Kotz, *Passion for Equality*, 271–77, 289, claim that 50,000 came to the Children's March. Police estimated 30,000. See "30,000, Many of Them Children, Protest Nixon Welfare Policies," *New York Times*, March 26, 1972, 20. Slavery quotation in Burke and Burke, *Nixon's Good Deed*, 183.

42. On SSI, James T. Patterson, *America's Struggle against Poverty in the Twentieth Century* (Cambridge, Mass.: Harvard University Press, 2000), 190–92; Bowler, *Nixon Guaranteed Income Proposal*, 147; and Burke and Burke, *Nixon's Good Deed*, 192–202.

43. Patterson, *America's Struggle against Poverty in the Twentieth Century*, 160; Martha Derthick, *Policymaking for Social Security* (Washington: Brookings Institution, 1979), 345–68; Sheldon H. Danziger and Daniel H. Weinberg, "The Historical Record: Trends in Family Income, Inequality, and Poverty," in Sheldon H. Danziger, Gary D. Sandefur, and Weinberg, eds., *Confronting Poverty: Prescriptions for Change* (New York: Russell Sage Foundation; Cambridge, Mass: Harvard University Press, 1994), 46–47; Quadagno, *Color of Welfare*, 155–73; and Twentieth Century Fund, *Social Security Reform: The Basics* (New York: Century Foundation Press, 1998).

44. Iric Nathanson, "How the Poor Got a Lucky Break," *The Nation*, January 31, 1976, 106–8; John McDermott, "And the Poor Get Poorer," *The Nation*, November 14, 1994, 576–80, for quoted phrases; Jonathan Peterson, "GOP Seeking to Curb Tax Break for the Poor," *Los Angeles Times*, May 13, 1995, A1, A22. Bradley R. Schiller, *The Economics of Poverty and Discrimination*, 9th ed. (Upper Saddle River, N.J.: Prentice-Hall, 2004), 210.

45. Stamps had restrictions. In 1970 Congress passed a work requirement for able-bodied adults who had no child-care duties and were not working thirty hours a week.

People who had significant assets besides a car and house lost eligibility. Also, the program was still run by local welfare departments, some of which liked to make life hard for the poor. See Patterson, *America's Struggle against Poverty in the Twentieth Century*, 160–63; Burke and Burke, *Nixon's Good Deed*, 116–22, 213; Kotz, *Let Them Eat Promises*; and Maurice MacDonald, "Food Stamps: An Analytical History," *Social Service Review* 51(December 1977): 642–58.

46. Section on CETA and Humphrey-Hawkins based on William Mirengoff, Lester Rindler, Harry Greenspan, and Charles Harris, *CETA: Accomplishments, Problems, Solutions* (Kalamazoo, Mich.: W. E. Upjohn Institute for Employment Research, 1982); Bonnie B. Snedeker and David M. Snedeker, *CETA: Decentralization on Trial* (Salt Lake City, Utah: Olympus Publishing Co., 1978); Grace A. Franklin and Randall B. Ripley, *CETA: Politics and Policy, 1973–1982* (Knoxville: University of Tennessee Press,1984); Laurie Bassi and Orley Ashenfelter, "The Effect of Direct Job Creation and Training Programs on Low-Skilled Workers," and Nathan Glazer, "Education and Training Programs and Poverty," and Christopher Jencks's reply (133–179), all in Sheldon H. Danziger and Daniel H. Weinberg, eds., *Fighting Poverty: What Works and What Doesn't* (Cambridge, Mass.: Harvard University Press, 1986); Carol Brightman, "The CETA Factor," *Working Papers*, May–June 1978, 34–42; Rebecca M. Blank, "The Employment Strategy: Public Policies to Increase Work and Earnings," and Hugh Heclo, "Poverty Politics," both in Danziger, Sandefur, and Weinberg, *Confronting Poverty*, 168–204, esp. 188, and 406–37; Margaret Weir, *Politics and Jobs: The Boundaries of Employment Policy in the United States* (1992; Princeton, N.J.: Princeton University Press, 1993), 130–40; David Vogel, *Fluctuating Fortunes: The Political Power of Business in America* (New York: Basic Books, 1989),137–56; Jerry Flint, "Jobless Rate of Blacks Still Rising despite a 25-Year Federal Effort," *New York Times*, March 13, 1979, A1, B6. *HT*, 267, shows that federal employment slipped by more than a million, most of that military. Most growth in government jobs was at the state and local level; Eli Ginzberg, "The Job Problem," *Scientific American*, November 1977, 43–51; Michael K. Brown and Steven P. Erie, "Blacks and the Legacy of the Great Society: The Economic and Political Impact of Federal Policy," *Public Policy* 29 (Summer 1981): 299–330. "What Humphrey-Hawkins Would Mean," *Business Week*, May 31, 1976, 66–67, cites prominent liberal economists against Humphrey-Hawkins.

47. Peter Goldman and Gerald C. Lubenow, "Mr. Small-Is-Beautiful," *Newsweek*, December 15, 1975, 47–50; Randall Rothenberg, *The Neoliberals: Creating the New American Politics* (New York: Simon and Schuster, 1984).

48. Bruce S. Jansson, *The Reluctant Welfare State: A History of American Social Welfare Policies* (Pacific Grove, Calif.: Brooks/Cole Publishing Co., 1993), 262–64; Gary Burtless, "Public Spending on the Poor: Historical Trends and Economic Limits," in Danziger, Sandefur, and Weinberg, *Confronting Poverty*, 22–40.

49. Noncash programs like Medicaid and food stamps helped poor people but did not cut poverty rates because they were not counted as income.

50. Carter aide Landon Butler quoted in James T. Patterson, "Jimmy Carter and Welfare Reform," in Gary M. Fink and Hugh Davis Graham, eds., *The Carter Presidency:*

Policy Choices in the Post–New Deal Era (Lawrence: University Press of Kansas, 1998), 117–35, esp. 134 n. 24. Also, Ferguson and Rogers, *Right Turn*, and Robert Bussel, " 'A Trade Union Oriented War on the Slums': Harold Gibbons, Ernest Calloway, and the St. Louis Teamsters in the 1960s," *Labor History* 44 (February 2003): 49–67.

51. Carter increased the number of CETA jobs and the number on food stamps, but he made it more difficult for the disabled to get SSI. In 1977 Congress also passed the Community Reinvestment Act to compel lending institutions to serve low- and moderate-income neighborhoods. See Helene Slessarev, *The Betrayal of the Urban Poor* (Philadelphia: Temple University Press, 1997), 169–73.

52. Lawrence E. Lynn Jr. and David deF. Whitman, *The President as Policymaker: Jimmy Carter and Welfare Reform* (Philadelphia: Temple University Press, 1981), 91; Jansson, *Reluctant Welfare State*, 261; Patterson, "Jimmy Carter and Welfare Reform."

53. Patterson, "Jimmy Carter and Welfare Reform," 125, 127 for quotations; Gordon L. Weil, *The Welfare Debate of 1978* (White Plains, N.Y.: Institute for Socioeconomic Studies, 1978), 20, 27, 73–74.

54. Patterson, "Jimmy Carter and Welfare Reform," 126–27. The plan also expanded the Earned Income Tax Credit.

55. Whitman, "Liberal Rhetoric and the Welfare Underclass," is a scathing attack on the Left.

56. O'Connor, "False Dawn of Poor Law Reform," 120–25; Patterson, "Jimmy Carter and Welfare Reform," 128–32; and Lynn and Whitman, *President as Policymaker*, esp. the chronology, 286–88. The farthest Program for Better Jobs and Income got was passage by a House subcommittee. Later a no-frills bill that would have raised welfare payments passed the full House but was never voted on in the Senate.

57. There was support for the welfare state, for aid to the needy, and for an attack on the oil companies; see Ferguson and Rogers, *Right Turn*, 12–20. But by the late 70s, liberal Democrats and unionists were not doing well pushing their agenda, and the Right had seized the media's attention. See Walter Dean Burnham, *The Current Crisis in American Politics* (New York: Oxford University Press, 1982), esp. 234–39.

58. Walter I. Trattner, *From Poor Law to Welfare State: A History of Social Welfare in America*, 5th ed. (New York: Free Press, 1994), 355.

59. Carter quoted in Bruce J. Schulman, "Slouching toward the Supply Side: Jimmy Carter and the New American Political Economy," in Fink and Graham, *Carter Presidency*, 66. Schulman notes that governments in Western Europe faced similar problems but did better at protecting the poor (64). Lester Thurow, "Carter's Economics: A Perilous Performance," *Los Angeles Times*, July 27, 1980, V, 1, 6. Thomas J. Sugrue, "Carter's Urban Policy Crisis," in Fink and Graham, *Carter Presidency*, 137–57, on Carter's almost nonexistent urban policy. On Carternomics, Judith Stein, *Running Steel, Running America: Race, Economic Policy, and the Decline of Liberalism* (Chapel Hill: University of North Carolina Press, 1998), esp. 229–65, 271, 318. Anthony S. Campagna, *Economic Policy in the Carter Administration* (Westport, Conn.: Greenwood Press, 1995), 98, concludes that "a cautious administration was unwilling to meet the challenges of inflation head-on, but offered only a poor substitute." See also Burton I.

Kaufmann, *The Presidency of James Earl Carter, Jr.* (Lawrence: University Press of Kansas, 1993).

Chapter Seven

1. William Julius Wilson, *The Truly Disadvantaged: The Inner City, the Underclass, and Public Policy* (1987; Chicago: University of Chicago, 1990), and Wilson, *When Work Disappears: The World of the New Urban Poor* (New York: Alfred A. Knopf, 1996).

2. Inflation might be moderated during fast growth and low unemployment through government-union-business agreements to restrain pay increases. Sweden tried this approach, but even then public employment was necessary to push jobless rates down to 2%. Robert Kuttner, *Everything for Sale: The Virtues and Limits of Markets* (New York: Alfred A. Knopf, 1998), 94.

3. Edward Banfield, *The Unheavenly City: The Nature and Future of Our Urban Crisis* (Boston: Little, Brown, 1970); Susan Sheehan, *A Welfare Mother* (New York: Mentor, 1977); "The American Underclass," *Time*, August 29, 1977, 14–18, 21–22; Herbert J. Gans, *The War against the Poor: The Underclass and Antipoverty Policy* (New York: Basic Books, 1995); Martin Anderson, *Welfare: The Political Economy of Welfare Reform in the United States* (Palo Alto, Calif.: Stanford University/Hoover Institution, 1978), 56; Walter Korpi, "Approaches to the Study of Poverty in the United States: Critical Notes from a European Perspective," in Vincent T. Covello, ed., *Poverty and Public Policy: An Evaluation of Social Science Research* (Boston: Published for the Committee on Evaluation of Poverty Research, Assembly of Behavioral and Social Sciences, National Research Council, National Academy of Sciences, by G. K. Hall and Co.; Cambridge, Mass.: Schenkman Publishing Co., 1980), 287–314. Vincent Fanelli, *The Human Face of Poverty: A Chronicle of Urban America* (New York: Bootstrap Press, 1990), xiii, 24, 29, 79, 45–48, 89, 121–25, links unstable employment and attitudes among Puerto Rican families in the 1970s and views welfare as a tool, not an addiction. "The welfare check is safer than the father's job," said one parent.

4. Support for the three bulleted items is in Gary Burtless, "Public Spending on the Poor: Historical Trends and Economic Limits," in Sheldon H. Danziger, Gary D. Sandefur, and Daniel H. Weinberg, eds., *Confronting Poverty: Prescriptions for Change* (New York: Russell Sage Foundation; Cambridge, Mass.: Harvard University Press, 1994), 51–84, esp. 51– 56; Christopher Jencks, "Is the American Underclass Growing," in Christopher Jencks and Paul E. Peterson, eds., *The Urban Underclass* (Washington: Brookings Institution, 1991), 28–100, esp. 82–83, 90; Kristin Luker, "Dubious Conceptions: The Controversy over Teen Pregnancy," *American Prospect*, Spring 1991, 73–83; Lawrence Mishel and Jared Bernstein, *The State of Working America, 1992–1993* (Armonk, N.Y.: Economic Policy Institute and M. E. Sharpe, 1993), 296.

5. Mary Jo Bane, "Household Composition and Poverty," in Sheldon H. Danziger and Daniel H. Weinberg, eds., *Fighting Poverty: What Works and What Doesn't* (Cambridge, Mass.: Harvard University Press, 1986), 211.

6. Bane, "Household Composition and Poverty."

7. Ruth Sidel, *Urban Survival: The World of Working-Class Women* (Boston: Beacon Press, 1978), 20.

8. Government study cited in Barbara Leyser, Adele M. Blong, and Judith A. Riggs, *Beyond the Myths: The Families Helped by the AFDC Program*, 2nd ed. (New York: Center on Social Welfare Policy and Law, 1985), 2. Anderson, *Welfare*; *SA, 1981*, 5, 343. Studs Terkel, *Working: People Talk about What They Do All Day and How They Feel about What They Do* (New York: Pantheon Books, 1974), 303–6; Diana Pearce, "The Feminization of Poverty: Women, Work and Welfare," *Urban and Social Change Review* 7 (February 1978): 28–36; Barbara Ehrenreich and Karen Stallard, "The Nouveau Poor," *Ms.* magazine, July–Aug. 1982, 217–24.

9. Lillian Breslow Rubin, *Worlds of Pain: Life in the Working-Class Family* (New York: Basic Books, 1976), 73. Ehrenreich and Stallard, "Nouveau Poor;" Greg J. Duncan et al., *Years of Poverty, Years of Plenty: The Changing Economic Fortunes of American Workers and Families* (Ann Arbor: Institute for Social Research, University of Michigan, 1984), 41, 75.

10. Mary Corcoran, Greg J. Duncan, Gerald Gurin, and Patricia Gurin, "Myth and Reality: The Causes and Persistence of Poverty," *Journal of Policy Analysis and Management* 4 (1985): 516–36; the 1965 *Economic Report of the President* (Washington: Government Printing Office, 1965), 164.

11. Barry Bluestone and Bennett Harrison, *The Deindustrialization of America* (New York: Basic Books, 1982), 5–6.

12. Ibid., 8–19.

13. "American Underclass," 18.

14. *HLS, 1983*, 8, 12, and *HLS, 1980*, 6; *SA, 1981*, 379; the 1999 *Economic Report of the President* (Washington: Government Printing Office, 1999), 282; Louise B. Russell, *The Baby Boom Generation and the Economy* (Washington: Brookings Institution, 1982), 50–90.

15. *HLS, 1980*, 13–14.

16. Paul Peterson, "The Urban Underclass and the Poverty Paradox," in Jencks and Peterson, *Urban Underclass*, 7. U.S. Department of Commerce, Bureau of the Census, Current Population Reports, series P-60, no. 127, *Money Income and Poverty Status of Families and Persons in the United States, 1980* (Washington: Government Printing Office, 1981), contained no category for Asian backgrounds. Varying uses of the terms "Hispanic" and "Spanish Origins" make it tough to determine whether poverty among Latinos was increasing in the 1970s; also, immigrants must have been underrepresented in the house-to-house sample on which poverty estimates were based. I used *SA, 1981*, 445–46, to estimate by how much 2 million poor immigrants increased poverty rates.

17. Greg DeFreitas, "Fear of Foreigners: Immigrants as Scapegoats for Domestic Woes," *Dollars & Sense*, January–February 1994, 8–9, 33–35; DeFreitas did find that older immigrants suffered from the job competition of new immigrants. See also Julie Quiroz, *Hispanic Poverty: How Much Does Immigration Explain* (Washington: National Council of La Raza, 1989), esp. 26; Michael Fix and Jeffrey S. Passel, *Immigration and Immigrants: Setting the Record Straight* (Washington: Urban Institute, 1994), 47–54, 77–

81; Frank Levy, *The New Dollars and Dreams: American Incomes and Economic Change* (New York: Russell Sage Foundation, 1998), 135; Vernon M. Briggs Jr., "Immigration and Poverty Reduction: Policy Making on a Squirrel Wheel," *Journal of Economic Literature* 37 (June 2003): 325–31.

18. Russell, *Baby Boom Generation and the Economy*, 50–90; *HLS, 1980*, 12–18.

19. *HLS, 1980*, 51; Emma Rothschild, "Reagan and the Real America," *New York Review of Books*, February 5, 1981, 12–18.

20. Chinhui Juhn, Kevin Murphy, and Robert H. Topel, "Why Has the Natural Rate of Unemployment Increased over Time," *Brookings Papers on Economic Activity* 2 (1991): 75–142, esp. 87, 98–101, 109–10, 124–25, 132, and *HLS, 1983*, 10–14.

21. This and preceding two paragraphs based on Edward D. Berkowitz, *Disabled Policy: America's Programs for the Handicapped* (Cambridge: Cambridge University Press, 1987), 79–154, esp. 111–13, 122–23; Michael B. Katz, *The Price of Citizenship: Redefining the American Welfare State* (New York: Metropolitan Books, 2001), 195–222, including 214 for the "purge" quotation from Martha Derthick; *SA, 1992*, 361; and *SA, 1981*, 329.

22. *HLS, 1980*, 14–15, 69–70.

23. Ibid., 67–70, 7–18.

24. Charles Murray, *Losing Ground: American Social Policy, 1950–1980* (New York: Basic Books, 1984), 69–82; Jencks, "Is the American Underclass Growing," 33, 66, 70–73; John Herbers, "Changes in Society Holding Black Youth in Jobless Web," *New York Times*, March 11, 1979, I, 1, 44, for the quotation.

25. Bradley R. Schiller, *The Economics of Poverty and Discrimination*, 6th ed. (Englewood Cliffs, N.J.: Prentice-Hall, 1995), 162.

26. Winston Williams, "Hopes Dim for Job Seekers Counting on Airline Plan," *New York Times*, March 13, 1979, B6, and Judith Cummings, "For Young People on a Street Corner in Harlem, Jobs Seem Few and Far Away," *New York Times*, March 12, 1979, B11; Mishel and Bernstein, *State of Working America, 1992–1993*, 166–71, 358–60; John Bound and Richard B. Freeman, "What Went Wrong?: The Erosion of Relative Earnings and Employment among Young Black Men in the 1980s," *Quarterly Journal of Economics* 107 (1992): 201–32, esp. 221–23.

27. Thomas Larson, "Black Youth Employment and Residential Location: A Study of Los Angeles County," unpublished article (1995). The unemployment rate for black male teens (16–19 years old) rose from 22% (1965–69) to 34% (1975–79). The rate for white male teens increased from 11% to 16%, according to the 1983 *Economic Report of the President* (Washington: Government Printing Office, 1983), 201.

28. Thomas A. Johnson, "Cost of Black Joblessness Measured in Crime, Fear, and Urban Decay," *New York Times*, March 12, 1977, A1, B10, for the quotation; Herbers, "Changes in Society," 44; Joleen Kirschenman and Kathryn M. Neckerman, " 'We'd Love to Hire Them, but . . .': The Meaning of Race for Employers," in Jencks and Peterson, *Urban Underclass*, 203–32.

29. "American Underclass," 18; Daniel R. Fusfeld and Timothy Bates, *The Political Economy of the Urban Ghetto* (Carbondale: Southern Illinois University Press, 1984),

124–33; Thomas J. Sugrue, "The Structures of Urban Poverty: The Reorganization of Space and Work in Three Periods of American History," in Michael B. Katz, ed., *The "Underclass" Debate: Views from History* (Princeton, N.J.: Princeton University Press, 1993), 85–117, esp. 103–4; Wilson, *When Work Disappears*, 34–35; *HLS, 1983*, 11, 39, 43; and Bound and Freeman, "What Went Wrong?" Levy, *New Dollars and Dreams*, 45, 73, 83–89, claims that the low dollar protected manufacturing jobs in the 70s, but blue-collar manufacturing jobs were slipping as a share of the total labor force (Jacobs, *Handbook*, 39, 109, 163–64), and the population of young adults looking for work was doubling.

30. "American Underclass," 18; Cummings, "For Young People on a Street Corner in Harlem"; Herbers, "Changes in Society"; *HLS, 1983*, 11, 15, 17, 19, 39. Black female teens did slightly better than their male counterparts. They raised their labor force participation rate from 32% to 37%, and their unemployment rate was not noticeably higher in 1979 than in 1972, although at around 40% it was very high. Of their additional 97,000 labor force participants in 1979, 63,000, or two-thirds, found work.

31. *HLS, 1980*, 73; Jacobs, *Handbook*, 113.

32. Jacobs, *Handbook*, 92. "The New Two-Tier Market for Consumer Goods," *Business Week*, April 11, 1977, 80, 82–83; the 1983 *Economic Report of the President*, 196; Mishel and Bernstein, *State of Working America, 1992–1993*, 230.

33. Sanford Rose, "We've Learned How to Lick Inflation," *Fortune*, September 1976, 100–105, 180, 182, 184; quotation, including italics, in the original. For the record, unemployment rates for black male teens rose from a range of 22–24% in the late 1960s to 31–37% in the late 70s; for black female teens, from 27–32% in the late 60s to 36–39% in the late 70s (the 1983 *Economic Report of the President*, 201).

34. Theda Skocpol, "Bringing the State Back In: Strategies of Analysis in Current Research," in Peter B. Evans, Dietrich Rueschmeyer, and Theda Skocpol, eds., *Bringing the State Back In* (Cambridge: Cambridge University Press, 1985), 3–37, esp. 11–12, 18.

35. Hugh Heclo, "The Political Foundations of Antipoverty Policy," in Danziger and Weinberg, *Fighting Poverty*, esp. 326, 328, 333, and Heclo, "Poverty Politics," in Danziger, Sandefur, and Weinberg, *Confronting Poverty*, esp. 402–3.

36. Meany quoted in Thomas Byrne Edsall, *The New Politics of Inequality* (New York: W. W. Norton and Co., 1985), 151. See, too, Foster Rhea Dulles and Melvyn Dubofsky, *Labor in America: A History*, 5th ed. (Arlington Heights, Ill.: Harlan Davidson, 1993), 361, and David Vogel, *Fluctuating Fortunes: The Political Power of Business in America* (New York: Basic Books, 1989).

37. Korpi, "Approaches to the Study of Poverty," and William C. Berman, *America's Right Turn: From Nixon to Bush* (Baltimore: Johns Hopkins University Press, 1994).

38. Vogel, *Fluctuating Fortunes*, 137–56. The growth rate of government jobs, which often paid better than private sector jobs, fell from 46% in the 60s to 24% in the 70s. See *HLS, 1980*, 151, and *HT*, 267.

39. Berman, *America's Right Turn*, 37–59; Bennett Harrison and Barry Bluestone, *The Great U-Turn: Corporate Restructuring and the Polarizing of America* (New York: Basic Books, 1990), 170–71; Margaret Weir, *Politics and Jobs: The Boundaries of Employment*

Policy in the United States (1992; Princeton, N.J.: Princeton University Press, 1993), esp. 99–129; Jerry Flint, "Jobless Rate of Blacks Still Rising despite a 25-Year Federal Effort," *New York Times*, March 13, 1979, A1, B6; and chapter 6 in the present volume.

40. U.S. Department of Commerce, Bureau of the Census, *Money Income and Poverty Status* (1980), 2, 28, 32. An excellent history of poverty lines is Gordon M. Fisher, "The Development and History of the Poverty Thresholds," *Social Security Bulletin* 55 (Winter 1992): 3–14.

41. Roger Friedland and Jimy M. Sanders, "Capitalism and the Welfare State," in Michael K. Brown, ed., *Remaking the Welfare State: Retrenchment and Social Policy in America and Europe* (Philadelphia: Temple University Press, 1988), 29–56, and Robert J. Lampman, *Balancing the Books: Social Spending and the American Economy* (Washington: National Conference on Social Welfare: 1985), which concludes that the loss of growth was inconsequential.

42. Mishel and Bernstein, *State of Working America, 1992–1993*, 434. See also Michael K. Brown, "Remaking the Welfare State: A Comparative Perspective," in Brown, *Remaking the Welfare State*, 3–28; David M. Cutler and Lawrence F. Katz, "Macroeconomic Performance and the Disadvantaged," *Brookings Papers on Economic Activity* 2 (1991): 1–74, esp. 54. It is true that the United States had a large hidden welfare state induced by tax breaks, favoring the affluent, not the poor and potentially poor. See chapter 10 in the present volume and Christopher Howard, *The Hidden Welfare State: Tax Expenditures and Social Policy in the United States* (Princeton, N.J.: Princeton University Press, 1997), 28–35.

Chapter Eight

1. A well-known example of the conservative counterrevolution was Thatcherism. See Rodney Lowe, *The Welfare State in Britain since 1945*, 3rd ed (New York: Palgrave Macmillan, 2005), 315–75.

2. Harries quoted in Robert A. Gorman, *Michael Harrington, Speaking America* (New York: Routledge, 1995), 159.

3. Fay Lomax Cook and Edith J. Barrett, *Support for the American Welfare State: The Views of Congress and the Public* (New York: Columbia University Press, 1992), 25–27, 63–65. Chapter 7 in the present volume has economic data that could have been used. Elsewhere the Left's defense of gay rights and affirmative action alienated some voters, but so did the Right's attack on equal pay and fair wages. Most Americans supported the Equal Rights Amendment, which the right wing fought. The conservative Family Research Council even opposed the child-care tax credit and the Equal Pay Act. See Ronald Brownstein, "Apple Pie Fight," *New Republic*, February 3, 1986, 20–22.

4. Barbara Ehrenreich, "The New Right Attack on Social Welfare," in Fred Block, Richard A. Cloward, Barbara Ehrenreich, and Frances Fox Piven, *The Mean Season: The Attack on the Welfare State* (New York: Pantheon Books, 1987), 161–95.

5. Thomas Byrne Edsall and Mary D. Edsall, *Chain Reaction: The Impact of Race, Rights, and Taxes on American Politics* (New York: W. W. Norton and Co., 1991).

6. David Vogel, *Fluctuating Fortunes: The Political Power of Business in America* (New York: Basic Books, 1989); John B. Judis, *The Paradox of American Democracy: Elites, Special Interests, and the Betrayal of Public Trust* (New York: Pantheon Books, 2000), 109–55; David Gordon, *Fat and Mean: The Corporate Squeeze of Working Americans and the Myth of Managerial "Downsizing"* (New York: Free Press, 1996), 204–37; and Ellen Reese, *Backlash against Welfare Mothers: Past and Present* (Berkeley: University of California, 2005), 150–71.

7. Judis, *Paradox of American Democracy*, 116–22.

8. Gregg Easterbrook, "Ideas Move Nations," *Atlantic Monthly*, January 1986, 66–80, quotation on 72. Sidney Blumenthal, *The Rise of the Counter-establishment: From Conservative Ideology to Political Power* (New York: Times Books, 1986).

9. Gertrude Schaffner Goldberg and Sheila D. Collins, *Washington's New Poor Law: Welfare Reform and the Roads Not Taken—1935 to the Present* (New York: Apex Press, 2001), 126. Valuable liberal scholarship that did not make a splash was Sheldon H. Danziger and Daniel H. Weinberg, eds., *Fighting Poverty: What Works and What Doesn't* (Cambridge, Mass.: Harvard University Press, 1986). See also Easterbrook, "Ideas Move Nations," 69; Michael B. Katz, *The Undeserving Poor: From the War on Poverty to the War on Welfare* (1989; New York: Pantheon Books, 1990), 138–39, 176. A fighting liberal was William Ryan, author of *Blaming the Victim*, rev. ed (New York: Vintage Books, 1976).

10. There were books about blue-collar whites who were not affluent: Andrew Levison, *The Working-Class Majority* (New York: Penguin Books, 1975), and Lillian Breslow Rubin, *Worlds of Pain: Life in the Working-Class Family* (New York: Basic Books, 1976). See also Charles Murray, "White Welfare, Families, 'White Trash,'" *National Review*, March 28, 1986, 30–34, and Jay MacLeod, *Ain't No Makin' It: Aspirations and Attainment in a Low-Income Neighborhood* (Boulder, Colo.: Westview Press, 1995), which compares the aspirations of white and black youths.

11. Blumenthal, *Rise of the Counter-establishment*, 191–93; Ann Evory and Linda Metzger, eds., *Contemporary Authors*, New Revision Series (Detroit: Gale Research Co., 1983), 9:16–17; Martin Anderson, *Welfare: The Political Economy of Welfare Reform in the United States* (Palo Alto, Calif.: Stanford University/Hoover Institution, 1978).

12. Anderson, *Welfare*, 25, quoting Edgar Browning. Conservative economists Browning, of the University of Virginia, and Morton Paglin, of Portland State, claimed that federal officials exaggerated the poverty rate by omitting unreported income and in-kind benefits like food stamps and Medicaid. Recalculations allegedly reduced poverty rates from 11% to 3%. Browning claimed that "there is practically no poverty—statistically speaking—in the United States today." Browning, "How Much More Equality Can We Afford?," *Public Interest*, Spring 1976, 90–110. Browning made no effort to determine whether the typical poor family received all benefits. See Timothy M. Smeeding, "The Anti-Poverty Effect of In-Kind Transfers: A 'Good Idea' Gone Too Far," *Policy Studies Journal* 10 (1982): 499–522; "Is Poverty Dead?," *Newsweek*, October 9, 1978, 85–86. Conservatives were not the only ones to criticize the welfare system. A report prepared under Michigan Democrat Martha Griffiths claimed that

average benefit levels for people who received every benefit were too high. See A Staff Study for the Subcommittee on Fiscal Policy of the Joint Economic Committee of the Congress of the United States, *Welfare in the 70s: A National Study of Benefits Available in 100 Local Areas* (Washington: Government Printing Office, 1974). See also Jean Stafancic and Richard Delgado, *No Mercy: How Conservative Think Tanks and Foundations Changed America's Social Agenda* (Philadelphia: Temple University Press, 1996), 83; in 1973–75 Congress compelled the states to reduce "overpayments" and enacted stricter child-support requirements. Lawrence M. Mead, *Beyond Entitlement: The Social Obligations of Citizenship* (New York: Free Press, 1986), 94, 224, 101.

13. Anderson, *Welfare*, 49–50, 56. Nathan Glazer, "Reform Work, Not Welfare," *Public Interest*, Summer 1975, 3–10, suggested that, instead of making welfare more unpleasant, work be made more attractive via national health care and child allowances.

14. Whether people just over the poverty line are "middle class," as Anderson claimed, is debatable. On government subsidies, work disincentives, and Carter's proposal, Anderson, *Welfare*, 54–55, 121, 123, 126, 175–207, and Lawrence E. Lynn Jr. and David deF. Whitman, *The President as Policymaker: Jimmy Carter and Welfare Reform* (Philadelphia: Temple University Press, 1981), 32, 42–43, 78–80.

15. William Julius Wilson, *The Declining Significance of Race: Blacks and Changing American Institutions*, 2nd ed. (Chicago: University of Chicago Press, 1980), 218 n. 72. On the PBJI, Gordon L. Weil, *The Welfare Debate of 1978* (White Plains, N.Y.: Institute for Socioeconomic Studies, 1978), 40, and Lynn and Whitman, *President as Policymaker*, 229–30.

16. Robert Lekachman, "Welfare Needs Help," *New York Times Book Review*, July 9, 1978, 13, 37–38.

17. Wilson, *Declining Significance of Race*, 92–97, 167, 160, 152–54.

18. Ibid., 160, 163–64, 166, 179, 219, 151.

19. Alphonso Pinkney, *The Myth of Black Progress* (New York: Cambridge University Press, 1984), 13–15; Charles Vert Willie, ed., *The Caste and Class Controversy on Race and Poverty: Round Two of the Willie/Wilson Debate*, 2nd ed. (Dix Hills, N.Y.: General Hall, 1989).

20. Willie, *Caste and Class Controversy*, 65, and in the same volume, Richard Margolis, "If We Won, Why Aren't We Smiling," 99–100, 110, 117; also, Joleen Kirschenman and Kathryn M. Neckerman, "'We'd Love to Hire Them, but . . .': The Meaning of Race for Employers," in Christopher Jencks and Paul E. Peterson, eds., *The Urban Underclass* (Washington: Brookings Institution, 1991), 203–32; Kenneth L. Kusmer, "African Americans in the City since World War II: From the Industrial to the Post-Industrial Era," *Journal of Urban History* 21 (May 1995): 458–504, esp. 476–77.

21. Wilson, *Declining Significance of Race*, 19. For Wilson's concept of class, ix, 156. Sociologists may wonder whether Wilson's conceptual lapse on the ruling class stems from the Chicago school's penchant for explaining social problems in terms of cultural lag rather than class conflict.

22. Wilson, *Declining Significance of Race*, 87.

23. Blumenthal, *Rise of the Counter-establishment*, 206–9; Charles Moritz, ed., *Current*

Biography Yearbook, 1981 (New York: H. W. Wilson, 1981), 166–69; J. David Hoeveler, *Watch on the Right: Conservative Intellectuals in the Reagan Era* (Madison: University of Wisconsin Press, 1991), 101.

24. Blumenthal, *Rise of the Counter-establishment*, 203–6; Moritz, *Current Biography Yearbook, 1981*; Gilder's *Wealth and Poverty* (1981; New York: Bantam Books, 1982) was reviewed by *Times* editor Roger Starr, "A Guide to Capitalism," *New York Times Book Review*, February 1, 1981, 10, 37.

25. Gilder made unsupported allegations about "the increasing reluctance of the American poor to perform low-wage labor" and the middle-class propensity for living off lavish unemployment insurance payments. He admitted that the inner cities lost jobs—but only because government affirmative action suits had driven them out. Gilder conceded that high school dropouts might not find work, but *government* emphasis on educational credentials kept poor people from jobs. Gilder, *Wealth and Poverty*, 150, 187–88, 173, 181. It was always government, never economic factors and business decisions. That stance was essential if conservative hostility to welfare programs was to be maintained.

26. Quotations in this and preceding paragraph, Gilder, *Wealth and Poverty*, 164, 149–52.

27. Ibid., 136–43. A critique of conservative arithmetic, especially on Medicaid, can be found in Michael Harrington, *The New American Poverty* (1984; New York: Penguin Books, 1985), 65–94. Federal minimum wage rates in *SA, 1981*, 408. Staff Study for the Subcommittee on Fiscal Policy of the Joint Economic Committee of the Congress of the United States, *Welfare in the 70s*, concluded from a survey of welfare officials in July 1972 that a family receiving all possible benefits might get $5,349; at that time the poverty line was $4,275. Most of Medicaid went to a small number of the elderly disabled, and a majority of the poor did not get housing benefits. See also Center on Budget and Policy Priorities, "The Cato Institute Report on Welfare Benefits: Do Cato's California Numbers Add Up?," March 7, 1996, at <www.cbpp.org>, accessed March 8, 1996.

28. Gilder's way of cutting welfare was that governments allow inflation to eat into the value of welfare payments; he seemed unaware that this was already happening. In his home state of New York, as Michael Kinsley pointed out, the real value of AFDC payments had fallen by 42% over 1974–80. Kinsley, "Tension and Release," *New Republic*, February 7, 1981, 25–31, esp. 28. Another view is Michael Walzer, "Life with Father," *New York Review of Books*, April 2, 1981, 3–4. Surprisingly, Gilder did support child allowances (*Wealth and Poverty*, 152–53).

29. Gilder, *Wealth and Poverty*, 46–51, 57–63, 321. A sound reason for criticizing contemporary Keynesianism was that it seemed to have failed to combine low inflation and high growth in the 1970s. See ibid., 265, 271, 230–42, and Lewis Beman, "The Chastening of the Washington Economists," *Fortune*, January 1976, 159–62, 165–66. In passing (*Wealth and Poverty*, 221), Gilder admitted that Kemp-Roth mirrored the Kennedy-Johnson tax cuts.

30. Conservatives used sleight of hand to make an obvious case of inadequate con-

sumption demand—one of the main causes of the Great Depression—disappear. In part they blamed the Smoot-Hawley Tariff, which, inconveniently for the argument, passed one year after the crash. See Gilder, *Wealth and Poverty*, 49. A sharp critique is Peter Temin, *Did Monetary Forces Cause the Great Depression?* (New York: W. W. Norton and Co., 1976).

31. As quoted in Blumenthal, *Rise of the Counter-establishment*, 195.

32. Useful is Herbert Stein, *The Fiscal Revolution in America: Policy in Pursuit of Reality*, 2nd rev. ed. (Washington: AEI Press, 1996), 384–430. On the Laffer curve, Gilder, *Wealth and Poverty*, 214. For other aspects of Gilder's approach, Frank Ackerman, *Hazardous to Our Health: Economic Policies in the 1980s* (Boston: South End Press, 1984), 1–48. Gilder ignored the highly regarded studies of Joseph Pechman, who demonstrated that all taxes taken together were barely progressive. Gilder, *Wealth and Poverty*, 104, also wildly exaggerated the negative impact of capital gains taxes on business formation and exaggerated the success of capital gains tax cuts.

33. Kinsley, "Tension and Release," 28.

34. Capitalists were still partly motivated by self-interest even in Gilder, *Wealth and Poverty*, 22, 31. Fred Hirsch, *The Social Limits to Growth* (Cambridge, Mass.: Harvard University Press, 1976), 117–22, argued that capitalism eroded the religious and moral cultures from which it emerged and which initially restrained capitalist amorality.

35. Carter's "Crisis of Confidence" speech is excerpted in William H. Chafe and Harvard Sitkoff, eds., *A History of Our Time: Readings in Postwar America*, 4th ed. (New York: Oxford University Press, 1995), 435–40.

36. In *A Welfare Mother* (1976; New York: Mentor, 1977) Susan Sheehan shows that Mrs. Santana had worked until child-care problems arose, but Sheehan does not make much of that or other job issues—for example, the loss of jobs in New York City in the 1970s. A case study that includes economic context is Elliot Liebow, *Tally's Corner: A Study of Negro Streetcorner Men* (Boston: Little, Brown, 1967). A sympathetic view of poverty-stricken Puerto Rican immigrants is Vincent Fanelli's recollections of the 70s, *The Human Face of Poverty: A Chronicle of Urban American* (New York: Bootstrap Press, 1990).

37. "The American Underclass," *Time*, August 29, 1977, 14–18, 21–22, 27, quotation on 14. Much of the article was less inflammatory than the magazine cover. Kennedy is quoted in Ken Auletta, *The Underclass* (1982; New York: Vintage Books, 1983), 26.

38. Auletta, *The Underclass*, 223, 244. Auletta's work first appeared in the *New Yorker* on November 16, 23, and 30, 1981.

39. Auletta, *The Underclass*, 27–30. Background in Mary Corcoran, Greg J. Duncan, Gerald Gurin, and Patricia Gurin, "Myth and Reality: The Causes and Persistence of Poverty," *Journal of Policy Analysis and Management* 4 (1985): 516–36; Erol R. Ricketts and Isabel V. Sawhill, "Defining and Measuring the Underclass," *Journal of Policy Analysis and Management* 7 (1988): 316–25; and Hugh Heclo, "Poverty Politics," in Sheldon Danziger, Gary D. Sandefur, and Daniel H. Weinberg, eds., *Confronting Poverty: Prescriptions for Change* (New York: Russell Sage Foundation; Cambridge, Mass: Harvard University Press, 1994), 396–437, esp. 418–19.

40. Auletta quoted in Herbert J. Gans, *The War against the Poor: The Underclass and Antipoverty Policy* (New York: Basic Books, 1995), 34. Auletta admitted that just 500 people committed 70% of the street robberies in Manhattan in 1979, and 1,862 multiple offenders committed 90% of the serious crimes in Philadelphia in 1973. Perhaps the underclass itself was not so large. See *The Underclass*, 45, 99.

41. Auletta, *The Underclass*, 50, 317–19, 11–12, 158–200, 213–14.

42. Marvin Harris, "Why the Underclass Can't Type," *Psychology Today*, June 1982, 81–84. See, too, Michael Harrington, "The Lower Depths," *New Republic*, June 9, 1982, 26–30; Andrew Hacker, "The Lower Depths," *New York Review of Books*, August 12, 1982, 15–20; Adolph Reed Jr., "The Underclass as Myth and Symbol: The Poverty of Discourse about Poverty," *Radical America* 24 (January–March 1990): 21–40; and Chester Finn, "At the Bottom," *Commentary*, August 1982, 72–74. Although he positioned himself between right and left, Auletta's title and arguments strengthened negative stereotypes of the poor and served conservative ends. The term "underclass" suggested people who were unwilling or unable to take advantage of job offers or social programs. See the epilogue in the paperback edition (1983) of *The Underclass*, 317–19, and Gans, *War against the Poor*, 33–35.

43. Auletta, *The Underclass*, 272.

44. In *Poor People's Movements: Why They Succeed, How They Fail* (1977; New York: Vintage Books, 1979), Frances Fox Piven and Richard A. Cloward argued that low-income Americans mainly had the power to disrupt during severe political crises. Over time, demonstrations and strikes gelled into bureaucratic organizations with "responsible" leaders and government connections; the poor lost their power to threaten politicians. As a result, they won less from government *after* they were well organized than before. But Piven and Cloward were flexible and pragmatic in their attitude toward elections and organization. In the 80s, they formed Human SERVE to increase low-income voter turnout. My section on Piven and Cloward is based on my reading of their books and articles and also Sanford D. Schram, *Praxis for the Poor: Piven and Cloward and the Future of Social Science in Social Welfare* (New York: New York University Press, 2002), 49–108.

45. Frances Fox Piven and Richard A. Cloward (*The New Class War: Reagan's Attack on the Welfare State and Its Consequences* (1982), rev. expanded ed. [New York: Pantheon Books, 1985], 4) admitted that a minority of welfare mothers were demoralized and dependent. A surprisingly evenhanded review from the right is Leslie Lenkowsky, "Social Policy," *Commentary*, July 1982, 80–82. In *New Class War* I am most concerned with chapters 1, 5, and 6. Chapters 2, 3, and 4 were not a political guide but a fascinating argument about the history of poor people's rights and the structures in the American system that favored the privileged. Although brilliantly written, these sections seemed Olympian, more concerned about which theory explained welfare state history than focusing people's emotions and ideas for action.

46. For critical responses to the earlier works, Walter I. Trattner, ed., *Social Welfare or Social Control: Some Historical Reflections on Regulating the Poor* (Knoxville: University of Tennessee Press, 1983).

47. Piven and Cloward, *New Class War*, 140, 162–68, 187, 24–26, 31, and Richard A. Cloward and Frances Fox Piven, "Workers and Welfare: The Poor against Themselves" and "Dissensus Politics: A Strategy for Winning Economic Rights," *The Nation*, November 25, 1968, and April 20, 1968, reprinted in Cloward and Piven, *The Politics of Turmoil: Essays on Poverty, Race, and the Urban Crisis* (New York: Pantheon Books, 1974), 141–50, 161–70. On the continuing political influence of unions, Taylor E. Dark, *The Unions and the Democrats: An Enduring Alliance*, updated ed. (Ithaca, N.Y.: Cornell University Press, 2001). Piven and Cloward might have added to the 1985 edition of *New Class War* a discussion of the big recession of 1981–82, which did exactly what they had hinted in chapter 1 would not occur—cut wages—and which was arguably the most important economic event of the Reagan years. They claimed that through the 70s "wages did not fall" (26), but for the first time since the 30s real wages stagnated, and at the end of the decade they were at slightly lower levels than those at which they began.

48. Quotation from Ann Withorn, "The Politics of Welfare," *Radical America* 16 (July–October 1982): 71. Piven and Cloward, *New Class War*, 181, find no evidence of public support for the right-wing attack on the welfare state. Agreed, but public support for the welfare state was not deep and often wavered on unemployment insurance and AFDC. As a result, highly organized minorities like the Reaganites cut programs in the 80s.

49. Blumenthal, *Rise of the Counter-establishment*, 294–96; Chuck Lane, "The Manhattan Project," *New Republic*, March 25, 1985, 14–15; Kathleen J. Edgar, ed., *Contemporary Authors* (Detroit: Gale Research, 1995), 147:319–21; Charles Moritz, ed., *Current Biography Yearbook, 1986* (New York: H. W. Wilson, 1986), 398–402.

50. Charles Murray, *Losing Ground: American Social Policy, 1950–1980* (New York: Basic Books, 1984), 125–29.

51. Gilder's words about liberal critics: "some of the most intellectually debilitated of Americans . . . mental incompetents . . . limp-minded and lame-prosed critics," quoted from the *American Spectator*, March 1985, in Blumenthal, *Rise of the Counter-establishment*, 296.

52. Daniel Patrick Moynihan, *Family and Nation* (1986; New York: Harcourt, Brace, Jovanovich, 1987), 129, and the introduction to the Tenth Anniversary Edition (New York: Basic Books, 1995) of *Losing Ground*, in which Murray claimed that everyone who worked in the streets knew that welfare caused illegitimacy. Only social scientists didn't know it.

53. Christopher Jencks, "How Poor Are the Poor?," *New York Review of Books*, May 9, 1985, 41–48; Robert Greenstein, "Losing Faith in 'Losing Ground,'" *New Republic*, March 25, 1985, 12–17; David T. Ellwood and Lawrence H. Summers, "Is Welfare Really the Problem?," *Public Interest*, Spring 1986, 57–78; Murray's retort, "No, Welfare Isn't Really the Problem," *Public Interest*, Summer 1986, 3–11; and Lawrence M. Mead, "Welfare: More Harm than Good?," *New York Times Book Review*, December 16, 1984, 7. Murray manipulated figures. He had to argue that the economy of the 70s was good; otherwise a bad economy was a better explanation for poverty and crime

than the liberal welfare state. But most people knew that 1974–75 had been the worst depression since the 30s. Murray set up a comparison that omitted the war boom of 1950–53 to make the 70s look about as good as the 50s, but there is no doubt growth in the 70s was weaker than in the 50s or 60s and that business practices had become harsher as well. Excellent critiques of Murray that probably did not reach large audiences are in Sara McLanahan et al., *Losing Ground: A Critique* (Madison, Wis.: Institute for Research on Poverty, 1985).

54. Barry Bluestone and Bennett Harrison, *The Deindustrialization of America* (New York: Basic Books, 1982).

55. Murray, *Losing Ground,* 69–84. Murray later penned a manifesto, *What It Means to Be a Libertarian: A Personal Interpretation* (New York: Broadway Books, 1997). Robert J. Samuelson, "The Way to Help the Poor Is Simple—but Troubling," *Los Angeles Times,* April 4, 1985, II, 5, noted that Murray "erred in blaming poverty's persistence mostly on welfare [while] the economy was the main problem."

56. See "Saving the Underclass, Ken Auletta Interviews Charles Murray," *Washington Monthly,* September 1985, 21.

57. Greenfield quoted in Moynihan, *Family and Nation,* 58.

58. Quoted in J. Patrick Lewis, "Willing Goodness," *The Nation,* October 20, 1984, 397.

59. Cook and Barrett, *Support for the American Welfare State,* 25–27, 60–65. Martin Gilens, *Why Americans Hate Welfare: Race, Media, and the Politics of Antipoverty Policy* (1999; Chicago: University of Chicago Press, 2000), 125–27, on how the effects of the depression of 1981–82 were so obvious and widespread that the media soft-pedaled their usual identification of poverty and blackness.

60. Sometimes Harrington aimlessly wandered around a subject. See, for example, *New American Poverty,* 73 and all of chapter 7, a confusing effort about the impact of large-scale immigration on the labor market.

61. Ibid., 42–60, 123–50, 179–206. Harrington could have gone further: over 1978–83, that is, adding just two years, *10 million* were added to the poverty rolls.

62. Palmer quoted in Charles Moritz, ed., *Current Biography Yearbook, 1988* (New York: H. W. Wilson, 1988), 233.

63. For three decades Harrington was the most prominent socialist in America. This, William Buckley chided, was like being the tallest building in Topeka, Kansas. See Bill McKibben, "The Other American," *Mother Jones,* July–August 1988, 40. Other evaluations include Katz, *Undeserving Poor,* 77; Lewis, "Willing Goodness"; Mitchell Sviridoff, "New Faces, Old Problem," *New York Times Book Review,* August 26, 1984, 7; and Tom Wicker, "The Other America Revisited," *Atlantic Monthly,* October 1984, 123–26. Joseph Sobran, "Harrington, D.C.," *National Review,* December 28, 1984, 38–39, criticizes Harrington for moving to the suburbs.

64. Mead, *Beyond Entitlement,* 57–58. Mead uncritically accepted estimates that the underclass numbered about 9 million, mostly black Americans (*Beyond Entitlement,* 22). He admitted that European nations had more permissive social programs than the United States but fewer dysfunctions (16).

65. Evaluations of government job and training programs, a sketch of the congressional forces for welfare reform, and Mead's research in twenty-two workfare offices in New York state.

66. Mead, *Beyond Entitlement*, 148–68. Sosin's devastating review is in *Social Service Review* 61 (March 1987): 156–59. More favorable is Mark Lilla, "A Way to Save Welfare," *New Republic*, April 14, 1986, 33–36.

67. Mead, *Beyond Entitlement*, 36–37, 71–90.

68. Quotation from Katz, *Undeserving Poor*, 165; see also Daniel Bell, *The Cultural Contradictions of Capitalism* (New York: Basic Books, 1976).

69. Ronald Brownstein, "Beyond Quotas," *Los Angeles Times Magazine*, July 28, 1991, 18, 38–43.

70. William Julius Wilson, *The Truly Disadvantaged: The Inner City, the Underclass, and Public Policy* (1987; Chicago: University of Chicago Press, 1990), 5–19. Research on ghetto ills after *The Negro Family* includes sources mentioned in Wilson's endnotes, 173–74 and nn. 41–52 on 217–19; Liebow, *Tally's Corner*; Carol Stack, *All Our Kin: Strategies for Survival* (1974; New York: Harper Colophon Books, 1975); and Douglas G. Glasgow, *The Black Underclass: Poverty, Unemployment and Entrapment of Ghetto Youth* (1980; New York: Vintage Books, 1981). Jesse Jackson combined the call for more government aid with the call for self-help. See Peter Kovler, "Black on Black Crime: A Taboo Broken," *The Nation*, October 23, 1976, 390, and Cynthia Jo Rich, "Young, Black and No Place to Go," *The Nation*, May 15, 1976, 592–95.

71. Adolph Reed Jr., "The Liberal Technocrat," *The Nation*, February 6, 1988, 167–70. Christopher Jencks, *Rethinking Social Policy: Race, Poverty, and the Underclass* (New York: Harper Perennial, 1993), 120–42, claims that only a fraction of black female-headed families can be attributed to male unemployment, but he agrees that unemployment is a big problem.

72. Wilson, *Truly Disadvantaged*, 82–106.

73. See ibid., 156, and William Greider, *Who Will Tell the People: The Betrayal of American Democracy* (New York: Simon and Schuster, 1993), for example, 183–91, 247–50, 260.

74. Wilson, *Declining Significance of Race*, 218. In 1996 Wilson was said to be Clinton's favorite sociologist, and he praised Clinton for including job creation in welfare reform, but in that same year Clinton signed off on welfare reform without the jobs. Gerald Early, "William Julius Wilson," *Mother Jones*, September–October 1996, 20–24.

75. For example, how racism in one realm such as education affected black people's chances in another, the job market. See Willie, *Caste and Class Controversy*, esp. 149, 151.

76. *Consensus* authors did not include such moderates as Richard Freeman of Harvard and Sheldon Danziger of the University of Wisconsin's Institute for Research on Poverty or anyone connected with the Catholic bishops' pastoral letter, *Economic Justice for All* (Washington: National Conference of Catholic Bishops, 1986). On the American Enterprise Institute, James A. Smith, *The Idea Brokers: Think Tanks and the Rise of the New Policy Elite* (New York: Free Press, 1991), 174–80.

77. Michael Novak et al., *The New Consensus on Family and Welfare: A Community of Self-Reliance* (Washington: American Enterprise Institute, 1987), 37, 88.

78. Novak et al., *New Consensus on Family and Welfare*, 17, 27, 36, 59, 45, 49.

79. Ibid., xiv, for the quotation 18 n. 1, 36, 48, 62; Easterbrook, "Ideas Move Nations," 68. And to help poor families, why not raise the minimum wage? In part because that approach alienated conservative business funders. It seemed at times that a right-winger like Gary Bauer might support a higher minimum wage, but nothing came of it. Extremely conservative business funders like Richard Scaife and Joseph Coors would not have supported a higher minimum wage or stronger unions, even for the sake of stronger families. Nor would the right-wing John M. Olin Foundation, which subsidized *The New Consensus on Family and Welfare*.

80. Gans, *War against the Poor*, esp. 37–51. See also Myron Magnet, "America's Underclass," *Fortune*, May 11, 1987, 130, 134, 138, 142, 144, 146, 148, 150. A reporter who kept his head about the harsh economy of the 1980s, even in a article with an inflammatory title, was Timothy Harper, "The Underclass-Squalid Existence in the Backwater of American Life," *Los Angeles Times*, April 19, 1984, pt. IB, 8.

81. Another example of using the underclass idea for liberal goals, in this case a jobs program for inner-city youths, was Richard Stengel, "The Underclass: Breaking the Cycle," *Time*, October 10, 1988, 41–42.

82. Pete Hamill, "America's Black Underclass: Can It Be Saved?," *Reader's Digest*, June 1988, 105–10. Condensed from the original in *Esquire*, March 1988.

83. On foreign policy, Moynihan became the darling of conservatives for his anti-communism, his strong support of Israel, and his attacks on third-world nations in the United Nations. After winning his Senate seat, he hired Elliott Abrams and Chester Finn, both of whom were very conservative. Philip Green, "The Wayward Social Scientist," *The Nation*, September 22, 1979, 231–32. In 1978 Moynihan was willing to trade away adequate welfare funding for fiscal relief to New York City. See Richard A. Cloward and Frances Fox Piven, "The Welfare Vaudevillian," *The Nation*, September 22, 1979, 236–39.

84. These became law in the Family Support Act of 1988 and 1986 tax reform. Reviews of *Family and Nation*: Dennis Wrong, "21 Years Later," *New Republic*, March 17, 1986, 30–33, and Glenn C. Loury, "The Family, the Nation, and Senator Moynihan," *Commentary*, June 1986, 21–26.

85. Moynihan, *Family and Nation*, 216–17, notes that a year after he first delivered the Godkin Lectures, he had evidence from a scholarly article to prove that AFDC, which he had once thought "*somewhat*" led to single-parent households, now "*more than somewhat*" led to them; Moynihan's emphasis.

86. Ibid., 126.

87. Ibid., 133, 184, for two places where the job issue races in and out of the book.

88. *SA, 1992*, table 640.

89. Jeff Chapman and Pamela S. Dear, eds., *Contemporary Authors, New Revision Series*, vol. 52 (Detroit: Gale Research, 1996), 324–28.

90. "The White House vs. CBS," *Time*, May 3, 1982, 24. Sympathetic reactions to

Moyers's 1986 film included Anthony Lewis, "State of the Union," *New York Times*, February 6, 1986, L23, and John Corry, "TV: 'CBS Reports' Examines Black Families," *New York Times*, January 25, 1986, L49. It is hard not to conclude that the political center had moved to the right: Corry found "no negative racial stereotypes" in the film, and he almost completely ignored what was happening to inner-city economies. See Richard B. Freeman and Harry J. Holzer, eds., *The Black Youth Employment Crisis* (Chicago: University of Chicago Press, 1986), and "Hard Times for Black America," *Dollars & Sense*, April 1986, 5–7.

91. A later effort to inventory facts about the underclass was Christopher Jencks, "Is the American Underclass Growing?," in Jencks and Peterson, *Urban Underclass*, 28–100. Linking teen pregnancy among poor people to low expectations rather than welfare is Thea M. Lee, "Rational Expectations: A New Look at the Economics of Teen Pregnancy," *Dollars & Sense*, March 1989, 10–11.

92. Gans, *War against the Poor*, 54–55. *The Business of America* played on a New York City station and received a notice by Steven Greenhouse, "Film Explores Steel Industry Decline," *New York Times*, May 8, 1984, C17. Apparently it caused no stir, but it soon found a home in college film libraries. In the 90s and early 2000s, Moyers did several programs about hardworking families striving to afford a decent living. He began to talk about the class war of rich on poor and middle America.

93. Four reports mentioned in Novak et al., *New Consensus on Family and Welfare*, some by liberals like Mario Cuomo, seemed to agree that the goal of social policy was to get people off welfare, not to solve poverty.

94. Richard G. Niemi, John Mueller, and Tom W. Smith, *Trends in Public Opinion: A Compendium of Survey Data* (Westport, Conn.: Greenwood Press, 1989), 89; William G. Mayer, *The Changing American Mind: How and Why American Public Opinion Changed between 1960 and 1988* (Ann Arbor: University of Michigan Press, 1992), 374, 444–58, 481; Cook and Barrett, *Support for the American Welfare State*, 60–65, 90; Lawrence Bobo and Ryan Smith, "Antipoverty Policy, Affirmative Action, and Racial Attitudes," in Danziger, Sandefur, and Weinberg, *Confronting Poverty*, 373–95; Robert Y. Shapiro and John T. Young, "Public Opinion and the Welfare State: The United States in Comparative Perspective," *Political Science Quarterly* 104 (Spring 1989): 59–89.

95. Thomas Ferguson and Joel Rogers, *Right Turn: The Decline of the Democrats and the Future of American Politics* (New York: Hill and Wang, 1986), 3–28; Cook and Barrett, *Support for the American Welfare State*, 90.

96. In 1984, for example, liberals presented vital research at a Department of Health and Human Services conference, but it was rather technical. The conference was published in Danziger and Weinberg, *Fighting Poverty*. See also Easterbrook, "Ideas Move Nations," 69. The Left added to its infrastructure in the 80s with the Center on Budget and Policy Priorities, and in the 90s, with the Economic Policy Institute.

97. On the class position of journalists, Trudy Lieberman, *Slanting the Story: The Forces That Shape the News* (New York: New Press, 2000), 151–61. A prime example of Republicans linking crime and race in an incendiary way was the Willie Horton story in the 1988 presidential election. On the media hyping crime despite falling crime

rates, Beth Shuster, "Living in Fear," *Los Angeles Times*, August 23, 1998, A1, 32–33, and Marc Mauer, *Race to Incarcerate* (New York: New Press, 2001), 171–77.

98. Wilson, *Truly Disadvantaged*, 6, 8 for the quotation, 173–74, 217–18, nn. 45, 46; Edsall and Edsall, *Chain Reaction*, 15–16, 55, 114, 122, 235, 258, 278–79, 286.

99. An exception was Harrison and Bluestone's *Deindustrialization of America*. Thomas J. Sugrue, *The Origins of the Urban Crisis: Race and Inequality in Postwar Detroit* (Princeton, N.J.: Princeton University Press, 1996), includes a historical critique of the Edsalls.

100. First quotation from David M. Ricci, *The Transformation of American Politics: The New Washington and the Rise of Think Tanks* (New Haven, Conn.: Yale University Press, 1993), 235; the second from Gans, *War against the Poor*, 50. See also Gans, *War against the Poor*, 50–51, 124–27. Some think tanks and foundations previously identified as liberal became less liberal. This was true of the Brookings Institution and the Urban Institute.

101. Poverty expert David Ellwood, *Poor Support: Poverty in the American Family* (New York: Basic Books, 1988), 98, claimed that nobody knew "how to recapture the dramatic growth of the 1960s," but that did not stop him from helping to push people off welfare and into a slow-growth labor market. On neoliberalism, Randall Rothenberg, *The Neoliberals: Creating the New American Politics* (New York: Simon and Schuster, 1984).

102. George Lakoff, *Moral Politics: How Liberals and Conservatives Think*, 2nd ed. (Chicago: University of Chicago Press, 2002), emphasizes the importance of telling a story linked to a moral view of the world.

103. Piven and Cloward, *New Class War*, 137. Piven and Cloward (188) label client and server resistance to welfare cuts "unadorned interest group liberalism," and that is different from a belief in a moral economy for all.

Chapter Nine

1. Michael Schaller, *Reckoning with Reagan: America and Its President in the 1980s* (New York: Oxford University Press, 1994); Ephraim Katz, revised by Fred Klein and Ronald Dean Nolen, *The Film Encyclopedia*, 5th ed. (New York: Collins, 2005), 1165; John Horn and Rachel Abramowitz, "Hollywood a Crucible for His Conservatism," and John Neuman, "Reagan Dies at 93," both in *Los Angeles Times*, June 6, 2004, A31, A35; A1, A36–A38.

2. Ronnie Dugger, *On Reagan: The Man and His Presidency* (New York: McGraw-Hill, 1983), 293–294. Reagan appointed an extreme right-winger, Lewis K. Uhler, to head the state poverty agency.

3. Schaller, *Reckoning with Reagan*, 27–33; Foster Rhea Dulles and Melvyn Dubofsky, *Labor in America: A History*, 5th ed. (Arlington Heights, Ill.: Harlan Davidson, 1993), 391; Carol Berkin et al., *Making America: A History of the United States*, vol. 2, *Since 1865* (Boston: Houghton Mifflin, 1995), 976–79; William Greider, *The Education of David Stockman and Other Americans* (New York: E. P. Dutton, 1982), 113 (first quotation); Howard E. Shuman, *Politics and the Budget: The Struggle between the President*

and the Congress, 2nd ed. (Englewood Cliffs, N.J.: Prentice-Hall, 1988), 246 (second quotation); William C. Berman, *America's Right Turn: From Nixon to Bush* (Baltimore: Johns Hopkins University Press, 1994), 103 (third quotation), 114.

4. Johnson was forced to give up his bid for reelection by the antiwar movement, Nixon resigned over Watergate, and Ford and Carter were derided as ineffectual. On Reagan's poor memory and his frequent lack of involvement, see Schaller, *Reckoning with Reagan*, 5 (Moyers quotation), 8–9, 53–54, 57.

5. Ibid., 33, 62.

6. Ibid., 56, 53; Martin Gilens, *Why Americans Hate Welfare: Race, Media, and the Politics of Antipoverty Policy* (1999; Chicago: University of Chicago Press, 2000), 126.

7. Frances Fox Piven and Richard A. Cloward, *The New Class War: Reagan's Attack on the Welfare State and Its Consequences* (New York: Pantheon Books, 1982).

8. "Why Supply-Side Economics Is Suddenly Popular," *Business Week*, September 17, 1979, 116, 118. In the late 70s *Business Week* admitted that corporations were sitting on $80 billion (Piven and Cloward, *New Class War*, 11), but business lobbyists used the capital shortage claim to get tax breaks.

9. Frank Ackerman, *Hazardous to Our Wealth: Economic Policies in the 1980s* (Boston: South End Press, 1984), 96; quotation, Doug Henwood, *Wall Street: How It Works and for Whom* (London: Verso, 1998), 201.

10. Piven and Cloward, *New Class War,* and Paul Krugman, *Peddling Prosperity: Economic Sense and Nonsense in the Age of Diminished Expectations* (1994; New York: W. W. Norton and Co., 1995), 82–169; Greider, *Education of David Stockman*, 7–8, 62–65, 86–96. There were divisions among Reaganites, for example, between extreme free marketeers like James Watt and flexible conservatives like James Baker and Donald Regan. But no one argued for a higher minimum wage to help the working poor. On one split, "Supply Siders vs. Monetarists," *Business Week*, August 24, 1981, 78, 80–82.

11. Ackerman, *Hazardous to Our Wealth*, 19–48, esp. 28–31 on Laffer, and the "What Was the Laffer Curve?" sidebar in chapter 8 of the present volume.

12. Schaller, *Reckoning with Reagan*, 26; Ackerman, *Hazardous to Our Wealth*, 1–32, 37–38; Anthony S. Campagna, *The Economy in the Reagan Years: The Economic Consequences of the Reagan Administrations* (Westport, Conn.: Greenwood Press, 1994), 41; Editorial, "Kicking a Trojan Horse," *Los Angeles Times*, November 12, 1981, II, 6.

13. Ackerman, *Hazardous to Our Wealth*, 44–48, quotation on 44; "Reaganomics Report Card," *Dollars & Sense*, May 1987, 6–8; George L. Perry, "Reaganomics's First Year a Failure," *Los Angeles Times*, November 24, 1981, IV, 3; Shuman, *Politics and the Budget*, 261. The buying and selling of tax breaks was scandalous; General Electric, with profits of $2.26 billion in 1981, bought enough tax breaks from other companies to get a tax refund of $100 million ("The Tilted Tax Structure," *AFL-CIO NEWS*, March 20, 1982, 4). The sale of tax breaks was abolished in 1982, and cigarette and phone taxes were raised.

14. John Aloysius Farrell, *Tip O'Neill and the Democratic Century* (Boston: Little, Brown, 2001), 589.

15. Paul Pierson, *Dismantling the Welfare State?: Reagan, Thatcher, and the Politics of Retrenchment* (New York: Cambridge University Press, 1995), 150, 152, 210 n. 22. See

also Robert Lekachman, "Deficit Aids Conservatives' Agenda," *Los Angeles Times*, January 22, 1985, VI, 3, and Allen Schick, "Reagan Sits Happily in Red-Ink Bath," *Los Angeles Times*, February 6, 1985, II, 5. In 1986, Stockman claimed that the tax cuts had been in part intended to limit social spending. See Barry Bluestone and Bennett Harrison, *Growing Prosperity: The Battle for Growth with Equity in the Twenty-first Century* (Berkeley: University of California Press, 2001), 119.

16. Sanford Rose, "We've Learned How to Lick Inflation," *Fortune*, September 1976, 100–105, 180, 182, 184; Dugger, *On Reagan*, 327 (for the quotation); William Tabb, "Zapping Labor," *Marxist Perspectives* 3 (Spring 1980): 64–77. The most important source for this section is Piven and Cloward, *New Class War*.

17. Campagna, *Economy in the Reagan Years*, 53–54; for the quotation, Lester C. Thurow, "Monetarists' Theory Didn't Work," *Los Angeles Times*, July 21, 1981, IV, 3; Greider, *Education of David Stockman*, 86–87, 139–59, for Stockman's wishful optimism, his worries about a recession, and his support of monetary tightening.

18. Schaller, *Reckoning with Reagan*, 49; U.S. Department of Labor, Bureau of Labor Statistics, *Employment and Earnings* 30 (April 1983): 61; "The Recovery Hype: False Claims and Shaky Gains," *Dollars & Sense*, October 1983, 3–5.

19. Michael Perelman, *The Pathology of the U.S. Economy: The Costs of a Low-Wage System* (New York: St. Martin's Press, 1996), 42; William Greider, *Secrets of the Temple: How the Federal Reserve Runs the Country* (New York: Touchstone Books, 1989), 429–43, 565–66.

20. Ackerman, *Hazardous to Our Wealth*, 96–97, 135; William J. Eaton, "Reagan Will Stand Firm in Recession," *Los Angeles Times*, December 6, 1981, I, 1, 17; Robert Magnuson, "Fed Urged to Ease Grip on Money, Credit," *Los Angeles Times*, October 16, 1981, IV, 1–2; William J. Eaton, "U.S. Jobless Rate Rises to 6-Year High of 8.4%," *Los Angeles Times*, December 5, 1981, I, 1, 16; Robert Lekachman, "Unemployment Crisis Is at Hand," *Los Angeles Times*, July 13, 1982, IV, 3. Economist James Tobin, in "Reaganomics 'Never Was a Consistent Policy,'" *U.S. News & World Report*, February 1, 1982, 46–47; Dugger, *On Reagan*, 325–27; Lou Cannon, *President Reagan: The Role of a Lifetime* (New York: Simon and Schuster, 1991), 268–71; Greider, *Education of David Stockman*, 65.

21. Krugman, *Peddling Prosperity*, 73–74; Dugger, *On Reagan*, 328. Why liberals weren't more successful defending unemployment insurance is not clear. See Pierson, *Dismantling the Welfare State?*, 102–3, 106, 119–28, 160–61; Piven and Cloward, *New Class War*, 13; and the 1983 *Economic Report of the President* (Washington: Government Printing Office, 1983), 47–49.

22. David Vogel, *Fluctuating Fortunes: The Political Power of Business in America* (New York: Basic Books, 1989), 256. The housing industry was one of several exceptions to business support for recession.

23. Ackerman, *Hazardous to Our Wealth*, 136–37. The Fed's high interest rates made imports cheap and exports expensive. That kept inflation down but hurt factory workers. Steel industry unemployment reached 23% in 1982. See "Subsidized Steel Imports Hit As Industry Job Losses Soar," *AFL-CIO News*, April 17, 1982, 3.

24. Ackerman, *Hazardous to Our Wealth*, 128, 130–34; Randy Albelda et al., *Real World Macro*, 8th ed. (Somerville, Mass.: Dollars & Sense, 1991), 95; Teresa Amott, "The 6% Solution: The Fed Redefines Full Employment," *Dollars & Sense*, November 1988, 6–8, 21, esp. 7; *SA, 1992*, table 664, 418.

25. Ackerman, *Hazardous to Our Wealth*, 99–100, and Michael B. Katz, *The Price of Citizenship: Redefining the American Welfare State* (New York: Metropolitan Books, 2001), 65–66.

26. Gordon Lafer, *The Job Training Charade* (Ithaca, N.Y.: Cornell University Press, 2002), 156–89.

27. Pierson, *Dismantling the Welfare State?*, 64–73; Edward D. Berkowitz, *Disabled Policy: America's Programs for the Handicapped* (Cambridge: Cambridge University Press, 1987), 111–51; *SA, 1981*, 329. Katz, *Price of Citizenship*, 209–15, claims only 83,000 of those kicked off stayed off, but figures in *SA, 1992*, 361, suggest the number was much higher.

28. Pierson, *Dismantling the Welfare State?*, 58–73; Katz, *Price of Citizenship*, 236–43; Edward D. Berkowitz, *America's Welfare State: From Roosevelt to Reagan* (Baltimore: Johns Hopkins University Press, 1991), 69–87; Sheldon Danziger and Peter Gottschalk, "The Impact of Budget Cuts and Economic Conditions on Poverty," *Journal of Poverty Analysis and Management* 4 (1985): 587–93. Century Foundation, *Social Security Reform: The Basics* (New York: Century Foundation Press, 2002), estimated that Social Security benefits constituted half of all income for two-thirds of the elderly.

29. Stockman quoted in Greider, *Education of David Stockman*, 46; emphasis in the original.

30. Paul Light, *Artful Work: The Politics of Social Security Reform* (New York: Random House, 1985); Pierson, *Dismantling the Welfare State?*, 64–73; Ackerman, *Hazardous to Our Wealth*, 118; and Edward D. Berkowitz, *Robert Ball and the Politics of Social Security* (Madison: University of Wisconsin Press, 2003), 214–323, a gold mine of information on program details and political maneuvering.

31. In the late 90s, Social Security actuaries, assuming weak economic growth (1.6% a year), predicted that the system might be unable to pay full benefits in 2029. By 2005 the day of doom had advanced to 2041. See Century Foundation, *Social Security Reform*, 4, 17.

32. Reagan quotations from Sylvester J. Schieber and John B. Shoven, *The Real Deal: The History and Future of Social Security* (New Haven, Conn.: Yale University Press, 1999), 190, 195. For "Unscathed," Berkowitz, *Robert Ball*, 322.

33. Thomas Ferguson and Joel Rogers, *Right Turn: The Decline of the Democrats and the Future of American Politics* (New York: Hill and Wang, 1986), 114–61. Statistics for Temporary Assistance for Needy Families (TANF, formerly AFDC) at <http://www .acf.dhhs.gov/news/stats/3697.htm> (June 21, 2000); and Andrew Hacker, "Getting Rough on the Poor," *New York Review of Books*, October 13, 1988, 12–17.

34. D. Lee Bawden and John L. Palmer, "Social Policy: Challenging the Welfare State," in John L. Palmer and Isabel V. Sawhill, *The Reagan Record: An Assessment of America's Changing Domestic Priorities* (Cambridge, Mass.: Ballinger Publishing Co.,

1984), 192, and James T. Patterson, *America's Struggle against Poverty in the Twentieth Century* (Cambridge, Mass.: Harvard University Press, 2002), 206.

35. Statistics for Temporary Assistance for Needy Families. The administration tried unsuccessfully to classify catsup as a vegetable (Ackerman, *Hazardous to Our Wealth*, 107); Palmer and Sawhill, *Reagan Record*, 367–70.

36. Quoted in Jerry Adler et al., "The Hard-Luck Christmas of '82," *Newsweek*, December 27, 1982, 12–16. On the limits of private charity, Rebecca M. Blank, *It Takes a Nation: A New Agenda for Fighting Poverty* (1997; Princeton, N.J.: Princeton University Press, 1998), 200–207.

37. Katz, *Price of Citizenship*, 300; Palmer and Sawhill, *Reagan Record*, 373.

38. See chapter 8 in the present volume; Erica B. Baum, "When the Witch Doctors Agree: The Family Support Act and Social Science Research," *Journal of Policy Analysis and Management* 10 (1991): 603–15; and Eleanor Clift, "Reagan Condemns Welfare System, Says It's Made Poverty Worse Instead of Better," *Los Angeles Times*, February 16, 1986, I, 4.

39. Baum, "When the Witch Doctors Agree"; Katz, *Price of Citizenship*, 57–56, 70–71; Pierson, *Dismantling the Welfare State?*, 122–25, 202 n. 80; and Hacker, "Getting Rough on the Poor."

40. Katz, *Price of Citizenship*, 71–76; Baum, "When the Witch Doctors Agree," 613. On the Manpower Demonstration Research Corporation, Alice O'Connor, *Poverty Knowledge: Social Science, Social Policy, and the Poor in Twentieth-Century U.S. History* (Princeton, N.J.: Princeton University Press, 2001), 231–37, 258–59.

41. Katz, *Price of Citizenship*, 73; Charles Nobel, *Welfare As We Knew It: A Political History of the American Welfare State* (New York: Oxford University Press, 1997), 122–23.

42. Berkowitz, *America's Welfare State*, 147; Pierson, *Dismantling the Welfare State?*, 125; Katz, *Price of Citizenship*, 75–76, 96–97; percentages calculated from Lawrence Mishel and Jared Bernstein, *The State of Working America, 1992–1993* (Armonk, N.Y.: Economic Policy Institute and M. E. Sharpe, 1993), 290; Mimi Abramovitz, "Why Welfare Reform Is a Sham," *The Nation*, September 26, 1988, 238–41; Michael Novak, "Will Welfare Bill Break the Cycle of Poverty?," *Los Angeles Times*, October 9, 1988, V, 5.

43. Stockman quoted in Pierson, *Dismantling the Welfare State?*, 125. The EITC is summarized in chapter 6 of the present volume.

44. Campagna, *Economy in the Reagan Years*, 80; Pierson, *Dismantling the Welfare State?*, 125. Gary Burtless, "The Supply-Side Legacy of the Reagan Years: Effects on Labor Supply," in Anandi P. Sahu and Ronald L. Tracy, eds., *The Economic Legacy of the Reagan Years: Euphoria or Chaos?* (New York: Praeger, 1991), 46.

45. Albelda et al., *Real World Macro*, 95; Lester C. Thurow, "Baseball Economics: Carter Whips Reagan 6 to 1," *Los Angeles Times*, May 20, 1984, V, 3.

46. Lawrence R. Klein, "Recovery May Be Partly an Illusion," *Los Angeles Times*, September 11, 1984, IV, 3, and Ackerman, *Hazardous to Our Wealth*, 138–41.

47. *Poverty, 1998*, B-2; Schaller, *Reckoning with Reagan*, 47; "Reaganomics Report Card"; Krugman, *Peddling Prosperity*, 108, 117, 125–27, 158.

48. Albelda et al., *Real World Macro*, 93; quotation in Bob Drogin, "True Victims of Poverty: The Children," *Los Angeles Times*, July 30, 1985, I, 11.

49. Paul Krugman, "The Right, the Rich, and the Facts: Deconstructing the Income Distribution Debate," *American Prospect*, Fall 1992, 19–31.

50. Mishel and Bernstein, *State of Working America, 1992–1993*, 50, for 1980–89.

51. Krugman, "Right, the Rich, and the Facts"; Kevin Phillips, *Boiling Point: Democrats, Republicans and the Decline of Middle-Class Prosperity* (New York: Harper Perennial, 1994), 103–22; Mishel and Bernstein, *State of Working America, 1992–1993*, 284, 432; Christopher Jencks, "Is the American Underclass Growing," in Christopher Jencks and Paul E. Peterson, eds., *The Urban Underclass* (Washington: Brookings Institution, 1991).

52. For quotations, Mishel and Bernstein, *State of Working America, 1992–1993*, 271–72. See also Rebecca M. Blank, "Why Were Poverty Rates So High in the 1980s?," in Dimitri B. Papadimitriou and Edward N. Wolff, eds., *Poverty and Prosperity in the Late Twentieth Century* (New York: St. Martin's Press, 1993), 21–57.

53. Mishel and Bernstein, *State of Working America, 1992–1993*, 286–88; quotation in Drogin, "True Victims of Poverty."

54. Mishel and Bernstein, *State of Working America, 1992–1993*, 32–41, 306. Real median family incomes rose 4.2% (1979–89).

55. "Sever labor shortage" from Novak, "Will Welfare Bill Break the Cycle of Poverty?" The 1999 *Economic Report of the President* (Washington: Government Printing Office, 1999), 41. In 1987 Massachusetts's unemployment rate was 2.7%, half the national average, and McDonald's was offering twice the minimum wage to entice employees (Krugman, *Peddling Prosperity*, 41, 209). But see chapters 5 and 10 in the present volume; Albelda et al., *Real World Macro*, 94; Mishel and Bernstein, *State of Working America, 1992–1993*, 216. For changing definitions of full employment, Bluestone and Harrison, *Growing Prosperity*, 155–65.

56. Benjamin Zycher, "Even the Poor Profited in the Reagan Years," *Los Angeles Times*, December 15, 1992, B7.

57. Morton Kondracke, "The Two Black Americas," *New Republic*, February 6, 1989, as quoted in Stephanie Coontz, *The Way We Never Were: American Families and the Nostalgia Trap* (New York: Basic Books, 1992), 235; chapter 8 in the present volume, esp. on Moyers; Coontz, *Way We Never Were*, 232–54; and Patterson, *America's Struggle against Poverty*, 209–16.

58. Mishel and Bernstein, *State of Working America, 1992–1993*, 206–7; Coontz, *Way We Never Were*, 245; Richard Child Hill and Cynthia Negry, "Deindustrialization and Racial Minorities in the Great Lakes Region, USA," in D. Stanley Eitzen and Maxine Baca Zinn, eds., *The Reshaping of America: Social Consequences of the Changing Economy* (Englewood Cliffs, N.J.: Prentice-Hall, 1989), 168–78.

59. Gilens, *Why Americans Hate Welfare*, esp. 146; *Poverty, 1998*, table B-2. Rates for non-Hispanic whites.

60. Barry Bearak, "Poor Share Work Ethic, U.S. Dream," *Los Angeles Times*, July 29, 1985, I, 1, 8–9.

61. Richard E. Meyer and Barry Bearak, "Poverty: Toll Grows amid Aid Cutbacks," *Los Angeles Times*, July 28, 1985, I, 7.

62. Ibid.; quotation from Robert Greenstein, in Sam Fullwood III and Stanley

Meisler, "Public Apathy Runs High As Problems of Poor Mount," *Los Angeles Times*, July 19, 1990, A1, A18–A19; Gilens, *Why Americans Hate Welfare*, 121–27.

63. Robin Wright, "Gimme Shelter: The Plight of the Homeless in Lands of Plenty," *Los Angeles Times*, October 4, 1994, World Report, 1, 5.

64. Christopher Jencks, *The Homeless* (1994; Cambridge, Mass.: Harvard University Press, 1995), 1–20; Jonathan Kozol, *Rachel and Her Children: Homeless Families in America* (New York: Fawcett Columbine, 1989), 3, 204.

65. Many of the 50s "bums" had housing—a tiny room in a cheap hotel. Joel Blau, *The Visible Poor: Homelessness in the United States* (New York: Oxford University Press, 1993), believes that veterans accounted for one-third of the adult male homeless, a proportion that was smaller than their representation (41%) in the general adult male population. Kozol, *Rachel and Her Children*, 206, claims that 60% of New York City homeless were in families, Blau that 40% were in families in Chicago and Boston.

66. Jencks, *The Homeless*, 21–40; Kevin Roderick, "Homeless—Left Behind by Recovery," *Los Angeles Times*, February 17, 1985, I, 1, 3, 32–34.

67. Kozol, *Rachel and Her Children*, 1–2, 8, 32.

68. Roderick, "Homeless—Left Behind."

69. Ibid., 34.

70. The 1999 *Economic Report of the President*, 377; *Poverty, 1998*, B-2.

71. Wright, "Gimme Shelter."

72. On single-room occupancy units, see Charles Hoch and Robert A. Slayton, *New Homeless and Old: Community and the Skid Row Hotel* (Philadelphia: Temple University Press, 1989), esp. 116–17; Blau, *Visible Poor*, 75. Five million households paid 60% of their income to rent (Kozol, *Rachel and Her Children*, 11). "Affordable housing" is that which does not cost a family more than 25–30% of its total income.

73. Kozol, *Rachel and Her Children*, 11–12, 17, 34, 36–37.

74. Blau, *Visible Poor*, 28, shows that depending on the city, between 2% and 40% of the homeless were employed. See also Press Release, Mayors' 16th "Annual Survey on Hunger and Homelessness in America's Cities Finds Increased Levels of Hunger, Increased Capacity to Meet Demand," December 14, 2000, at <http://www.usmayors .org/uscm/news/press_releases/documents/hunger_release.htm> (November 2, 2001); National Alliance to End Homelessness, "A Plan: Not a Dream, How to End Homelessness in Ten Years," at <http://www.naeh.org/pub/tenyear/demograp .htm>, accessed November 2, 2001; and Volunteers of America, "Many Working Families Are Joining the Ranks of the Homeless, New Survey Says," January 10, 2001, at <http://www.voa.org/tier3_cd.cfm?content_item_id=1098&folder_id=124>, accessed November 5, 2001. On disasters and scandals in federal housing programs under Reagan, see Pierson, *Dismantling the Welfare State?*, 87–99; Palmer and Sawhill, *Reagan Record*, 372–73; Jencks, *Homeless*, 95–97; Katz, *Price of Citizenship*, 120–23; and Kozol, *Rachel and Her Children*, 133–34.

75. Kozol, *Rachel and Her Children*, 194–204; Blau, *Visible Poor*, 113–14, on the McKinney Act (1987). Why not rely on organizations like Habitat for Humanity for low-cost housing? Since 1976, Habitat has built only 30,000 houses in the United

States, about 1,000 a year. On how the boom of the 90s made people housing poor by raising the demand for housing, Steven Greenhouse, "Janitors Struggle at the Edges of Silicon Valley's Success," *New York Times*, April 18, 2000, A12.

76. Berman, *America's Right Turn*, 138–49; E. J. Dionne Jr., *They Only Look Dead: Why Progressives Will Dominate the Next Political Era* (New York: Touchstone Books, 1997), 68–69.

77. He went shopping for socks to show that he was a regular guy, but he did not know what a scanner was. See also George Will, "Ahoy! Is That a Middle Class?" *Newsweek*, November 4, 1991, 80, and "Bush Sinks to Modern Low in Stewardship," *Los Angeles Times*, October 30, 1991, B7.

78. Quotation in William H. Chafe, *The Unfinished Journey: America since World War II*, 4th ed. (New York: Oxford University Press, 1999), 504. As the election of 1992 approached, Bush and Brady berated Greenspan for high interest rates, but by then Greenspan had begun to cut interest rates to counteract recession. See Justin Martin, *Greenspan: The Man behind the Money* (Cambridge, Mass.: Perseus Publishing, 2000), 181–98.

79. Few works on the Bush administration explain the recession. See, for example, John Robert Greene, *The Presidency of George Bush* (Lawrence: University Press of Kansas, 2000), 161–63.

80. Bluestone and Harrison, *Growing Prosperity*, 128–29.

81. For the quotation, Amott, "6% Solution," 6. On union contracts, *SA, 1992*, table 664; inflation rates, U.S. Department of Labor, Bureau of Labor Statistics, *CPI: Detailed Report, Data for February 1997* (Washington: Government Printing Office, 1997), 84. John Miller, "Soft Landing, Hard Times: The Fed Brings the Economy Down," *Dollars & Sense*, November 1989, 6–8, 21; James Risen, "Slow Growth Seen Plaguing Economy for Years to Come," *Los Angeles Times*, November 25, 1991, A1, A14. See also the 1999 *Economic Report of the President*, 412; Krugman, *Peddling Prosperity*, 122–23; Henwood, *Wall Street*, 158–59; James K. Galbraith, *Created Unequal: The Crisis in American Pay* (New York: Free Press, 1998), 222–26. John Miller, "The Speculative Bubble Bursts," *Dollars & Sense*, June 1991, in Albelda et al., *Real World Macro*, 5–8.

82. Paul S. Boyer, *Promises to Keep: The United States since World War II* (Lexington, Mass.: D. C. Heath and Co., 1995), 501.

83. Ibid.; Teresa Amott, "A Recession by Any Other Name," *Dollars & Sense*, December 1990, 6–8; and Karen Tumulty, "Jobs Vanish—and May Not Return," *Los Angeles Times*, November 29, 1991, A1, A22. According to Martin, *Greenspan*, 198, Greenspan cut federal funds rates twenty-seven times over 1989–92 and got them down to 3%, below inflation rates.

84. Some economists believed heavy borrowing for the deficit raised long-term interest rates and discouraged investment.

85. The 1999 *Economic Report of the President*, 376–78.

86. Greene, *Presidency of George Bush*, 169; James H. Johnson Jr. and Walter C. Farrell Jr., "The Fire This Time: The Genesis of the Los Angeles Rebellion of 1992," in John Charles Bolger and Judith Welch Wegner, eds., *Race, Poverty, and American Cities*

(Chapel Hill: University of North Carolina Press, 1996), 166–85; Gerald Horne, *Fire This Time: The Watts Uprising and the 1960s* (Charlottesville: University of Virginia Press, 1995), 355–64.

87. Ashley Dunn and Shawn Hubler, "Unlikely Flash Points for Riots," *Los Angeles Times*, July 5, 1992, A1, A18–A19.

88. Johnson and Farrell, "Fire This Time," 168–71.

89. Dunn and Hubler, "Unlikely Flash Points for Riots."

90. Johnson and Farrell, "Fire This Time," 172–75.

91. Ibid., 166.

92. Laura D'Andrea Tyson, "U.S. Needs New Spending Priorities," *Los Angeles Times*, November 10, 1991, D2.

93. James Risen, "History May Judge Reaganomics Very Harshly," *Los Angeles Times*, November 8, 1992, D1–D11, and Mishel and Bernstein, *State of Working America, 1992–1993*, 106.

Chapter Ten

1. Jonathan Peterson, "Poverty Rate Falls to 11.3%, but Trouble Looms," *Los Angeles Times*, Sept 26, 2001, A25; Lawrence Mishel, Jared Bernstein, and John Schmitt, *The State of Working America, 1998–1999* (Ithaca, N.Y.: Cornell University Press, 1999), 291.

2. The Enterprise Foundation estimated that Los Angeles rents averaged $933 a month, or $11,196 a year. Jim Newton, "Program to Help Poor Buy Homes Is Unveiled," *Los Angeles Times*, December 8, 2000, B1, B7.

3. *Poverty, 1998*; Garth Mangum, Andrew Sum, and Neeta Fogg, "Poverty Ain't What It Used to Be," *Challenge: The Magazine of Economic Affairs* 43 (March–April 2000): 97–130. My $21,000 line is about what Americans believed was the minimum for necessities.

4. Contrast Charles Murray, "And Now for the Bad News," *Commentary*, November–December 1999, 12–15, and chapters 7–9 in the present volume. Rebecca M. Blank, "Why Were Poverty Rates so High in the 1980s?," in Dimitri B. Papadimitriou and Edward N. Wolff, eds., *Poverty and Prosperity in the Late Twentieth Century* (New York: St. Martin's Press, 1993), 21–57, showed that poverty stayed high in the 80s not because people avoided work but because jobs paid poorly.

5. Quotation in Robert A. Rosenblatt, "Economic Surge Adds 348,000 Jobs to U.S. Work Force," *Los Angeles Times*, June 8, 1996, A1, A13. See also Stuart Silverstein, "Jump in Jobless Rate Spurs Rally in Nasdaq, Dow," *Los Angles Times*, June 3, 2000, A1, A14.

6. Don Bauder, "Count on It, the Good Times Will Be a Long Time Coming," *San Diego Union-Tribune*, March 9, 2003, H1–H2; Mary Williams Walsh, "Economic Growth, Labor Costs Fan Inflation Fears," *Los Angeles Times*, April 28, 2000, A1, A25; Jared Bernstein and Dean Baker, *The Benefits of Full Employment: When Markets Work for People* (Washington: Economic Policy Institute, 2003), 13–40; and Jeff Faux, "The Fed's Unnecessary Assault on Wages," Economic Policy Institute Issue Brief #136, March 2, 2000, at <www.epinet.org.>

7. Mark T. Hooker, *The History of Holland* (Westport, Conn.: Greenwood Press, 1999), 143–55.

8. Timothy M. Smeeding, Lee Rainwater, and Gary Burtless, "U.S. Poverty in Cross-national Context," in Sheldon H. Danziger and Robert H. Haveman, eds., *Understanding Poverty* (New York: Russell Sage Foundation; Cambridge, Mass.: Harvard University Press, 2001), 162–89.

9. Chuck Collins, Betsy Leondar-Wright, and Holly Sklar, *Shifting Fortunes: The Perils of the Growing American Wealth Gap* (Boston: United for a Fair Economy, 1999), 17; Steven Greenhouse, "A Rising Tide, but Some Boats Rise Higher Than Others," *New York Times*, September 3, 2000, Wk, 3.

10. Rebecca M. Blank, *It Takes a Nation: A New Agenda for Fighting Poverty* (1997; Princeton, N.J.: Princeton University Press, 1998), 65–68, asserts that low-skill workers are not in demand. For skepticism on the skills hypothesis, Jeff Madrick, "Computers: Waiting for the Revolution," *New York Review of Books*, March 26, 1998, 29–33; David R. Howell, "The Skills Myth," *American Prospect*, Summer 1994, 81–90, and Howell, "Skills and the Wage Collapse," *American Prospect*, June 19, 2000, 74–77. James K. Galbraith, *Created Unequal: The Crisis in American Pay* (New York: Free Press, 1998), 23–36; Michael J. Handel, "Is There a Skills Crisis?," Levy Institute Public Policy Brief, no. 62A, 2001, available at <www.levy.org>; Handel, "The Skills of American Workers in Today's Labor Market," *Focus* 23 (Winter 2004): 17–25; and chapters 4 and 7 in the present volume.

11. Even Greenspan admitted that we had to look beyond skill and technological explanations to fully understand growing wage inequalities. See Barry Bluestone and Bennett Harrison, *Growing Prosperity: The Battle for Growth with Equity in the Twenty-first Century* (Berkeley: University of California Press, 2001), 193.

12. Jeff Madrick, "The Treadmill Economy," *American Prospect*, November–December 1998, 60; Aaron Bernstein, "Inequality: How the Gap between Rich and Poor Hurts the Economy," *Newsweek*, August 15, 1994, 78–83, on how poverty makes it difficult for people to acquire skills.

13. Mishel, Bernstein, and Schmitt, *State of Working America, 1998–1999*, 120–21; Frederic L. Pryor and David L. Schaffer, *Who's Not Working and Why: Employment, Cognitive Skills, Wages, and the Changing U.S. Labor Market* (Cambridge: Cambridge University Press, 2000); Urban Institute, "Are There Good Jobs for Low-Skilled Workers," January 4, 2004, event transcript at Urban Institute Web site, <www.urban.org>. See also Alan Tonelson, *The Race to the Bottom: Why a Worldwide Worker Surplus and Uncontrolled Free Trade Are Sinking American Living Standards* (Boulder, Colo.: Westview Press, 2000), 28–33; Bluestone and Harrison, *Growing Prosperity*, 193.

14. Zeynep Tufekci, "They Can Point and Click, but Still End Up Painting Walls," *Washington Post*, January 25, 2004, B04. Michael J. Handel, *Trends in Direct Measures of Job Skill Requirements*, Working Paper No. 301 (Annandale-on-Hudson, N.Y.: Jerome Levy Economics Institute, 2000), found that employer skill demands have risen no faster than the skill levels of the workforce.

15. Wall Street Journal Reports, Executive Pay, *The Wall Street Journal*, April 9, 1998,

esp. Joann S. Lublin, "Pay for No Performance," R1–R4. Executives who didn't perform but came away with millions included Jill Barad at Mattel and Michael Ovitz at Disney.

16. Howell, "Skills and the Wage Collapse," 77.

17. Benjamin Ross, "Democratic Misalliances," *Dissent*, Spring 2003, 7–10.

18. Helene Slessarev, *The Betrayal of the Urban Poor* (Philadelphia: Temple University Press, 1997), 175–81. The Children's Health Insurance Program (CHIP) serves children whose families have too much income for Medicaid but are too poor to buy health insurance. See Alexandra Starr, "Chipping Away at the Uninsured," *American Prospect*, May 22, 2000, 18–19.

19. David Moberg, "Martha Jernegons's New Shoes," *American Prospect*, June 19, 2000, 50–53; Jared Bernstein and Jeff Chapman, "The Living Wage: A Progressive Movement in Action," *Poverty and Race* 13 (January–February 2004): 1–2, 6–7, 10–11. On other Clinton efforts, Elizabeth Shogren, "White House Fighting a Quiet War on Poverty," *Los Angeles Times*, November 28, 1993, A1.

20. Robert Pollin, "Anatomy of Clintonomics," *New Left Review* 3 (May–June 2000): 25.

21. The 1999 *Economic Report of the President* (Washington: Government Printing Office, 1999), 112–14; Gary Burtless, "Growing American Inequality: Sources and Remedies," *Brookings Review*, Winter 1999, 34; and Christopher Jencks, "The Hidden Paradox of Welfare Reform," *American Prospect*, May–June 1997, 33–40. For poverty lines, *Poverty, 1998*, A–4.

22. Twentieth Century Fund, *Social Security Reform: The Basics* (New York: Century Foundation Press, 1998), esp. 11–12.

23. Neil Gilbert, "The Size and Influence of the Underclass: An Exaggerated View," *Commentary*, November–December 1999, 45.

24. For "virtually," Pollin, "Anatomy of Clintonomics," 20; for the longer quotation, Bluestone and Harrison, *Growing Prosperity*, 128, 158. On the liberal side were appointments to the National Labor Relations Board and verbal support for a ban on striker replacements. But those actions were the minimum expected of a Democratic president. On NAFTA as an effort to clamp down on prices and wages, Bluestone and Harrison, *Growing Prosperity*, 15.

25. For a defense of Clinton, Ronald Brownstein, "Clinton's Biggest Gains Not on the Conservative Critics' Radar," *Los Angeles Times*, June 28, 2004, A10.

26. Gary Bryner, *Politics and Public Morality: The Great American Welfare Reform Debate* (New York: W. W. Norton and Co., 1998), 11, 17, 67–78, 107, 152; Edward D. Berkowitz, *America's Welfare State: From Roosevelt to Reagan* (Baltimore: Johns Hopkins University Press, 1991), 100–111; Anthony S. Campagna, *Economic Policy in the Carter Administration* (Westport, Conn.: Greenwood Press, 1995), 157–66; Paul Pierson, *Dismantling the Welfare State?: Reagan, Thatcher, and the Politics of Retrenchment* (New York: Cambridge University Press, 1995), 115–28; Ed Gillespie and Bob Schellhas, eds., *Contract with America: The Bold Plan by Rep. Newt Gingrich, Rep. Dick Armey and the House Republicans to Change the Nation* (New York: Times Books, 1994), 65–77, 169–96.

27. Bryner, *Politics and Public Morality*, 114–15.

28. Ron Haskins, "Effects of Welfare Reform on Family Income and Poverty," in Rebecca Blank and Ron Haskins, eds., *The New World of Welfare Reform* (Washington: Brookings Institution, 2001), 103–36, esp. 106, 120. Liberals who supported welfare reform hoping to get job and training programs did not get much. Some scholars in government seemed to think that rational arguments would carry the day, but without political pressures for the poor, conservatives often got their way, regardless of what was rational and humane. Some liberals resigned their positions in the Department of Health and Human Services to protest Clinton's signing of the final bill. See Peter Edelman, "The Worst Thing Bill Clinton Has Done," *Atlantic Monthly*, March 1997, 43–58, and Frances Fox Piven and David Ellwood, "Was Welfare Reform Worthwhile?," *American Prospect*, July–August 1996, 14–15. Ellwood had been co-chair of Clinton's welfare reform task force and had written books that proposed strict time limits on welfare benefits.

29. See Public Law 104–193, 104th Cong., 2nd sess. (August 22, 1996), and Bryner, *Politics and Public Morality*, 106–82; Anne Marie Cammisa, *From Rhetoric to Reform: Welfare Policy in American Politics* (Boulder, Colo.: Westview Press, 1998), 117–31, and David A. Super, Sharon Parrott, Susan Steinmetz, and Cindy Mann, *The New Welfare Law* (Washington: Center on Budget and Policy Priorities, 1996). Although there were no new training funds in the 1996 law, in 1997 Clinton got $3 billion for welfare-to-work programs that included public service jobs to cover two years, 1997–98. See Bryner, *Politics and Public Morality*, 185–86. The 1996 law allowed states to exempt 20% of the rolls from the five-year limit for special cases. As the economy sank in 2001, some states implemented exemptions. See Peter T. Kilborn, "Recession Is Stretching the Limit on Welfare Benefits," *New York Times*, December 9, 2001, A28.

30. Sarah Brauner and Pamela Loprest, "Where Are They Now?: What States' Studies of People Who Left Welfare Tell Us," Urban Institute, Assessing the New Federalism Project, series A, no. A-32, May 1999, 8; accessed at <www.urban.org>.

31. Patrick Burns, Mark Drayse, Daniel Flaming, and Brent Haydamack, *Prisoners of Hope: Welfare to Work in Los Angeles* (Los Angeles: Economic Roundtable, 2003), and next note.

32. Little was done for fathers in poverty. Leslie Kaufman, "Are Those Leaving Welfare Better Off Now? Yes and No," *New York Times*, October 20, 2003, B1; Heath Foster, "Hard Reality of Welfare Reform Surfaces As Caseloads Creep Up," *Seattle Post Intelligencer*, May 26, 2000, at <http://seattlep-i.nwsource.com/local/welf26.shtml>; Amy Goldstein, "Forgotten Issues; Welfare Reform's Progress Is Stalled," *Washington Post*, June 1, 2000, A1, available on LexisNexis; "States Lag in Promoting Responsible Dads as Social Norm," *News and Issues* (National Center for Children in Poverty) 9 (Summer 1999): 1–2; Mary Jo Bane, "Welfare As We Might Know It," *American Prospect*, January–February 1997, 47–53; Blank, *It Takes a Nation*, 42–47; Ron Haskins, "Welfare Reform Works," and Wendell Primus, "Success of Welfare Reform Unclear," both in *News and Issues* (National Center for Children in Poverty) 10 (Winter 2000): 4–6; Carla Rivera, "5 Years Later, Welfare Reform Draws Fire from Recipients and

Advocates," *Los Angeles Times*, August 23, 2001, B3; Stephanie Simon, "Welfare Reform Offers Paradox," *Los Angeles Times*, December 30, 2001, A22.

33. Jason DeParle, "Bold Effort Leaves Much Unchanged for the Poor," *New York Times*, December 30, 1999, A1, A12–A13; Randy Albelda, "What Welfare Reform Has Wrought," *Dollars & Sense*, January–February 1999, 15–17; and Sam Mistrano, "Welfare Clock Will Run Out before Job Supply Catches Up," *Los Angeles Times*, July 16, 1999, B7; Sheldon Danziger and Jeffrey Lehman, "How Will Welfare Recipients Fare in the Labor Market?," *Challenge*, March–April 1996, 30–35; Karen Houppert, "You're Not Entitled!: Welfare 'Reform' Is Leading to Government Lawlessness," *The Nation*, October 25, 1999, 17.

34. For a more upbeat assessment, see Haskins, "Effects of Welfare Reform."

35. Center on Budget and Policy Priorities, "Average Incomes of Very Poor Families Fell during Early Years of Welfare Reform, Study Finds," <www.cbpp.org./8-22-99 wel.htm>. See also Christopher Jencks and Joseph Swingle, "Without a Net: Whom the New Welfare Law Helps and Hurts," *American Prospect*, January 3, 2000, 37–41.

36. Pamela Loprest, "How Families That Left Welfare Are Doing: A National Picture," Urban Institute, Assessing the New Federalism Project, series B, no. B-1, August 1999, accessed at <www.urban.org>.

37. Work, Welfare and Families and the Chicago Urban League, *Living with Welfare Reform: A Survey of Low-Income Families in Illinois* (Chicago, 2000).

38. Associated Press, "Wisconsin Welfare Reform a Mixed Bag, Study Shows," *Los Angeles Times*, April 12, 2001, A31; Simon, "Welfare Reform Offers Paradox." Wisconsin officials operated a Catch-22 system. People who found jobs upon leaving welfare but lost them in the recession were deemed not worthy of cash aid because they had shown themselves job-ready.

39. Robert L. Jackson, "Family Welfare Rolls Show Slight Drop," *Los Angeles Times*, September 6, 2001, A14; Blaine Harden, "2-Parent Families Rise after Change in Welfare Laws," *New York Times*, Aug. 12, 2001, I, 1, 24.

40. Sheldon Danziger and Rucker C. Johnson, "From Welfare to the Low-Wage Labor Market," May 27, 2004, at <http://www.lowwagework.org/Sheldon%20Danzi ger%20paper%205-27-04.htm>.

41. Burns et al., *Prisoners of Hope*, 134–40. On a different state with equally troubling results, see Marilyn Edelhoch, "Welfare Reform in South Carolina: 'Roughly Right,'" 7–14; Sheila D. Collins and Gertrude Schaffner Goldberg, "South Carolina's Welfare Reform: More Rough than Right," 16–33; Frances Fox Piven, "What's Really Happening in South Carolina?," 34–37; and Marilyn Edelhoch with Linda S. Martin, "Rebuttal," 42–46, all in *Social Policy* 29 (Spring 1999).

42. Estimate based on previously mentioned sources and Sharon Hays, *Flat Broke with Children: Women in the Age of Welfare Reform* (New York: Oxford University Press, 2004), 50, 224, and Gregory Acs and Pamela Loprest, *Leaving Welfare: Employment and Well-Being of Families That Left Welfare in the Post-Entitlement Era* (Kalamazoo, Mich.: W. E. Upjohn Institute for Employment Research, 2004), 41–42, 74–76.

43. Michael Massing, "The End of Welfare?," *New York Review of Books*, October 7,

1999, 22–26; Tony Perry, "Rise in Homeless Families Strains San Diego Aid," *Los Angeles Times*, January 24, 2000, A3–A20; and Center on Budget and Policy Priorities, "Low Unemployment, Rising Wages Fuel Poverty Decline," <www.cbpp.org/9-30-99pov.htm>. According to Pollin, "Anatomy of Clintonomics," 26, 4.4 million Americans were cut from the Food Stamp Program over 1995–97.

44. Manpower Demonstration Research Corporation, "Los Angeles's Jobs-Focused Welfare Program Meets Its Major Goals—Further Progress Lies Ahead," August 1, 2000, press release, at <http://www.mdrc.org/PressReleases/LAGAIN-NEWWS-7-2000PR1.htm>, accessed August 5, 2000; Burns et al., *Prisoners of Hope*, 69–126. Gordon L. Berlin, "Welfare That Works: Lessons from Three Experiments That Fight Dependency and Poverty by Rewarding Work," *American Prospect*, June 19, 2000, 71. See also Marlene Cimons, "Welfare Plan Gives Families Surer Footing, Study Says," *Los Angeles Times*, June 1, 2000, A1, A21; Judith Graham, "Study Finds Welfare Plan Surprise," *Chicago Tribune*, June 1, 2000, accessed at <http://chicagotribune.com/news/printedition/article/0,2669,SAVE-0006010213.FF.html> on June 25, 2000; William Raspberry, "Two Takes on Welfare Reform," *Washington Post*, June 5, 2000, A17, accessed at <http://washingtonpost.com/wp-dyn/articles/A62489-2000Jun4.html> on June 25, 2000; Manpower Demonstration Research Corporation, "Minnesota's Welfare Reform Brings Dramatic Results for Long-Term Recipients and Their Children," press release, at <http://www.mdrc.org/PressReleasesmfippr.htm>, accessed June 23, 2000; and Virginia Knox, Cynthia Miller, and Lisa A. Gennetian (Manpower Demonstration Research Corporation), "Reforming Welfare and Rewarding Work: A Summary of the Final Report on the Minnesota Family Investment Program," at <http://www.mdrc.org/Reports2000/MFIP/MFIPSummary.htm>, accessed June 23, 2000.

45. A careful reading of *Losing Ground* shows that ending poverty was less important than getting people off government support. The same could be said of Clinton administration officials who publicized declines in the rolls but acknowledged as "unanswered the question of what happens to individual welfare recipients when they leave the rolls. Do they get jobs and prosper? . . . Are they driven deeper into poverty?" Melissa Healy, "Welfare Cases Drop 20% in U.S., Study Finds," *Los Angeles Times*, May 10, 1997, A1, A9.

46. Vicki Lens, "TANF: What Went Wrong and What to Do Next," *Social Work* 47 (July 2002): 279–90. Houppert, "You're Not Entitled!," 17. On Idaho and South Carolina, Joshua Green, "Holding Out" and "Tough Sanctions, Tough Luck," *American Prospect*, June 19, 2000, 33, 38.

47. In New York City, low-wage jobs grew more rapidly than high-wage jobs. Factory jobs vanished, and people leaving welfare and immigrants flooded the labor market. See Steven Greenhouse, "Low-Paid Jobs Lead Advance in Employment," *New York Times*, October 1, 2000, I, 1, 56. Kenneth Hanson and Karen S. Hamrick, *Moving Public Assistance Recipients into the Labor Force, 1996–2000*, U.S. Department of Agriculture, posted at <www.ers.usda.gov>, accessed May 21, 2004, estimated that 2 million people leaving welfare helped depress wages for low-income workers by between 2.3% and 7.2%.

48. John Miller, "1994, As the Economy Expands, Opportunity Contracts," *Dollars & Sense*, May–June 1994, 8–11, 37, and Tonelson, *Race to the Bottom*, 19–23.

49. Clinton quoted in Charles O. Jones, "Campaigning to Govern: The Clinton Style," in Colin Campbell and Bert A. Rockman, eds., *The Clinton Presidency: First Appraisals* (Chatham, N.J.: Chatham House Publishers, 1996), 29. See, too, Paul J. Quirk and Joseph Hinchliffe, "Domestic Policy: The Trials of a Centrist Democrat," in Campbell and Rockman, *Clinton Presidency*, 262–89; Robert B. Reich, *Locked in the Cabinet* (New York: Alfred A. Knopf, 1997), 26–31; and Bluestone and Harrison, *Growing Prosperity*, 13–15, 118–22. Congressional Republicans filibustered Clinton's modest stimulus package to death.

50. U.S. Department of Commerce, Bureau of Economic Analysis, "Gross Domestic Product, in Current Dollars and in Chained (1996) Dollars," at <http://www.bea .doc.gov/bea/dn/gdplev.htm>. The site is now without "doc" in its name and uses 2000 dollars to track real value.

51. Lawrence Mishel, Jared Bernstein, and John Schmitt, *The State of Working America, 2000–2001* (Ithaca, N.Y.: Cornell University Press, 2001), 130; Greg Krikorian, "Living Wage Hard to Find in the Northwest," *Los Angeles Times*, January 10, 1999, A12; John Schmitt, Lawrence Mishel, and Jared Bernstein, "Dangers for European Workers in the U.S. Model," *Working USA*, May–June 1998, 73–85; and Bernstein and Baker, *Benefits of Full Employment*, 41–45. The record economic expansion lasted from spring of 1991 until spring of 2001.

52. Louis Uchitelle, "Companies Try Dipping Deeper into the Labor Pool," *New York Times*, March 26, 2000, I, 1, 26. Peter G. Gosselin, "Job Picture Still Rosy As Hiring Gets Creative," *Los Angeles Times*, August 30, 1999, A1, A15, noted that in many occupations wages were not rising, despite alleged labor shortages. For higher wages, Jerry Hirsch, "Costco's Profit Warning Sends Major Retail Stocks Plunging," *Los Angeles Times*, May 25, 2000, C1, C4.

53. Peter G. Gosselin, "A Rising Tide Puts the Nation to Work," *Los Angeles Times*, April 11, 1999; Warren Vieth, "Layoffs Push Jobless Rate to 6-Year High," *Los Angeles Times*, December 8, 2001, C1, C3.

54. Mishel, Bernstein, and Schmitt, *State of Working America, 2000–2001*, 125–27, 157; the 1999 *Economic Report of the President*, 101–9. By 1997, the median annual earnings of full-time, year-round female workers had grown by only 3% over the 1989 level. Men's were still 4% *below* the 1989 level. Economic Policy Institute, "Jobless Gaps Still Wide despite Strong Recovery," *QWES* (*Quarterly Wage and Employment Series*) 3 (1999), at <www.epinet.org>. Also, Paul Osterman, *Securing Prosperity: The American Labor Market: How It Has Changed and What to Do about It* (Princeton, N.J.: Princeton University Press, 1999), 74.

55. DeLong quoted in Gosselin, "Rising Tide Puts the Nation to Work," A30. See also these articles in the *Los Angeles Times*: Don Lee, "Labor Supply Falling Short," September 23, 1998, D1, D6; Lee, "Labor Pinch Has Midwest Pitching Woo," December 7, 1999, A1, A24; Stuart Silverstein, "Missing the Boom-Time Bandwagon," July

30, 1998, A1–A16; and Peter G. Gosselin, "Boom Times Elude Workers with Modest Educational Skills," November 27, 1999, A1, A32.

56. The 2004 *Economic Report of the President* (Washington: Government Printing Office, 2004). Tables B-35, B-40 at <www.gpoaccess.gov/eop/tables04.html>. Job growth was just under 16% for Reagan (1980–88) and Clinton (1992–2000).

57. Mary Williams Walsh, "Sizzling Economy, Fears of Inflation Put Stocks in Dive," *Los Angeles Times*, January 29, 2000, A1–A15, highlights rising labor costs, in particular health insurance. According to Bernstein and Baker, *Benefits of Full Employment*, 82, international and other crises kept the Federal Reserve Board from activities that would have led to recession in the 90s. In other words, the people lucked out.

58. Don Lee, "2 Years, 6 Layoffs, Zero Expectations," *Los Angeles Times*, November 11, 1998, C1, C7, and other pieces in the same issue.

59. Data on involuntary job loss are from Mishel, Bernstein, and Schmitt, *State of Working America, 1998–1999*, 235.

60. Quoting the 1999 *Economic Report of the President*, 126. On 1998, Osterman, *Securing Prosperity*, 49–53, 125. Even Greenspan admitted that much success against inflation came because of "a heightened sense of job insecurity and, as a consequence, subdued wages"; quoted in Pollin, "Anatomy of Clintonomics," 39. Opposing views on whether workers were more insecure are Davan Maharaj, "Layoffs: A Company's Strategy of First Resort," *Los Angeles Times*, November 11, 1998, C1, C7, and Sanford M. Jacoby, "Most Workers Find a Sense of Security in Corporate Life," *Los Angeles Times*, September 7, 1998, B5.

61. Mishel, Bernstein, and Schmitt, *State of Working America, 1998–1999*, 226–50, and Osterman, *Securing Prosperity*, 45–60. I have not found evidence for a long-term increase in the number of independent contractors, and the trends of full-time/part-time shares are complex. Over the 1990s, the share of all workers who were full-time, year-round employees rose. Lawrence Mishel, Jared Bernstein, and Sylvia Allegretto, *State of Working America, 2004–2005* (Ithaca, N.Y.: Cornell University Press, 2005), 256–57.

62. Bronfenbrenner cited in Tonelson, *Race to the Bottom*, 47.

63. Economic experience in the late 90s threatened the theory of the nonaccelerating inflation rate of unemployment (NAIRU), which assumed that once unemployment dipped below 6%, wages and inflation would soar. In the 90s unemployment fell far below 6% without boosting inflation much, and NAIRU appeared dead. However, if I am right, the nearby labor force and hidden unemployment saves NAIRU, for there were still millions ready to go to work.

64. Government distributed two monthly job numbers, and they sometimes differed by millions. See Elise Gould, "Measuring Employment since the Recovery: A Comparison of the Household and Payroll Surveys," December 2003, <www.epinet.org>.

65. Bluestone and Harrison, *Growing Prosperity*, 98.

66. The U.S. Labor Department and Census Bureau create broader unemployment rates. U-6, which includes discouraged workers and part-timers wanting full-time work, may be double the official unemployment rate. Check table A-12, "Alternative

Measures of Labor Underutilization," on the Bureau of Labor Statistics site, at <www
.bls.census.gov/cps/empsit.t12>. These higher rates are not widely publicized. An
exception is Uchitelle, "Companies Try Dipping Deeper."

67. Bluestone and Harrison, *Growing Prosperity*, 285 n. 87.

68. For numbers 5 to 14, Gosselin, "Rising Tide Puts the Nation to Work," and Don
Lee, "A Rising Tide Puts the Nation to Work: The Real Winners," *Los Angeles Times*,
April 11, 1999, A1, A30, A31. Jeff Madrick, "How New Is the New Economy," *New
York Review of Books*, Sept. 23, 1999, 49. On older Americans, "Employment's New
Age," *New York Times*, July 30, 2000, IV, 14; and Bluestone and Harrison, *Growing
Prosperity*, 246. Don Lee, "L.A. County Jobs Surge since '93, but Not Wages," *Los
Angeles Times*, July 26, 1999, A1, A19, suggested that immigration caused jobs paying
under $15,000 to grow twice as fast as others in the 1994–98 recovery; also Tonelson,
Race to the Bottom, 48; Louis Uchitelle, "I.N.S Is Looking the Other Way As Illegal
Immigrants Fill Jobs," *New York Times*, May 9, 2000, C1; Bruce Western, "Incarcera-
tion, Unemployment, and Inequality," *Focus* 21 (Spring 2001): 31–36; David H. Autor
and Mark G. Duggan, "The Rise in Disability Recipiency and the Decline in Unemployment," Center for Retirement Research at Boston College, September 2002; on
engineers and scientists, Lisa Girion, "Millions of Jobless Are Uncounted, New Study
Says," *Los Angeles Times*, September 4, 2000, C1–C2. On H-1B, Jube Shriver, "U.S.
Tech Firms Abusing Visa Program, Critics Say," *Los Angeles Times*, November 21,
2001, A1, A29. On increased hours of work, Barry Bluestone and Stephen Rose, *The
Unmeasured Labor Force: The Growth in Work Hours* (Annandale-on-Hudson, N.Y.:
Jerome Levy Economics Institute, 1998). On hiring the urban poor, Uchitelle, "Com-
panies Try Dipping Deeper." On independent contractors, Bluestone and Harrison,
Growing Prosperity, 98, and Lester Thurow, "The Crusade That's Killing Prosperity,"
American Prospect, March–April 1996, 56. On the global workforce, Tonelson, *Race to
the Bottom*, 53–80, esp. 56.

69. Marc-Andre Pigeon and L. Randall Wray, "Did the Clinton Rising Tide Lift All
Boats?," *Challenge*, May–June 1999, 14–33; Thurow, "Crusade That's Killing Pros-
perity"; Timothy Bartik, *Jobs for the Poor: Can Labor Demand Help?* (New York: Russell
Sage Foundation, and Kalamazoo, Mich.: W. W. Upjohn Institute for Employment
Research, 2001); Bob Herbert, "In America: Going Nowhere Fast," *New York Times*,
December 1, 1995, A33, for the Newman Study.

70. On the nearly poor, who were above federal poverty lines but dependent on
charities, Stephanie R. Niedringhaus, *Welfare Reform: How Do We Define Success?*
(Washington: Network: A National Catholic Social Justice Lobby, 2001).

71. Based on percentage of people in households below 40% of each nation's median
income. For more recent data of the same kind, see Mishel, Bernstein, and Allegretto,
State of Working America, 2004–2005, 407–12.

72. Smeeding, Rainwater, and Burtless, "U.S. Poverty in Cross-national Context,"
178; for the Canadian comparison, Lane Kenworthy, "Do Social Welfare Polices Reduce Poverty: A Cross-National Assessment," *Social Forces* 77 (March 1999): 1135. In
"Bulls Run Riot over the Unemployed," *Los Angeles Times*, June 6, 2000, B6, Robert

Scheer asked, "If the health of the economy requires a permanent pool of the under-paid and unemployed, should the well-off not return the favor by letting a few more of the crumbs fall off the table?" Antipoverty unionism is described in Harold Meyerson, "A Clean Sweep: The SEIU's Organizing Drive for Janitors Shows How Unionization Can Raise Wages," *American Prospect*, June 19, 2000, 24–29.

73. This section was instigated by a searching critique of my book by Professor Edward Berkowitz of George Washington University.

74. Christopher Howard, *The Hidden Welfare State: Tax Expenditures and Social Policy in the United States* (Princeton, N.J.: Princeton University Press, 1997), 26; Jacob S. Hacker, *The Divided Welfare State: The Battle over Public and Private Social Benefits in the United States* (Cambridge: Cambridge University Press, 2002), 14–15. The United States ends up above Ireland, Italy, Australia, Canada, and Denmark and below Finland, Sweden, the Netherlands, Germany, and the United Kingdom.

75. See also Mishel, Bernstein, and Allegretto, *State of Working America, 2004–2005*, 407–8.

76. A progressive tax break that benefits middle and lower incomes is the Earned Income Tax Credit. But most categories were regressive. See Howard, *Hidden Welfare State*, 28–32, 106, and Hacker, *Divided Welfare State*, 23–24, 36–39.

77. Randy Lowe, *The Welfare State in Britain since 1945*, 3rd ed. (New York: Palgrave Macmillan, 2005), 18–22, 337–48, and 431–38.

78. Richard Bernstein and Mark Landler, "Only Marginal Reforms Are Expected in Germany," *New York Times*, October 12, 2005, accessed at <www.nytimes.com> on October 12, 2005. Also Hooker, *History of Holland*, 147–55, for ample information that there was not much of a decline in the Dutch welfare state.

79. John-Thor Dahlburg and Richard Boudreaux, "Europe's Cheaper Rx for Health," *Los Angeles Times*, October 21, 2000, A1, A14, and Nicholas George and Nicholas Timmins, "Swedish Health System Feels Economic Pinch," *Los Angeles Times*, December 7, 2003, C4.

80. Howard, *Hidden Welfare State*, 4, 30–31, 204 n. 4.

Chapter Eleven

1. Alexander Cockburn, "The Crash," *The Nation*, October 29, 2001, 8; Peter Gosselin, "Job Losses in September Highest in a Decade," *Los Angeles Times*, October 6, 2001, C1, C8; Jeff Faux, "Bait and Switch: How Alan Greenspan Snookered the Democrats," *American Prospect*, February 25, 2002, 17–18.

2. Ricardo Alonso-Zaldivar, "Many New Jobs Going to Noncitizens," *Los Angeles Times*, June 16, 2004, A15; Louis Uchitelle, "Blacks Lose Better Jobs Faster As Middle-Class Work Drops," *New York Times*, July 12, 2003, A1, B14; Jeffrey Gettleman, "It's Like Getting Fleeced," *Los Angeles Times*, February 20, 2002, A1, A14.

3. Edmund L. Andrews, "A Growing Force of Nonworkers," *New York Times*, July 18, 2003, BU4; Lee Price and Yulia Fungard, "Understanding the Severity of the Current Labor Slump," Economic Policy Institute Briefing Paper #146 at <www.epinet.org>,

November 7, 2003 (revised February 19, 2004); Jared Bernstein and Yulia Fungard, "Jobs Picture: September's Job Growth Weaker Than Expected," at <www.epinet .org>, October 8, 2004.

4. The 2004 *Economic Report of the President* (Washington: Government Printing Office, 2004), tables B-35, B-40, at <www.gpoaccess.gov/eop/tables04.html>; Walter Hamilton, "Company Layoffs Taking a Less Damaging Toll," *Los Angeles Times*, February 3, 2001, A15. The soaring cost of health insurance is also a disincentive to hiring.

5. Edmund L. Andrews, "Report Finds Tax Cuts Heavily Favor the Wealthy," *New York Times*, August 13, 2004, A16; Andrews, "Two Countries, Two Tales of Jobs," *New York Times*, April 18, 2004, BU6; Warren Vieth, "Are Bush's Tax Cuts Doing the Job?" *New York Times*, September 29, 2004, A22; Paul Krugman, "Dooh Nibor Economics," *New York Times*, June 1, 2004, A19.

6. Louis Uchitelle, "As Stimulus, Tax Cuts May Soon Go Awry," *New York Times*, November 30, 2003, BU4; Joseph E. Stiglitz, "That Was Then," *American Prospect*, February 2004, 14–16; David Kamin and Isaac Shapiro, "Studies Shed New Light on Effects of Administration's Tax Cuts," revised September 13, 2004, esp. table 3 (accessed at <www.cbpp.org/8-25-04tax.htm>).

7. William G. Gale, Peter R. Orszag, and Isaac Shapiro, "The Ultimate Burden of the Tax Cuts," June 2, 2004, at <www.cbpp.org>, accessed June 2, 2004.

8. Jared Bernstein, "Critiquing Misleading White House Statements about the Economy: Part 1: Income Growth and Median Earnings," at <www.epinet.org>, accessed May 13, 2006. See also the 2004 *Economic Report of the President*, T-47; Michelle Conlin and Aaron Bernstein, "Working and Poor," *Business Week*, May 31, 2004, 58–68; Eduardo Porter, "Hourly Pay in U.S. Not Keeping Pace with Price Rises," *New York Times*, July 18, 2004, 1, 19.

9. Stephanie Simon, "Homeless, Helpless, Hopeless," *Los Angeles Times*, January 12, 2002, A12, A16; Center on Budget and Policy Priorities News Release, "Census Data Show Poverty Increased, Income Stagnated, and the Number of Uninsured Rose to a Record Level in 2003," August 26, 2004, at <www.cbpp.org>, accessed August 26, 2004; and Joel Havemann and Ricardo Alonso-Zaldivar, "U.S. Poverty Rate Rose Again in 2004," *Los Angeles Times*, August 31, 2005, A13.

10. Center on Budget and Policy Priorities News Release, "Census Data Show Poverty Increased."

11. "CPBB Response to HHS's Announcement that TANF Caseloads Fell in 2003," August 23, 2004, at <www.cpbb.org>, accessed August 23, 2004; Center on Budget and Policy Priorities News Release, "Census Data Show Poverty Increased." Isaac Shapiro, Robert Greenstein, and Leighton Ku, "Will Poverty, Income, and Health Insurance Coverage Improve Significantly in 2004?," August 27, 2004, at <www.cpbb .org>, accessed August 28, 2004. The number on food stamps jumped by 7.1 million (42%), indicating rising need; see Joseph Llobrera, "Food Stamp Caseloads Are Rising," August 16, 2004, at <www.cpbb.org>, accessed October 4, 2004.

12. Katha Pollitt, "$hotgun Wedding," *The Nation*, February 4, 2002, 10; Jonathan

Peterson and James Gerstenzang, "Bush Proposes 'Ethic of Work' in Welfare Plan," *Los Angeles Times*, February 27, 2002, A1, A10. There would not, for example, be much more money for child care.

13. Among the many articles I consulted on Katrina, these were especially useful: Tomas Alex Tizon, "Images of Evacuees Spark a Racial Debate," *Los Angeles Times*, September 3, 2005, A11; Jason DeParle, "Liberal Hopes Ebb in Post-Storm Poverty Debate," *New York Times*, October 11, 2005, accessed at <www.nytimes.com>; De-Parle, "What Happens to a Race Deferred," and John M. Barry, "The Prologue, and Maybe the Coda," both under "Broken Levees, Unbroken Barriers," *New York Times*, September 4, 2005, IV, 1, 4.

14. Conlin and Bernstein, "Working and Poor," 63; Peter Gosselin, "If America Is Richer, Why Are Its Families So Much Less Secure?," *Los Angeles Times*, October 10, 2004, A1, A26–A29. Elizabeth Warren and Amelial Warren Tyagi, *The Two-Income Trap: Why Middle-Class Mothers and Fathers Are Going Broke* (New York: Basic Books, 2003), for example, 84, 106.

15. Gordon Lafer, "Bush's Call for Job Training: Cruel Joke on Unemployed," *Los Angeles Times*, January 25, 2004, M5. In Sheldon H. Danziger and Daniel H. Weinberg, eds., *Fighting Poverty: What Works and What Doesn't* (Cambridge, Mass.: Harvard University Press, 1986), 173–79, "Comment by Christopher Jencks."

16. Gene Sperling, "The Road to Zero: Still Not There Yet, Private Sector Job Growth under President Bush," Center for American Progress, June 3, 2005, at <www .americanprogress.org>, accessed September 26, 2006. Aaron Bernstein, "Waking Up from the American Dream," *Business Week*, December 1, 2003, 54–58.

17. Ralph Nader, in "Liberalism Regained: Building the Next Progressive Majority," *Harper's*, August 2004, 34.

18. Jeff Chapman and Jared Bernstein, "Immigration and Poverty: Disappointing Income Growth in the 1990s Not Solely the Result of a Growing Immigration Population," Briefing Paper #130 (Washington: Economic Policy Institute, 2002). I suspect that immigrants were undercounted; if fully counted, they might have added a bit more to poverty rates.

19. Eduardo Porter, "Cost of Illegal Immigration May Be Less Than Meets the Eye," *New York Times*, April 16, 2006, BU3.

20. Eduardo Porter and Teresa Watanabe, "L.A. Workers Join Fierce Debate over Immigration," *Los Angeles Times*, February 20, 2006, A1, A18.

21. John M. Broder, "Immigrants and the Economics of Hard Work," *New York Times*, April 2, 2006, Wk, 3.

22. "Unemployment Is Harder Here," *Labor Party Press*, September 2001, 5.

23. Paul Krugman and Robin Wells, "The Health Care Crisis and What to Do about It," *New York Review of Books*, March 23, 2006, 38–43.

24. The California Budget Project, *Making Ends Meet: How Much Does It Cost to Raise a Family in California* (Sacramento: California Budget Project, 2005), estimated that a single parent with two children in California needed about $54,000 a year to pay for the

basics. See also Denton R. Vaughan, "Exploring the Use of the Views of the Public to Set Income Poverty Thresholds and Adjust Them over Time," at <http://www.census.gov/hhes/www/povmeas/approaches.html>, accessed February 2, 2006.

25. Relevant is Anita Mathur, Judy Reichle, Julie Strawn, and Chuck Wiseley, *From Jobs to Careers: How California Community College Credentials Pay Off for Welfare Participants* (N.p.: California Community Colleges Chancellor's Office and Center for Law and Social Policy, 2004).

26. Robert G. Lynch, *Exceptional Returns: Economic, Fiscal, and Social Benefits of Investment in Early Childhood Development* (Washington: Economic Policy Institute, 2004); Richard Rothstein, "Cheapskate Conservatives Cheat Students," *Los Angeles Times*, April 3, 2005, M1, M3; a special report, "Starting Young: The Case for Investment in America's Kids," in *American Prospect* 15 (November 2004): A1–A24; and James J. Heckman, "Doing It Right: Job Training and Education," *Public Interest*, Spring 1999, 86–107.

27. Center on Budget and Policy Priorities News Release, "Census Data Show Poverty Increased."

28. Joan Williams and Ariane Hegwisch, "All Work and No Play Is the U.S. Way," *Los Angeles Times*, August 30, 2004, B9; John de Graaf, "Gimme a Break!," *Los Angeles Times*, September 4, 2005, M3.

29. Karen Christopher, "Family Friendly Europe," *American Prospect*, April 8, 2002; Timothy Smeeding, "Why the U.S. Anti-Poverty System Doesn't Work Very Well," *Challenge*, January–February 1992, 30–35.

30. Conlin and Bernstein, "Working and Poor," 63.

Appendix Two

1. Office of Planning, Research, and Evaluation, Office of Economic Opportunity, *The Poor in 1970: A Chartbook* (Washington: Government Printing Office, 1972), 18. The rural percentage of all the poor was 47.6%. The rest of the poor lived in central cities (32%) or suburbs (20.4%).

2. Sar A. Levitan, *The Great Society's Poor Law: A New Approach to Poverty* (Baltimore: Johns Hopkins University Press, 1969), 227–70; Henry Hampton's PBS series *America's War on Poverty, In Service to America* (pt. 4), on Kentucky and California Rural Legal Assistance; and Lee Romney, "End of Welfare Leaves Rural Poor in a Bind," *Los Angeles Times*, April 6, 2003, B1, B10.

3. Office of Planning, Research, and Evaluation, Office of Economic Opportunity, *The Poor in 1970*, 30–31; Richard Parker, *The Myth of the Middle Class* (New York: Harper Colophon Books, 1974), 105; Bradley R. Schiller, *The Economics of Poverty and Discrimination*, 8th ed. (Upper Saddle River, N.J.: Prentice-Hall, 2001), 105–6.

4. Mollie Orshansky, "Counting the Poor: Another Look at the Poverty Profile," *Social Security Bulletin*, January 1965, 16–43.

BIBLIOGRAPHICAL ESSAY

The notes to each chapter in this book open avenues for further research. Here I highlight works of history. What follows is a sketch, not the full-blown article that someone might write on the historiography of poverty in modern America.

One should start with two basic sources. The first is the Census Bureau's annual report on poverty lines and poverty thresholds. The report appears in late August and covers the previous year. The 2001 edition was called *Poverty in the United States: 2000*. In recent years the bureau has broadened the title of these annual reports, and the 2005 edition was called *Income, Poverty, and Health Insurance Coverage in the United States: 2004*. One may purchase hard copies from the Government Printing Office, but it is easy to print a copy from the U.S. Census Bureau's Web site, <www.census.gov>. A second valuable reference work that includes dozens of articles, source listings, and a minihistory on the modern period is Gwendolyn Mink and Alice O'Connor, eds., *Poverty in the United States: An Encyclopedia of History, Politics, and Policy* (2004).

Three books offer historical surveys: James T. Patterson, *America's Struggle against Poverty in the Twentieth Century* (2000), Michael B. Katz, *The Undeserving Poor: From the War on Poverty to the War on Welfare* (1989), and Alice O'Connor, *Poverty Knowledge: Social Science, Social Policy, and the Poor in Twentieth-Century U.S. History* (2001). Although it lacks much conceptualization, Patterson's book is valuable because it packs one hundred years of history into 250 pages. Katz writes mostly an intellectual history of the 60s, 70s, and 80s; he examines how Americans constructed negative stereotypes of the undeserving poor and the underclass. O'Connor's book is high-level intellectual history and, in its grasp of the subject, authoritative. The next step will be for historians to explain why American researchers and intellectuals have so often taken the low road, blaming the poor and ignoring class structures that channel people into poverty. Maurice Isserman's *The Other American: The Life of Michael Harrington* (2000) is a well-researched biography of a leading socialist who usually avoided the low road, except in his most famous book, *The Other America: Poverty in the United States* (1962).

While there is a fair amount of serious historical work on ideas and—as we will see—politics and policy, there is not so much history of poor people from the bottom up. It is as though the call for the history of the common people in the 1960s helped to shape women's history, ethnic history, and labor history but never got to the subject of poor people in the postwar era. Examples of what can be done include journalist Nicholas

Lemann's *The Promised Land: The Great Black Migration and How It Changed America* (1992), which blends a history of the common people with stories of the War on Poverty; sociologist Nancy Naples's *Grassroots Warriors: Activist Mothering, Community Work, and the War on Poverty* (1998); and Jacqueline Jones's *The Dispossessed: America's Underclass from the Civil War to the Present* (1992).

Undoubtedly, others have written histories of poor people that I do not know about, but there does not seem to be much in published books and articles. An adequate history of the poor in the postwar era would have to be written as part of a history of the working class, or, to use a softer term, that majority of Americans who, while not poor, lived close to the edge. The poor should not be isolated in a separate history that assumes that they are fundamentally different from the nonpoor.

A subtopic one might study, for example, is how blue-collar workers felt about poverty, poor people, and their own situation in the 40s and 50s. We all know the sentiment that in the old days "we were poor but did not know it," but was it true? A related topic involves the way union leaders and union activists thought about the poor and how that affected their politics. An adequate history of poor people would have to study the apparently nonpoor working class. The lines were not rigid, and many who were poor would become not poor and vice versa. Also, histories of the poor and the working class would have to study people's real incomes and their experience with unemployment and underemployment. I do not think such a history of the economics of daily life has been written for the postwar era. Some of the data for such a study are presented clearly in Frank Levy, *The New Dollars and Dreams: American Incomes and Economic Change* (1998).

Frances Fox Piven and Richard A. Cloward were not historians, but in two books they wrote brilliant synthetic histories in which they attended to poor people *and* to massive economic change and the dynamic situation of politicians interacting with the poor. *Regulating the Poor: The Functions of Public Welfare* (1971) tried to comprehend the poor as a part of the working class. *Poor People's Movements: Why They Succeed, How They Fail* (1977) included for the 30s and 60s four of the most provocative historical sketches of poor people in action that I have ever read. Readers might not agree with all of Cloward and Piven's conclusions, but they could not find a better introduction to poverty history than these two works by a political scientist and a sociologist. Cloward and Piven explored big explanations of why things turned out the way they did in America.

In contrast to the scarcity of historians writing about the poor from the bottom up, there is a fair amount of history on the development of policy, welfare, and the welfare state. A good place to begin is Edward D. Berkowitz's informed and compact survey, *America's Welfare State: From Roosevelt to Reagan* (1991). A politically engaged study of the welfare program itself is Gertrude Schaffner Goldberg and Sheila D. Collins, *Washington's New Poor Law: Welfare Reform and the Roads Not Taken, 1935 to the Present* (2001). Robert C. Lieberman, *Shifting the Color Line: Race and the American Welfare State* (1998), is one of several books arguing that racism and sexism were built into America's welfare state from its beginning in the 30s. Jill Quadagno, *The Color of Welfare: How Racism*

Undermined the War on Poverty (1994), does not always convince, but she asks significant questions about social programs in the modern era.

Anyone thinking deeply about the history of government's role should consult the many works of Theda Skocpol and also Charles Noble, *Welfare As We Knew It: A Political History of the American Welfare State* (1997). Two books about why economic policy went bad are Gary Mucciaroni, *The Political Failure of Employment Policy, 1945–1982* (1990) and Judith Russell, *Economics, Bureaucracy, and Race: How Keynesians Misguided the War on Poverty* (2004).

There are two well-lit paths to the history of the War on Poverty in the 1960s. First, Allen J. Matusow's chapters in *The Unraveling of America: A History of Liberalism in the 1960s* (1984) are the best scholarly introduction to the subject. Second, Henry Hampton's six-part video series *America's War on Poverty* (1995) is a watchable and provocative piece of historical investigation.

An emerging subfield attends to the balance of public and private welfare and why the United States devotes an unusually large amount of resources to the private side. Much of the focus is on the years before the 1950s and 1960s, but both of these books are essential to historians of the postwar era: Jacob S. Hacker, *The Divided Welfare State: The Battle over Public and Private Social Benefits in the United States* (2002), and Jennifer Klein, *For All These Rights: Business, Labor, and the Shaping of America's Public-Private Welfare State* (2003).

Of the many other works of value to historians of poverty in the postwar era, three are noteworthy. Edward D. Berkowitz's *Disabled Policy: America's Programs for the Handicapped* (1987) disentangles elements of a complex issue. Gareth Davies, *From Opportunity to Entitlement: The Transformation and Decline of Great Society Liberalism* (1996), is too pessimistic in my view but is a probing examination. Finally, sociologist Ellen Reese has written a history that reaches back to the 1940s in her well-researched *Backlash against Welfare Mothers, Past and Present* (2005).

Area Redevelopment Act (1961), 38
Association of Community Organizations for Reform Now, 243
Auletta, Ken, 165–67
Automation, 1, 26, 38, 41, 84, 160
Automobile industry, 26, 190

Baby boomers, 67, 79, 96, 107, 146, 150, 239
Baldwin, James, 48
Ball, Robert, 192
Banking industry, 203
Bankruptcies, 190, 203, 229
Bannister, Walter, 201
Baran, Paul, 29
Bartik, Timothy, 226
Bateman, Worth, 122
Berg, Ivar, 92, 93
Beyond Entitlement (Mead), 172–73
Bigart, Homer, 48
Birth control, 58, 75
Black, William, 166
Black Arts Theater, 74
Black Power movement, 100, 111, 112
Blair, Tony, 228
Blank, Rebecca, 220
Blue-collar workers, 25–26, 47, 109, 138–39, 150. *See also* Job Corps
Bluestone, Barry, 60, 92, 94
Boeing, 223
Boggs, Mary Sue, 166
Boone, Richard, 53
Borjas, George, 237
Bowles, Sam, 96
Brady, Nicholas, 203
Braverman, Harry, 96
Bronfenbrenner, Kate, 223
Bronfenbrenner, Urie, 69
Brown, Jerry, 117
Buchanan, Pat, 132
Bureau of the Budget, 56
Burns, Arthur, 29, 123, 188
Burton, Phillip, 127

Bush, George H. W., 186, 193, 195, 202–3, 204
Bush, George W., 3, 86, 231–35, 239, 243
Business of America, The (documentary), 178
Business sector, 5, 29, 81, 129, 210; anti-poverty solutions and, 236, 238, 242; conservatives and, 158, 162, 176, 180, 242; corporate taxes and, 185; Democrats and, 180, 185; deregulation of, 136, 145, 203; government regulations and, 2, 158, 163, 183, 186; investment tax credits for, 39; 1970s and, 145, 151–52, 158; 1980s and, 185, 187, 189–90, 195–97, 198, 205, 206; political/lobbying activities by, 158, 187; tax cuts/subsidies for, 10, 39, 60, 186, 187, 197, 205, 232

Califano, Joseph, 137
California, 120, 138, 184, 205; immigration effects in, 146, 224, 237
California Rural Legal Assistance, 77
California Welfare Rights Organization, 130
Capital flight, 139, 160
Capitalism, 13, 29, 153, 163, 175, 179; Democrats and, 180, 181; Marxist view of, 44; poverty and, 96, 98, 101, 227; unemployment and, 4, 44, 96
Carmichael, Stokely, 111
Carter, Hodding, III, 71
Carter, Jimmy, 117–18, 135–39, 164, 184, 190; welfare reform and, 137–38, 153, 160, 174
Castle, Mike, 194
Catholic Conference, U.S., 126
Catholic Worker movement, 44
Caudill, Harry, 48
CBS, 133, 177
CDGM. *See* Child Development Group of Mississippi

Census Bureau, U.S., 106

CETA. *See* Comprehensive Employment and Training Act

Chamber of Commerce, U.S., 126, 189

Chaney, James, 70

Chicago, Ill., 17, 26, 73, 118, 145, 150

Child care, 57, 104, 193–95, 227

Child Development Group of Mississippi, 70–72, 73

Children: nutrition programs and, 193; poverty rates and, 72, 136, 197. *See also* Education; Head Start; Welfare

Children's Health Insurance Program, 214, 233

Children's March for Survival, 129

Child support, 175, 194

China, 238

Church, Frank, 131

Civil rights, 14–15, 24, 60, 62, 84, 100, 111–12, 137, 138; Democrats linked with, 95, 180; Eisenhower and, 28; Johnson and, 41, 49, 50, 70–71, 84, 86; Kennedy and, 37–38, 41, 48; welfare rights activists and, 119

Clark, Joseph, 133

Clark, Kenneth, 88

Class, 5, 55, 89, 167, 176, 180; Marxist theory of, 95, 96–100, 101; 1950s view of, 13, 31; prejudice and, 113–14; Reagan programs and, 205; as social handicap, 14, 59–60; tax cuts and, 39, 197, 206, 232–33, 234, 240. *See also* Middle class; Underclass; Working class

Clendenin, Sam, 166

Cleveland, Ohio, 118, 120

Clinton, Bill, 3, 28, 214–23, 232; health care reform and, 86, 214, 215; welfare reform and, 194, 209–10, 216–20

Cloward, Richard, 41, 42–43, 118, 119, 128, 167–68, 181, 182

Cold War, 12, 13, 15, 50, 184, 202

Coleman, James, 69

College-level education, 53, 213, 235–36, 240

Common Cause, 127

Community action programs, 42, 53–54, 55, 60, 68, 70, 86, 121; evaluation of, 61, 72–76

Community development programs, 14, 48–49

Comprehensive Community Health Centers, 75

Comprehensive Employment and Training Act (1973), 95, 112, 134–35, 139, 153, 167, 190, 205

Congress, U.S., 15, 59, 158, 179; community action agencies and, 75–76; disability insurance reform and, 148, 191; guaranteed income program and, 2, 127–28, 129, 131; job-and-training programs and, 95, 134, 135; Kennedy and, 38; Nixon and, 121–22; Reagan and, 187, 189; Social Security and, 2, 131, 192

Congressional Black Caucus, 135

Congressional Budget Office, 232

Conservatives, 1, 6, 50, 57, 90, 97; anti-poverty policy and, 2–3, 61, 78, 82, 158, 242, 243; basic assumptions, 176–77; deficits and, 29, 164, 187; job issue and, 171–74; public debate framing by, 3, 152, 157–82, 198–99, 205, 206, 234; 1970s and, 117–18, 127, 129, 136–52 passim, 156, 157; 1980s and, 157, 183, 198–99; social programs and, 15, 129, 158, 164, 191, 198; Social Security and, 192; welfare and, 3, 117, 118, 123, 127, 133, 157, 194, 209, 216–17, 234; welfare state attacks by, 158, 159. *See also* Reagan, Ronald

Construction industry, 10, 109, 110

Consumption, 29, 106

Contingent workers, 223, 225

Conway, Jack, 48

Cottrell, Leonard, 42

Council of Economic Advisors, 20, 216

Crime, 88, 100, 106, 120; community action programs and, 73, 76; as conservatives' concern, 143, 156, 174, 179, 193, 198; media portrayals of, 179–80

Culture of poverty, 36, 88, 165; Dissenters and, 91–92, 93; Harrington's view of, 45–47; Johnson initiatives and, 51, 54, 58–59, 73

Daley, Richard, 73

Dalton, Shirley, 130

Day, Dorothy, 44

Debt, 203, 204, 205

Declining Significance of Race, The (Wilson), 160–61, 173, 174

Deficit spending, 29–30, 204; Bush and, 239; Clinton and, 221; Kennedy and, 39; Reagan and, 138, 164, 187, 191, 196, 205, 221

DeFreitas, Greg, 146

Deindustrialization, 25–28, 139, 141, 205; as poverty cause, 3, 82, 171; unions and, 117, 153

DeLong, Bradford, 222

Democratic Leadership Council, 214

Democratic Party, 15, 29, 30, 83–85, 99, 117, 135, 153, 158, 168, 184, 185, 193, 206; antipoverty solutions and, 243; civil rights and, 95, 180; community action initiatives and, 72, 73; deficit spending and, 29; guaranteed income and, 122, 127–28; Harrington and, 44, 171; tax cuts and, 39–40, 162–63, 171. *See also* Liberals

Denmark, 155

Depression: 1930s, 13, 187; 1973–75, 117, 145; 1981–82, 105, 138, 170–71, 187, 195–96, 201, 205, 223

Deregulation, 136, 145, 203

Desegregation, 121, 122

Detroit, Mich., 26, 27, 82, 118, 237

Disability insurance, 11, 12; Social Security, 136, 147–48, 188, 191

Disabled people, 217, 225, 249; benefit reform for, 147–48, 191, 193; Supplemental Security Income and, 131, 139

Discouraged workers, 106–7, 108, 109, 110, 224

Disraeli, Benjamin, 123

Dissenters, 85, 91–95, 96, 100, 112

Doering, Edith, 130

Doeringer, Peter, 93

Dole, Robert, 192

Domestic abuse, 197, 217

Douglas, Paul, 15, 19, 30, 38

Dropout rate, 149

Drug addiction, 106, 178, 217; conservative debate framing and, 156, 174, 198; homelessness and, 200, 202

Dukakis, Michael, 202

Earned Income Tax Credit, 2, 132, 139, 219, 227, 239; expansion of, 195, 205, 211, 214–15

Eastland, James, 70, 133

Economic growth, 61, 181; aggregate, 16–18, 24, 25, 28, 30–31; antipoverty solutions and, 2, 103, 104–6, 113, 142, 151, 209, 210, 211, 212, 226–27, 235; full employment and, 4, 20, 24, 104; 1950s and, 9, 10, 11, 15, 22, 28; 1960s and, 24, 39, 62, 78–79, 80, 103, 104, 106, 109, 113; 1970s and, 145, 181; 1980s and, 24, 196, 205; 1990s and, 24, 203, 218, 220–22, 226; tax cuts and, 2, 10, 39–40, 163; 2000–2005 and, 232

Economic inequality, 59–60, 212

Economic insecurity, 6, 13, 19, 26, 28, 62, 97

Economic Opportunity Act (1964), 51, 53

Economic structures, 1, 37, 92–95, 96, 99, 166

Edsall, Mary, 180

Imports, 3, 6, 145, 158, 190, 196; anti-poverty solutions and, 236, 238

Income: of African Americans, 11, 26, 48, 67, 197, 198; antipoverty solutions and, 240–41; cash transfers and, 49, 78–79; Family Assistance Plan and, 121–29, 131; 1950s and, 10, 11, 26, 28–29; 1970s and, 145; 1980s and, 197, 198; 1990s and, 203, 218; rich-poor gap in, 5–6, 13, 49, 101–2, 197, 202, 210, 211–12, 232–33, 240; skills/education linked with, 212–14. *See also* Guaranteed income; Wages

Income taxes, 39, 186–87

Inequality, 10, 13, 36, 49, 57, 60, 102, 197, 211–12, 237, 240, 243

Infant mortality, 72, 136

Inflation, 2, 152; antipoverty solutions and, 235; economic growth and, 4, 24, 104, 105, 142; interest rates and, 30, 103, 105, 113, 142, 186; 1970s and, 118, 122, 135, 138, 139, 145, 158, 185–86; 1980s and, 171, 187–88, 195–96, 205, 206; Social Security and, 131; unemployment and, 102, 105, 135–36, 171, 185–86, 187–88, 210

Inland Steel, 124

Inner city, 136, 173–74, 198; female-headed families and, 87, 90; riots and, 2, 67, 80, 87, 93, 99, 100, 121, 204–5; subemployment and, 108–9, 111; sub-urbanization effects on, 26, 149, 150; unemployment and, 2, 67, 150

Interest rates: inflation and, 30, 103, 105, 113, 142, 186; 1970s and, 138, 139, 186; 1990s and, 105, 203, 210, 222, 226; 2000–2005 and, 231, 232

Interior, U.S. Department of, 64

Investment, 28–29, 73, 142, 183, 232; overproduction and, 24, 29; recessions and, 106; supply-side economics and, 187, 196; tax credits and, 39

Iran hostage crisis (1979), 138, 184, 185

Iraq, 202, 234

Italy, 83, 229

Jackson, Jesse, 178

Jacobs, Paul, 49

Jencks, Christopher, 169, 200

Job Corps, 51, 53, 55, 121; evaluation of, 63–65, 67

Job creation: antipoverty solutions and, 4, 235; government and, 2, 3, 5, 36, 49, 58, 67, 80–81, 90, 110–12, 113, 134, 137, 153, 190, 227, 235; Head Start and, 70; private sector and, 3, 112, 236

Job flight, 26, 41, 43, 215, 223

Job Opportunities and Basic Skills Training, 194–95

Job Opportunities in the Business Sector, 51, 81

Job Partnership Training Act, 190

Jobs, 37, 51, 114, 120, 121; antipoverty solutions and, 4, 235–36, 240; community action programs and, 74; exporting of, 158, 170, 225; guest worker programs and, 238; 1970s and, 145, 149–51; part-time, 67, 107, 151, 198, 224, 239; public service, 95, 112, 134, 137, 190; Right vs. Left on, 171–74; shortage of, 4, 25, 62, 63, 65, 92, 104, 148, 167, 172, 189, 213, 214, 226, 235; suburbanization of, 26, 141, 149, 150; 2000–2005 and, 232, 236; workers' rights enforcement and, 236, 242; young people and, 43, 53, 63–65, 150. *See also* Labor force; Labor glut; Labor markets; Unemployment

Job training, 16, 25, 61, 62–68, 212–14; antipoverty solutions and, 235–36; 1950s and, 13–14, 15; 1960s and, 2, 38–39, 41, 51, 53, 81, 104, 120; 1970s and, 133–36, 139, 153; 1980s and, 171, 194–95; 1990s and, 217

Job vacancies, 25, 110, 189, 197–98

ness in, 200, 201; job loss in, 150;
Mobilization for Youth program in,
42–43, 73; public housing in, 201–2;
welfare rights movement in, 118
New York State, 13, 38, 118–19
New York Stock Exchange, 124
New York Times, 48, 71, 138
Nicaragua, 185
Nisbet, Robert, 13
Nixon, Richard, 2, 29, 30, 37, 39, 112,
159, 183; deficit spending and, 29;
food stamps and, 122, 124, 133; guaranteed income plan and, 2, 86, 90, 99,
121–29, 159; job-and-training programs and, 134, 135, 139; Moynihan
and, 85, 86, 90, 122, 123; Social Security and, 131; social welfare spending
by, 136; welfare system and, 117, 119,
121, 139
Non-accelerating inflation rate of unemployment, 105
North American Free Trade Agreement,
215
Novarro, Jesusita, 144
Nowak, Marion, 9
Nutrition, 68, 133, 193. *See also* Food
stamps

Oakley, J. Ronald, 9
OEO. *See* Office of Economic
Opportunity
Office of Economic Opportunity, 51, 53,
55, 56, 59, 61, 68, 74, 77–78, 84, 121
Ohio, 237
Ohlin, Lloyd, 42–43
Oil crises (1970s), 138, 164, 185
Oil industry, 60
Old Age, Survivors, and Disability Insur-
ance, 11, 12. *See also* Social Security
Disability Insurance
Older people, 193, 232; poverty and, 11,
12, 20–22, 143, 197; Supplemental
Security Income and, 131, 139; unem-

ployment and, 225. *See also* Social
Security
Olin Foundation, 181
O'Neill, Tip, 192
O'Neill, William, 9
Orshansky, Mollie, 56–57
Osterman, Paul, 223
Other America, The (Harrington), 2, 43–
48, 49, 91, 170

Packard, 17, 25
Packard Bell, 223
Palmer, Thomas, 171
Parker, Richard, 94
Part-time jobs, 67, 107, 151, 198, 224, 239
Patterson, James, 11
Pells, Richard, 13
Pennsylvania, 15
Perry School (Ypsilanti, Mich.), 69
Personal Responsibility and Work
Opportunity Reconciliation Act
(1996), 217
Philadelphia, Pa., 120
Phillips curve, 105
Pigeon, Marc-Andre, 226
Pines, Burton, 158
Piore, Michael, 92, 93
Pittsburgh, Pa., 74
Piven, Frances Fox, 41, 118, 119, 128,
167–68, 181, 182
Plant shutdowns, 145, 158, 170, 178,
196, 203
Police brutality, 204, 205
Political structures, 1, 103, 166, 243
Poor people, 99, 136, 158; attitudes of,
36–37, 43, 45–46, 51, 88, 93, 106,
174, 234; blaming of, 1, 2, 3, 18–19,
88, 97, 103, 104, 199; community
action agencies and, 53–54; "deserving," 12, 82, 129, 131; Harrington's
view of, 45–47, 170–71; social handicaps and, 45, 59–60, 103–4; work
experience of, 67, 68. *See also* Culture

Socialism, 13, 83, 98

Social policy, 84, 86, 114, 159

Social programs, 5, 228–29; business sector and, 2, 129; conservatives and, 14, 129, 158, 164, 191, 198; European nations and, 83, 114, 155, 227–29, 235; Johnson and, 2, 50, 80; 1950s and, 11–12; 1970s and, 129, 155; Reagan and, 138, 148, 166, 171, 178, 185, 186, 188, 191, 193, 197, 201, 205, 206

Social Security, 4, 60, 81, 168, 179; antipoverty solutions and, 239, 241; benefit increases, 2, 11, 12, 22, 36, 37, 58, 131, 139; Clinton and, 215; Johnson and, 50, 51, 53; 1950s and, 11, 12–13, 22; 1960s and, 36, 37, 50, 51, 53, 55, 61, 79; 1970s and, 131–32, 136, 139; 1980s and, 86, 191–92, 199, 205; privatization proposal for, 86, 215, 239

Social Security Act (1935), 118

Social Security Administration, 56, 131, 167, 191

Social Security Disability Insurance, 136, 147–48, 188, 191

Social services, 73, 75, 119, 211

Social workers, 38, 123

Sosin, Michael, 172

Soviet Union, 15, 184

Sparer, Edward, 77–78

Sparkman, John, 14–15

Speakes, Larry, 188

Spring, William, 92, 94

Sprinkel, Beryl, 188

Sprint, 221

SSI. See Supplemental Security Income

Stahl, Leslie, 185

Stalinism, 96, 98

Steel industry, 190

Stennis, John, 70

Stockman, David, 186, 187, 188, 189, 191, 192, 206

Student movement, 60, 62, 111, 136

"Stues," 16–17, 23–24, 25, 26

Subemployment, 67, 108–9, 111, 112

Suburbanization, 26, 137, 141, 149, 150, 153

Supplemental Security Income, 131, 139, 179, 241

Supplemental Unemployment Benefits, 81–82

Supply-side economics, 163, 186–87, 188, 195–96

Swados, Harvey, 19, 20

Sweden, 83, 155, 227, 241

Sweezy, Paul, 29

TANF. See Temporary Assistance for Needy Families

Tax breaks, 81, 228, 229. See also Tax subsidies

Tax cuts, 4, 37, 145; Bush and, 202, 232–33, 234, 240; conservatives and, 161, 162–63; economic growth and, 2, 10, 39–40, 163; full employment and, 102; Johnson and, 2, 49, 80, 163; Kennedy and, 39–40, 163; Reagan and, 162–63, 164, 171, 186–87, 191, 196, 197, 205, 206

Taxes: antipoverty solutions and, 240–41; conservatives and, 159, 176, 180, 183; corporate, 185; gas, 193; income, 39, 186–87; income inequality and, 29, 211–12, 240–41; Laffer curve and, 164; negative income tax, 124, 132; 1990s and, 205–6, 211, 214, 221; poor people exemptions, 122; progressive, 158, 211, 214, 240–41; Social Security, 192; on unemployment benefits, 189

Taxpayer Relief Act (1997), 214

Tax Reform Act (1986), 195

Tax subsidies, 4, 10, 60

Technology, 29, 38

Teen pregnancy, 143, 178

Teen unemployment, 107, 149, 150, 198

Temporary Assistance for Needy Families, 217, 233–34, 241